DISASTER
SPIRITUAL
CARE

Other Professional Resources from SkyLight Paths

How to Be a Perfect Stranger
The Essential Religious Etiquette Handbook
Edited by Stuart M. Matlins and Arthur J. Magida

The Perfect Stranger's Guide to
Funerals and Grieving Practices
A Guide to Etiquette in Other People's Religious Ceremonies
Edited by Stuart M. Matlins

Interactive Faith
The Essential Interreligious Community-Building Handbook
Edited by Rev. Bud Heckman with Rori Picker Neiss

DISASTER SPIRITUAL CARE

Practical Clergy Responses to Community, Regional and National Tragedy

Edited by Rabbi Stephen B. Roberts, BCJC
and Rev. Willard W. C. Ashley Sr., DMIN, DH

Walking Together, Finding the Way®
SKYLIGHT PATHS®
PUBLISHING
Woodstock, Vermont

Disaster Spiritual Care:
Practical Clergy Responses to Community, Regional and National Tragedy

2008 First Printing
© 2008 by Stephen Roberts and Willard W. C. Ashley

Library of Congress Cataloging-in-Publication Data
Disaster spiritual care : practical clergy responses to community, regional, and national tragedy / edited by Stephen Roberts, Willard W.C. Ashley.
    p. cm.
ISBN-13: 978-1-59473-240-9 (hardcover)
ISBN-10: 1-59473-240-X (hardcover)
1. Disaster victims—Pastoral counseling of. 2. Church work with disaster victims. 3. Disasters—Religious aspects. 4. Disasters—Psychological aspects. I. Roberts, Stephen, 1958– II. Ashley, Willard W. C., 1953–
HV554.4.D57 2008
259—dc22
                                                                        2008000726

10   9   8   7   6   5   4   3   2   1
Manufactured in the United States of America
♻ Printed on Recycled Paper
Jacket design: Melanie Robinson

SkyLight Paths Publishing is creating a place where people of different spiritual traditions come together for challenge and inspiration, a place where we can help each other understand the mystery that lies at the heart of our existence.

SkyLight Paths sees both believers and seekers as a community that increasingly transcends traditional boundaries of religion and denomination—people wanting to learn from each other, *walking together, finding the way.*

SkyLight Paths, "Walking Together, Finding the Way," and colophon are trademarks of LongHill Partners, Inc., registered in the U.S. Patent and Trademark Office.

Walking Together, Finding the Way®
Published by SkyLight Paths Publishing
A Division of Longhill Partners, Inc.
Sunset Farm Offices, Route 4, P.O. Box 237
Woodstock, VT 05091
Tel: (802) 457-4000   Fax: (802) 457-4004
www.skylightpaths.com

To Ron and Hyman, whose work of writing and publishing has inspired and encouraged me in this undertaking.

To Dayle, who encouraged me to push my limits of safety by writing a book chapter that, over time, has led to this book.

To Stuart, who lives his values every day. Without his active mentoring while I was a rabbinic student, I would not be doing this work today.

To JP, who encourages both those he works with and those he encounters in his daily life to strive to change the world for the better. He is a living example of a rabbi's rabbi.

—*Rabbi Stephen B. Roberts*

To Evelyn, Edith, Will, Clara, Annette, Tina, Eunice, Tanya, and Chris—you taught me about disaster spiritual care and encouraged me to share this wisdom with others.

To Earl, Kirk, and David, whose friendship and accomplishments pushed me to press on.

To Anita and Raiford—you model every day how to be an effective caregiver.

To Bruce—without our friendship of over forty years, I may have been another statistic.

To the late Revs. Samuel D. Proctor, William A. Jones, and Frederick G. Sampson—there is not one day that I do not remember some lesson you taught me. Thank you.

To Revs. Eddie O'Neal and Gardner C. Taylor—our conversation in the hallway of the Harvard Chapel at the Black Seminarians Conference has guided my ministry.

To the late Rev. Oscar George Phillips (O. G.)—you were a pastor's pastor.

—*Rev. Willard W. C. Ashley Sr.*

Contents

PART II
SPECIAL NEEDS

Preface

Disasters are a given in the human experience. Various sacred scriptures from all over the world chronicle disasters. Floods, plagues, storms, and a host of other disasters are common occurrences in the human realm. Trauma is part of the human condition. Disasters fall into the paradoxical category of the "expected unexpected." Each individual disaster is unexpected, but disasters and trauma in general are expected.

We, the leaders of our faith communities, are known by dozens of names—priest, reverend, rabbi, imam, nun, pastor, father, minister, rector, preacher, monk, sister, brother, chaplain, and dozens more. Regardless of what we are called, when a disaster strikes, people most often turn to us for leadership, advice, comfort, compassion, and faith. People turn to us with the expectation that we will be able to provide a wide range of disaster spiritual care.

Repeated studies have shown that significant numbers of people having difficulties in the wake of disaster turn either *first* or *only* to spiritual care providers for help. An American Red Cross poll taken almost a month after the September 11, 2001, terrorist attacks indicated that close to 60 percent of Americans polled were likely or very likely to seek help from a spiritual counselor as opposed to only 40 percent who were likely or very likely to turn to a mental health professional.[1]

In our task as caring and effective leaders of our faith communities, we must expect the unexpected. Further, we must plan for the unexpected. It is through resources such as seminars, professional training programs, and this book that we should prepare ourselves to provide disaster spiritual care. This book is intended to offer the practical tools to allow us to do our work in a disaster with skill and compassion.

Intended Use of This Book

This book is designed to allow leaders of individual faith communities to plan and prepare for the unexpected. It is, first and foremost, intended to be concrete and useful by covering a wide range of situations, time frames, and areas. Many of our contributors have extensive academic backgrounds and often write in academic journals. They were asked to make their chapters more practical than academic. Contributors were encouraged to include concrete examples to help bring to life that which they are teaching. Further, our contributors were asked to include easy-to-use checklists and charts.

We expect that you will first become familiar with this book before ever facing a disaster, and then add it to your bookshelf. When a disaster does occur, you will then pick up this book again for specific suggestions, ideas, practices, and advice. Thus, there is intentional repetition within the book. You may open to a specific chapter looking for information and then put the book down for a period of time. To allow you to easily find the information you seek, it may occur in one chapter and then be repeated by another author with a different perspective in a different chapter.

We also expect that this book will become a teaching resource for those devoting significant time to the field of disaster spiritual care. This book is intended to be a primary teaching and reference tool to train our colleagues entering the field.

Finally, it is our hope that seminaries around the country will use this resource to better prepare the next generation of faith community leaders. All leaders of faith communities will encounter disasters sometime during their career. It is important that future leaders, while still in theological formation, struggle with the various theological implications of disasters, think about the practical aspects of responding, and begin to think of self-care as part of their "mission" before entering religious leadership full-time.

The Structure of This Book

The book is divided into two sections. The first is chronological; the second focuses on a variety of issues that are not time related. Chapters in both sections are written by a cross section of leaders in this developing field who come from a wide range of religions and cultures.

The first section focuses on disasters as they unfold. The size of a disaster serves as a variable as to the scope of issues that will confront you. We have devoted more than one chapter to some time periods in order to address the needs of you and your faith community for local, regional, and national disasters. We also recognize the multiyear impact of disasters and have developed this book with the intent that it be a resource you can reference over a long period of time or at a single time of urgent need.

The second section of the book focuses on issues you will face throughout the course of a disaster that will not arise on a set time line. These topics range from compassion fatigue, how best to provide spiritual care at different stages of human development, recovering bodies in the field and working in a morgue environment, and working with and providing spiritual care to first responders.

The work after a disaster is both holy and challenging. We pray that you find this book a valuable resource increasing your skills and comfort level, thus helping you engage in the sacred task of disaster spiritual care response and recovery better prepared.

Notes

1. American Red Cross national poll, October 5–8, 2001, by Caravan ORC Int. 1,000 adults over the age of 18 living in private homes; +/-3 percent; release date: October 16, 2001.

Introduction

Disasters and Spiritual Care

Rabbi Stephen B. Roberts, BCJC,
and Rev. Willard W. C. Ashley Sr., DMin, DH

A disaster at its most basic level is an event that severely disrupts the everyday lives of individuals and communities. It almost always involves the loss of life and/or extreme, widespread property damage. The American Red Cross defines a disaster as "an event of such destructive magnitude and force as to dislocate, injure or kill people, separate family members, and damage or destroy homes."[1] Further, disasters often overwhelm the initial coping capacities and resources of an individual, a family, or a community. Disaster disruptions can be spiritual, emotional, economic, physical, and ecological. The larger the disaster, the more likely it is that a community will need outside assistance with recovery and healing, both short- and long-term.

Disasters produce a ripple effect. The number of individuals affected by disaster and in need of spiritual care is often dramatically greater than the number of people killed or injured. In various studies regarding terror attacks, research showed that there were between two and ten mental health victims for every physically injured person.[2] When disaster strikes people will be traumatized; their spirits will require healing. But the pool of individuals who would normally provide support may decrease, as potential helpers may themselves be traumatized and require assistance.

There is a spectrum of disasters. Small, common disasters that you may deal with on a regular basis can include building fires, acts of violence, accidents, or localized flooding from a severe weather system.

Slightly larger disasters that are less common but may occur at some point in your career can include regional flooding, small tornadoes or hurricanes, mud slides, or transportation accidents involving planes, buses, or trains.

Medium-scale disasters often overwhelm a geographic area beyond just one community. You may not encounter this scale of disaster within your own geographic area, but it may hit a region near you. These can include large tornadoes or hurricanes, wildfires affecting residential areas, earthquakes, terror attacks, cruise ship or ferry accidents, flooding that impacts multiple states, an explosion at a chemical plant, or a nuclear reactor accident.

Large-scale disasters often require a national or international response. Though you may never be directly affected by a large-scale disaster, you will likely be aware of them no matter where they strike. You may help your community provide financial or volunteer support to those affected. Large-scale disasters can include drought, nuclear accidents, pandemics, major tsunamis, flooding impacting large areas of a country, or multiple large hurricanes within a short period of time.

Types of Disasters

Disasters are commonly defined by two categories: natural or human-caused; accidental or intentional. The "category" of a disaster affects how those experiencing it make meaning of what has happened and integrate the impact of it into their lives. Unfortunately, it is usually difficult to clearly categorize disasters.

Natural disasters are frequently referred to as "acts of God." We often think of tornadoes, hurricanes, heat waves, flooding, tsunamis, and earthquakes as within this category. As people of faith, we often view these disasters as devastating but within our religious or spiritual understanding of the nature of the world. With the technology we have today, natural disasters are commonly believed to be uncontrollable but predictable. Thus, any resulting loss of life from the disaster can often theoretically be avoided through advance warning or other mitigation preparations.

Human-caused disasters often have a technological component. They include transportation disasters, hazardous materials accidents, and nuclear catastrophe. It is with human-caused disasters that the categories of intentional act or accident come into play.

An intentional human-caused disaster may include loading a virus onto a computer network, hacking into secret files, shutting down electrical power, acts that disrupt public transportation or access to roads, a chemical or nuclear attack, or other acts of terrorism and civil disturbance. The goals of such intentional acts are to create terror, foster panic and chaos, and disrupt daily functioning.

Mission of Disaster Spiritual Care

The mission of disaster spiritual care is to provide appropriate short-term and long-term care for people who have been affected by both the initial trauma and the ongoing disaster situation. The goal is to provide sensitive spiritual and emotional care to affected individuals and families by respecting a person's culture, religious tradition, and faith commitments.

As care providers we serve as a spiritual resource through our presence, our referrals to other responders and aid agencies, and our prayers. Through our presence (and sometimes through our words) we hope that people will feel God's love, care, and comfort.

The role of the spiritual care provider in a disaster is not to shelter people or to help them escape, but *to help those affected draw upon their own emotional and spiritual resources* in the midst of their pain. Our goal is not necessarily to take away their grief, but to help them work through their grief. Our work involves presence, prayer, and at times religious ritual (according to the individual's religious tradition). Another key goal is to know who is most at risk for short- and long-term readjustment problems—whether spiritual, emotional, or physical—and to offer help.

Defining Spiritual Care in a Disaster

Spirituality is a term that has many meanings. Its definition is broad and varies depending on whom you ask. In this book we often use *spirituality* to describe a person's path to finding meaning in his or her life experiences, in light of a relationship to the Transcendent. In today's multicultural environment, those who provide spiritual care must be sensitive to and aware of the varied expressions of faith and belief.

Spiritual care in the context of a disaster responds to this poignant need for spiritual meaning and comfort by providing accompaniment and prayer, both individual and communal. In the midst of the chaos of the crisis we can stand with others, pray with them, accompany them at the hardest times (such as notification of confirmation of death), and provide a sacred space where the person can sit quietly with his or her God and experience comfort. It is often the simple presence of a person of God that provides healing and comfort. The ministry of solidarity and accompaniment, of silence in the face of tragedy, of surrender to the God of our understanding, is often the most we can do in such situations.

Defining Religious Care in a Disaster

The *Oxford English Dictionary* defines religion as "a particular system of faith and worship."[3] Religious care in a disaster is particularly focused on facilitating the ability of people to practice their own particular faith without fear of intimidation or proselytizing. Care is focused on both those directly affected by a disaster and those responding to a disaster.

Disasters often separate people from their own faith community— their church, synagogue, mosque, or temple—and also from their faith community's leaders. After a disaster people tend to turn to religion to help stabilize their lives. Religious care after a disaster is focused on helping people access this important element in their lives by providing:

- Access to religious worship
- Access to sacred scripture and texts (in a way that others will not find proselytizing)
- Access to food that meets a person's religious needs
- A multifaith sacred space that can be used for meditation and prayer
- Appropriate timely religious care to the dead

Key Principles of Disaster Spiritual Care

1. Basic needs come first. Particularly in the immediate hours and days after a disaster, before helping with the spiritual needs of those affected, assess that the person you are working with is not hungry, has access to and has taken any medications that they normally require,

and has a safe place to sleep. Most people are unable to focus on spiritual issues when their basic physical needs are in doubt.

2. Do no harm.
3. Each person you work with is unique and holy.
4. Do not proselytize, evangelize, exploit, or take advantage of those affected by a disaster, and don't allow others to do so.
5. Respect the spiritual, religious, and cultural diversity of those you are working with—ask questions about things you do not understand.
6. Presence—meet the person you are working with wherever they may be in their spiritual and religious life. Accept them as they are and where they are.
7. Help victims and survivors tell their story.
8. Be aware of confidentiality.
9. Make neither promises nor something that even sounds like a promise.
10. Grief, both short- and long-term, looks different in different cultures and religions—ask before you assume.
11. Be sensitive to language barriers. Remember that it is often difficult to express yourself effectively in a second language. If possible, provide spiritual care in the person's native language by finding a spiritual care provider who speaks their language. Allow the person or family you are working with to choose their own translator. Ideally, do not use children as an interpreter, though it is sometimes necessary to do so.
12. Remember when working with immigrants that both legal and illegal immigrants often fear or distrust the government due to their life circumstances.
13. Practice active listening—listen with your ears, eyes, and heart. Do far less talking than you do listening. Never respond with, "I know how you feel," or, "You think that is bad, let me tell you my story."

Disasters and Spiritual Health

Spirituality is a complex and intricately personal experience. Each person's spiritual life is a unique and marvelous journey. Each spiritual journey follows its own course; nevertheless, lives that are spiritually whole exhibit similar trends. Such lives express:

- **A sense of awe and wonder:** Feelings of awe and wonder are the personal response to our awareness of and relationship to the Transcendent, to the Mystery, to That-Which-Is-Greater-Than-Myself.
- **A sense of community:** Feelings of belonging and connectedness nurture our souls and our physical and mental health. The "soul food" of communal identity promotes connectedness, compassion, and the desire to serve others.
- **A sense of personal mission:** People who have a strong sense of purpose and direction for their lives seem better able to remain focused and grounded in spite of disruptions and changes.
- **Enthusiasm for continuous discovery and creativity:** A mark of the presence of spiritual reflection is an adventurous spirit that is willing to risk new experiences.
- **A sense of well-being and joy:** Feelings of satisfaction and happiness reflect a balanced life; care for ourselves and others; accountability to ourselves and others; and the ability to celebrate life and the Source of Life even in the worst of times.[4]

Many of these trends of healthy spirituality need to be nurtured and attended to after disaster. Faced with any loss, but especially the sudden and profound loss that accompanies disaster, our sense of meaning and purpose—indeed everything we may have thought about how the world works—is turned upside down.

The symptoms of spiritual dis-ease that may be exhibited during disaster include:

- Reconsidering core tenets of religious beliefs
- Asking questions such as "Why did God do this?"
- Questioning justice and meaning
- Feeling far from previously held beliefs
- Feeling a need to be cleansed
- Closing oneself off from loved ones
- Feeling despair and hopelessness
- Feeling guilty
- Wondering about life and death
- Feeling shame

Differences between Disaster Spiritual Care and Other Forms of Spiritual and Religious Care

Disaster spiritual care is different from other forms of spiritual and religious care, particularly when we are working in the larger community. In non-disaster times, we often spend our days speaking about our faith and guiding others in how to live their faith. People come into our worship spaces voluntarily to hear us preach and teach. These spiritual and religious seekers actively, freely, and with full ability give their consent to be challenged in their spiritual beliefs and to change the way they live their religious lives.

After a disaster, however, people are often extremely vulnerable and fragile. They are easily taken advantage of in many ways, including spiritually. A multitude of people descend upon the disaster area, including those offering spiritual "help." While many are well intentioned, they often come with agendas that can exploit a person's fragility and vulnerability.

Victims of a disaster tend to be lonely, afraid, scared, homeless, and hopeless. Their cognitive abilities are diminished; their brains just shut down. They often lack the true moral capacity to consent to be evangelized or proselytized.

After a disaster, we often open up our houses of worship to become shelters for those displaced. The people who enter may have no other options for a place to go. They are worried about being able to eat and sleep, and are concerned about their loved ones. It is at these times that we must be extremely vigilant not to take advantage of this vulnerability. The normal practices in our house of worship may become inappropriate during a disaster. Following are some examples of how things change:

- Many houses of worship commonly put religious tracks on tables during community dinners and gatherings. This common practice should be examined and possibly forgone if the congregation becomes a shelter following a disaster. People are no longer voluntarily a part of the congregation; the building has become their shelter of last resort. While never explicitly stating it, those staying often feel that if they do not read the material, they will be asked to leave.

- Faith communities commonly offer a faith-specific prayer prior to eating communally. It may be necessary to eliminate this practice following a disaster, or to offer a simple moment of silence before a meal instead, in order to make those taking shelter with your congregation feel welcome. The people staying with you need a place over their head and food in their belly; they are seeking shelter, not a change in their religious lives.

Grief Is a Common Positive Spiritual Coping Reaction

Finally, we wish to note what most religious leaders already know, that grief is a common positive spiritual coping reaction. Each faith tradition has their own rituals to encourage mourning and grief. It is even more important than usual to allow mourning and grieving after a disaster, as the losses sustained by individuals, families, and communities are often substantial. Losses may include family members and friends dying, jobs and careers vanishing, homes being destroyed, and whole neighborhoods being wiped out.

What is mourning?[5] At its most basic, mourning is adaptation to loss. The first, and often hardest, step is to accept the reality of the loss. The second step is to walk through the spiritual, emotional, and physical pain of grief. The spirit, mind, and body all hurt from the loss. Religious rituals in particular help people get to a point where they can cope with their pain and not be overwhelmed in day-to-day living. The third step is learning to adjust to an environment in which the people or things lost are no longer present. The final step is to emotionally and spiritually "relocate" the losses and then continue on with living.

Mourning and grief after a disaster can become particularly complicated if common religious rituals do not occur in a timely manner or do not occur at all. People may be physically uprooted from their religious communities and leaders. They are stripped of their spiritual coping mechanism and lose their vital spiritual connections at a time when they are most in need. Very large disasters can further complicate the mourning process because it may take months to get the deceased back, or their remains may never be recovered. As religious leaders, we need to be aware of the challenges disasters present and work hard to help those in our community grieve and mourn their losses in a timely way and a spiritually appropriate fashion. If people are not able to mourn and grieve appropriately, they may never be able to rebuild their spiritual and emotional lives, even after they have rebuilt their physical lives. In the chaos after a disaster, helping people mourn is one of the hardest challenges we will faces as leaders of faith communities.

"Common" versus "Normal"

Most of us providing disaster spiritual care are not trained mental health workers. Our field is faith. We are trained spiritual care providers. That is why people seek us out. But when working with those affected by disaster, it is important that we use our own field's language.

Normal and *abnormal* are clinical psychological terms with therapeutic implications and judgments. Very few clergy are trained in the field of pastoral counseling. Use of these words when describing reactions to disasters should be avoided by leaders of faith communities. Rather, we encourage the use of the phrases "common reactions to uncommon situations" and "uncommon reactions to uncommon situations." *Common* is a nonjudgmental word. After a disaster, whether in the immediate hours or months or years later, there are a wide range of common reactions that people have. By using the word *common* instead of *normal*, a person who doesn't experience these reactions feels no judgment for not responding a certain way.

For example, in the immediate days after a disaster it is common for a person's ability to focus and do "easy" tasks to be lower. Many people also experience changes in their sleep patterns. Those of us working with victims of disaster often relieve worry by letting people know these reactions are common. If we say they are "normal" and other people are still functioning at the same level they were prior to the disaster, they might hear themselves defined as "abnormal," with all the negative implications that word has. The "abnormal" label can be deeply troubling; it can easily cause internal reactions of doubt and worry about what reactions a person should or should not be experiencing.

Key Assumption: Resilience—Most People Do Find a New Balance Without Outside Help

Research has demonstrated what leaders of faith communities have long known: the vast majority of the people we serve are resilient. After a disaster, most affected individuals and communities return to a state of equilibrium on their own. They do not require a referral for acute emotional or spiritual care.

To say people are resilient is to say that while they may have a large range of reactions to a disaster, they also have the spiritual and emotional resources to find a new place of balance without needing professional help. People affected by disaster are often changed by the experience. Part of the return to balance in life is their ability to incorporate the experiences they have gone through into their spirit in some meaningful fashion.

It is important to assume resiliency when we work with those affected by disaster; this should be the bedrock of our faith. When we assume resilience, it means we work as a partner in helping the people we serve to look both within and without for the resources they need—spiritually, emotionally, and physically—to rebuild their lives. When we treat people as partners, we encourage them to look within and find their own spiritual and emotional tools that will get them through the impact of the disaster. When we believe, consciously or unconsciously, that those we are working with are not resilient, the opposite occurs. Once people perceive our paternalistic attitude, they lean on others and do not exercise their own resources. This leads to a vicious cycle of dependence instead of independence, health, renewal, and healing. We must remember to treat those we work with as our partners in rebuilding, not as people lesser than ourselves that must be treated gingerly or as children.

Numerous studies have documented that the overwhelming majority of people who experience even the most devastating of disasters do *not* develop serious spiritual or emotional infirmity.[6] Further, when we find ways to support one person's spiritual and emotional life after a disaster by providing resiliency training and support, even more people benefit, which is a key goal of the work of disaster spiritual care.

Research in the Field of Disaster Spiritual Care

One of the major obstacles in preparing this book was the lack of research into "best practices" in the provision of disaster spiritual care. In doing a background search into the subject, we found only a handful of articles involving research of any sort. Only a small percentage of these were actual peer-review articles, the highest level of research.

In similar fields, such as disaster mental health, hundreds of research projects have been completed and written up. The research focuses on determining the most effective way to provide care so that "best practices" can be developed within the field.

Research takes our "hunches" and puts them to the test. It confirms and supports our work, or it alerts us that our hypotheses are not supported by fact. Either way, we have concrete knowledge. For disaster spiritual care to develop and grow, and more important, for us to be effective leaders of our faith communities, we need to systematically engage in research to develop a series of "best practices" supported through professional and unbiased research.

Disaster Spiritual Care Wisdom Sayings and Insights

The following wisdom sayings are intended to help spiritual care providers remember the basics of disaster spiritual care. This list was developed by many of the contributors to this book, all leaders in the field of disaster spiritual care. We encourage you to look at this often, especially when faced with a disaster. Keep a copy above your desk or in your car.

DISASTER SPIRITUAL CARE
WISDOM SAYINGS*

OVERVIEW

1. No one who "witnesses" a disaster is untouched by it.

SELF-CARE

2. Everyone responding to a disaster needs to practice self-care and seek the support of others so that they leave the disaster experience changed but not damaged.

3. Self-care is a religious mandate particularly for leaders of faith communities. According to most Western religions, even the Creator of the Universe rested on the seventh day. Practice what we preach about time off!

BASICS

4. The first order of business is helping meeting people's base need of human care—food, water, shelter, medical. Only then are they even able to focus on spiritual needs.

5. Disaster spiritual care is more about team and less about lone ranger.

6. Spiritual care and mental health are most effective when working cooperatively for the benefit of the client.

7. When in doubt, check it out.

DIVERSITY

8. The disaster spiritual caregiver must recognize the unknown god in diversity.

9. Spiritual care must be uniquely tailored to the spiritual community and/or individual affected.

10. Every disaster survivor must be treated as an individual created in the image of God. Some will require minimal assistance to regroup and move on, while others will need intensive support.

DISASTER SPIRITUAL CARE
WISDOM SAYINGS* (CONTINUED)

CONNECTIONS

11. People do not care how much you know until they know how much you care.

12. Healing happens within human relationships.

I AND THOU

13. Listening to and being with are more important than talking at and doing for. If you cannot improve on silence, do not try.

14. Ministry of presence, not pressure.

15. Always ask, and re-ask: "Whose needs am I trying to meet?"

16. Disaster spiritual caregivers must struggle with the victims as they ask their questions...not answer them. True wisdom is not in the answer when someone asks "Why?"

PRACTICAL TOOLS

17. The best initial spiritual assessment tool in the midst of the initial stages of a disaster begins with open-ended questions such as "How are you doing?" or "How are things going today?"

18. Let them pound on God's chest; the Creator of the Universe can take our anger.

19. Draw the lines before you jump or you will end up in an overwhelming sea of need.

20. We, as helpers, may not have the power to "heal" but we can through our work as disaster spiritual caregivers plant a seed of hope. Hope is an essential part of all forms of healing.

21. Ritual is an important and effective means of healing.

*Contributors to Disaster Spiritual Care Wisdom Sayings:

Stephen B. Roberts, Willard W. C. Ashley Sr., George Abrams, Yusuf Hasan, John Kinsel, Charles R. Lorrain, Pamela Norris Norwood, Naomi Paget, Tanya Pagan Raggio, Timothy G. Serban, Frederick J. Streets, and Julie Taylor

Notes

1. American Red Cross, "Definition of Disaster." Available online at www. redcross.org.
2. In discussing the sarin gas attacks on Tokyo on March 20, 1995, the following was written: "Part of what overwhelmed the medical system was a category of affected people called the 'worried well.' The worried well included exposed and unexposed individuals who sought—but did not really require—medical treatment.... Of the more than 5,000 patients who hospital visits were directly related to the attack, less than 20 patients were admitted and treated in intensive care units.... People who did not exhibit symptoms of exposure—easily over one half of the patients seen." R. Pagni, "Consequence Management of the 1995 Sarin Attacks on the Japanese Subway System," *BCSIA Discussion Paper* 2002–2004, *ESDP Discussion Paper* 2001–2002, John F. Kennedy School of Government, Harvard University (February 2002): 30–31.
   A study on the affect of Iraqi missile attacks on Israel reported the following: "During the period 18 January–28 February 1991, a total of 39 Iraqi modified SCUD missiles landed in Israel, most of them in densely populated Tel Aviv Area. These attacks caused 1,059 cases of injury. Acute Anxiety was the reason for admission of 544 patients." E. Karsenty et al., "Medical Aspects of the Iraqi Missile Attacks on Israel," *Israel Journal of Medical Sciences* 27, nos. 11–12 (November–December 1991): 603–07.
3. *Compact Oxford English Dictionary of Current English*, 3rd ed. (Oxford: Oxford University Press, 2005).
4. This complete section comes from K. Massey, *Light Our Way: A Guide for Spiritual Care in Times of Disaster* (Washington, D.C.: National Voluntary Organizations Active in Disaster, 2006), 5–6; chart by Rev. John A. Robinson, Jr.
5. These concepts come from the following: J. W. Worden, *Grief Counseling and Grief Therapy: A Handbook for the Mental Health Practitioner* (New York: Springer, 1991), 10–18.
6. "Most trauma experts agree that the psychological outcome of the country will be resilience, not psychopathology." National Center for PTSD, 2001.

About the Contributors

Rabbi Stephen B. Roberts, BCJC, is coeditor of this book. He is the associate executive vice president of the New York Board of Rabbis overseeing the Jack D. Weiler Chaplaincy Program. He is a past president of the National Association of Jewish Chaplains. Two years prior to September 11, 2001, he founded a partnership organization within the American Red Cross in Greater New York of what is now Disaster Chaplaincy Services, New York (DCS-NY), an independent 501(c)3. He serves DCS-NY as chairman emeritus. Since 2000, Rabbi Roberts has served as one of the five official representatives overseeing the American

Red Cross's national Spiritual Care Response Team. Following 9/11, he was the first national officer to set up American Red Cross spiritual care response in New York City. On June 17, 2002, in New York City, Rabbi Roberts envisioned and then chaired an American Red Cross one-day conference for clergy and other religious leaders with over 650 participants. This resiliency training specifically addressed the impact of 9/11 and the tools needed to better understand and work with those affected. He has taught extensively on disaster spiritual care and was the primary researcher for the only published peer-review research on the impact of disasters on spiritual care providers.

Rev. Willard W. C. Ashley Sr., DMin, DH, is coeditor of this book, a psychotherapist, and founder and senior pastor of the Abundant Joy Community Church in Jersey City, New Jersey. He envisioned and implemented the largest clergy resiliency program in the United States following the attacks on September 11, 2001, the Care for the Caregivers Interfaith Program, a ministry of the Council of Churches of the City of New York. His ministry also includes roles as an adjunct professor; a consultant on disaster recovery and clergy self-care to congregations and Fortune 100 companies; a board member of Disaster Chaplaincy Services, New York City; a board member of Christ Hospital, Jersey City, New Jersey; a former assistant dean of students and director of recruitment for Andover Newton Theological School; and past president of the Blanton Peale Graduate Institute, Alumni Association. Ashley is an ordained minister in the National Baptist Convention, USA, Inc.; Disciples of Christ; and the American Baptist Churches, USA.

PART I

The Life Cycle of a Disaster

1

The Life Cycle of a Disaster

Rabbi Stephen B. Roberts, BCJC

L ife and the way life is lived are unique for each person. Yet there is much commonality in the way we spiritually and religiously mark the cycles of our lives. There are common ebbs and flows in life—birth, growing up, finding and committing to life partners, and dying. Most religious and spiritual communities have their own unique practices that mark these occasions.

Leaders of faith communities are deeply involved with these "life cycle" events. We often perform rituals, worship services, and other spiritual practices associated with them. Different religious, spiritual, and cultural groups mark birth differently, with different customs, worship services, religious practices, and spiritual traditions. The range of customs includes naming ceremonies, ritual immersion in water of the baby or mother, circumcising practices, naming backup guardians who are not blood relatives, tattooing, and much more. When we look across the spectrum of beliefs and religious practices, we see that most groups have some sort of clearly identified ritual to mark this beginning of the cycle of life.

Life cycles are what leaders of faith communities often know best. Life cycle events mark both the happy and sad occasions within a spiritual and religious community. They provide meaning in our lives as leaders of faith communities and in the lives of those whom we serve.

Each Disaster Is Unique

Like life itself, each disaster is unique. No two floods inundate communities and individuals the same way. No two hurricanes or tornadoes follow the exact same paths. No two large transportation disasters touch the same families, businesses, and communities. Yet, like life itself, all disasters have a common set of phases. Figure 1.1 is a graphic representation that lays out the common phases of a life cycle of a disaster.[1]

Individuals and communities progress through these phases at different rates depending on the type of disaster and the degree and nature of disaster exposure. This progression may not be linear or sequential, as each person and community brings unique elements to the recovery process. Individual variables such as psychological resilience, social support, and financial resources influence a survivor's capacity to move through the phases. While there is always a risk of aligning expectations too rigidly with a developmental sequence, having an appreciation of the unfolding of reactions to disaster is valuable.[2]

Phases of the Life Cycle of a Disaster

Pre-disaster Phase—Threat and Warning

A man lived in a known flood plain. He turned on the TV and the weatherman was announcing that extreme rain was taking place and that all people should evacuate to higher ground. The man said to himself: "God will take care of me." The next morning a policeman knocked on his door and told him he was in a mandatory evacuation area and should leave immediately. The man responded: "God will take care of me." By late afternoon the water was up to his second story window. A boater saw him in his house and offered to take him out of harm's way. The man responded: "God will take care of me." Finally, as night was falling and the man was on his roof a helicopter flew over and offered to rescue him. The man responded yet again: "God will take care of me." The man then drowned in the flood and came before God. The man was angry and demanded to know of God: "I was a man of deep faith. Why did you not take care of me?" God responded: "I

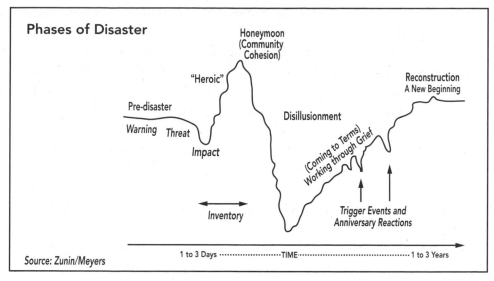

Figure 1.1

had the weather man alert you with plenty of time to get out with all your possessions. I then sent a policeman to alert you with time to take some of your possessions. I then sent a boat to get you out. Finally, I sent a helicopter. Why did you not have faith in me to accept the help I offered? Faith works both ways."

Some disasters, such as earthquakes and explosions, come with no immediate warning. Some, such as hurricanes, come with lots of warnings. Some, such as tornadoes and floods, fall in between. Yet, in almost every case, people and communities can make plans and preparations to lessen the impact of a potential disaster.

There is a known relationship between an actual risk and an individual's threat assessment, which greatly influences that person's disaster preparedness. There are many stories of survivors of multiple hurricanes who ignored mandatory warnings to evacuate extremely large and dangerous storms. They assessed the risk as low: "I survived many storms in my home. I can survive this as well." Their own threat assessment led to tragic consequences for them and, many times, for their families. Further, how someone reacts has long-term implications for their spiritual, physical, and emotional health.

Leaders of faith communities play an extremely important role in the time prior to a disaster. Experience has repeatedly shown that people often downplay the risks involved because thinking about all of the various risks can overwhelm them. One of the most common expressions heard prior to a disaster, and a common excuse for not preparing properly, is "God will take care of me." Our responsibility as leaders of faith communities is to be agents for God in taking care of God's flock. It is first our responsibility to help our communities prepare. Then we must guide them to appropriate reactions when a threat occurs.

The work of preparation is familiar to us. Prior to a wedding, many of us counsel the couple about the changes they will experience in their lives. We take a proactive role. We must equally be proactive in our preparation for disasters. With warning of impending disaster comes anticipatory stress. What shall I do? Where shall I go? Will my family be safe? Will my property be safe? Will I live? Will I die? People are often overwhelmed with worry and do not prepare or react proactively. Our job in the warning or threat phase is to mobilize our communities to prepare. There is always planning and preparations that our communities can do to lessen the impact of disaster. Ultimately, when the phone call comes, we need to be prepared to lead. Further, we need to be able help keep our communities from neither panicking nor becoming so frightened that they are immobilized with fear.

Impact

The actual time in which a disaster occurs can be seconds, minutes, hours, or even days. Depending on the disaster and the warnings involved, a community's reactions to the actual event range from confusion to disbelief to shock. As stated by D. Myers and D. Wee in *Disaster Mental Health Services*, "In disasters of discreet and rather sudden impact, people may experience intense fear but rarely panic."[3]

Common spiritual reactions to disasters that occur suddenly and are short in duration include spontaneous prayer, calling out to God, and reciting a fixed prayer from memory. Common spiritual reactions to disasters longer in length, such as a hurricane, include reading sacred texts, forming prayer circles, meditating, religious singing, and holding more formal worship services.

Common physical reactions to a disaster include increased pulse, rapid shallow breathing, sweating, chills, and time distortion (where time "slows down").[4] People tend to focus initially on their own survival and the survival of their family, and then the physical well-being of others. When families are separated by geography during the impact of a disaster, survivors will often experience considerable anxiety until they know their loved ones are safe.[5]

Rescue/Heroic/Miracle Phase

The period immediately following a disaster is known as either the "rescue" or "heroic" phase. It commonly lasts between a day and a week, except in the largest of disasters. This is a moment of action when adrenaline flows. It is a period of search and recovery. To leaders of faith communities, this period can also be known as the "miracle" phase. This is the time when miracles of survival take place, when those who thought they were going to die are rescued.

Once people realize they are alive, they move into action. It is common to see victims helping other victims, and to see people live their faith at this time. Strangers step in to help first responders save lives and rescue property. Chain saws, moving equipment, boats, and other rescue items suddenly appear and are put into action. Communities pull together. Shelters are opened, people are housed and fed.

> People are grateful to be alive, and often report a feeling of euphoria and sense of personal vulnerability. While people are shocked and horrified by damages and losses, morale is typically high for people directing their energy into concrete, necessary, and meaningful tasks. Psychological arousal results in high level of activity but cognitive impairment (confusion, difficulty comprehending, problem solving, and setting priorities) often contribute to a low level of efficiency and effectiveness. People rushing to help others are often inattentive to safety, and injuries frequently occur in this phase.[6]

It is also during this period that people begin to take inventory and try to locate loved ones. Frantic phone calls are placed, which often overwhelms the phone system and renders it inoperative. Electricity is often out, so people may not have access to e-mail. Survivors who have found their families to be unharmed try to find out about the state of their property, about where they work, about their friends, and about their houses of worship.

> "The contribution of the recovery environment to individual and community responses to traumatic events cannot be overemphasized. Community leaders and families can critically influence the

speed and direction of recovery by first constructing an environment of rest, respite and safety."[7]

Figure 1.2 provides common responses exhibited during this phase of a disaster. If these reactions last a significant length of time (weeks or months), they are no longer common and the person experiencing them should be referred to a professional.

Honeymoon or Remedy Phase— Community Cohesion

In the days, and sometimes weeks, immediately after a disaster communities come together. People flock to the affected area with offers of help. Government officials publicly proclaim that they will assist with disaster aid. People who have insurance think it will cover their losses. Those without insurance often think that government aid or donations will help them recover. Survivors and their families are often grateful just to be alive when others were not so fortunate; they have a sense that God is watching over them and taking care of them. Those who lost loved ones are often comforted by large community outpourings of support.

There is a strong sense of having shared with others a dangerous, catastrophic experience and having lived through it.[8] There is a sense the worst is over. Leaders of faith communities are exhaustingly busy and visible during this phase. First they lead funerals for those who have died and provide direct spiritual care to the families and friends of the deceased. Multiple hospital visits take place to tend to both the wounded and their loved ones. Prayer vigils continue for those injured and in need of healing. Multifaith memorial services for those who died are organized and held. If there are not multifaith disaster response organizations to help focus on unmet needs, this is the phase in which they are often created. There are extensive meetings with both governmental and private industry leaders to focus on needs and on beginning the healing process and then reporting back to their own communities on what is taking place. And finally, if their own house of worship was damaged or destroyed in the disaster, they must organize their own faith community to begin the process of deciding the next steps.

COMMON EARLY RESPONSES TO DISASTER IN IMPACT/INVENTORY PHASES

SPIRITUAL	EMOTIONAL	THOUGHTS/ COGNITIVE	BEHAVIORAL	PHYSICAL
Guilt, shame	Depression	Memory loss	Tearful	Fatigue
Anger at God	Grief	Lowered Concentration	Prolonged silences	Dizzy spells
Religious reappraisal	Hopelessness	Confusion in thinking	Changes in eating	Headaches
Questioning the power of prayer	Helplessness	Loss of attention span	Decreased libido	Chest pain **
Feeling need to be punished	Panic feelings	Difficulty making decisions	Changes in sleep patterns	Light-headedness
Questions about reality/meaning/ justice/fairness	Withdrawal, lack of enjoyment	Calculation problems	Overly alert, startle easily	Muscle tremors
Feelings of hopelessness and fatalism	Anger, intense irritability	Problems with abstract thinking	Avoidance behaviors	Sensitivity to noise
Questioning core faith and spiritual values	Feeling overwhelmed	Reconstructing events in mind to change outcome	Withdrawal from others	Rapid breathing **
Changing assumptions about life and afterlife	Fear and heightened anxiety	Lowering of all higher cognitive functions	Decreased personal hygiene	Chills or Sweating
Needing acts/rituals of purification	Emotional numbness and shock	Recurrent thoughts, dreams and nightmares about event	Overly protective of self and family	Hunger and/or thirst
Needing reassurance of God's presence and power			Increased conflict at work and home	Difficulty breathing **
Asking core questions: "Why me?" "Why would God...?"			Increased alcohol and drug use *	Increased heart rate **
			Discarding treasured objects *	Elevated blood pressure **
			Changes in ordinary behavior patterns	Nausea and/or gastrointestinal distress
			Increased or decreased association with fellow workers	

These should be discouraged. They are common but often unhealthy.
** *These symptoms should be referred to a physician immediately.*

Figure 1.2

Disillusionment Phase—
Coming to Terms, Working through Grief

This phase is often the most difficult one, and a small number of survivors never get beyond it. This phase is full of grief, one of the most basic spiritual issues in which most leaders of faith communities have extensive experience. We have an essential healing role during this period.

The disillusionment phase starts just days or weeks after the disaster. People realize that their insurance may be inadequate or that it will take months or years to recover money. They grieve the loss of their hopes and dreams for a quick rebuilding. In the previous phase they had been hopeful and full of joy; now they are despondent and discouraged.

The media quickly moves on to the next "big event." The survivors discover that both the private and the government disaster relief programs that promised to help them are generally bureaucratic with red tape, delays, changing rules, a host of agencies to connect with, and pages of paperwork to fill out, often requiring documents they do not have. Their savings begin to disappear, and they grieve the loss of financial stability. They tire of the temporary housing, which is often cramped. They become weary and fatigued. They grieve their lost lives.

They discover that their destroyed homes may not be able to be rebuilt due to changes in zoning or lack of money. Mortgages may still need to be paid. They may find themselves the victim of price gouging and unethical builders. Their jobs may have disappeared. Their schools may have closed. It dawns on them just how much they have truly lost.

Within what seems a short period of time, relief agencies close their doors. People suddenly may feel abandoned and alone, full of sorrow and grief. Life is *not* better for them, and yet people act as if it is or it should be.

> A frequently overlooked aspect of trauma is the stigmatization of victims. As individuals, families, or communities, we frequently wish to avoid the victims of trauma or disasters. These victims remind us of our own profound vulnerability to unexpected and unplanned events. Such stigmatization increases the isolation of the victims and frequently their experience of self-blame. Often the stigmatization of the victim is the result of the expectation and wish of others that the individual "be all better now."[9]

Figure 1.3 lists just some of the issues people face during this difficult and critical period. As spiritual leaders, we are often in a unique position to observe these problems. It is imperative that we provide referrals and support when we witness these problems. In this phase, if we are proactive, we can often find volunteers from within our faith communities to help strategize ways to deal with the myriad issues our congregants and communities face.

One of the most imperative issues faced during the disillusionment phase is a significant rise in suicide rates. You should alert your congregants that people often think about suicide at this time, and that you and other leaders of faith communities are there for them. Use sermons, newsletters, and special mailings to get this information out. Emphasize they are not alone, even if they feel they are alone. Take talk of suicide seriously.

PROBLEMS FACED BY SURVIVORS IN DISILLUSIONMENT STAGE

- Spiritual struggles of faith and meaning, including a sense of abandonment by either God or their faith community

- Divorce

- Suicide

- Physical exhaustion from a lack of recreation or leisure time

- Medical, due to preexisting conditions or a lack of insurance, doctors, medicine, healthy eating

- Fatigue, due to crowding and noisy living conditions in "temporary" shelters

- Increased drug use and domestic violence—a common but unhealthy way that some people handle their situations

- Greater emotional and psychological problems, including depression

- Financial ruin caused by a lack of adequate insurance, timely payment by insurers, loss of job and prospect for work in the area, bureaucratic hassles

Figure 1.3

The larger community less impacted by the disaster often returned to business as usual, which is typically discouraging and alienating for survivors. Ill will and resentment may surface in neighborhoods as survivors receive unequal monetary amounts for what they perceive to be equal or similar damage. Divisiveness and hostility among neighbors undermine community cohesion and support.[10]

People realize during this phase that life is never going to be the same—they have lost much. Our role as leaders of faith communities during this period is essential. We are the experts in grief, and people often seek us out in their grief. We must work hard to be available, to reach out, and to be visible. The world has changed and moved on for worse or for better. In their grief, survivors make great effort to find meaning. We, the leaders of faith communities, are the trained professionals to guide them in this struggle and to ensure they are not alone and abandoned when they are so vulnerable.

It is during this phase that survivors decide how best to rebuild given their new realities. It becomes apparent to them that they must take personal responsibility for moving forward to rebuild their spiritual, emotional, and physical lives, including their home, work life, and religious community. We need to be able to offer them spiritual support and spiritual resiliency guidance to help them in this work of rebuilding.

Chapter 11 deals with the "trigger events" that can affect disaster survivors, such as birthdays, weddings, wedding anniversaries, the anniversary of the disaster, or major news articles about the disaster.

Like most people filled with grief after loss, the majority of people affected by a disaster realize at some point that they do have the strength, faith, hope, and ability to cope. They discover parts of themselves they may not have been aware of. They pass through the darkest periods and then begin to move back toward the brighter future. Their journey is not a continuous climb. There are many setbacks and roadblocks—both internal and external—but the work of rebuilding has really begun now.

As our final comment on the disillusionment phase, we offer an important reminder about self-care: you, as a leader of a faith, *are* vulnerable to compassion fatigue and burnout! You must take care of yourself. Chapter 2 provides extensive information on self-care; chapter 13 provides detailed information on compassion fatigue and secondary traumatic stress. We strongly encourage you to read and implement the suggestions for both. The disillusionment phase is when you are most needed. The only way to get through it is by being proactive with self-care.

Reconstruction Phase—A New Beginning

New beginnings really happen when both the individuals and the community as a whole have worked through the worst of their loss, grief, and anger. A mindset of "moving on" sets in. In this phase your spiritual care work should be proactive. We need to be mindful of the two kinds of trigger events that can add stress to our community. The first is predictable events, such as anniversaries of the disaster or the dedication of memorials. The second is unpredictable events, such as a similar disaster striking another community and bringing up reminders and images of the community's own experience.

No matter our faith traditions, we know that life after a disaster is never the same. Our various sacred texts all teach this lesson. When calamity strikes, we look to rebuild lives of stability and meaning. This final phase leads back to a "new beginning" in people's lives.

Dynamics That Contribute to the Length of a Disaster Life Cycle

The following factors have an impact on the life cycle—the time line and duration—of a disaster. It is important to be aware of these factors and to assess them when responding to a disaster.

Scope

The scope of a disaster refers to its size. The larger the disaster, the more lives lost or put at risk and the larger the loss of property. A tornado that does physical damage to a community without injuring people is small in scope. Hurricane Katrina affected the whole of the southeastern United States and thus was extremely large in scope.

Small-scale disasters leave most of a community's infrastructure in place. The larger the scope, the more infrastructure destruction takes place. After a large-scale disaster it is often hard to shop for food and other vital materials, to find clean water to drink, to be in contact with family and friends, and to get reliable information.

As a general rule, the larger the scope of a disaster, the longer the life cycle.

Intensity

The intensity of a disaster refers to the emotional, spiritual, and psychological impact. It also refers to the physical destruction caused by a disaster. Power outages often have a large scope and often cause large losses of property, but most people are not worried for their lives once they realize what has caused the outage. Thus, a power outage would be considered low in intensity.

In genereal, the more intense a disaster, the longer the life cycle.

Duration

The duration of a disaster refers to the total time period a disaster is actually taking place and for which people are affected by the disaster. The longer the duration, the longer people are in a state of hyper vigilance. A tornado has a relatively short duration. A major hurricane has a long duration. A major earthquake has a short duration, but when all of the aftershocks are included, it has a much longer duration. Cold and heat waves often have long durations lasting days and sometimes even weeks.

A key consideration with duration is the cumulative impact over time. The 2004 hurricane season had a very long duration in Florida. The state was hit by four different storms. The overall impact of four storms was much greater than a single storm, or even two, would have been. Its duration was extremely long.

In general, the longer the duration of a disaster, the longer the life cycle.

Multiplicity and Situational Importance

The multiplicity of a disaster refers to the amount of personal exposure or number of times a person is exposed to different disasters and trauma. There is often a cumulative effect to exposure of trauma and disaster. Situation importance refers to how significant a person perceives an event will be in their own personal life. The same event will often be perceived as having different situational importance for different people. A hurricane that destroys most of a city will have high situation importance for most people in the town, but to a homeless person, who is already on the edge, it might have a lower situation importance. The greater a person's perception of situational importance regarding an event, the greater his or her reaction. High multiplicity, high situational importance events include the death of a family member or close friend; the loss of a home and possessions; and the physical destruction of the larger local community including residential neighborhoods, shopping areas for food, houses of worship, and work locations.

In general, the higher the multiplicity and situational importance of a disaster, the longer the life cycle.

You have heard the saying, "knowledge is power." Sharing with you the life cycle of a disaster is an attempt to give you back the power a disaster steals from you. My hope is that with the knowledge of what to expect following a disaster you will be able to discern what are common responses to uncommon events.

It is also my prayer that you will heed the strategies and suggestions offered throughout this book. Adhering to the principles of this book, following good self-care practices, and maintaining a healthy support network can be a very positive use of your time and a source of healing following a disaster. Finally, knowing the life cycle of a disaster allows you to keep track of your journey and to look at the benchmarks in your recovery process. May this book lead you to finding that joy that King David said comes following weeping.

Notes

1. L. M. Zunin and D. Meyers, in D. J. DeWolfe, *Training Manual for Mental Health and Human Service Workers in Major Disasters,* 2nd ed., DHHS publication no. ADM 90-358 (Washington, D.C.: U.S. Department of Health and Human Services: Substance Abuse and Mental Health Services Administration, Center for Mental Health Services, 2000).

2. Ibid., 12.

3. D. Meyers and D. Wee, *Disaster Mental Health Services* (New York: Brunner-Routledge, 2005), 19.

4. Ibid., 20.

5. Ibid.

6. Ibid.

7. R. J. Ursano, B. G. McGaughey, and C. S. Fullerton, *Individual and Community Responses to Trauma and Disaster* (Cambridge: Cambridge University Press, 1994), 404.

8. N. L. Faberow and C. J. Frederick, *Training Manual for Human Service Workers in Major Disasters* (Rockville, MD: National Institute of Mental Health, 1978).

9. Ursano, *Individual and Community Responses to Trauma and Disaster,* 404.

10. D. J. DeWolfe, *Training Manual for Mental Health and Human Service Workers in Major Disasters*, 12.

Further Reading

Flynn, B. W., and A. E. Norwood. "Defining Normal Psychological Reactions to Disaster," *Psychiatric Annals* 34 (2004): 597–603.

Myers, D., and D. Wee. "Disasters and Their Impact." *Disaster Mental Health Services: A Primer for Practioners*. New York: Brunner-Routledge, 2005.

About the Contributors

Rabbi Stephen B. Roberts, BCJC, is editor of this book. He is the associate executive vice president of the New York Board of Rabbis overseeing the Jack D. Weiler Chaplaincy Program. He is a past president of the National Association of Jewish Chaplains. Two years prior to September 11, 2001 he founded a partnership organization within the American Red Cross in Greater New York of what is now Disaster Chaplaincy Services (DCS-NY), New York, an independent 501(c)3. He serves DCS-NY as chairman emeritus. Since 2000, Rabbi Roberts has served as one of the five official representatives overseeing American Red Cross's national Spiritual Care Response Team (SRT). Following 9/11 he was the first national officer to set up American Red Cross spiritual care response in New York City. On June 17, 2002, in New York City, Rabbi Roberts visioned and then chaired an American Red Cross one-day conference for clergy and other religious leaders with over 650 participants. This resiliency training specifically addressed the impact of 9/11 and on providing tools to better understand and work with those affected. He has taught extensively on disaster spiritual care and was the primary researcher for the only peer-reviewed research on the impact of disasters on spiritual care providers that has been published.

2

Self-Care—Not an Option

Tanya Pagán Raggio, MD, MPH, FAAP,
and Rev. Willard W. C. Ashley Sr., DMin, DH

Weeping may endure for a night, but joy cometh in the morning.

PSALM 30:5B, KJV

What happens when weeping lasts for more than a night or joy does not come in the morning? When a disaster occurs it may last only briefly, but the impact of a traumatic experience may continue for days, months, years, or even a lifetime. As clergy responding to a disaster or a series of disasters, when is it permissible to take care of ourselves?

Self-care during the impact, rescue, or heroic phase[1] is a challenge. Clergy are busy caring for others or attending to the dead and the dying (including mass casualties, which most of us are ill prepared to handle). As clergy we are providing last rites and observing other rituals of the deceased's respective religion. We find ourselves working with a team of first responders to tend to those who are maimed. We are in concert with police officers, firefighters, and emergency and medical personnel trying to maximize their chances of survival by providing a wide range of assistance and, most important, hope, when they (or even we) feel there is none. If we are not preoccupied with these tasks, we are trying to provide solace to the family members or friends who are grieving for lost, injured, or missing loved ones, and directly supporting those who have been injured.

Such was the case for clergy who responded to the World Trade Center attacks of September 11, 2001. Clergy were also called to respond to the crash of flight 587, which was flying from New York City to the Dominican Republic on November 12, 2001. Clergy were first responders during the rescue and recovery period from the back-to-back hurricanes Rita and Katrina, which devastated the Gulf Region of the United States in August and September of 2005. Clergy responded following the tsunami that struck eleven countries in the Indian Ocean on December 26, 2004, and following the unexpected tornado that hit Bay Ridge, Brooklyn, in August of 2007. Responding to these types of disasters, which often include mass casualties for which most clergy are ill prepared, creates additional stress in a profession already noted for its high levels of stressful experiences.

The need for self-care becomes even greater when clergy members themselves are personally affected by a disaster. Deborah DeWolfe, author of the *Training Manual: For Mental Health and Human Service Workers in Major Disasters*, notes how survivors of disasters, including clergy, react to a disaster and how the stress they experience is affected by a range of factors: "Natural vs. human causation, degree of personal impact, size and scope, visible impact/low point, and probability of recurrence contributes to dynamics that have potential psychosocial implications."[2] In addition to an individual's constellation of disaster preparedness, personal experiences, culture, and resilience will affect how he or she responds to a disaster.

Physiologically, our body's response during the impact and rescue phases of a disaster is to secrete adrenaline or epinephrine, which causes the heart to race and blood pressure to rise, giving us the strength or energy we need for a fight or flight response.[3] (A "freeze," or hypervigilant, response has also recently been added prior to the flight and fight responses.[4]) These hormones enable us to make split decisions, run away from a disaster site, and stay awake for long periods of time with little sleep or nourishment. This "rush" makes it difficult to calm down, psychologically and physiologically, or take a respite during the impact and rescue phases of a disaster.

Though we feel full of energy, our work may not be as effective due to being in shock, extreme fatigue, and anxiety. Therefore, even brief periods of rest, prayer, meditation, and sleep can provide us with additional emotional, spiritual, and physical strength and energy. It is easier to engage in these practices if we have made self-care a pattern prior to the disaster. With self-care a part of our vocational tool kit, we are more likely to be in better physical, psychological, and spiritual shape. Equally important, we will be more prepared to deal with the extraordinary responsibilities we will encounter as a consequence of a disaster. As our friend Rev. Kirk Jones wrote, we must "rest in the storm."[5]

It is essential to give ourselves permission to rest, not only to prevent burnout and compassion fatigue (a topic covered more thoroughly in chapter 13), but also to safeguard against physical and mental illness. Resting and caring for ourselves will enable us to better preserve our relationships with our families, partners, friends, congregations, and acquaintances.

Studies have shown that clergy are at high risk for poor health outcomes. This tendency is exacerbated during times of extreme stress, such as disasters. According to D. W. Hager and L. C. Hager, "Approximately 70%–75% of illnesses (physical and emotional) and doctor's visits are related to stress."[6] Persons under the extreme acute stress of a disaster, as well as the prolonged chronic stress that frequently follows, are at increased risk of illnesses such as hypertension, stroke, and sudden cardiac death.

During a disaster, clergy will be called upon to provide an increased load of pastoral counseling to both their own congregation and the wider community.[7] Besides coping with grief, depression, and anxiety, people who have survived a disaster, including clergy, may also find themselves questioning their faith, a side effect that may be most apparent during the post-disaster phase of disillusionment.[8] This questioning of faith is so significant that there is even a Diagnostic and Statistical Manual (DSM-IV) category for religious or spiritual problems titled "Spiritual Emergency" (V62.89), which includes those questioning their faith and those having near-death experiences.[9] To get through a spiritual emergency, David Lukoff, coauthor of "Spiritual Emergency," suggests the following:

- Simplify your life
- Limit your use of all stimulants
- Create a sacred space
- Find a means of expressing your experience

- Develop internal support
- Seek external support
- Flow with the process
- Know your limits[10]

It is also common after a disaster to experience anxiety, depression, acute traumatic stress disorder (ATSD, diagnosed within the first thirty days of a disaster), and posttraumatic stress disorder (PTSD, diagnosed thirty days after the disaster).[11]ATSD occurs in the first two to four days following a traumatic event and lasts no longer than four weeks. PTSD develops over a longer period of time.[12]

During the phases after the impact of a disaster, clergy, like others, are usually going through the process of grief and mourning. Most of us are familiar with the stages of grief: denial, anger, bargaining, depression, and acceptance. Mourning addresses the tasks of grief. Dr. Ibrahim Abdul-Malik says, "The first of four tasks is that the griever ACCEPT the reality of the loss, both intellectually and emotionally. It is not enough that the person simply speaks the words. Surely the 'saying' is the necessary first step. But acceptance is not complete until it is felt at a deeper level of the emotions."[13] The way and length that a person grieves and mourns varies. If you find yourself going through grief and mourning following a disaster, remember to allow yourself time to rest—observing the Sabbath can become an essential aspect of your self-care.

You may become a victim (some prefer to use the term *survivor*) during a disaster. Like the people we serve, clergy also have different coping mechanisms and levels of resilience. We may become victims either through direct exposure to or observation of the disaster; physical or emotional injury; the loss of loved ones; loss or damage to our property, or the weight of the devastation of entire communities (primary traumatization); the experiences of family and friends (secondary traumatization); or through repetitive exposure via listening to and counseling others (vicarious traumatization). As a result of these traumas, people go through stages of crisis that are quite similar to the stages of grief and include immobilization, denial, anger or anxiety, self-doubt, depression, testing, and acceptance.[14]

The experiences of disaster survivors (including clergy) lead to high levels of long-term stress during the post-disaster period, which causes the adrenal glands to release heightened levels of cortisol (a hormone that, when secreted at elevated levels for prolonged periods of time, can elevate blood pressure; create ulcers; impair the immune system, predisposing us to infections and cancer; and increase abdominal girth (fat) and cause us to crave "comfort foods" high in fats, carbohydrates, and sugar, predisposing us to diabetes and cardiovascular disease).[15] Chronically elevated levels of cortisol can result in increased rates of obesity and diseases such as metabolic syndrome, a constellation of abdominal obesity, elevated blood pressure, elevated triglycerides, low HDL (a condition that fosters plaque buildup in arterial walls), and insulin resistance or glucose intolerance (which means the body can't properly use insulin or blood sugar), as well as heart disease and stroke.[16] The long-term affects of trauma and subsequent chronic stress associated with the acute and chronic release of hormones such as adrenaline, norepinephrine, and cortisol may also adversely affect the brain, contributing to neuropsychiatric disorders such as memory loss, depression, anxiety, acute traumatic stress disorder, posttraumatic stress disorder, hypervigilance, and loss of sleep, fatigue, substance abuse, and dissociative response.[17] In a national survey conducted by Pulpit and Pew of 2,500 religious leaders, they found 76 percent of clergy were either overweight or obese compared to 61 percent of the population. Ten percent shared they were depressed and 40 percent depressed at times, or worn out "some of the time." Because of these factors, clergy have one of the highest risks of heart disease.[18] In addition to the effects of trauma, clergy and their spouses are also stressed due to high rates of congregational intrusiveness, a term Dr. Lee Cameron, professor of marriage and family studies at Fuller Theological Seminary, classifies as "presumptive expectations, personal criticism, family criticism and boundary ambiguity."[19]

In the face of the emotional and physiological responses to disasters and other stressors, how can you take care of yourself while still caring for others? We will address (1) why self-care (2) the spiritual basis for self-care (3) self-care during different phases of a disaster, and (4) returning to overall good self-care.

Now that you know the types of emotional and physical obstacles you may face when you are affected by or respond to a disaster, we can examine the why and how of self-care.

Besides helping the clergyperson, good self-care is also beneficial to the congregation. Good self-care practices allow clergy to be productive leaders and to be at their best, especially during disasters. It is a two-way street. Clergy need to support and encourage their congregation to engage in self-care. However, the congregation needs to support and encourage their clergy to develop and maintain good self-care practices.

It would be easy to provide a to-do list for clergy self–care, such as observing the Sabbath, eating well, exercising, training for disaster situations, and the like. We have actually provided such a list at the end of this chapter. You can also probably come up with your own additions to this list. We encourage you to take a few minutes right now to create your own list, specific to your interests and needs.

The Spiritual Basis for Self-Care

Once we've tackled the question of what we should do, we have to address how we can "schedule" ourselves for activities such as exercise, play, good nutrition, rest, Sabbath, and time with loved ones. How do we make these practices become part of our daily routine? How do we justify taking time for ourselves? What is the spiritual basis for self-care?

The answer may lie in activities clergy engage in frequently (or so we hope): spiritual disciplines such as prayer, meditation, and reading sacred literature.[20] Most, if not all, sacred literature (the Bible, the Torah, the Qur'an, and the like) encourages spiritual leaders to take care of themselves. Where is it written that we should care for others to the exclusion of our own spiritual, emotional, and physical health? Indeed, most religions recommend the opposite, that we should care for ourselves—our bodies, our minds, and our souls—in order to be effective leaders.

Sacred literature teaches about spiritual health, prayer, meditation, and fasting. In the Ten Commandments, for example, we are encouraged to observe the Sabbath, a time of rest and renewal. The Sabbath has now become a workday for clergy due to many and varied responsibilities, therefore, we need an additional day of rest. Yet some clergy find taking additional rest extremely difficult, especially if they are bi-vocational (if they have a full-time job in addition to their full-time pastoral responsibilities).

Our sacred texts also usually speak about our physical health. Most (if not all) religious texts instruct us on the importance of taking care of our bodies, telling us what types of food to eat or avoid and sometimes prescribing times we should fast (with exceptions for those who are ill, pregnant women, small children, and infants). Please check with your physician before fasting as you may have a medical condition you are unaware of which does not allow you to fast or you may need to modify your fasting.

In addition to these more prosaic issues, most religious texts also address the impact of despair, distress, and cataclysmic disaster on individuals, communities, nations, and the world, usually in the form of plagues, floods, wars, rape, incest, or murder. Religious texts encourage us to have hope and not to worry; they tell us that there are seasons for all phases of life, including both grief and happiness. In short, religious texts and sacred literature are not silent about self-care.

With the background of our religious texts' advocacy for self-care, we can look at the practice of self-care in the context of the phases of disaster, as depicted by Leonard M. Zunin and Diane Meyers, as well as the responses to these phases of disaster, according to Deborah DeWolfe.[21] Leonard M. Zunin, MD, is senior psychiatric consultant for the California Department of Mental Health. Diane Meyers, RN, MSN, is a licensed clinical nurse specialist with twenty-five years of experience in disaster mental health and a member of the California Governor's Office of Emergency Services. Deborah J. Dewolfe, PhD, MSPH, is the author of books and articles on mental health.

Self-Care during the Impact, Rescue, and Honeymoon Phases

During the impact phase of a disaster we are immediately concerned about survival and safety for our families, friends, and communities. Depending on the nature of the disaster, this concern may continue for days or weeks, into the phase known as rescue and heroic. However, we must also be concerned about our own safety and survival in these two phases of the disaster. We are certain you have heard of clergy who have survived a disaster, only to become hurt, severely injured, or killed during the rescue efforts.

Depending on the nature of the disaster, we may be concurrently seeking out the basic necessities of life—food, water, and shelter—during the first two phases of the disaster. It is important to remind ourselves to engage in the basic activities we are encouraging others to do: drinking water, eating, sleeping, praying, trying not to lose hope, and if possible, basic grooming such as washing, combing our hair, and changing clothes.

Some would say that once basic needs and safety are attended to it is extremely important to maintain some semblance of spirituality through prayer, observation of the Sabbath and other religious traditions, and observation of major holidays. However, it is important to acknowledge that as the finality of the affects of a disaster hits, you may not feel like engaging in any religious activities, including prayer. You may even become angry, questioning God, or even asking if there is a God at all, while simultaneously feeling guilty about these thoughts. It is a common response to have such feelings, and it is very important to share your reactions with people you trust and who understand you.

During the weeks to months that follow, also known as the remedy or honeymoon phase, disaster volunteers, assistants, and mental health workers are often available to assist individuals and the community, including clergy. You may not want to seek their assistance, thinking that others need them more than you, but it is important to use their services and to encourage others to do so.

Self-Care during the Disillusionment Phase

During the disillusionment phase, which may last from months to years, the recognition of what has been lost hits home, and many of the resources previously available may be withdrawn, creating a tremendous void that further exacerbates stress, fatigue, depression, and anxiety. During this time you may depend more on the assistance of family members, friends, and others in your community who may be equally as strained and stressed.

If you live in a community that has been totally destroyed, such as the ninth ward in New Orleans following Hurricane Katrina, and you have become homeless and displaced, you are far more likely to be disillusioned, depressed, anxious, and downright angry than if you lived in another community that is rapidly being rebuilt or at least showing some progress.

The amount of stress we experience during this time will vary and can adversely affect our physical and mental health, families, finances, and living conditions. It is important, though difficult, to do all we can to maintain our family units; this may mean seeking mental health services, if available. We may also face the challenges of compassion fatigue from helping others, and ATSD or PTSD from our own experiences during the disaster. Please read chapter 13 in this book for more on compassion fatigue. The Substance Abuse and Mental Health Services Administration (SAMHSA) has excellent resources for assessing and dealing with ATSD and PTSD, and general disaster training.[22]

If you have a chronic illness such as asthma, diabetes, or heart disease you may experience an exacerbation of this condition during this time. It is important to seek health care wherever you can, and to obtain and take your medications. You may need to seek health and mental health care from city or state agencies. Even if you are not chronically ill, it is important to maintain your health by trying to eat nutritionally; get some exercise, even if it is just walking outside (which exposes you to sunlight and helps improve your mood); and avoiding self-medication through alcohol or other drugs. It may be extremely difficult to care for yourself properly if you are feeling severely depressed and overwhelmed, but it is important to push yourself to do so. You need to do whatever you can to improve your living conditions. This may mean applying for and accepting resources you never thought you would need, such as shelter accommodations; unemployment insurance; city, state, federal, and charity disaster funds; and food stamps. It is essential to remember that you have worked all your life and paid for most of these resources through your taxes, tithes, and other donations.

Self-Care during the Reconstruction Phase

During the reconstruction or recovery phase, spiritual and mental health continues to be an extremely important component of self-care since fatigue, depression, and emotional exhaustion may continue. It may take years to be able to "accept" what has happened to you and your family, friends, and community. Some people say they are unable to accept what has transpired, but they deal with their profound losses by finding a special place in their hearts and minds where they will never forget the experience or their lost loved ones. Some individuals have great difficulty overcoming their despair and may require long-term support and mental health treatment. Many start to reevaluate their lives and use their unimaginably traumatic experiences to positively change their living conditions and communities.

Starting a Self-Care Routine before a Disaster Hits

The goal of self-care is to keep yourself healthy. The constitution of the World Health Organization defines health as "the state of complete physical, mental, and social well-being and not merely the absence of disease or infirmity." We would add spiritual well-being to this list. One of the best ways to achieve good health is through self-care.

A major way to establish emotional and psychological well-being is by minimizing our level of stress, when possible. We will spend a lot of time on this topic because it is clearly the root of almost all physical and psychological illness, and even death! There is even stress that is secondary to positive experiences (eustress) such as getting married, having a baby, or receiving a promotion. Clearly, some stress is unpreventable, such as the stress of a disaster, trauma, or the sudden death of a loved one. How we deal with stress secondary to a disaster will be different from, but rooted in and related to, how we deal with the stress of everyday life. Thus, the following recommendations about managing and preventing stress will address both types of stress and their relationship.

An important component of self-care is discerning what causes stress in your life and, if possible, what you can do about it. Another good way to overcome stress is to consider what brings you joy or pleasure. What causes stress or joy in your professional life? What causes stress or joy in your personal life? Consider conducting a time budget to discern how many things you do that are stressful and how many bring you joy. How does your stress affect your family, partners, and friends? How does their stress affect you? When are the times you feel like saying, "Helping you is hurting me!"[23] What do you do to decrease your stress and your reaction to the stress of those around you?

You might want to make a list of your stressors and work toward decreasing them one at a time by prioritization.

Another objective way to view the impact of stress and where modification may be needed is to complete a stress scale of everyday experiences such as the Social Readjustment Rating Scale developed by Drs. Holmes and Rahe.[24] The doctors examined the medical records of over 5,000 medical patients as a way to determine whether stressful life events might cause illnesses and found that as the cumulative level of stress increased, the percentage of people who became physically, psychologically, or psychosomatically ill increased dramatically.[25] There are other stress scales designed specifically for post-disaster and trauma assessment, such as the Florida Secondary Traumatic Stress Scale and the Compassion Fatigue Self-Test.[26]

In addition to conducting a stress inventory, other stress management techniques can also be helpful, such as slow and deep breathing, stretching, cognitive techniques, relaxation, meditation, imagination, humor, creative expression, time management, conflict resolution, resistance building, and lifestyle adjustments (changing your work schedule, getting enough rest, eating properly, exercising, reaching out for social support, and taking time for relaxation and recreation).[27]

Stress Reactions during a Disaster

Specific recommendations for those who have experienced a disaster are a little different, since there are reactions during a disaster that are common in the short-term but uncommon in the long-term. Some of these reactions have already been addressed in this chapter, some are delineated below, and still others appear in chapter 13, on compassion fatigue.[28] If these symptoms are not resolving they may also be a reason to seek additional care.

If you experience a disaster it is important to express your feelings and share your stories with other clergy and perhaps other first responders in a safe, supportive, confidential environment. Sometimes we find our friends, family, and even our colleagues are not enough! *It is important to know when you should seek additional professional help from a mental health provider, such as a licensed clinical social worker, psychologist, psychotherapist, or psychiatrist.*

After a disaster or severe trauma it is common to be in denial, to be hypervigilant, to be preoccupied with thoughts of the deceased, to exhibit avoidant behavior, to feel sad, lonely, fearful, abandoned, depressed, anxious, frightened, withdrawn, guilty, angry, irritable, lonely, or tearful, to have difficulty sleeping, concentrating, or making decisions, to experience changes in appetite and weight, and just to feel lousy. However, if these symptoms persist more than a month, or if you find yourself using alcohol, tobacco, or other drugs to calm down, they may be indicative of PTSD or compassion fatigue. You should seek mental health assistance.

Seek immediate attention if you have any thoughts of suicide or homicide, any delusions or hallucinations. It is important to know these are different from feeling the presence of loved ones or friends or feeling that they may be communicating with you after their death, which is common.

Some advise anyone who has experienced severe trauma such as a disaster to proactively seek counseling or psychotherapy before you experience the symptoms listed above. Some people have mixed feelings about going to mental health practitioners; they may have had a negative experience in the past, or worry about confidentiality issues, or think they will be labeled "ill" in some way. If you are reluctant to see a behavioral health specialist, at least see your primary care physician, nurse practitioner, or physician's assistant and talk with them about your concerns. Remember that poor mental health status and extreme and prolonged stress can lead to many physical illnesses, including sudden cardiac death.

What Else Can You Do for Yourself?

Find your own oasis—a peaceful, quiet place that you can retreat to on a daily basis and engage in some physical exercise. You might choose a place near running water or where there is grass or trees, parks, rivers, beaches, or mountains. Perhaps your oasis would be swimming laps in a pool. Or perhaps you would enjoy regular trips to the gym to play basketball or lift weights. Whatever your choice, engage in an activity that enables you to relax your mind and participate in an aerobic exercise for thirty minutes a day, at least five days a week.

Take time to pray and meditate daily. In addition, consider a sabbatical to a spiritual retreat or some other form of respite.

Some people find writing in a journal helpful. If you are more verbal, you could speak into a tape recorder. There are even computer programs that will automatically transcribe for you. Perhaps you fancy yourself a poet or writer of fiction. Go ahead and write. Explore your artistic side by drawing, painting, or sculpting. Maybe knitting, crocheting or quilting are more your speed. Explore or renew activities you enjoy. Go on an outing to the theater, musical event, or a museum. If you are a sports enthusiast, go for a bike ride or run a race or even complete a triathlon (please consult your physician or other primary care provider first, especially if you have been sedentary). Perhaps you are more of the observer and you find it relaxing to watch tennis matches, baseball, soccer, football, basketball, or ice skating. Try to listen to relaxing music, sing, or read for pure enjoyment.

Take time to be with your friends and family. You may want to schedule a regular time to meet with some of your clerical colleagues to discuss life and your vocation. Some clergy find these moments together entertaining, relaxing, and life giving. As in any profession, there are some things only insiders understand.

Take a vacation from work! Spend time away from both your house of worship and, if you have another vocation, your other job. Have a date night with your partner or spouse. Try to take even a brief mini-vacation once every three months. Delegate to others you trust. People tend to appreciate the opportunity to participate and contribute in your absence.

Take good care of yourself because you are special and deserve it. You will be a healthier caregiver. Remember, change is difficult. Do not feel like a failure if you cannot maintain all of your desired changes. It is usually easier and more successful in the long run to introduce changes incrementally. Also, whenever starting an exercise program, please consult your health care provider first and start slowly!

Nutrition

Healthy eating is a great way to provide self-care, especially since many Americans are overweight. In certain demographics, we are nurtured by our congregations with wonderful treats of baked goods, candies, and other sweets or fat-laden delicacies. And that's okay once in a while. But the majority of foods we eat should consist of fresh fruits and vegetables. Think of your plate as a clock: one-half should be filled with vegetables, one-fourth with grains and breads, and one-fourth with protein (beans, fish, or meat; especially low-fat organic). We provide some basic suggestions for healthy eating in this section, but there are many comprehensive resources available. We encourage you to seek them out. The U.S. Department of Agriculture is one such resource. They have developed a new food pyramid and a fun and interesting website to go with it: www.mypyramid.gov. This site helps you evaluate the quality of your diet, how much you need to eat, how much physical activity you should be doing, and the steps you can take to achieve a healthier lifestyle.

Balance is the key to eating well. Most people benefit from eating breakfast, lunch, dinner, and two to three healthy snacks consisting of fruits and vegetables daily. But not everyone is comfortable eating this way. Eat when you are hungry and try to stop eating about three hours before bedtime. If you eat out, consider placing half your meal in a container to take home, before you start eating. Most restaurant portions are double the amount of calories we require.

Drink water when you are thirsty. Most adults need about sixty-four ounces, or eight eight-ounce glasses, of water a day. Try drinking water before coffee, tea, sodas, or juices. Breads and cereal that are high in fiber and nuts are also a very important component of our diet. A good general rule about ingredients is if you can't spell it, then most likely it's not natural and you probably shouldn't eat it! Try to keep refined sugars, white flour, and other white foods to a minimum, and especially try to avoid them at night.

Protein is extremely important to our diet. Good non-animal sources of protein include nuts and beans. Fish is also a good source of protein and an excellent source of omega-3 fatty acids. Try to eat fish two to three times a week.

Regarding vegetables, we are learning more and more about how they help to decrease risk for a wide range of cancers. For example, tomatoes contain lycopene, also known as carotenoids or antioxidants, which is associated with decreasing the risk of cancer, especially breast cancer. Vegetables such as broccoli, brussels sprouts, cauliflower, and cabbage are also associated with decreased cancer rates.

Blueberries are also an excellent antioxidant that are delicious and a great addition to most cereals.

Although it is recommended for adults to have two eight-ounce glasses of milk a day, many people cannot drink milk either because of lactose intolerance or an allergy to cow's milk protein. As an alternative, fortified soy milk is a good source of calcium and vitamin D. Some people prefer to obtain their calcium from cheese and yogurt, but be aware of the sugar content of your yogurt if it is premixed fruit. You might buy plain low-fat or fat-free yogurt and add your own fruit instead. Also be aware of the fat content of your cheese and consider buying low-fat varieties.

Vitamin supplements are also a very important component of the diet since most of us do not obtain an adequate amount of vitamins from our food. Most women need supplemental calcium and vitamin D. Sunlight is the best source of vitamin D. If you are a woman of child-bearing age, you will need additional folic acid before and during your pregnancy. Consider taking a multivitamin every day.

If you are not allergic, some doctors recommend that those over age forty take a baby aspirin daily to prevent heart attacks, strokes, and some cancers. However, please consult your physician about this recommendation since it may be contraindicated for some people.

Limit your intake of stimulants such as the caffeine found in chocolate, coffee, and soft drinks. Consider drinking decaffeinated herbal tea instead. Try not to self-medicate with alcohol or other drugs. If you drink, limit your intake of alcohol to one glass of red wine a day. Red wine may actually help prevent heart disease, but more than one glass a day on a regular basis is not helpful and can actually cause harm. If you smoke or chew tobacco, stop! You may need help to discontinue. Avoid the use of illegal substances.

Physical Self-Care

An excellent, more in-depth, resource about clergy health is a book by Dr. Gwen Washington Halaas titled *The Right Road: Life Choices for Clergy*.[29] Exercise! You should have a checkup by your physician or other health care provider before starting an exercise program. You do not have to run a marathon. In fact, brisk walking is great aerobic exercise. If you have not exercised in a while, you should start with five to ten minutes a day and build up slowly to thirty minutes a day, at least five days a week. You want to consider working with a health professional who can design a program for your needs and current state of health.

You can climb the stairs at work—even one flight a couple of times a day helps. Gardening is a great physical activity and also relaxing for the soul. You could plant some tomatoes and blueberries, perhaps even some wine grapes, and work on your nutrition at the same time. Doing home repairs is also good exercise, though not necessarily aerobic. Stretching is wonderful for the body and very relaxing. Stretching before and after you exercise also helps to prevent injuries.

Strength or resistance training three times a week is very helpful, especially for building bone strength and preventing osteoporosis and injuries such as hip fractures. You do not have to use very heavy weights. Exercise produces hormones called endorphins that help to relax your mind and body. They give you a natural high!

Another good way to relax your body is to just do as the expression suggests: "take a deep breath."It really is helpful to inhale and exhale slowly several times a day. Try closing your eyes and raising your arms while breathing in, and lowering your arms while breathing out. It is really quite relaxing!

There is a wonderful book written by Drs. Mehmet C. Oz and Michael F. Roizen entitled *You—The Owner's Manual: An Insider's Guide to the Body that Will Make You Healthier and Younger.*[30] It is fun, easy to read, and user friendly, while still being accurate and very informational. It a book about everything you wanted to know about how your body works, accompanied by some diet and exercise suggestions. Another good resource, though one more oriented toward clinicians, is the *U.S. Preventive Task Force Guide to Clinical Preventive Measures.*[31]

Eye health and oral health are also very important aspects of your physical well-being. It is important to get a baseline assessment of your visual acuity from an ophthalmologist or optometrist. Your doctor will also check for glaucoma, or increased pressure in the eye, and signs of other eye problems such as macular degeneration. Poor oral hygiene, cavities, and periodontal (gum) disease have been associated with a range of other medical problems such as heart attacks, stroke, and low birth weight. See your dentist annually and get your teeth cleaned by a hygienist regularly. Engage in daily brushing and flossing in the morning after breakfast and at night before you go to bed.[32]

Getting a little older and not hearing well? Consider getting your hearing checked. Many of us need hearing aids as well as glasses as we mature.

Talk to your family about inherited medical problems such as heart disease, diabetes, and cancer so you can obtain appropriate early screening and detection. If you are getting ready to start a family, ask about genetically transmitted diseases such as sickle-cell anemia (most common in African-Americans), thalassemia (most common in people of Mediterranean heritage), and Tay-Sachs disease (most common in Jewish people of Ashkenazi descent).

Undergo routine annual physical exams. Schedule an appointment using holy days such as during Ramadan, the Hebrew month of Elul, between Ash Wednesday and Easter. Making an annual physical exam an integrated part of your spiritual life means you are less likely to skip or forget to schedule your exam.

Know your numbers! Your blood pressure should be checked every time you go to the doctor. Obtain age-appropriate lab tests and screening exams such as lipid profiles (cholesterol, HDL, LDL, and C-reactive protein, a test that evaluates inflammation in your arteries) to prevent, detect, and treat heart disease. You should also get a random blood sugar and hemoglobin A1c test (essentially, a three-month reading of your blood sugar) for diabetes (many people have undiagnosed diabetes).

For cancer prevention we suggest routine self-examination and the use of screening tests through your physician or other health care provider. Use sunscreen to prevent skin cancer; examine your skin and if you notice any lesions that are changing color, irregular, or bleeding, please contact your physician. If you can, prevent cervical cancer by requesting a vaccine called Gardasil, which prevents several types of human papillomavirus, the major cause of cervical cancer. Unfortunately this vaccine is only available for females ages nine to twenty-six. Detect early cervical cancer early by having your Pap smear done regularly on the schedule recommended by your health care provider. Detect early breast cancer by conducting monthly self breast exams and go to the doctor immediately if you feel anything unusual or see a discharge. Have your clinician conduct a breast exam and order mammograms annually (annual mammograms should start at age forty unless you have a family history of breast cancer, in which case additional genetic testing may also be indicated). Digital rectal exams and a blood test called prostate-specific antigen (PSA) should be conducted to detect prostate cancer for men over fifty years of age. Detect early testicular cancer by conducting a self examination and go to the doctor immediately if you feel or see anything unusual. A testicular exam should also be part of your routine physical. Of note, testicular cancer is more common among younger men, twenty to thirty-nine years of age. During the rectal exam a fecal occult blood test can be conducted to detect colorectal cancer. A colonoscopy should be conducted every five years starting at fifty years of age, forty-five for African-Americans, and earlier if there is a family history of colon cancer.

Keeping immunizations such as tetanus, hepatitis B, and influenza up to date is extremely important, especially in the event of a disaster. In addition, you may want to obtain a tuberculosis test, especially if you work with immigrants, the homeless, prisoners, or immunosuppressed persons, or if you travel overseas. Although the hepatitis A vaccine is not routinely given in the United States, it is very helpful to have during a disaster when sanitary conditions may be poor.

If you have a chronic disease such as asthma, heart disease, or diabetes, make sure you keep your appointments and try to have an extra month of medication on hand. Do not wait until you have symptoms to go to the doctor; if you do experience symptoms, go right away. In addition to the vaccines already mentioned, make sure you obtain a vaccination to prevent pneumonia (pnuemococcal vaccine). People with diabetes should be sure to get an annual eye (ophthalmology) exam and foot (podiatry) exam. Your regular health care provide can conduct your foot exam, but if possible, see a podiatrist.

Do not avoid seeing the doctor because you do not want to be a burden to or worry your spouse, partner, children, or congregation. They want you to be healthy as much as you do! Please do not avoid seeing a doctor because you are uninsured. Yes, many of us (clergy) are uninsured or underinsured (that is, our insurance does not adequately cover preventive measures, medication, or mental and oral health services). Every state has health centers, funded by the federal government, that provide care to you on a sliding fee scale.[33] States have insurance programs for children who are not eligible for Medicaid called State Child Health Insurance Programs, and some have similar programs for adults. States and some cities have health departments that may provide vaccinations and other health services for a low cost or for free.

Many pharmaceutical companies also have programs now to help with the cost of medications.

There are complementary or alternative forms of therapy, also known as holistic medicine, that are practiced by people around the world and can be very helpful. These include, but are not limited to, homeopathic, naturopathic, traditional Chinese medicine such as acupuncture, Ayurveda, herbs foods, vitamins, osteopathic manipulation and massage, therapeutic touch, Reiki, qigong, mind-body medicine such as prayer, mental healing, yoga, tai chi, art, music, or dance. An excellent online resource for information about complementary medicine is the National Center for Complementary and Alternative Medicine.[34] If you use complementary and alternative therapies, especially herbs, it is important to remember to share this information with your medical doctor since herbs and other medical plants may interact with your other medications and are not always innocuous. In fact, many of our medications are refined products made from plants and herbs.

A delicate but important issue to discuss, since this is a book about clergy dealing with disaster and trauma, is having a living will or advance health care directives. These documents allow your loved ones and health care providers to know your desire for your health care, such as the extent of resuscitation efforts, if for some reason you become incapacitated and unable to make decisions for yourself. Let your loved ones and health care providers know you have a living will, and provide them with a copy. A financial will is also important, and don't forget to keep your beneficiaries up to date if you have a pension or life insurance. Last, but not least, put in writing what kind of services you would like to have done in the event of your death.

Final Words

We live in a time of tension, terror, and turbulence. We need healthy clergy to help us navigate a world where human evil and natural disasters grab the headlines. Self-care is not an option; it is a requirement that should start before the disaster occurs so we can give our best to our families and our vocation.

Notes

1. L. M. Zunin and D. Meyers, "Phases of Disaster," in D. J. DeWolfe, "Responses to Disaster," in *Training Manual for Mental Health and Human Service Workers in Major Disasters*, 2nd ed., DHHS publication no. ADM 90-358 (Washington, D.C.: U.S. Department of Health and Human Services: Substance Abuse and Mental Health Services Administration, Center for Mental Health Services, 2000), 5.

2. DeWolfe, "Responses to Disaster," 6–8.

3. W. B. Cannon, *Bodily Changes in Pain, Hunger, Fear and Rage: An Account of Recent Research into the Function of Emotional Excitement*, 2nd ed. (New York: B. Appleton. 1929).

4. J. A. Gray, *The Psychology of Fear and Stress*, 2nd ed. (Cambridge: Cambridge University Press, 1988).

5. B. K. Jones, *Rest in the Storm: Self-Care Strategies for Clergy and Other Caregivers* (Valley Forge, PA: Judson Press, 2001).

6. D. W. Hager and L. C. Hager, *Stress and a Woman's Body* (Grand Rapids, MI: Fleming H. Revell, 1996).

7. W. S. Sage, *Spiritual and Emotional Care Resource* Church World Service, 3.

8. R. W. Roukema, *Counseling for the Soul in Distress: What Every Religious Counselor Should Know about Emotional and Mental Illness*, 2nd ed. (New York: Haworth Pastoral Press, 2003), 1.

9. See chapter 9, "From Honeymoon to Disillusionment to Reconstruction: Pastoral Counseling—Thinking Outside the Box."

10. D. Lukoff, "From Spiritual Emergency to Spiritual Problem: The Transpersonal Roots of the New DSM IV Category," *Journal of Humanistic Psychology* 38, no. 2 (1998): 21–50.

11. "Clinical depression is a profound alteration in mood marked by sadness, despair, feelings of hopelessness, and disturbances in sleep and appetite. It has mental, psychological and physical effects." Roukema, *Counseling for the Soul in Distress*, 34.

12. http://mentalhealth.samhsa.gov/dtac/FederalResource/table_of_contents.htm.

13. I. Abdul-Malik, "Preparing for the Future: Upcoming Anniversaries, Reminders, Holidays," in *The Life Cycle of a Disaster: Ritual & Practice* (American Red Cross of Greater New York, June 17, 2002).

14. National Volunteer Organizations Active in Disaster, *Emotional and Spiritual Care: An Introduction on Basic Concepts*, May 24, 2004, 9, 18. A working document from the emotional and spiritual care committee of the NVOAD. See C. L. Hacker's "How Faith Communities Can Respond to Crises and Disasters" for more on the stages of crises.

15. D. J. Bremmer, *Does Stress Damage the Brain? Understanding Trauma Related Disorders from a Mind-Body Perspective* (New York: W. W. Norton and Company, 2005); and Hager, *Stress and a Woman's Body*.

16. American Heart Association, "Metabolic Syndrome." http://www.americanheart.org/presenter.jhtml?identifier=534.

17. Bremmer, *Does Stress Damage the Brain?*; National Center for Posttraumatic Stress Disorder, "Helping Survivors in the Wake of a Disaster,"27; and National Volunteer Organizations Active in Disaster, *Emotional and Spiritual Care: An Introduction on Basic Concepts.*

18. B. Wells, "Which Way to Clergy Health?" http://www.divinity.duke.edu/programs/spe/resources/dukediv-clergyhealth.html.

19. A. C. Darling, E. W. Hill, and L. M. McWey, "Understanding Stress and Quality of Life for Clergy and Clergy Spouses," *Stress and Health* 20 (2004): 261–77.

20. R. J. Foster, *Celebration of Disciple: The Path of Spiritual Growth* (New York: HarperCollins, 1978, 1988, 1998).

21. Zunin and Meyers, "Phases of Disaster"; and DeWolfe, "Responses to Disaster."

22. DeWolfe, "Responses to Disasters,"14.

23. This is the title of a seminar given by Rev. Ashley, the coauthor of this chapter.

24. H. T. Holmes and R. H. Rahe "The Social Readjustments Rating Scales," *Journal of Psychosomatic Research* 11 (1967): 213–18.

25. H. Clinebell, *Basic Types of Pastoral Care and Counseling: Resources for Ministry of Health and Growth* (Nashville: Abingdon Press, 1984).

26. C. R. Figley, *Treating Compassion Fatigue* (New York: Brunner-Routledge, 2002), 91, 115–17.

27. D. Meyers and D. F. Wee, *Disaster Mental Health Services* (New York: Brunner-Routledge, 2005), 121.

28. S. Roberts, "Jewish Spiritual Care in the Wake of a Disaster," in *Jewish Pastoral Care: A Practical Handbook from Traditional and Contemporary Sources,* 2nd ed., ed. Dayle Friedman (Woodstock, VT: Jewish Lights, 2005), 447.

29. G. W. Halaas, *The Right Road: Life Choices for Clergy* (Minneapolis: Augsburg Fortress, 2004).

30. M. C. Oz and M. F. Roizen, *You—The Owner's Manual: An Insider's Guide to the Body that will Make You Healthier and Younger* (New York: HarperResource, 2005).

31. U.S. Preventive Services Task Force, http://www.ahrq.gov/clinic/uspstfix.htm#Recommendations.

32. "Oral Health in America: A Report of the Surgeon General," http://www.surgeongeneral.gov/library/oralhealth/.

33. http://ask.hrsa.gov/pc.

34. National Center for Complementary and Alternative Medicine, http://nccam.nih.gov.

Further Reading

Levine, Peter A., with Ann Frederick. *Waking the Tiger: Healing Trauma.* Berkeley, CA: North Atlantic Books, 1997.

Milam, James R., and Katherine Ketcham. *Under the Influence: A Guide to the Myths and Realities of Alcoholism.* New York: Bantam Books, 1983.

Nouwen, Henri J. M. *The Wounded Healer.* Garden City, NY: Image Books, 1972.

Oswald, Roy M. *Clergy Self-Care: Finding a Balance for Effective Ministry.* New York: Alban Institute, 1991.

Rothschild, Babette, with Marjorie Rand. *Help for the Helper: Self-Care Strategies for Managing Burnout and Stress.* New York: W. W. Norton, 2006.

Schwartz, Richard C. *Internal Family Systems Therapy.* New York: Guilford Press, 1995.

Yalom, Irvin D. *The Gift of Therapy: An Open Letter to a New Generation of Therapists and their Patients.* New York: HarperCollins, 2002.

About the Contributors

Tanya Pagán Raggio, MD, MPH, FAAP, is board-certified in preventive medicine and pediatrics. She was awarded her bachelor's of science and doctor of medicine from Rutgers University. She completed her masters in public health and fellowship in cardiovascular epidemiology at the University of Pittsburgh. She has extensive experience in developing and implementing health care services for persons of all ages throughout the country. She has also served as an associate professor of medicine at several universities.

Rev. Willard W. C. Ashley Sr., DMin, DH, is coeditor of this book, a psychotherapist, and founder and senior pastor of the Abundant Joy Community Church in Jersey City, New Jersey. He envisioned and implemented the largest clergy resiliency program in the United States following the attacks on September 11, 2001, the Care for the Caregivers Interfaith Program, a ministry of the Council of Churches of the City of New York. His ministry also includes roles as an adjunct professor; a consultant on disaster recovery and clergy self-care to congregations and Fortune 100 companies; a board member of Disaster Chaplaincy Services, New York City; a board member of Christ Hospital, Jersey City, New Jersey; a former assistant dean of students and director of recruitment for Andover Newton Theological School; and past president of the Blanton Peale Graduate Institute, Alumni Association. Ashley is an ordained minister in the National Baptist Convention, USA, Inc.; Disciples of Christ; and the American Baptist Churches, USA.

3

Pre-disaster Phase

No One Is an Island: How to Prepare Your Congregation and Congregants through Cooperation, Collaboration, and Community

Pamela Norris Norwood, LCSW, and Rev. Lorraine Jones, MDiv,

> *Pre: A prefix occurring originally in loanwords from Latin, where it meant "before" (preclude; prevent); applied freely as a prefix, with the meanings "prior to," "in advance of," "early," "beforehand," "before," "in front of," and with other figurative meanings.*
>
> OXFORD ENGLISH DICTIONARY

The Western Hemisphere is plagued with the conundrum of not having had to endure the sustained and widespread destruction that often cuts a swatch through countries in the 10/40 window.[1] Countries in the 10/40 window are the indigenous people located in northern Africa and Asia. Christian missions strategist Luis Bush started calling this rectangular area or band "the 10/40 window." He used that easy-to-remember name because it lies across Africa and Asia from 10 degrees latitude north of the equator to 40 degrees latitude north of the equator. Two-thirds of the world's population—more than 3.2 billion people—live in the 10/40 window. Furthermore, 85 percent of those living in the 10/40 window are the poorest of the world's poor. Those countries often do not have the benefit of interconnected infrastructures that can preplan, implement, and respond to full-scale emergencies in numerous places at once. Deteriorating or nonexistent roadways, sporadic rail systems, and inconsistent supplies of energy all wreak havoc on already fragile economies and even more frayed nerves as people seek adequate shelter, food, and medicines.

In the West, the very existence of such infrastructures have given certain nations—including our own—a false sense of security in our ability to foresee and respond to emergencies of varying degrees. The effects of the North American power grid brown-out, July 2006, the terrorist attacks of September 11, 2001, well-publicized mudslides and mining accidents, flooding in the Midwest, and hurricanes Katrina and Rita all illustrate poignantly that no region or nation is immune to the devastating effects of disaster. Through these events, the West officially joined the human family and found itself in solidarity with pain and purpose that will either propel it into a period of greater development or cripple it and subject it to increased isolation and paranoia.

Congregations of all religious persuasions need to expand their level of preparedness knowledge. All too often they have an abundance of "nice to know" information but not enough of the "need to know" information that will save their lives. Their level of knowledge must go beyond a recitation of facts to an understanding of how to translate those facts into a form of action. Religious leaders can accomplish this by providing detailed instruction on the type of pre-disaster preparedness required in this final dispensation. Your job is to lead, but your congregation and community have free agency to either act or not. People and resources have been placed at the world's disposal to save lives, but as in the days of Noah, each person can choose to get on board or not.

Utilizing Collective Memory

When our vulnerabilities and weaknesses are exposed, we are reminded that we are all members of the genus Humanity. Ancient proverbs and traditional folk songs remind us that "no one is an island, entire of itself."[2] In the face of widespread destruction and colossal human need, technological prowess, organized people-power, and adequate resources must be coupled with practical know-how and effective implementation early in the response process. We are only as strong as the weakest link in the chain.

One of the greatest weapons in the arsenal of emergency preparedness is memory, for it is memory that tells the story of how we fared the last time something unexpected happened. Memory shapes our actions—for better or for worse—in the aftermath of an event. Everything is interpreted in light of the last impactful thing that happened to us. That incident becomes part of the cultural folklore and collective memory. The required attitudes and knowledge associated with pre-disaster phase planning involve utilizing that collective memory to the best advantage. The one thing that memory reminds us of is that our culture is often reactionary rather than proactive. Across social, economic, political, and religious distinctions, being proactive is at a premium. Survivability depends on a number of factors including, but not limited to, physical condition, mental acumen, performance under pressure, resource availability, and strategy. Billie Holiday, the late jazz singer, put it this way in a song, "God bless the child that's got his own."

Disasters come in all forms and are caused by both humans and nature. Sacred texts of almost all traditions warn us of impending earthquakes, hail storms, fires, volcanic eruptions, pollution of waters, decimation of sea life, famine, and pestilences. Terrorist threats warn us of roadside bombings, nuclear explosions, and biochemical and biological warfare. As horrific as the thought of these occurrences may be, we are blessed with foreknowledge of what is to come and therefore have advance notice to prepare. Knowledge is power, and in this case knowledge provides the power to act proactively to save lives. Now let's look at what it will take to survive and the detail planning required.

Discovering Your Congregational Strategy

A key element in developing a helpful and meaningful strategy involves thoughtful preplanning. Congregations often labor under the false perception that "everyone in my congregation believes what I believe, ergo, our needs are the same." While we may share common ideals and religious precepts, we are still individuals. Proper questioning that gets to the underlining root of what the congregational thinking and needs are in reference to disaster is paramount to the process. For example, in this country, oil, gas, and electricity are our major modes of energy. We all have our own ideas of where these resources come into play in our everyday lives, and we take a lot of the goods and services we use for granted. We may not be cognizant of the inter-relationship of supply and demand of resources to panic, specifically, if supply lines are disrupted for any appreciable amount of time. Peruse the following list (figure 3.1) and make a mental note of how many of these things you could live without for twenty-four hours, one week, a month, or longer.

- Household electric appliances
- Internet/cable TV
- Cars/vans
- Elevators/escalators
- Food/water
- Sewerage/trash disposal
- Newspapers

- Telephones/cell phones
- Computers/laptops
- ATMs/credit/debit cards
- Air conditioner/heat
- Cleaners
- Police/fire/EMT
- Coffee shops

Figure 3.1

How well did you do? Sobering isn't it?

Congregational Resource Checklist

Nilikuonyesha nyota (mwezi) na uliangalia kidole tu. (Swahili) I pointed out to you the stars (the moon) and all you saw was the tip of my finger.[3]

The next step in pre-disaster preparedness involves uncovering the resources that your congregation has at its disposal in tangible terms (see figure 3.2). While faith and spiritual fortitude are intangibles that may inform the planning activity and extend the mental acumen of your body of believers, practicality is the foundational cornerstone that needs to be laid during this phase of congregational strategy development. An important element in this process is the inclusion of and respect for the contributions and insight of children and elders. Each person has valuable contributions; the more involved everyone is in the planning stages, the more invested they become in its successful implementation.

SAMPLE CHECKLIST

I. CONGREGATIONAL PROFILE
   a. Age groups identified
   b. Physical mobility profile
   c. Spiritual muscle
   d. Congregational picture profile

II. EDUCATIONAL RESOURCES
   a. Journaling exercises
   b. Resource agency research materials
   c. Up-to-date preparedness library
   d. Multilingual resources

III. RESOURCE MEETING ROOM
   a. Map of vicinity in fifteen-mile radius increments
   b. Strategic mapping of congregant residences, schools, and workplaces
   c. Emergency / Evacuation routes / Modes of transportation
   d. Phone numbers to key services and agencies
   e. Ham radios and flashlights—self-powered, hand-cranked
   f. Batteries and battery-operated equipment
   g. Generators and secured fuel and alternative fuel sources
   h. Bunks and blankets
   i. Water, water, water, water
   j. Dehydrated food supplies
   k. Bathroom supplies
   l. Whistles and compasses

IV. PRE-DISASTER ESSENTIALS
   a. Family activity day
        i. Multigenerational activity days that emphasize an important principle in preparedness
        ii. Sponsor community health fair to assess the needs of the neighborhood the church resides in
        iii. Promote physical fitness as a means of bolstering congregational fitness
        iv. Collect and distribute food supplies at holidays
   b. First responders training and certification
   c. Bolster the foundation of the meeting place to withstand disaster
        i. Make repairs
        ii. Apply for matching grants to enact needed training
        iii. Construct / Expand existing supply space
        iv. Check / Update emergency supplies
   d. Denominational resources
   e. Collaborate with congregations one hundred miles away
   f. Exchange phone chain congregant calling lists

Figure 3.2

Congregation, Where Art Thou?

One of the first activities for emergency preparedness planning is to know and map where every congregant family lives. How will you communicate in a disaster?

Step 1: To carry out this procedure today requires getting out detailed street maps and marking where every family lives. This provides the framework for assigning leaders (walkers and drivers) who will be responsible for checking on designated families in their area in the event of a disaster.

Step 2: Select leaders who are in good physical health (in order to walk) and/or have a vehicle they can drive. Collect the name, address, and telephone number of each leader. Leaders should never go to bed without a full tank of gas and toilet tissue in their car.

Step 3: Leaders should be assigned to check on selected families in reasonable walking distance from their home (the walkers) or within reasonable driving distance from their residence (the drivers). Make those family assignments.

Step 4: Have the leaders take a dry run to their assigned families to collect the following information about their members: name, ages, medical needs, and other special needs. This dry run enables an accurate accounting of every person and enables leaders to anticipate potential needs in the event of a disaster. Leaders must also calculate how long it takes to get to each house. Your house of worship can then approximate how long it will take to hear back from each leader about the status of their assigned families and, ultimately, how long it would take to learn about the well-being of all members.

Step 5: Leaders are also responsible for teaching their assignees how to store food, water, medicine, and financial resources, and to help them establish an emergency travel plan should evacuation become necessary. Needless to say, this necessitates that the leaders receive training. At least once a year, hold an emergency preparedness drive within your congregation for all congregants to check their supplies and pick up new supplies if needed.

Step 6: Create a master telephone list of the physicians, nurses, mental health professionals, and pharmacists in your congregation. These are critical occupations, and leaders may need to consult them should they find their assigned families are in extreme distress.

Step 7: Establish a backup communication system should the phone lines go down and cell towers become overloaded. Use ham radio operators and walkie-talkies to keep the lines of communication open. During Hurricane Katrina the Vietnamese community in the Gulf Region successfully used ham radios to keep their congregants and community informed.

Step 8: Conduct a dry run of the emergency preparedness plan every six months. This enables everyone to practice their role, engage in a discussion of food, water, medical, and financial preparedness, evaluate evacuation contingencies, and improve the efficiency of the process of accounting for all members of the congregation. All congregants should be instructed to add their assigned leader to the list of phone numbers they will contact to let others know they are all right in case of disaster. This will prevent leaders from losing precious time and resources looking for members who are away from home when tragedy strikes.

Bring the Food into Your Storehouse

Houses of worship and congregants must begin storing food for extended periods of potential scarcity. Faith groups often help members by giving them food when unexpected financial challenges surface. If each house of worship kept these emergency rations of food stored in their facility, they could rotate them effortlessly by replacing it when they give to members who are in need throughout the year. People turn to the churches, temples, and mosques in their community for more than just spiritual assistance during a disaster. Since no one knows the day or hour when tragedy will strike, how prepared would you be if it occurred during service and none of your members could leave the building to go home? How long could you provide food and water for the masses within your walls?

We encourage congregations to hold food drives to collect dry goods that can be distributed in the event of a disaster. We believe religious leaders have a responsibility to cooperate and collaborate with their congregants and other religious leaders in the community to ensure every household has a "Go Bag"[4] filled with emergency supplies, clothes, blankets, important documents, and food (see later in this chapter for details).

Individual families also need to store as much food as their living space will accommodate. It is advisable for them to store a year's supply of food, if possible. If economics or space does not allow such storage, three to five days' worth of supplies and food is the minimum to keep on hand. Remember, having some stored resources is better than having none. If storage space is limited, consider dividing storage with relatives or friends who live within walking distance. In this case, one family would be responsible for storing only water, another only food, and another paper supplies and first aid materials. Should disaster arrive, the families would pool their supplies.

Each family in your congregation should rotate rations during their weekly shopping trip. Rotating rations among family groups involves taking an inventory of the common items—e.g., dried milk, canned beans, freeze-dried noodles, paper goods, etc.—and then tasking each family unit to take responsibility for providing a specific amount. This amount could be a number of packages per person or a specific dollar amount assigned to the items.[5] For families with young children this could become an excellent way of introducing the concept of preparedness in a proactive and educational manner that includes spelling, math, and penmanship. Assign the young persons with age-appropriate tasks that include counting the available items, labeling the units, calculating the days of supply, etc. In this way, family units are budgeting essentials in their weekly grocery lists, thus minimizing the potential for persons becoming overwhelmed if the items had to be purchased at the last minute. In addition, everyone is buying into the process before trouble comes. Encourage your membership to begin growing crops in their backyard, or on their windowsill if they live in an apartment. There are many devices available now that enable you to grow fruits and vegetables on your kitchen counter. Through cooperation and collaboration with others in the congregation and the community you can increase your available resources.

We do not live by food alone and water must be remembered. Should drinking water become polluted or disrupted, a water supply will be critical for survival. Water is needed for taking medicine, cleaning wounds, cooking food, bathing, and general consumption. It is advisable to have enough water stored to provide two gallons of water per person per day for at least one week. Water is a commodity that is receiving increased attention worldwide. The news highlights the devastation that extended drought periods have on arid regions of the world. People and animal groups move to follow the flow of the water, which means the possibility of crossing tenuous borders and testing fragile peace agreements in the process. Some analysts predict that the scarcity of clean and abundant water sources will soon eclipse border violations and control of vital resources as the major cause for armed conflicts.

According to the 2nd United Nations World Water Development Report, "The global water crisis is the leading cause of death and disease in the world, taking the lives of more than 14,000 people each day, 11,000 of them children under age 5. Survival without water is usually limited to three or four days."[6] This is a vital and sobering statistic when coupled with the fact that many of us do not currently drink enough water. The human body is comprised of mostly water so life would cease to exist without it. Thus, paying attention to this vital resource includes not just cleaning up the available rivers and streams, but getting into the habit of stockpiling one's own personal supply while it is available. Most of the pristine water sources are either privately owned or largely inaccessible due to terrain or other obstacles. If the available water supply is contaminated then what one has on hand may very well determine the length of survival.

No One Makes Change during Disasters

Your congregation needs to begin saving money at home. Many disasters cause electrical outages, which means the banks close down. This means no access to your safe deposit box, bank cashiers, or ATMs. In other words, this means *no access to money*. What you have in your possession is all you may have available. So let's examine how to ensure your members have enough financial resources to meet their family's needs. First and foremost, have them come up with a plan to get out of debt so they can begin saving money.[7] It is best to set a target of financial reserves equal to six months of their living expenses. Remind them that if they wait until the first warning of a potential natural disaster to go and withdraw money from the bank, they will not be the only ones in line. There are other more important things they need to be doing with their time in the days or hours before a disaster strikes. And if disaster comes at night—too late, the banks will be closed. So, once again, preparedness is the strategy needed.

Begin by putting aside five one-dollar bills and one roll of quarters every week, more if you are able. Having small denominations of money allows you to make cash reserves go farther. Since cash registers are electronically controlled and cannot be opened if the electricity goes out, most grocery stores will only allow you to buy items if they don't have to provide change. As stores run out of supplies, your congregants will be forced to buy on the street at scalper prices. Advise your members to hide the money in various locations both inside and outside their house, in case their house is somehow damaged or destroyed during the disaster. Money can be buried in the yard, but remember to mark the spot. The rolls of quarters should be attached with duct tape under the front seat of their car or in the trunk's spare tire, which gives them reserve cash even if they are away from home when tragedy strikes.

One woman who is the executive director of an emergency preparedness agency said she carries two or three one-hundred-dollar bills (hidden), a whistle, and a mini-flashlight on her at all times. Her rationale is, first, that she could blow her whistle if someone she did not invite to do so was following her to her car. Second, in the event of a building collapse, she could blow her whistle and shine her flashlight so the rescue workers could identify her location. Third, she said, "You are wondering why the one-hundred-dollar bills? If the rescue workers have room for only one more person and need to make a choice, being a woman of color I need to level the playing field. I have two hundred or three hundred dollars cash. Who do you think will get that final seat?"

Preserving Medication Integrity

In the middle of an emergency is not the time to discover you have run out of your medication, don't know where to locate it in the house, or have no way to keep cold any medications requiring refrigeration. To ensure that your congregants do not run out of medication quickly, advise them to start stockpiling by asking their physician for samples of the medication they use. They can also request that their physician write a three-month prescription, as opposed to a thirty-day prescription (if allowed by law for their particular prescription). Many insurance companies will not pay for more than a thirty-day supply of medication at a time, which will require individuals to pay by cash to have the additional emergency supply of their medicine. Costly, yes, but important for survival. There are regulations that dictate how much medication your doctor will prescribe as well as how much the pharmacy will dispense that is dependent upon pharmacological type and dosage level. An estimated amount of medication that should be explored is a sixty-day supply. Each individual has a responsibility to discuss his or her medication requirements with his or her medical provider. Here are some helpful questions that can be included in that discussion: (1) what is the life cycle of the medication; (2) how warm is too warm (or, too cold); (3) are there acceptable generics available for me to use instead of name-brand products? The use of generics and the rise of megapharmaceutical carriers in retail chains (e.g., Wal-Mart) are making prices lower as competition for consumers increases; (4) how long can I forego using my medication; what are the side effects that let me know that I am in the danger zone and need emergency attention?; (5) can I take my medication with other fluids if water is not available; does the fact that I use another fluid to take with my medication impact my medication's integrity and effectiveness?; (6) does the medication become toxic or unsafe to use if it cannot be refrigerated? At what point does the medication reach the danger threshold? Is there some type of color coding that can visibly show me that the medication has become unstable and unsafe to use?

Everyone should prepare a list of all medication prescribed, the dosage, and the time of day it is to be taken. They should also retain one set of the pill bottles provided by the pharmacy even if they transfer their medication into pill dispenser cases. This is important to prove that they are being prescribed this medication and by which physician. In extreme emergencies, pharmacies will provide limited quantities of certain drugs if patients can prove their physician has prescribed it and if their usual pharmacy and pharmaceutical records have been destroyed.

There are over thirty medications that require refrigeration. They are for conditions such as diabetes, cancer, glaucoma, HIV/AIDS, and schizophrenia. Some medications become ineffective when they become warm, but others become poisonous when they get hot. It is therefore critical that medication requiring refrigeration be kept cool in the event of an electrical outage. The resource list at the end of this chapter will direct you to a product that will keep your medications cool in the event of an electrical outage. This product is called an Ice Buddy™ System. In addition to keeping your medications cool, an Ice Buddy™ System also provides a source of clean water for seven days and comes equipped with a first aid kit that contains 170 over-the-counter medications, supplies and necessities needed in an emergency.

Community, Where Art Thou?
Twenty-First-Century Response to Preparedness

Disasters such as wildfires, hurricanes, mudslides, and tsunamis are clear illustrations of the need for cooperation and collaboration within the faith community. Interfaith and intrafaith relationships have very practical and lifesaving applications for the twenty-first century. Your congregants may need to evacuate or relocate with little to no warning. Where will they go? What will they take with them?

We encourage every congregation to have a partner congregation that is located at least one hundred miles away. If you need to evacuate, your partner congregation will welcome you as your "ready receiving center." Every faith community has in its sacred literature wisdom about hospitality. Congregational partnerships are a practical application of that wisdom. They are about building community.

We also suggest that you form cooperative interfaith relationships with other local religious leaders as part of your pre-disaster planning. We are well aware of how race and other prejudices can rear their ugly heads at times of stress and great need. Interfaith cooperation among religious leaders can offer a new model of collaboration to both their congregants and the larger community.

The American Red Cross, governmental agencies, and ecumenical emergency response organizations all strongly recommend that each household within your community will do well to be equipped with a Go Bag and Ice Buddy™ System that contains medications, food, water, blankets, clothes, important documents, emergency equipment, and other necessities needed in the event of a disaster. Figures 3.3–3.6 list the recommended items to include in your Go Bag and Ice Buddy™ System.

GO BAGS AND ICE BUDDY™ SYSTEMS

Have a Go Bag and Ice Buddy™ System for each person in the house. Keep them by your bed. If you need to evacuate, grab them and go.

ADULT GO BAG AND ICE BUDDY™ SYSTEM

- Flashlight, batteries, and light sticks
- Portable radio and batteries
- Keys (house and car)
- Money (coins and bills)
- Glasses, contacts lenses, and solution
- Medications (at least one-week supply)
- Comfortable shoes, two pairs of socks
- Comfortable clothing (sweats, extra underwear)
- Jacket or sweatshirt
- Whistle (call for help if trapped)
- Pocket knife
- Paper and pencil
- "Okay" and "Help" signs (provided by CERT)
- Emergency phone list, out-of-state contact numbers
- Lists of people to notify if you are injured
- Copies of important documents: insurance, identification, social security, etc.
- Small first aid kit
- Toilet articles: comb, toothbrush, toothpaste, soap, washcloth, face towel, shampoo, lotion, razor, lip balm, emery board, nail clipper, sanitary products, tissue, sunscreen, etc.
- Toilet paper
- Resealable plastic bags, plastic grocery bags
- Good book, playing cards, crossword puzzles
- Work gloves, several pairs of latex gloves
- Blanket
- Plastic ground cloth
- Dust mask
- Crow bar (to remove debris)
- Drinking water—store in a separate place (minimum one gallon per person)
- Food
- Snacks (granola bars, trail mix, peanut butter)

Figure 3.3

SENIORS OR DISABLED GO BAG AND ICE BUDDY™ SYSTEM

These items are in addition to the Adult Go Bag and Ice Buddy™ System.

- Food for special diet needs
- Batteries for hearing aids, wheelchair, etc.
- List of style and serial number of medical devices
- Special supplies: oxygen, catheters, etc.
- Prescriptions for eyeglasses (not older than one year)
- Personal sanitary items (adult diapers, disposable bags, ties, wipes)
- For guide dogs, see Pet Go Bag.

Figure 3.4

INFANT AND TODDLER GO BAGS AND ICE BUDDY™ SYSTEMS

These items are in addition to the Adult Go Bag and Ice Buddy™ System.

- Formula, disposable bottles, nipples
- Diapers and wipes
- Instant baby cereal
- Bowl and spoon
- Sunscreen
- At least two changes of clothes
- Light jacket
- Thermometer
- Medicine dropper
- Electrolyte replacement solution such as pedialyte
- Children's medications
- Firm-soled slippers or shoes
- Toys, books, stuffed animals
- Comleted consent to treatment of a minor form

Figure 3.5

PET GO BAG AND ICE BUDDY™ SYSTEM

Keep your Pet Go Bag and Ice Buddy™ System in an easily accessible location near your own emergency supplies.

- Food, water—three-day supply for each pet
- Bowls—non-spillable
- Collar and leash for dogs and cats
- Muzzle
- Poop scooper, bags
- Treats, toy
- Blanket, towel, or newspaper for warmth
- ID tag should always be on pet
- Extra name tag
- License number
- Pet carrier or crate for each pet labeled with pet and owner's information (keep near your bag)
- Name, address, and phone number of veterinarian, animal control agency, and shelters
- People to contact to take care of the animal
- Vaccination and medical records
- Keep inoculations current. In an emergency, pets may come in contact with diseased animals.
- Allergy or other special instructions

Figure 3.6

It is important to remember that each member of the house needs his or her own Go Bag and Ice Buddy™ System. Different people have different needs. We have included additional recommendations of needed supplies for both the youngest and the oldest in our communities, as well as our pets.

CAR EMERGENCY KIT

- Water
- Food (canned, dehydrated, snacks)
- Sweater or jacket, extra clothing
- Comfortable walking shoes
- Money (coins and bills)
- Flashlight (extra batteries)
- Blanket
- First aid kit (bandages, gauze, etc.)
- Pocket knife
- Matches (waterproof)
- Tools (screwdriver, pliers, wire, crowbar, rope, etc.)
- Emergency phone numbers, including your contact person
- Maps of your most traveled routes
- Personal items (eyeglasses, toothbrush and toothpaste, soap, tissues, hand wipes, toilet tissue, etc.)
- Special needs (medication, diapers, infant formula, etc.)
- Favorite book, crossword puzzles, or games
- Flares
- Fire extinguisher
- Work gloves
- Jumper cables
- Pencil and paper

Figure 3.7

Finally, you could at almost any time find yourself stranded in your car in a disaster. Figure 3.7 shows the standard recommendations of that which is needed in your automobile at all times.

Final Words

This is, by no means, an exhaustive list but it begins the very real and practical conversation that each congregation ought to have among its membership. One critical item to remember is that resources must be kept in accessible places in order to actually be useful in a disaster. At its best, pre-disaster planning can demonstrate the resourcefulness of its membership. You may have resources in your midst that you had not have even realized existed. It can spark a revival among the membership to use its collective gifts and talents in tangible ways, which conveys the message that disaster preparedness is not an exercise in futility but a change in lifestyle.

Faith leaders are tasked to prepare their members for potential disaster. It is time to know where your flock lives, teach them how to be self-sufficient, have a plan for rescuing those in need, and gather lifesaving products before it is too late.

Notes

1. Window of Opportunity, http://www.1040window.org.
2. Donne, J. "Meditation XVII," in *Devotions Upon Emergent Occasions* (Whitefish, MT: Kessinger Publishing, 2004).
3. African Proverb of the Month, June 1998, http://www.afriprov.org/resources/explain.htm.
4. The term "Go Bag," is used by a number of emergency preparedness websites. Other terms used are, "Grab and Go Bag" and "Ready to Go Bag." FEMA and other emergency preparedness agencies and organizations suggest the same list of items to include in your bag. "Go Bag" is also the term used for a solar panel emergency bag that can be purchased through World Life Savers, Inc., and works in tandem with Ice Buddy™ Systems, Inc. See the Resources section below for contact information.
5. Church Educational System, *The Life and Teachings of Jesus & His Apostles* (Salt Lake City: The Church of Jesus Christ of Latter-day Saints, 1979), 278.
6. The 2nd United Nations World Water Development Report: "Water, a Shared Responsibility," 2006, online article, http://www.unesco.org/water/wwap/wwdr2/ http://www.unesco.org/water/wwap/wwdr2/.
7. N. H. Leash, "Food Storage Chart," in *Prophetic Statements on Food Storage for Latter-day Saints,* (Springville, UT: Horizon Publishers & Distributors, 2005), 187–88.

Further Reading

Church Educational System. *The Life and Teachings of Jesus & His Apostles.* Salt Lake City: The Church of Jesus Christ of Latter-day Saints, 1979.
Donne, John. "Meditation XVII," in *Devotions Upon Emergent Occasions.* Whitefish, MT: Kessinger Publishing, 2004.
Leash, Neil H., "Food Storage Chart," in *Prophetic Statements on Food Storage for Latter-day Saints.* Springville, UT: Horizon Publishers & Distributors, 2005.

Resources

ICE Buddy™ Systems, Inc. 14720 Fourth Street, Suite 411, Laurel, Maryland 20707 (301) 367-4519 www.icebuddysystems.com.
Go Bag: World Life Savers, Inc., (201) 400-3166 www.worldlifesavers.com.

About the Contributors

Rev. Lorraine Jones, MDiv, relishes the challenge of solving problems in a creative manner. Her educational background includes a degree in electrical engineering from Vanderbilt University and a master of divinity from Andover Newton Theological Seminary. Her career includes work in stewardship and missions training/fundraising on a denominational level and providing instruction on cutting-edge biohazard detection systems. Rev. Jones currently serves as senior vice president of design and production for ICE Buddy Systems, Inc., a company that designs, patents, and markets emergency preparedness items. She serves as an associate minister and outreach pillar leader at Parker Memorial Baptist Church, a Covenant Community ministry in Burtonsville, Maryland.

Pamela Norris Norwood, LCSW, received her degrees from Tufts University and Atlanta University. She is a member of the Church of Jesus Christ of Latter-day Saints, where she also serves as a Sunday school teacher. She also served as a member of the church's emergency preparedness team in Los Angeles. She is a clinical social worker with over thirty years of private practice experience, and also formally directed two outpatient mental health centers in the District of Columbia and Maryland. She served for over eighteen years as CEO of a security consulting firm providing extensive security and emergency preparedness services to law enforcement, educational systems, and business and faith groups. She currently serves as CEO of ICE Buddy Systems, Inc., a company that designs, patents, and markets emergency preparedness items.

4

Impact and Heroic Phases— Small Disaster

What Do I Do Now? Congregational and Community Work

Rev. Kevin Massey, BCC

The sound of the telephone ringing was the same as always, the voice on the other end, however, was not. "Pastor, did you hear what happened? The charter bus taking the cross-country team to their meet was hit by a train. My son was on the bus, and called me to tell me he's OK, but he says that the accident is bad ... really bad...."

When we think of disaster, we may tend to think of big events like hurricanes or major terrorist attacks. Indeed, the next chapter of this book will treat the faith community leaders' role in responding to these significant occurrences. However, the more common and crucial kind of experience is a small-scale disaster. Nearly every leader of a faith community will at one time or another be involved in responding to this kind of disaster. In this chapter we will examine the practical preparations and responses that faith community leaders can perform to be the best support to their own faith communities and wider communities during small-scale disasters.

Scales of Disaster

You can think of disasters as falling into three categories:

- A disaster that affects only your faith community, such as a building fire or an accident on the premises
- A disaster that affects your whole community—your town, city, or state
- A disaster that affects the whole nation

In some ways, the emotional and spiritual reactions of your faith community and the wider community may be the same regardless of the scale of the disaster. For example, if your worship building was destroyed by a fire or by a natural disaster that affected a wider area of your community, your faith community would still have the same challenges and needs emotionally and spiritually. In fact, sometimes the effect on your faith community by a small-scale disaster can be more acute because it will be evident that very limited external resources are going to come to help. The whole community looks to faith community leaders for support and guidance in the aftermath of these events.

Preparing Yourself and Your Faith Community for Disaster

Chapter 3 of this book detailed the importance of preparedness before disaster. Small-scale disasters require even more preparedness and attention than large-scale events specifically because limited external resources become part of the response. There are a number of important activities that you should do to prepare yourself and your faith community for small-scale disasters.

Get to know emergency management leaders in your community. Sometimes clergy are hesitant to introduce themselves to government leaders, feeling that they are only a minor player in the community. This is not the case. Many government leaders consider clergy and other faith community leaders essential in their task of communicating with the wider community. Request meetings with leaders from the mayor's office, the fire department, the police or sheriff's department, and other emergency management leaders in your community. Be persistent. It may take time to schedule meetings with busy people, but it will be worth it. A disaster is the worst time to be exchanging business cards. Chapter 19, "Working with Police, Fire, and Other Uniformed Personnel" gives great detail about how to attend to this important area of preparedness.

Get to know other faith community leaders in your area. Develop a regular schedule of meeting other faith community leaders in your area. Regular ministerial and interfaith events in your area are a good time to make connections, but also try to have one-on-one meetings with as many leaders as possible. Especially try to meet leaders from faith traditions other than your own. This will be very important in a time of disaster in your community because you may meet members of your community from other faith traditions who will look to you for support. You will want to build a referral list of other faith community leaders so that you can sensitively and appropriately refer people to leaders from their own faith communities. Additionally, other faith community leaders will be a valuable source of support and collegiality in the difficult days of coping with the aftermath of disaster. Again, be persistent! Faith community leaders can be very busy, but most will appreciate you taking the initiative to get better acquainted.

Get to know chaplains at the hospitals that service your community. When disaster strikes, you may need to be able to access congregants in area hospitals to visit and provide spiritual care. The chaplains at the hospitals in your communities can help you in this work and also want to know you so that they can refer you to provide care and support to patients in the hospital who may share your religious tradition. Again, a disaster is the wrong time to just be meeting each other! Chapter 6 introduces the unique role and skills clinical chaplains bring to trauma and disaster.

Make a congregational disaster response plan and regularly review it. Ask the members of your congregation who are responsible for issues around your building to map out topics such as evacuation plans, facility safety and security, and data and information backup. Additionally, determine the key services and activities that your congregation provides that you would consider "mission critical," that is, essential to who you are and what you do. These may include worship and important social ministries upon which your members and the community rely. All mission critical activities need to be planned for in a way that allows you to continue providing them even if you lose your building.

Attending to these topics will take you a great way forward in being ready to respond to a disaster that may affect your faith community or your wider community. Let's consider now the best steps and responses to take when a disaster actually occurs. We'll start by imagining how you might best respond in the scenario introduced at the start of this chapter.

> *The sound of the telephone ringing was the same as always, the voice on the other end, however, was not. "Pastor, did you hear what happened? The charter bus taking the cross-country team to their meet was hit by a train. My son was on the bus, and called me to tell me he's OK, but he says that the accident is bad ... really bad...."*

Begin to learn what happened. In the immediate aftermath of disaster, there may not be certainty as to the scale and scope of what happened. Early reports of a disaster can be contradictory and can change quickly from minute to minute. You should understand this dynamic and simultaneously seek accurate information and plan for how to respond to a range of occurrences. In this scenario, at the moment of this phone call, you cannot know how many people may be injured or killed. You only know that an event has occurred that has the potential to seriously impact the community. Begin to monitor local media. Don't immediately call the fire or police departments because they may still be assessing and responding themselves and need to keep their own lines of communication available.

Stay where people can find you; don't rush to the scene. There is a natural impulse to want to rush to the scene of an emergency to see if you can be helpful and to learn more quickly what happened. It is very important for all members of a community, including faith community leaders, to resist this impulse. Roads and paths to and from an emergency scene need to be as open as possible to help emergency medical services and police and fire officials to have immediate access. Additionally, people often reach out to their faith community leaders for emotional and spiritual support in times of emergency. Stay where people know they can most easily contact you. If you have made previous connections with local emergency management officials, you can trust that they will contact you if the scale and scope of the event warrants your involvement.

> *"Pastor, I heard there was a terrible accident," a congregant screamed into the phone on the other end. "Do you know anything? I heard that twenty kids were killed! My nephew was on that bus!"*

Only publicly state verified and up-to-date information. Many people looking for information will call their faith community leader, hoping to learn something about what has happened. It is therefore crucial for you to only share information that has been verified through trusted sources. Rumors and reports of disaster can wildly inflate the numbers of people affected. You must be clear and concrete and accurate. Well-grounded statements and questions can be helpful:

- "That's not information I've heard."
- "I'm monitoring this news right now too. When I hear anything for certain, I'll let you know too."
- "Where did you hear that? Do you know where they heard it?"

As a disaster unfolds, accurate information eventually comes into focus. People remember and appreciate when their faith community leaders are understood to have been concrete, accurate, and available.

> *"Pastor, I'm glad I was able to contact you," the fire chief began. "I suppose you heard there was an accident. We're still responding at the scene, but I fear that a number of young people in the community were killed. We're setting up a family reception area over at city hall to give updates and make notifications. I'm looking for leaders from the faith community to be on hand to help give support."*

Offer your partnership to emergency management leaders. Many leaders in emergency management and government appreciate the role that the faith community can play in supporting those affected by disaster. They may value that spiritual and emotional support *for themselves* in times of disaster, even if they don't ask for it. Be as available as possible when invited to support the community. Balance this responsibility with your primary responsibility to care for the needs of your own faith community.

Spiritual care in crisis and disaster can be an overwhelming experience for a caregiver. Chapter 1 introduced the life cycle of a disaster and how different phases bring specific challenges to the caregiver.

Figures 4.1 and 4.2 are a reminder of the profound physical, emotional, and spiritual effects of trauma.

Common Reactions after Disaster and Trauma

Following a traumatic event, people typically describe feeling relief to be alive, followed by stress, fear, and anger. They also often find they are unable to stop thinking about what happened. Having stress reactions is what happens to most people and has nothing to do with personal weakness. Many people will also exhibit high levels of arousal. For most, if the following symptoms occur, they will slowly decrease over time. Most people will recover from trauma naturally, but if their emotional reactions are getting in the way of their relationships, work, or other important activities, you may want to refer them to a counselor or their doctor. Good treatments are available.[1]

Remember that most trauma survivors (including veterans, children, and rescue or relief workers) experience common stress reactions. Understanding what is happening when you or someone you know reacts to a traumatic event will help you be less fearful and better able to handle things. These reactions may last for several days or even a few weeks. They are included in figure 4.1.

In addition to these profound physical and emotional symptoms, spiritual reactions to trauma are common. Figure 4.2 presents some of the common spiritual reactions you could expect to see.

Be aware that when called upon to give support to the wider community you must be sensitive to the religious diversity of the community. Never proselytize or evangelize in the context of disaster response. Chapter 14 gives helpful guidelines on how to work effectively and appropriately in an interfaith setting.

> "Chief, I'll be right over to city hall. I'm going to arrange for another minister to staff my office here for any needs that come up. Are there other leaders from the faith community that you've been able to contact?"
>
> "The rabbi is on her way over to city hall too. Can you help me contact other leaders from the faith community that we should involve?"

Partner with other faith community leaders. If you have already established good working relationships with other local faith community

COMMON SHORT-TERM REACTIONS
AFTER TRAUMA AND DISASTER

GENERAL REACTIONS

- Feeling hopeless about the future
- Feeling detached or unconcerned about others
- Having trouble concentrating, indecisiveness
- Jumpy and startle easily at sudden noise
- On guard and constantly alert
- Having disturbing dreams, memories, or flashbacks
- Work or school problems

PHYSICAL REACTIONS

- Stomach upset, trouble eating
- Trouble sleeping and exhaustion
- Pounding heart, rapid breathing, edginess
- Severe headache if thinking of the event, sweating
- Failure to engage in exercise, diet, safe sex, regular health care
- Excess smoking, alcohol, drugs, food
- Worsening of chronic medical problems

EMOTIONAL REACTIONS

- Feeling nervous, helpless, fearful, sad
- Feeling shock, numb, unable to experience love or joy
- Avoiding people, places, and things related to the event
- Being irritable or outbursts of anger
- Becoming easily upset or agitated
- Self-blame or negative views of oneself or the world
- Distrust of others, conflict, being overcontrolling
- Withdrawal, feeling rejected or abandoned
- Loss of intimacy or feeling detached

Figure 4.1

COMMON SPIRITUAL REACTIONS TO A TRAUMATIC EVENT*

- Feeling guilty
- Feeling shame
- Feeling a need to be cleansed
- Questioning justice and meaning
- Feeling despair and hopelessness
- Wondering about life and death

- Closing oneself off from loved ones
- Feeling far from previously held beliefs
- Reconsidering core tenets of religious beliefs
- Asking questions such as "Why did God do this?"

* Reproduced from K. Massey, *Light Our Way—
A Guide for Spiritual Care in Times of Disaster* (Washington D.C.:
National Voluntary Organizations Active in Disaster, 2006), 6

Figure 4.2

leaders, it is easier to be in contact and work collaboratively in a time of community crisis. It is important that when faith community leaders respond to disaster in partnership with emergency management they involve as many faith community leaders as will be necessary to reflect the religious diversity of the community. There is a role for everyone.

Be yourself. Every faith community leader will experience responding to their very first disaster. For most it will be a smaller-scale disaster that affects a local community. Some training and education can prepare us to respond to emergency, but ultimately, you just have to respond when called upon. The best way to respond to disaster survivors is to just be yourself. Your faith community values you and your leadership and the spiritual and emotional support that you give. Don't try to think about how someone else would do something, or how someone else would say something better. Do, be, and say what comes naturally to you. That said, figure 4.3 gives some helpful guidelines for approaching these sensitive conversations.

Your role as a faith community leader is not to make the disaster all better. It's never going to be all better. Your role is to be present and available to your faith community and the wider community for support in time of crisis. An important role for faith community leaders is to shepherd the telling of the stories. Every disaster survivor has a story to tell. Telling the story is part of fitting the disaster experience

WHEN RESPONDING TO VICTIMS/SURVIVORS ABOUT SPIRITUAL ISSUES*

1. Use reflective listening and active listening techniques when working with victims/survivors.

2. Be honest, with compassion, and do not assume you know what they will say or believe.

3. If you do not feel comfortable discussing spiritual/religious issues, listen quietly and refer them to someone who can help them appropriately.

4. Do not try to explain or give answers to spiritual questions.

5. Do not argue with their beliefs or try to persuade them to believe as you do.

6. Do not respond with platitudes or clichés to victims/survivors. "It will be okay." "It is God's will." "They are in a better place."

7. Let them tell you what their religious/spiritual beliefs are. Do not assume anything.

8. Help them use their spiritual/religious beliefs to cope.

9. They may need reassurance that it is "common" to ask questions about God and/or their religious beliefs. However, some faiths do tell their members not to question God.

10. Allow expressions of anger toward God or others—in healthy, nondestructive ways.

11. Do affirm their search for spiritual/faith-based answers. Do not impose your thoughts or beliefs on them.

12. Do affirm the wrongness, evil, and/or injustice of what has happened, especially if the trauma was caused by humans.

13. Give them the materials that can help them in their search for meaning or their search for spiritual answers.

14. Emphasize that everyone has to find their own answers and way of understanding in traumatic events.

* From C. Hacker, *Too Much, Too Ugly, Too Fast! How Faith Communities Can Respond in Crisis and Disasters* (Chicago: Lutheran Disaster Response, 2003), 11

Figure 4.3

into the wider story of that person's life, which is the only way to move on to a healthy future after trauma. Some people have to tell the same stories over and over and over. Clergy can be helpful by being the few people who never tire of listening.

What you do well every day as a member of the clergy should be the cornerstone of the care you give in disaster. Listening, companioning, and helping people connect their story with their wider life and faith tradition are all crucial healing gestures in disaster (see figure 4.3).

Dr. Carol Hacker, a nationally recognized expert on reactions to crisis and trauma, compiled a useful set of issues on ministry leadership in disaster and crisis (see figure 4.4). These issues highlight the ways clergy are accustomed to being leaders in common times, and how this leadership role can be both challenged and strengthened in disaster. Consider keeping figure 4.4 with you when navigating faith community leadership in disaster.

You also don't have to do everything or be good at everything. You may find that responding to disaster isn't something you feel comfortable with. This doesn't mean that you are a bad leader, it just means that this one aspect of ministry isn't what you're best at. We all have areas of ministry that aren't our strong suit.

Remember that you aren't alone. You aren't the only person responding to the disaster. Lean on the support of other local faith community leaders. Stay in close contact with emergency management officials and governmental leadership. Model partnership and interconnectedness to others and it will be reciprocated.

> Dozens of people crowded the room for the press conference. "Thank you all for coming," the mayor began. "Yesterday was a day that will always mark our community. At this time, we are reporting that eleven people were killed in this horrible accident. We are still investigating what happened and will report fully when any determination is made. I want to personally thank the leaders from the faith community today for the support they have been giving to the whole community since this tragedy began to unfold. Let us all work together to support each other as we continue to struggle in these difficult days.

Remember that a small-scale disaster is still a disaster. Keep in mind that everybody in disaster is on edge. Even seasoned emergency management officials can feel overwhelmed and pressed to the limit when responding to even a small-scale disaster. Tempers can flare. People can be deeply upset. This is normal.

MINISTRY LEADERSHIP ISSUES
WHEN DISASTERS OR CRISIS OCCUR

CLERGY…	HOWEVER, IN A CRISIS OR DISASTER, THE CLERGY MAY…
• Are used to being in charge and being the strength of the congregation/faith community. • Are used to asking the questions and/or knowing the answers	• Not know what to do, what to ask, or what the answers are. • Be personally impacted and not have the strength to be a leader

CONGREGATION NEEDS ITS CLERGY TO…	HOWEVER, IN A CRISIS OR DISASTER, THE CLERGY MAY…
• Be strong, be the anchor, be the leader. • Have the answers and be confident. • Continue to do the daily, routine tasks and activities while also meeting the needs of the victims. • Meet the needs of all members, even when the needs are totally different from each other. ("We need to continue to focus on and discuss the tragedy" vs. "It is over and we need to move on").	• Have more questions than answers and not know what to say or do. • Feel lost, confused, anxious, and angry and not want to be the leader. ("Take this cup from me.") • Not have the energy or time to do routine tasks as well as minister to victims. • Find it impossible to make everyone happy or feel heard and become discouraged or frustrated.

OTHER ISSUES FOR CLERGY…	
• Taking care of their families. • Intrusion by and seductiveness of the media.	• Taking care of themselves. • Conflict and disagreements within the faith community.

WAYS CLERGY CAN HELP AND SUPPORT…

• Have support group meetings with other clergy.

• Respite leaves.

• Get extra help for daily, routine tasks (volunteers, retired clergy, people from the church not impacted by the disaster).

• Have training on crisis response, the emotional effects of tragedy, disaster preparedness.

• Set up a crisis response and disaster preparedness plan for the church.

• Know community resources and set up relationships with them (fire, police, paramedics, mortuaries, hospitals, mental health centers, etc.).

• Have ideas and suggestions for prayers, services, liturgies, Bible studies, and newsletter and bulletin articles and announcements for various types of crisis.

• Prepare and plan for anniversaries, similar catastrophic events, and other possible triggers.

• Have a lay group prepared to support the church staff physically and emotionally.

* From C. Hacker, *Too Much, Too Ugly, Too Fast! How Faith Communities Can Respond in Crisis and Disasters* (Chicago: Lutheran Disaster Response, 2003), 9

Figure 4.4

A small-scale disaster is just as significant to the people that it immediately affects as a large-scale event of national scope. Chapter 1 explored the life cycle of a disaster. One life cycle dynamic unique to small-scale disasters is a frustrating feeling of abandonment that comes even earlier than in large-scale events. Small-scale disasters sometimes get very little, if any, national media attention, and yet they are just as traumatic to the people and communities affected as large-scale disasters. People in communities affected by small-scale disasters sometimes feel that outsiders are dismissive of their pain because of their lack of knowledge about an event. Faith community leaders have an important role to accompany communities struggling to name how profound a small-scale disaster is to them.

Pace yourself. Chapter 2 introduced us to the importance of self-care for disaster responders. In small-scale disasters it is important to continually remind ourselves that this event may have affected us as significantly as a large-scale event would have. We have to be just as vigilant in caring for ourselves as we are in caring for our faith communities and the wider community. Be sure to stay in close contact with judicatory leaders and share with them how you are and whether you need any support as you work through these difficult times.

Nothing Is Ever the Same

> *"It doesn't seem possible that it's been a year since the accident,"* the rabbi said. *"It still seems so fresh in my mind. And the rest of the world acts like nothing even happened here! No one else remembers this; it was just a sidebar story for one day. We remember, however, and will always remember our loved ones we lost."*

When any community is affected by a tragedy such as a small-scale disaster, nothing is ever the same. The event will be remembered profoundly and will always be part of the story of that community. Chapters 11 and 12 of this book will help you understand the nature of anniversaries and reminders of disaster, and also how you can be part of shaping appropriate and inclusive memorials of the disaster. Small-scale disasters need to be ascribed all the attention and importance to the local community as large-scale disasters do to the wider community.

In addition, nothing is ever the same as the relationship you have with your congregation and community. People will always remember the care and support you gave in a time of crisis and disaster. When you have been genuinely yourself and offered what you have, you will be appreciated and honored and valued for your role in offering disaster spiritual care that helped people through such difficult times.

Notes

1. National Center for Posttraumatic Stress Disorder, "Common Reactions after Trauma," http://www.ncptsd.va.gov/ncmain/ncdocs/fact_shts/fs_commonreactions.html.

Further Reading

Erikson, K. T. *Everything in Its Path: Destruction of a Community in the Buffalo Creek Flood.* New York: Simon and Schuster, 1976.

Hacker, C. *Too Much, Too Ugly, Too Fast! How Faith Communities Can Respond in Crisis and Disasters.* Chicago: Lutheran Disaster Response, 2003.

Koenig, H. G. *In the Wake of Disaster: Religious Responses to Terrorism and Catastrophe.* Philadelphia: Templeton Foundation Press, 2006.

Massey, K. *Light Our Way: A Guide for Spiritual Care in Times of Disaster.* Washington D.C.: National Voluntary Organizations Active in Disaster, 2006. http://www.nvoad.org/articles/Light_Our_Way_LINKS.pdf.

National Center for Posttraumatic Stress Disorder, http://www.ncptsd.va.gov.

Shelp, E. "Pastoral Care as a Community Endeavor," *Park Ridge Center Bulletin*, issue 21, (2001).

Zinner, E., and M. Williams, eds. *When a Community Weeps: Case Studies in Group Survivorship.* Philadelphia: Brunner/Mazel, 1999.

About the Contributor

Rev. Kevin Massey, BCC, is an ordained pastor of the Evangelical Lutheran Church in America. He is a board-certified chaplain with the Association of Professional Chaplains. Rev. Massey was a chaplain and spiritual care trainer and coordinator with Advocate Health Care in Chicago from 1999 to 2005. Rev. Massey has worked extensively in the field of disaster spiritual care administration and training with the American Red Cross and Church World Service, including service at Ground Zero in New York City in the fall of 2001. Rev. Massey has been the assistant director of domestic disaster response for the Evangelical Lutheran Church in America since 2005. Rev. Massey has written numerous articles, curricula, and book chapters on such diverse topics as spiritual care, clinical ethics, disaster response, linguistics, archaeology, and interreligious dialogue.

5

Impact and Heroic Phases—
Large Regional and National Disasters

What Do I Do Now? Congregational
and Community Work

Rev. Naomi Paget, DMin, BCC, BCETS

If you're reading this, you're probably in one of two situations: (1) you've just been through a major disaster and are hoping to find some quick tips on what to do now, or (2) you know major disasters will happen and you want to be prepared. I hope you're in the second group. In either case, this chapter will give you strategic methodology for responding to large regional and national disasters as a congregation or as a community. You will find strategic ideas in planning, implementation, evaluation, and education as you provide disaster spiritual care. Nothing will take the place of preplanning, but following some of these guidelines will help you as you quickly begin to respond to large regional and national disasters.

> *No one expected the kind of destruction that Hurricane Katrina would bring to our city. No one expected the kind of weakness our churches would experience after the flood. No one expected the overwhelming sense of inadequacy we would feel as a community of believers. We should have had an emergency plan and a way to get some ministry done. We weren't ready and we made a lot of mistakes. Now we know that planning and education are essential. Now we know that we need to train laity to be leaders in crisis*

> *situations. Now we know that we must learn from our mistakes and we must teach others to be prepared.*
>
> PASTOR E. S., NEW ORLEANS, 2005

The history of major disasters is as ancient as war, pestilence, and catastrophe. These incidents of disaster include natural disasters and human-caused disasters that may be intentional or accidental. Each major disaster creates myriad complicating factors—loss of lives, destruction of property, feelings that range from anger to relief, and the certainty that life will never be the same again.

In recent history, thirty-three people died in the Virginia Tech campus shooting on April 16, 2007; and almost exactly twelve years prior, 168 lives were lost when terrorists bombed the Alfred P. Murrah Federal Building in Oklahoma City. In the 1990s, over 800 families were evacuated and relocated as a result of toxic chemical dumping at the Love Canal neighborhood near Niagara Falls, New York.[1] World War II resulted in 52,199,262 deaths; and on September 11, 2001, almost 3,000 people perished as a result of coordinated attacks by terrorists.[2] Human-caused major disasters create great losses and a wide array of feelings among victims, survivors, and onlookers.

According to Deborah DeWolfe, "In human-caused disasters such as bombings and other acts of terrorism, technological accidents, or airline crashes, survivors grapple with deliberate human violence and human error as causal agents. The perception that the event was preventable, the sense of betrayal by a fellow human(s), the externally focused blame and anger, and the years of prolonged litigation are associated with an extended and often volatile recovery period."[3] The issue of culpability causes a deep feeling of anger that often results in blame, resentment, a refusal to forgive, and hostility. The human heart interprets meaning in much different ways after human-caused disasters than after natural disasters. There are deep spiritual implications as victims and survivors grapple with values clarification and beliefs that have suddenly become ambiguous. Theological issues become evident as people struggle with grief, sin, revenge, justice, or God's sovereignty. The wail of lamentations and mourning are heard throughout the land.

Natural disasters include floods, hurricanes, earthquakes, and tornadoes. They may also include the lesser-considered avalanches, wildfires, and ice storms. The Southeast Asia tsunami of 2004 was the worst tsunami to ever impact the world. There were 8,212 fatalities, there are still 2,817 people missing, and over 6,000 people were displaced.[4] According to the National Interagency Fire Center, "The 2006 wildland fire season set new records in both the number of reported fires as well as acres burned. A total of 96,385 fires and 9,873,429 acres burned were reported. This season [2006] was 125 percent above the 10-year average."[5] The third most deadly hurricane in recorded history—Katrina—was also over three times more expensive than the next most expensive (Hurricane Andrew in 1992). Never before had an entire major American city been evacuated as a result of a disaster; never before had we seen the resulting massive governmental issues, including transportation, shelter, food, medical assistance, financial aid, jurisdiction, and permanent housing. In some cases, natural disasters may even act in concert with disasters caused by human error such as icy roads and inexperienced driving that causes a multicar, multifatality pileup. Like human-caused disasters, natural disasters cause loss of lives, destruction of property, psychological trauma, and spiritual distress. These major disasters can overwhelm congregations, communities, states, and even nations.

Strategic Planning:
Disasters Will Happen—Get Ready

Life is full of "should-a, would-a, could-a." When disaster strikes and chaos ensues, most congregations wish they had been better prepared. They wish they had planned for the possibility of a major disaster, but somehow the daily crises of congregational life usurped time, energy, and resources from strategic planning for major disasters. After the disaster hits, knowing the basics of planning will at least provide a framework for filling the gaps.

J. T. Mitchell cites, "In the International Critical Incident Stress Foundation (ICISF) model, strategic planning for group crisis intervention includes five key points: categorizing the threat or theme of the critical incident, classifying the target population to assist or support, selecting the types of interventions that will be utilized, determining the implementation timing, and selecting the right team to provide the intervention."[6] Using this model as a guide, congregational strategic planning for disasters could include variations of those same five points.

Congregations must first identify the immediate needs. Are there lives to be rescued? Do people need basic survival resources—medical attention, water, food, temperature-appropriate clothing, shelter? These needs must be met in the initial aftermath of a disaster, and congregations are usually in the best physical location to provide assistance since congregations are usually located in neighborhoods where people live. The first hours or days following the impact of the disaster will be devoted to rescue and meeting survival needs. All congregations should have some resources and supplies in place for these immediate needs. What can your congregation do?

Next, congregations must determine who their target group is. Who will be the recipients of spiritual care? Will it be the congregation, the neighborhood (the immediate area surrounding the congregational facility), the rescue and relief workers who have responded to the disaster, people with special medical needs, people who have been displaced, relief agencies that need staging areas (a place from which to conduct the business of providing relief), or another identified group? Most congregations cannot minister to everyone. Making the decision of a target group prior to disasters will enable the congregation to provide focus to their planning and will help eliminate the problem of making a hasty emotional decision to help everyone when there are inadequate resources and skills. If congregations in the community made specific assignments prior to disasters—using the team-assignment approach for effectiveness—each could offer some specialized assistance without being overwhelmed. Preplanning with a community clergy association could assist in this process.

Each congregation must determine what spiritual care resources they have to provide after a major disaster. Perhaps the resources are physical—space for sheltering, a kitchen for mass feeding, a large parking area for emergency relief vehicles, an education building for a temporary emergency day care facility. Or perhaps the resources are human—a staff of mental health professionals, a staff of licensed children's workers, volunteers willing to do emergency tasks that don't require extensive previous training (handing out water, sorting clothing, answering phones, and the like), people with construction skills and experience, people who speak foreign languages, trained crisis or disaster chaplains. People resources could include volunteers, listeners, encouragers, planners, counselors, or financial supporters.[7] Or perhaps the resources are a diminutive combination of these. Providing ministry to a particular target group will necessitate knowing what resources are available for that ministry. Congregations will be frustrated when they identify a target group and then realize they do not have the resources to provide appropriate spiritual care.

If your congregation will be providing direct care to congregants, victims, and relief workers, it will also be necessary to identify what ministry interventions you are able to provide. In other words, now that you know what resources you have, you must decide what you will do. Most congregations cannot do everything for everyone. It will be helpful to decide who you will be helping and what, specifically, you will be doing. For example, will you provide the evening meal for one hundred disaster relief workers? Will you provide emergency day care for fifty children, from infant through five years old, from 9 a.m. to 5 p.m., Monday through Friday? Will you provide disaster mental health services to children and teenagers for the next six months? Will you provide shelter (with or without meals) for one hundred people for the next three months? While it may be unrealistic to rigidly hold to these plans, without planning it will be difficult to make good decisions in the middle of overwhelming chaos and crisis needs. "Members of your congregation need to share in the ministry of disaster recovery. Share the work with your congregation. Know your limitations," states *Prepared to Care*, a booklet on disaster spiritual care.[8]

When congregations are also affected (they usually are also "victims" in major disasters), there are often some vacancies in congregational leadership. Good planning will include some specific identification of who will lead and manage the disaster spiritual care interventions that are being provided. These leaders and managers are not necessarily congregational staff (the staff usually have a myriad of other responsibilities during the aftermath of disasters), but are often congregants who are appointed to lead and manage the disaster spiritual care operations. Depending on the target group and the interventions you have decided to provide, these leaders may be predetermined (for example, the day care director may supervise the emergency day care or the kitchen director may supervise the mass-feeding operations). Planning the leadership and management structure prior to a disaster will help prevent leadership vacuums and conflicts in crisis decision making.

Appointing leaders and managers will be pointless if there are no followers or workers. Congregations must enlist volunteers who will be providing the interventions. Obviously, if pre-disaster strategic planning is occurring, there will be time for enlistment, orientation, training, and skill building. If leadership is recruiting volunteers post-disaster, training will be a little more complicated. It is very likely that many of the congregants will also be victims of the disaster. While this could make them unavailable to provide interventions, it might also make some more available to serve as volunteers. If they are being sheltered, they could help with shelter management. If they have no gas or power, they may assist in mass feeding while eating meals with other victims. Someone must be assigned the job of actively recruiting volunteers.

When congregations and communities are overwhelmed after major disasters, it may become necessary to identify regional and national resources. If you have already done this, good; you have completed some essential strategic planning. *The Work of the Chaplain* advises, "To minister effectively in community crisis and disaster relief, chaplains' [congregations] must familiarize themselves with the dynamics of relief organizations and their partnerships with other agencies. Many of these relationships are formalized through statements of understanding, but an equal number are informal agreements to 'work together for the good of the community.'"[9] Congregations must know which organizations and agencies provide assistance and what the parameters for assistance are. Congregants and victims often call the congregational office for information about housing, government assistance, free medical care, missing persons, and other emergency concerns. Good disaster spiritual care includes providing accurate information during emergencies. Use the information in the Resources section at the end of this chapter to make contact with your local, regional, and national resources online. Know what services they provide and whom to contact if necessary.

Good strategic planning includes training and education to prepare participants for their role in disaster spiritual care. If you are reading this pre-disaster, you have many possibilities to consider. The National Voluntary Organizations Active in Disaster (NVOAD) is comprised of many faith-based organizations that have various training programs to prepare congregations and individuals to respond in the event of major disasters. Many of these faith-based organizations also have online resources to help prepare disaster volunteers for various roles in response. If you are in the middle of a major disaster, one possible contact might be the American Red Cross Spiritual Response Team. The task force liaison could provide some contacts who could assist with emergency field training. One of the most urgent training components will be preparing clergy and laity to provide appropriate disaster spiritual care in the context of religious and cultural diversity. Spiritual care must be perceived as helpful, caring, and sensitive to the diversity of the population being served. Disaster spiritual care should never be perceived as an opportunity to proselytize, preach, or convert victims as a requirement for care. Learning to demonstrate respect for differences, sensitivity to unfamiliar needs, and awareness of common trauma responses will be essential learning components for all spiritual care providers.

According to *Church Preparedness for Disaster*, a congregation "must plan how it will respond to disasters, large and small, in the community. The plan needs to be well-thought-out and discussed by the church [congregation] leaders. The people in the congregation need to discuss the plan and determine how they, as individuals, can become part of this ministry. The unprepared church will miss valuable opportunities to minister if not prepared."[10]

Strategic Implementation: How Will We Provide Disaster Spiritual Care?

Have you started your preplanning? If not, you are now doing strategic implementation on the fly. An old adage says, "Timing is everything." While timing might not be everything to everyone, timing is still essential for effective spiritual care. Knowing the optimal time for beginning, executing, and ending disaster spiritual care will create among the volunteers a sense of urgency to begin and a sense of accomplishment when completed.

Know when your congregation will begin each type of intervention. During which phase of disaster will you provide your interventions? By necessity, some interventions will take place directly after impact—rescue, providing medical attention, water, food, and shelter, and providing spiritual comfort. Some interventions will take place during the early impact phase—sheltering, mass feeding, clothing distribution, helping to locate family members, or holding prayer services and vigils. Some interventions will be used after most of the rescue workers have left—rebuilding, finding jobs, small group interventions, memorial services, or pastoral counseling. Other interventions may continue for years. Two years after the destruction caused by Hurricane Katrina in New Orleans, organizations such as Operation Noah Rebuild, sponsored by the Southern Baptist Convention's North American Mission Board, were still working and had gutted 600 homes, built 37, and were working on over 160 more, with almost 1,500 families on their waiting list for help.[11]

Know when your congregation will continue interventions and know when your congregation will transition to pre-disaster ministry. Establishing the timetable for disaster spiritual care will be helpful for both the providers and the recipients.

> After weeks of serving three meals a day to victims of hurricanes Katrina and Rita, mass-feeding kitchens in Sabine Pass began to close the kitchen. A woman who had lost her home and was still living in a tent, ranted and raved, "How can you abandon us like this? You'll be killing us without food and water. How can you just pack up and leave?"

There's less guilt involved in terminating your intervention work if it has been planned and announced in advance. Furthermore, victims can begin making the physical and emotional transitions without being shocked when relief workers suddenly pack up and leave. Congregations need to make the public aware of their timetable—when they will begin ministry services and when they will end those services. There's an appropriate time to begin and an appropriate time to end. There's never an appropriate time to pull the rug out from under hurting people. There will come a day when the congregation will say, "We've done our part. We need to get back to our normal routines."[12]

Congregations must clearly understand their implementation processes. Preplanning is a bonus, but if you are reading this in the middle of a disaster, make some of these decisions immediately. Select one person to lead the team process—someone to initiate the process after some of the decisions in the strategic planning stage are completed. This person might also be the one who monitors the process and facilitates course changes, establishing specific points at which the process is evaluated. The process leader establishes the chain of command and makes it clearly understood by the entire congregational participants. There must clearly be one leader, but leadership means listening to wise counsel, being willing to make changes, and staying calm during chaos. The process will continue until all the evaluations and post-event education is completed. It will be helpful for future leaders if someone is assigned to keep an accurate record of timetables, processes, and personnel.

Another essential part of the process is thanking the participants during and after the event. This could take the form of verbal acknowledgment, recognition of group performance, or information in newsletters, bulletins, or during the worship service. After the event, leadership must individually acknowledge volunteers with written thanks. This could be accomplished by group leaders, team leaders, or staff. Keeping accurate records of volunteers and their contact information will be essential to this portion of the implementation phase. A helpful time of closure might include a thank you banquet or certificates of appreciation. Written thanks and certificates are often treasured for years after the event. Sometimes, community acknowledgment may be accomplished through news articles or radio interviews. Whatever the form, an appropriate thank you is essential. A sincere thank you is good manners and strategic planning for future events.

Strategic Evaluation: We'll Probably Make Mistakes, but We Can Improve

After the event has come to a close or is in the final process of closing, it will be important to begin the strategic evaluations. You will have been doing smaller evaluations throughout the process as you considered course changes. After the event is over, you may feel so exhausted that evaluations are left for "later." Typically, later will never come and strategic evaluations will be relegated to an insignificant optional detail as other responsibilities and crises take precedence. Make it a priority to complete the evaluations. One less painful way to complete the evaluations is to have each part of the team complete some part of the evaluations and then meet together to review the conclusions. Follow this with a celebratory meal and service. It will be a halleluja day for everyone!

Effectiveness in future events will increase as strategic evaluations are completed and shared. Some of the areas to be evaluated might include the following: providers of disaster spiritual care (for example, congregational and community volunteers or service providers), results of disaster spiritual care (How many were sheltered? How many spiritual care contacts were made? How many religious rites and rituals were provided? How effective was the use of church property?), implementation process (How was our timing? Did we have the right leadership? What could we have done differently? Did we recognize our volunteers?), scope of ministry provided, resources used (Did we duplicate ministry or pool resources with other agencies?), and collaboration with regional and national resources (How could we prevent future turf wars? What other training do our leaders need to be a part of? What did we learn by working with the Red Cross or the NVOAD organizations?).

Pre-event strategic planning includes a specific process for completing evaluations *after* the event. Many national relief organizations evaluate their participation in disasters and follow up with a document that states lessons learned, or best practices, in order to refine and improve their disaster services for the future.

Strategic Education: We Want to Teach Others about Providing Disaster Spiritual Care

If knowledge is power, specialized training in disaster spiritual care issues could empower congregations to be more effective in future disaster events. One of the primary issues in the aftermath of a major crisis is trauma and the distress that follows. Training volunteers and congregations about basic disaster trauma helps prepare them for the trauma issues they will encounter in victims and volunteers, reducing their personal anxiety while increasing their ability to provide appropriate disaster spiritual care. Learning the basics of stress mitigation and how to develop coping strategies will help caregivers provide essential ministry to victims.

> The impairment of human functioning has serious implications for not only the individual, but for every context within which that individual functions. Therefore, the impact of crisis can easily extend beyond the individual into the family, the work group,

and even the community. Thus, psychological crisis can become a public health challenge by virtue of its ability to reach far beyond the individual who initially experiences the crisis. Perhaps the most severe and disabling crisis context is that of psychological trauma. It has been argued that psychological trauma can leave in its wake the most severe and disabling of the adult-onset mental disorders.[13]

The International Critical Incident Stress Foundation, one of the major training organizations in the field of disaster response, offers several courses that could be helpful in training volunteers in the basics of responding to trauma. Everyone working in disaster spiritual care could benefit from these courses.

Volunteers and congregations need to acquire basic skills in disaster spiritual care. This may include learning skills related to ministering in cultural and religious diversity, how to effectively listen to people's stories, how to provide compassionate care when people are grieving, how to communicate care through presence and *being* even when they are unable to *do* very much, and how to provide age-specific ministry that will be helpful to individuals. Spiritual care providers in disasters usually function in the chaplain model—they make themselves available to provide ministry to all people. Some people may profess a specific faith tradition, others may profess no faith.

Perhaps the congregational training will be to prepare volunteers in specific disaster ministry disciplines—how to do mass feeding, how to run a shelter, how to assemble printed resources, how to help victims negotiate the governmental systems, how to complete assessments, how to undertake disaster cleanup, and how to deal with the media. All of these disciplines require specific training, and the most effective training is completed long before the disaster occurs.

A growing interest among laity is in the area of disaster chaplaincy—providing intentional spiritual care directly to victims. With appropriate training, laity and clergy are able to provide compassionate care that is welcomed and appreciated by many victims. Without coercing victims to convert or radically change their beliefs, well-trained laity and clergy have many opportunities to listen to the sacred stories of victims and other opportunities to share their own faith when asked. Many victims perceive unwanted religious discussions as unethical violations of their vulnerable status, so training is vital in order to provide effective, appreciated care.

Disaster relief chaplains are often volunteers who have collegial relationships with chaplains representing a variety of agencies and organizations. According to the *Southern Baptist Relief Chaplain Training Manual*, "The growing awareness of spiritual needs in crisis has begun to formalize the response of disaster relief chaplains. National and international disaster relief agencies are beginning to work together to coordinate spiritual care response in disasters of many kinds."[14] Many of these agencies also have well-developed training programs to prepare laity and community clergy to function in the chaplain role during disaster spiritual care.

> Crisis and disaster chaplains are highly trained in stress mitigation, trauma response, and victim psychology. Like other chaplain specialties, they are expert listeners and well acquainted with grief therapy and comforting grief. Previous education, training, and experience are the foundations for their ministry in this very specialized setting.[15]

Congregations must also be trained in individual disaster preparedness. Each family must have a clear understanding of how to prepare themselves for the possibility of disaster. See chapter 3 for more about individual preparedness. NVOAD, the Federal Emergency Management Agency, the American Red Cross, Lutheran Disaster Response, the North American Mission Board, and other faith-based organizations all have online resources to guide individuals, congregations, and dioceses in disaster preparedness. When individual family units are prepared, the congregation will have increased ability to provide ministry to others while suffering fewer inconveniences of their own disaster impact.

Pre-event training may be comprehensive and thorough, but on-the-job training is often a matter of touching on the most basic principles. Even if your congregation is trained and ready, there is always the possibility that some will be affected by the event and unable to fill their roles. Therefore, it is always prudent to have a mini-training format planned. This would be a fast-track field training version of the ideal training. It is training that provides some empowerment for the brave volunteers who step forward when there is a disaster need.

Policies and protocols must be in place to manage and train the spontaneous volunteers who arrive on the scene of disaster to "lend a hand," "provide disaster relief," or "just help whereever I can."

Final Words

Most congregations have never experienced a major disaster. Most congregations have not planned to react to a major disaster. Unfortunately, many congregations will be involved in the aftermath of a major disaster at some point. The most effective means of surviving the chaos of a major disaster is to plan ahead—create specific strategies prior to the event. But, if now is the time, begin with *strategic planning*:

- Identify the immediate needs (medical services, water, food, shelter, clothing)
- Identify the target for your disaster spiritual care ministry
- Identify what resources you have to provide disaster spiritual care
- Identify the ministry interventions you are able to provide
- Identify who will lead and manage the interventions
- Identify who will provide the interventions
- Identify regional and national resources
- Identify the training and education that you will provide to prepare participants

Next, employ *strategic implementation*:

- Identify the timetable for your participation
- Create the implementation process
- Thank your participants

When the event is over, apply *strategic evaluation*:

- Evaluate the effectiveness of the disaster spiritual care ministry provided
- Evaluate the providers of disaster spiritual care
- Evaluate the results of disaster spiritual care
- Evaluate the implementation process
- Evaluate the scope of ministry provided

- Evaluate the resources used
- Evaluate the collaboration with regional and national resources

Finally, provide *strategic education*:

- Educate volunteers about basic trauma issues
- Train volunteers in basic skills for disaster spiritual care
- Train volunteers in specific disaster ministry disciplines
- Train volunteers to lead and manage disaster ministry teams
- Train the congregation and dioceses in disaster preparedness

Congregations must also train and develop volunteers who will become the leaders and managers of disaster ministry teams. These people must have a working knowledge of the incident command system and how other relief agencies operate and interrelate. Leadership style inventories may be helpful in assessing specific roles for individual leaders. Being the rabbi, pastor, priest, imam, chairman of the deacons, or elder in the presbytery does not automatically qualify a person to be a disaster spiritual care team leader.

Remember that all the strategy in the world cannot account for the unexpected. Disasters are chaos, and change is always imminent. Hope for the best and plan for the worst. *Blessed are the flexible, for they shall not be broken.*

No congregation is ever fully prepared. No one anticipated the impact of Hurricane Katrina or the immediacy of hurricanes Rita and Wilma, or the catastrophe of September 11, 2001. With historical evidence that disasters are on the increase and that the possibility of great impact on local communities is possible, be strategic and don't be the congregation who cries out, "What do we do now?"

Notes

1. Wikipedia, "Love Canal," http://en.wikipedia.org/wiki/Love_Canal.
2. The History Place, www.historyplace.com/worldwar2/timeline/statistics.htm.
3. D. J. DeWolfe, *Training Manual for Mental Health and Human Service Workers in Major Disasters,* publication no. ADM 90-538 (Washington, D.C.: U.S. Department of Health and Human Services: Substance Abuse and Mental Health Services Administration, Center for Mental Health Services, 2000), section 2.

4. United Nations Office of the Special Envoy for Tsunami Recovery, http://www.tsunamispecialenvoy.org/country/thailand.asp.

5. National Interagency Fire Center, http://www.nifc.gov/stats/summaries/ summary_2006.html.

6. J. T. Mitchell, *Critical Incident Stress Management (CISM): Group Crisis Intervention*, 4th ed. (Ellicott City, MD: International Critical Incident Stress Foundation, 2006), 71–74.

7. *Preparing for Disasters: A Guide for Lutheran Congregations*, online manual (Chicago: Lutheran Disaster Response); http://www.ldr.org/resources/PrepDisaster.pdf.

8. *Prepared to Care: A Booklet for Pastors to Use in the Aftermath of a Natural Disaster* (Chicago: Evangelical Lutheran Church in America, 2004), 8.

9. N. K. Paget and J. R. McCormack, *The Work of the Chaplain* (Valley Forge, PA: Judson Press, 2006), 81–82.

10. *Church Preparedness for Disaster* (Alpharetta, GA: North American Mission Board, 2004): 1.

11. L. Szabo, "Faith Rebuilds House and Soul," *USA Today*, July 20, 2007.

12. Personal contact by author (Paget) with hurricane victim.

13. G. S. Everly and J. T. Mitchell, *Critical Incident Stress Management: A New Era and Standard of Care in Crisis Intervention*, 2nd ed. (Ellicott City, MD: Chevron, 1999), 21–22.

14. N. Paget, *Southern Baptist Disaster Relief Chaplain Training Manual* (Alpharetta, GA: North American Mission Board, 2004), 2.

15. Paget and McCormack, *The Work of the Chaplain*, 81.

Further Reading

Associational Preparedness for Disaster Relief. Alpharetta, GA: North American Mission Board, 2004.

Church Preparedness for Disaster. Alpharetta, GA: North American Mission Board, 2004.

DeWolfe, D. J. *Training Manual for Mental Health and Human Service Workers in Major Disasters,* publication no. ADM 90-538. Washington, D.C.: U.S. Department of Health and Human Services: Substance Abuse and Mental Health Services Administration, Center for Mental Health Services, section 2.

Everly, G. S., and J. T. Mitchell. *Critical Incident Stress Management: A New Era and Standard of Care in Crisis Intervention,* 2nd ed. Ellicott City, MD: Chevron, 1999.

History Place, The. www.historyplace.com/worldwar2/timeline/statistics.htm.

Massey, K. *Light Our Way*. National Voluntary Organizations Active in Disaster. Washington, DC: 2006.

Mitchell, J. T. *Critical Incident Stress Management (CISM): Group Crisis Intervention*, 4th ed. Ellicott City, MD: International Critical Incident Stress Foundation, 2006.

National Interagency Fire Center, http://www.nifc.gov/stats/summaries/summary_2006.html

Paget, N. K., and J. R. McCormack. *The Work of the Chaplain*. Valley Forge, PA: Judson Press, 2006.

Paget, N. K. *Southern Baptist Disaster Relief Chaplain Training Manual*. Alpharetta, GA: North American Mission Board, 2004.

Prepared to Care: A Booklet for Pastors to Use in the Aftermath of a Natural Disaster. Chicago: Evangelical Lutheran Church in America, 2004.

Preparing for Disasters: A Guide for Lutheran Congregations, online manual. Chicago: Lutheran Disaster Response, 2007); http://www.ldr.org/resources/PrepDisaster.pdf.

Szabo, Liz. "Faith Rebuilds House and Soul," *USA Today*, July 20, 2007.

United Nations Office of the Special Envoy for Tsunami Recovery, http://www.tsunamispecialenvoy.org/country/thailand.asp.

Wikipedia, "Love Canal," http://en.wikipedia.org/wiki/Love_Canal.

Resources

To secure a disaster spiritual care handbook, contact the National Voluntary Organizations Active in Disasters (NVOAD) at www.nvoad.org.

To secure online manuals for church and associational (diocesan) disaster preparedness, contact the following:

North American Mission Board at www.namb.net

Lutheran Disaster Response at www.ldr.org

United Methodist Organization for Relief at www.umcor.org

To obtain training in specific areas of disaster preparedness, contact your local chapter of the American Red Cross.

To obtain guidelines for disaster preparation, request the U.S. Department of Homeland Security Government Guide at www.ready.gov.

About the Contributor

Rev. Naomi Paget, DMin, BCC, BCETS is a Mission Service Corps missionary for the North American Mission Board of the Southern Baptist Convention. Rev. Paget's field of service is as an FBI chaplain and crisis interventionist with extensive training and experience in crisis intervention in law enforcement, community services, corporate institutions, and in multiple disaster relief organizations. She is a certified member of the national American Red Cross Spiritual Response Team, the Denver Seminary Critical Incident Stress Management Team, and several other national and international crisis response teams. She is a disaster chaplain trainer and curriculum writer for Southern Baptist Disaster Relief and serves on the National Volunteer Organizations Active in Disasters committee. She has served as a crisis chaplain consultant and instructor for multiple denominations, communities, institutions, and agencies throughout the country. Rev. Paget earned her DMin from Golden Gate Theological Seminary and her MDiv from The Southern Baptist Theological Seminary. She is board certified by the Association of Professional Chaplains and board certified by the American Academy of Experts in Traumatic Stress wherein she has achieved Diplomate status and is listed in the National Registry of the American Academy of Experts in Traumatic Stress. She is an adjunct professor at Golden Gate Baptist Theological Seminary and at Denver Seminary and has authored two books, *Disaster Relief Chaplain Training* (North American Mission Board, 2005) and *The Work of the Chaplain* (Judson Press, 2006). She is a passionate supporter of higher education for women and enjoys reading, ranching, and fly-fishing in her leisure.

6

Impact and Heroic Phases

Disaster Chaplains and Chaplaincy

Chaplain Therese M. Becker, MA, MDiv; Greg Bodin, BCC, MDiv; and Rev. Arthur Schmidt, DMin, BCC

We have entered the third millennium through a gate of fire.

KOFI ANNAN[1]

The events of September 11, 2001, propelled the need for disaster spiritual care into the public consciousness. The breadth and depth of human suffering and death, the violence done to a nation, had almost no precedent in our lived history here in the United States. Suffering and death, intentionally caused in the name of God, brutalizes our souls. Hurricane Katrina, an act of God, brought destruction beyond our imagination. The call has gone out. We respond.

Getting Ready—Preparing to Enter the Gate of Fire

What do we, as disaster chaplains, have to offer in the midst of this maelstrom? The whisper of God.

Prepare for the role. Disaster chaplaincy is a new venue for leaders of faith communities, one that in many ways is the inverse of a congregational setting. If we are involved with a congregation, we may have experience with individual or family disasters, death by disease, or in the normal course, unanticipated tragedy, the death of a child, or death by violence. However, as disaster chaplains, the incidents we respond to normally involve many people—a community or even a nation. The scope is much larger. In a disaster there are people from a multiplicity of denominations and of faith traditions, and those who have no religious beliefs at all. They may not understand God as we do, or pray in familiar ways. They do not come to us; we go to them.

We are not the preacher or teacher at this time; we accompany them as the listener, the compassionate silent one. We are a part of an interdisciplinary command structure, not in an authoritative position. Our role is somewhat inverted. We pray to have the ability and courage to be present.

Prepare spiritually. What does God ask in the midst of a disaster? What do our holy texts tell us? What does our tradition tell us? What motivates us to reach out our hearts, to stand with another in deep suffering, to risk our own suffering? "You too must befriend the stranger, for you were strangers in the land of Egypt" (Deut. 10:19). "For I was hungry and you gave me food, I was thirsty and you gave me to drink, I was a stranger and you welcomed me.... Just as you did it to one of the least of these, you did it to me" (Matt. 25:35). Remember. Hold your holy texts close. Stay "prayed up."

When we should not serve in a disaster. There are times when we are less effective in a disaster setting and should not offer to serve. When we are in the process of grieving a recent loss, or when we are recovering from a traumatic event, we have fewer inner resources to offer. When we ourselves are victims—for example, when we have experienced an earthquake and are in need ourselves of spiritual care—our ability to be available for others is diminished. And if we find that this particular disaster evokes emotions from a past trauma or loss, it is wise to offer support and care in another way. If you are in the care of a mental health provider, consult with him or her about volunteering to do this work.

Do not self-deploy to a disaster scene. Unless you are a part of a group that is invited or expected at a disaster, your presence can be a burden to those who are helping the victims. You will have to be housed and fed and perhaps helped to find transportation home. All of this takes away from the care of those affected by the disaster.

Consider your dress, work locations, and religious identification. Prepare clothing appropriate to the location in which you will be working. You may be at a family assistance center, a shelter, a respite center, a feeding site, a disaster assistance service center, disaster head-quarters, the disaster site (unusual), the morgue (rare), or you may be doing home visits in difficult terrain. You may wear clothing that is professional and considered normal clerical attire such as a Roman collar, a habit, or a prayer cap. Religious symbols worn around the neck, such as a cross, star, or crescent, should be no larger than three inches. Anything larger may give the appearance of proselytizing. Do not wear clothing that has a religious message written on it.

Enter the Fire—Working the Disaster

Flexibility and patience. When you first enter a disaster area, or even just the staging area for volunteers of a disaster, chaos is only slightly organized. Expect to wait; expect delays. The greatest virtue in getting to the site is flexibility. That should be your second mantra (the first is prayer). Flexibility, patience, flexibility, patience, flexibility, patience.

Cultural, racial, and religious diversity. At a disaster there will be people of cultures and races and backgrounds that are different from yours. This is both exciting and dangerous; exciting because it offers an opportunity to learn, dangerous because we may not know how to be with people whose culture or beliefs we do not understand.

Culture is "broadly defined as a common heritage or set of be-liefs, norms, or values … a system of shared meanings."[2] Culture influ-ences the way the cause or the meaning of a disaster is understood. Culture also affects coping styles. Some cultures value self-control and emotional restraint in the face of adversity. Other cultures encourage, or even require, the outward expression of grief, loud wailing, or throwing oneself over the deceased or on the floor. As disaster chap-lains, it is crucial that we are aware of our own culture's style and val-ues, and that we recognize and honor the differences in those we serve, as Therese Becker illustrates:

> While in New York after 9/11 accompanying a Chinese family to Ground Zero on a ferry, I stayed at a distance, respecting their pri-vacy, yet staying alert to their potential needs. At Ground Zero I guided them on the route and quietly answered questions. On the way back another disaster worker, unaware of my watchful pres-ence, approached the family and put her arm around the woman

who had lost her sister. This was not a culturally appropriate expression of solidarity with her suffering. I caught the other person's eye and invited her over. I explained that I was with the family and that being at a respectful yet caring distance was probably more appropriate than physical contact. She was receptive to this feedback.

Race is not a biological category; it is a social category that is given meaning in the context of a society, and that is "especially potent when certain social groups are separated, treated as inferior or superior, and given differential access to power and other valued resources."[3] Race is encoded in every aspect of our daily lives; such is our history. We all are members of a race, and race plays a primary role in interpersonal relationships. *It is critical that as disaster chaplains we are aware of our assumptions, biases, and values as we interact with people of another race.*

Religious diversity is a given in a disaster. We must be capable of ministering to those outside our own tradition. If our theology insists that we proselytize, we cannot minister at a disaster site. Period. "Religious predators" is the rather harsh name given to people who come to a disaster site for their own reasons—to further their beliefs or to engage others in their belief system. They are not welcome. It is unethical to prey upon vulnerable people.

EGYPTAIR 990

She sat on the sofa by herself against the back wall. Hair covered with a black hijab, she was observing all that was going on around her outside the briefing hall where the families received the latest information about the recovery of bodies from the plane crash. Her aloneness struck me even during my busy task of placing a notice board designating the beautiful cream, dew-covered roses to be distributed to the family members as they exited the briefing hall opposite.

I had to brush lightly by her to hang the sign on the wall about the flowers and felt a tug on my jacket as I did so. I stopped, turned and our eyes met. Jadwa. Her eyes sparkled through the tears that she worked hard to keep under control, and yet those same eyes had observed me very closely as I moved about the area.

"And who are you?" she said in excellent English.

"My name is John and I am a minister here with the church. And you?"

"My husband and son were on the plane. I know they are dead."

"I am so sorry. Please accept my sympathies for your sad and tragic loss."

"What does a minister do?" she queried.

"I'm a Christian Baptist and I am a counterpart of an imam. My work here is to help people to care for one another using our various faith beliefs whatever they are."

"Oh, I understand. So you can help me?

"I will try," I said. "How can I help you?"

Jadwa continued, "I know that it is the will of Allah that my husband and son are gone. I have done what my faith requires of me. I have surrendered them to Allah. That is what I have done, but what I need from you is help with my grief and pain as a mother and wife. It is too much to carry on my own."

Jadwa now had my full attention as I squatted down to be at her eye level. This ten-second conversation already had us both focused on each other, she ready to talk and I ready to listen.

"Tell me about what is happening to you," I ventured.

"My husband and I are from Syria and six months ago we told our six-year-old son, Hassan, that he would be going to Damascus to stay with his grandparents during the summer. I thought he would have liked that but he told us he didn't want to go. He was very insistent he wasn't going. I was as insistent that he would be going. You will enjoy your grandparents and they are looking forward to seeing you. I asked him why he did not want to visit Grandma and Granddad. Surely they love you and you love them. He yelled back at me that the plane will crash.

I told him no, and these planes don't crash. He argued with his father and me for a long time but he just wouldn't listen. I told him that he would be all right and that we had purchased his plane tickets with Omar, his father."

Jadwa, with remarkable clarity, told her story in detail. I had not for a long time been so wrapped up in another's story to this depth. My tears, a sign of my involvement, became evident to me and to her. Sometimes she spoke through open sobbing, through silence, and speaking with her hands, describing the last six months of her son's life. He was their only child.

The conversation moved through its sequences to where her experience and grief began to be retold. She stopped and reaching into her purse asked tentatively if I would like to see her pictures.

The pictures were from one roll of film, starting with the first picture taken at their house the morning the flight was to leave. Dad was smiling; Hassan looked subdued and quiet. The journey to the airport and the sequential series of photos right up to the departure gate were shared, but now along with an added deeper human experience of her grieving motherhood. It was easy to see that Hassan had become very withdrawn at the airport, but when time came to board the plane he became inconsolable, yelling and screaming, crying, and saying for all to hear, "The plane is going to crash."

"No! Mommy! No! No! No! I don't want to go! The plane will crash." Feeling embarrassed at her son's outburst, Jadwa picked him up off the ground, holding him tight, and said, "You will be all right, Hassan. I love you." She kissed him all over and Hassan became quiet. She placed his hand in his father's hand, and stepped back.

The next picture showed Hassan and his father walking backwards down the Jetway waving at her.

A crowd of about forty people had gathered around by this time, all silent, just listening and grieving. Silence reigned but emotions ruled. Sensing the story had been told and relived, we both stood at the same time, not breaking the contact we maintained through our teary eyes. I took two roses from the table beside us, handed them to her, and we embraced and held each other across culture, theology, and experience.

"Thank you for telling me about you, Omar, and Hassan," I said through a breaking voice. She smiled, and reflected that she needed to show someone the pictures and tell about what she had just lost on the plane crash.

"I needed someone to listen. Thank you, you have helped. Can I pray for you and the work you do?" she said in parting.

"If you will allow me to pray for you and your family," I responded.

We parted, the two white roses stood out in front of her black hijab. She carried them for the next six days finally placing them in the basket to be taken to the plane crash site where Hassan, Omar, and over two hundred souls died on the plane that crashed.

REV. JOHN C. WILSON, PHD

Breathing Fire—Working with the Victims and Families

Listen, listen, listen. That is the mantra for this time, the moment when we finally get to the site where the victims and families are. The way to provide spiritual care is ultimately a question about theology, as our theology shapes both what we see and the manner in which we make ourselves available to others. Spiritual care at this place is accompaniment, witness, solidarity. *Being* with another at the point of their suffering is far more significant than your words or actions. When people are deeply heard, they heal. St. Francis is said to have implored, "Preach the Gospel at all times; use words when necessary."

Spiritual care is not a facile prayer or scripture quotation or hollow words spoken prematurely to cover a broken heart. Spiritual care is a painful accompaniment, a deep listening to the rawest expression of human suffering. It may or may not include prayer. It may or may not include words. We respect, even humbly learn about faith in God, from those whom we serve. It is important to stick very closely to the experience of the person, and to listen for the "music behind the words," as one of my early mentors says. For only by this kind of listening (which, by the way, is very hard work) can we hear what is truly at stake. Most often the anger at God and the alienation from God that those affected by a disaster experience, is more a profound cry of pain than evidence of an endangered relationship with God.

In our experience as disaster chaplains, the more effective helpers are those who allow the people they help to instruct them about what or who was lost and the meaning of the loss. Spiritualities that are not grounded in the truth of personal experience can encourage those injured to move ahead of themselves and thereby do damage to their spirits—for example, by advising them to forgive prematurely or to rely on narrow interpretations of scripture.[4] We must know ourselves.

Realities we cannot abide in ourselves will be denied in the world and in others, leading to abandonment of those who suffer.

COMPANIONING

Companioning is about honoring the spirit; it is not about focusing on the intellect.

Companioning is about curiosity; it is not about expertise.

Companioning is about learning from others; it is not about teaching them.

Companioning is about walking alongside; it is not about leading.

Companioning is about being still; it is not about frantic movement forward.

Companioning is about discovering the gift of sacred silence; it is not about filling every painful moment with words.

Companioning is about bearing witness to the struggles of others; it is not about directing those struggles.

Companioning is about being present to another's pain; it is not about taking away the pain.

Companioning is about respecting disorder and confusion; it is not about imposing order and logic.

Companioning is about going into the wilderness of the soul with another human being; it is not about thinking you are responsible for finding the way out.[5]

Judith Herman, a writer in the field of trauma and recovery, wrote, "The traumatic event challenges an ordinary person to become a theologian, a philosopher, and a jurist. The survivor is called upon to articulate the values and beliefs that she once held and that the trauma destroyed. She stands mute before the emptiness of evil, feeling the insufficiency of any known system of explanation. Survivors of atrocity of every age and every culture come to a point in their testimony where all questions are reduced to one, spoken more in bewilderment than in outrage: Why? The answer is beyond human understanding."[6] Listening to the stories of those who have been traumatized is in itself healing. Creating and telling stories helps us to order our experience, to make meaning, as well as to create community. In both Chile and El Salvador psychologists and psychiatrists developed the use of testimony as a therapeutic tool. People who have experienced their worst fantasies, who have lost their grounding in reality because of this worst conceivable thing that could happen again, tell their story, not only as catharsis, but as denunciation. "By giving individual pain and suffering a social characteristic, the testimony allows its value to be recovered."[7] This tool is both individual and social—both parts are necessary for recovery. Figure 6.1 illustrates some of the ways spiritual care providers can help those affected by a disaster recover.

SPIRITUAL CARE INTERVENTIONS

Spiritual care interventions are designed to **mitigate** the impact of spiritual, physical, emotional, and behavioral crisis experienced by survivors, family members, rescue/ recovery personnel, and the community at large in the aftermath of a disaster.

APPROPRIATE SPIRITUAL CARE INTERVENTIONS AFTER A TRAUMA OR DISASTER

- Practice active listening skills (silence is golden)—**listen more than you speak!**

- Encourage people to tell their stories.

- Be swift to hear and slow to speak as appropriate to the needs.

- Refrain from imposing an explanation as to "why."

- Connect people with personal support community.

- "Commonize" intrusive thoughts and feelings.

- Help the individual accept the reality of the loss.

- Allow individuals to share memories of their loved one.

- Mention their loved one by name.

- Offer hope.

- Do not be afraid to weep with those who weep.

- Acknowledge an individual's/ family's grief

- Provide sacred space.

- Facilitate appropriate rituals.

- Pray with/for them.

- Provide guidance on transition issues.

- Respect confidentiality.

- Avoid clichés.

- Most disaster and trauma spiritual care provided is short-term. Be prepared to refer for longer-term spiritual care.

- Suggesting other support services such as health services or mental health, as needed.

- Do not attempt to solve problems, but rather to support them in coming up with their own answers.

Figure 6.1

In the aftermath of the massacres that occurred in Rwanda in the early 1990s, a woman psychologist was asked to visit one of the many refugee camps of Rwandan in Tanzania. It seemed that the women of the camp, though safe from slaughter, were not sleeping. During her visit to the refugees, the psychologist learned that the women, who had witnessed the murder of family and friends, had been told by camp officials not to speak of such atrocities in the camp. The women followed this instruction, but the memories of the carnage haunted them, and they could not sleep.

The psychologist decided that in response to this situation she would set up a story tree: a safe place for the women to speak of their experiences. Every morning she went out to the edge of the camp and waited under the canopy of a huge shade tree. The first day no one came. On the second day one woman appeared, told her story, and left. Another showed up the following day, then another and another. Within the span of a few days, scores of women were gathering under the tree each morning to listen and to share their tales of loss, fear, and death. Finally, after weeks of listening, the psychologist knew that the story tree was working. Reports confirmed that the women in the camp were now sleeping.[8]

If hope is something that is a dimension of the soul, an orientation of the spirit and heart, we cannot impart it, or offer it as if it were an hors d'oeuvre. We can perhaps evoke it through our caring presence and the evidence of our own faith. We can allow the person to borrow our strength until they have their own.

Basic Guidelines for Good Listening[9]

- **Prepare to listen. Make sure you have a time and place to truly listen. If the time is limited, acknowledge that fact and make the most of the time you have. Choose a quiet place. Cut down distractions and interruptions.**
- **Show interest.** Sit down facing the person. Keep a relaxed posture. Lean forward a bit. Maintain eye contact. Encourage communication with gestures (a nod of the head), phrases ("I see," or, "go on"), or facial expressions.

- **Respect the phases of crisis the person is in.** Do not probe too hard for feelings when a person is still in shock; do not try to talk a person out of their feelings of anger. Also, respect the times when the individual may not want to talk about how things are going. Talking with a person in a crisis does not always mean talking about the crisis. People usually "dose" themselves in dealing with pain and sorrow, and periods of normalcy and respite are important. Talking about ordinary events and laughing at life's humorous points are also healing. If in doubt, ask the person what they would like at the moment. For example, you might say, "I'm interested in how you're doing. Do you feel like talking?"

- **Provide comfort.** Touch the person if it seems appropriate: a touch on the hand or shoulder, a hug, or even holding the person in your arms may be helpful, depending on the circumstances. This should not be done if you feel uncomfortable, if there is some danger in physical closeness, or if the person is a victim of assault. Help to make the person physically comfortable. Offer food, something to drink, a blanket, or whatever else might seem comforting.

- **Focus attention.** Center on the person and their situation. Give your undivided attention. Be alert, present, and receptive.

- **Listen carefully.** Listen not only to words, but also to the person's tone of voice, body language, and emotion. Respond to nonverbal communications, such as a questioning look. Try to listen without judging, moralizing, condemning, making assumptions, or drawing conclusions. Do not lose track of what the person is saying while you think of what your response is going to be.

- **Avoid interrupting.** Allow the person to finish speaking before responding. Try not to jump in at any pause, finish a statement for the person, or hurry the person along.

- **Respect silence.** Silences can be remarkably eloquent, and can allow the person important time and space to think something through, or to allow a feeling to surface. It is especially important to be silent when an individual stops speaking because of strong feelings.

- **Allow expressions of emotion.** Do not try to forestall expression of emotion, such as crying, by interrupting. The expression of feelings can be therapeutic, and it is likely that the person will be better able to continue after intense emotions have been released. A touch or a nod of the head can indicate that you empathize.

- **Tolerate repetition.** Often, a person in crisis needs to tell the same story, or go over certain information many times. It is an important part of working through the trauma and "making sense" of what has happened. In addition, the person may need for you to repeat what you have said to them, or to repeat specific instructions or questions. A person in crisis often feels overloaded, and memory lapses and confusion can interfere with the ability to take in what you are saying.

- **Ask clear, simple questions.** Ask questions one at a time. Keep them understandable and focused. Avoid questions that can be answered with a yes or no. "How" and "what" questions bring out more information. Always wait for a response. Questions can be general ("Tell me more about it.") or specific ("How did you find out?").

- **Be sure you understand what is being communicated.** Periodically check to be sure you clearly understand what the person is telling you. By doing so, you will be validating the person's remarks, demonstrating your attentiveness, and confirming your interest. The following methods can be helpful:
  - **Paraphrasing.** Making a statement that puts into your words what you have heard. For example: "I look at my kids and wonder what they're thinking"; "You're really concerned about how your children are taking all of this."
  - **Reflective questioning.** Repeating back part or all of what you heard in the form of a question. For example: "I feel like a real jerk"; "A real jerk?"
  - **Asking for clarification.** Asking a simple question when the person's meaning is unclear. For example: "I'm concerned about my wife"; "What is it that concerns you?"

- **Summarizing.** Reviewing major points that have been covered in order to ensure you have heard what's most important.
- **Wait-think-respond.** Waiting helps you to think, and thinking increases the chance that the response will be appropriate. A short pause is usually all that is needed.

Examples of Insensitive or Unhelpful Remarks When Functioning as a Disaster Chaplain

- Claiming that you fully understand the survivor's situation
- Expecting someone to function normally almost immediately
- Trying to tell people how they should or should not be feeling, even though there may be times when their feelings seem inadequate or inappropriate to you. Many people experiencing major loss criticize themselves and believe their feelings are abnormal by saying they shouldn't be feeling the way they feel, they should have gotten over their feelings already, or they should be feeling more or less deeply.
- Telling survivors they are better off than others, or comparing their loss to that of others
- Brushing aside their feelings abruptly or rudely in order to get down to the business at hand, such as filling out their answers on an application
- Giving religious explanations for their misfortune
- Showing excessive sympathy. This may only make the survivor feel more hopeless and reinforce feelings of inadequacy.
- Playing down the crisis or the magnitude of their particular losses
- Claiming that a substitute item will replace what has been lost, such as pets, furniture, cars, or keepsakes
- Assuring a survivor that everything will be OK
- Complaining about the government or the "system" rather than giving solid and positive input while acknowledging system-processing requirements
- Making false promises
- Taking anger personally or responding angrily to the survivor
- Being intolerant, prejudging, moralizing, or accusing

See figure 6.2 for more examples of what or what not to say during or after a crisis.

AS A DISASTER CHAPLAIN ...

DON'T SAY:

- "I know how you feel."
- "Be happy for what you had."
- "Life is for the living."
- "At least you had him/her for ___ years."
- "I almost feel worse than you."
- "You're young; you can always marry/have more children."
- "They are in a better place."
- "Life must go on—you'll feel better before you know it."
- "Thank God you have other children."
- "You must be strong for your family."

DO SAY:

- "You have my heartfelt sympathy."
- "My heart goes out to you."
- "Friends here share your grief."
- "No words can express my sorrow."
- "I cannot imagine the pain you must feel."
- "I feel for your loss."
- "My prayers are with you at this time."
- "Please accept my sympathy."
- "You have the focus of our loving prayers at this time."
- "What can I do to help you at this time?"
- "I am here to help you in any way I can."

Figure 6.2

Disaster Chaplaincy—A Brief History

Spiritual care responders have been present at disasters since the dawn of civilization. Many human beings have a desire to express their faith in their day-to-day existence. Many human beings seek a deeper meaning to their life through their faith. In the day of disaster, those feelings and needs often intensify. Human beings are meaning makers; we try to find meaning in the events that surround us. Disasters are complex events and often challenge people physically, emotionally, and spiritually. Spiritual care providers have responded when their communities have been hit by disaster and have consistently tried to help people who have been affected.

The profession began through the leadership of Anton Boisen in the 1920s. Clinically trained institutional and community-based spiritual care providers have been there to support hurting people. Chaplains have been out on the streets responding to small- and large-scale disasters through police and fire departments for decades. Military chaplains have a long and brave history of walking beside soldiers, sailors, and Marines, going into harm's way with them. Health care institutions and the chaplains who serve them have provided care for the ill and injured after disasters in their community.

Professional chaplaincy began its formal disaster response on a national level in 1998. The Aviation Disaster Family Assistance Act was passed by Congress on October 9, 1996, to standardize and improve the quality of support for family members after an aviation crash. Embedded in this act was the right of family members to receive appropriate spiritual and emotional support. The National Transportation and Safety Board (NTSB), an engineering and technical investigation organization, was assigned to coordinate this response. The NTSB reached out to the American Red Cross to help them provide the appropriate emotional and spiritual support. The Red Cross, which already had a strong history of emotional support, agreed to this partnership. The problem was that neither the Red Cross nor the NTSB had the history or resources to provide spiritual support.

In the winter of 1998, an organization that was then called the College of Chaplains (today's Association of Professional Chaplains, or APC) stepped in to help provide these spiritual support services. The APC is a national organization of board-certified clinically trained chaplains. Chaplain Greg Bodin, from Minneapolis, was asked to attend the formative meetings between the Red Cross and the NTSB to create the Aviation Incident Response Team (the AIR Team). Chaplain Bodin had responded to five air crashes in his community and had some local experiences to draw from. He attended the initial planning meeting in Washington. As the AIR Team was being formed, the team decided to listen to the experts and organized a three-day planning retreat at the Red Cross National Headquarters; the experts were family and friends of airplane crash victims.

The first two days of this planning retreat were spent listening to the family and friends of airplane crash victims tell their story. In honest and painful ways, they spoke of what was helpful and hurtful at their time of crisis. Unfortunately, well-meaning but untrained helpers, some of them spiritual care providers, said and did things that only added to the pain of already hurting people. These two days were tearful and humbling, but very informative. As people told their stories it was, as Anton Boisen said, "Like reading living human documents." Victim's families became the teachers and told the team what they needed and did not need in this crisis.

That winter, the College of Chaplains began a formal relationship with the American Red Cross to respond to transportation disasters. Greg Bodin was asked to continue on as their liaison. At the encouragement of Bodin, the Association of Clinical Pastoral Education (ACPE) and the National Association of Catholic Chaplains (NACC) were asked by the Red Cross to also enter into this partnership. As training and board-certifying organizations, they brought additional chaplains and clinical expertise to the AIR Team. The ACPE and NACC asked Chaplains Arthur Schmidt and Therese Becker to represent them on this team. Bodin, Schmidt, and Becker together helped the Red Cross in the formation of the spiritual care branch of the AIR Team. This branch became the Spiritual Aviation Incident Response Team (SAIR Team) within the AIR Team. As advocates, teachers, and coaches, these three helped the Red Cross and NTSB organizations understand the important role of spiritual care in disaster response.

At the encouragement of Bodin, Schmidt, and Becker, other chaplain organizations entered into this partnership, starting with the National Association of Jewish Chaplains, with Rabbi Stephen B. Roberts, one of the editors of this book, as their liaison. Several years later, the International Association of Police Chaplains and the Federation of Fire Chaplains joined this partnership. The liaisons from each of these organizations have formed the Spiritual Care Task Force within the Red Cross. With each other and with other disaster response disciplines, they have modeled good communication, cooperation, and coordination of skills representing their diverse organizations and always championing the cause of professional chaplaincy. Developing training and professional standards both for their own team and the community has been a big challenge for this task team.

In the years to follow, professional chaplains have responded to one transportation incident after another, demonstrating in each situation the importance of spiritual support, and earning the trust of other disaster response disciplines. It was on this foundation of trust that the chaplain response expanded from transportation disasters to terrorist and natural disasters. From Ground Zero in New York to New Orleans after Katrina, this response team of clinically trained chaplains has been a key responder. Each time guided by their high ethical and professional standards, they have helped to coordinate the delivery of spiritual support for the hurting. Working side by side with local clergy and spiritual care providers, they have gone to the places where people are hurting and have been a helpful presence. Because of its broader mission, the AIR Team has now become the Critical Response Team of the American Red Cross. Since shortly after 9/11, Chaplain Earl Johnson has worked and volunteered within National American Red Cross headquarters on behalf of the professional chaplaincy associations involved in the Spiritual Care Response Team (SRT) overseeing and coordinating operations.

In New York City, two years prior to 9/11, Rabbi Stephen B. Roberts started working with the American Red Cross in Greater New York, creating a local group of professionally trained chaplains to respond to aviation incidents. They had completed all planning only a couple weeks prior to 9/11. When the terrorist attacks occurred, they immediately responded, helping to set up the New York City operations and then handing them over to the national SAIR Team for three months. At the end of three months they again took over the operations. Chaplain Zahara Davidowitz-Farkas was hired to oversee the operations full-time. Over eight hundred chaplains responded to 9/11 through the American Red Cross, working with the families and friends at the Family Assistance Center, with the workers at respite centers and Ground Zero, and with the victims by providing spiritual care at the hospitals morgues. With Chaplain Roberts as a founder and Chaplain Davidowitz-Farkas as the first executive director, disaster spiritual care was officially spun off into a separate 501(c)3 organization, which is now known as Disaster Chaplaincy Services, New York. The organization continues to respond to a wide range of disasters. The board is composed of members of the various New York faith communities. Their chaplain team of almost two hundred is represented by the full spectrum of faiths, races, and cultures.

Final Words

Disaster chaplaincy is a precious and privileged ministry, a burden of love. Abraham Verghese, the physician-writer, wrote of his care for Hurricane Katrina victims in San Antonio, Texas. As he drove in "for the 2 a.m. to 8 a.m. shift, riding down dark, deserted streets, [he] thought of driving in for night shifts in the ICU as an intern many years ago, and how [he] would try to steel [him]self, as if putting on armor." He cared for person after person, finally realizing that "as the night wore on, I understood that they needed me to ask [them where they had spent the previous five days]; to not ask was to not honor their ordeal. Hard men wiped at their eyes and became animated in the telling." It reminded him of the work he had done in India and Ethiopia, where "the careful listening, the thorough exam, the laying of hands was the therapy." He knew that in the same way here, the illnesses he was treating were inextricably linked to the bigger problem of homelessness, disenfranchisement, and despair. On his way home he knew that "the years have shown that there is no armor. There never was. The willingness to be wounded may be all we have to offer."[10] And so it is.

Notes

1. Nobel Peace Prize Lecture, Oslo, December 10, 2001. http://nobelprize. org/nobel_prizes/peace/laureates/2001/annan-lecture.html.
2. U.S. Department of Health and Human Services, *Mental Health: Culture, Race and Ethnicity—A Supplement to Mental Health: A Report of the Surgeon General* (Rockville, MD: U.S. Department of Health and Human Services, Substance Abuse and Mental Health Services Administration, Center for Mental Health Services, 2001), 9.
3. Ibid.
4. R. Grant, *The Way of the Wound: A Spirituality of Trauma and Transformation* (self-published), 128.
5. From Alan D. Wolfelt, "Companioning Versus Treating: Beyond the Medical Model of Bereavement Caregiving (Part 3)," *Forum Newsletter Association for Death Education and Counseling* (November/December 1998).
6. J. L. Herman, *Trauma and Recovery*, rev. ed. (New York: BasicBooks, 1997), 178.
7. L. Aresti, "Political Reality and Psychological Damage," *Flight, Exile and Return: Mental Health and the Refugee*, ed. Adrianne Aron (San Francisco: Committee for Health Rights in Central America, 1988), 59–61.
8. H. Anderson and E. Foley, *Mighty Stories, Dangerous Rituals: Weaving Together the Human and the Divine* (San Francisco: Jossey-Bass, 1998), 3.

9. From "Disaster Counseling," SAMHSA Publication KEN-01-0096.
10. A. Verghese, "Close Encounter of the Human Kind," *The New York Times,*
    September 18, 2005.

Further Reading

American Red Cross. *Providing Red Cross Disaster Health Services* (ARC 3076).
    December, 1982.
Hafen, B. Q., and K. J. Frandsen. Psychological Emergencies and Crisis Intervention.
    Englewood, CO: Morton, 1985.
Mitchell, J. T., and G. Bray. Emergency Services Stress: Guidelines for Preserving the
    Health and Careers of Emergency Services Personnel. Englewood Cliffs, NJ:
    Prentice Hall, 1990.
Mitchell, J. T., and H. L. P. Resnick. *Emergency Response to Crisis.* Bowie, MD:
    Robert J. Brady, 1981.
Zunin, L. M., and H. S. Zunin. *The Art of Condolence: What to Write, What to Say,
    What to Do at a Time of Loss.* New York: HarperCollins, 1991.

About the Contributors

Chaplain Therese M. Becker, MA, MDiv, is the manager of Spiritual Care Services at Kaiser Permanente in Santa Clara, California. She is a (joyful) Jew by choice. Her interest in disaster spiritual care began when she was doing her theological studies in earthquake country twenty years ago. A certified chaplain, she has worked in community hospitals and trauma centers. Previously, she was a machinist for United Airlines and a welfare worker in Manhattan. She was the first chaplain formally deployed by the American Red Cross to a train crash in Bourbonnais, Illinois, in March 1999. For her, disaster chaplaincy is an honoring of God in the stranger, the *ger,* which also means "convert."

Greg Bodin, BCC, MDiv, is the director of pastoral care at North Memorial Health Care and is an ordained pastor with the Evangelical Covenant Church. He has extensive experience in the field of disaster chaplaincy, starting in 1980 as a fire chaplain and then in 1981 as the disaster team pastoral care coordinator for the Metropolitan Airports Commission in Minnesota. He has responded to four aviation disaster crashes as well as two hurricanes; he was an officer for the American Red Cross in New York City overseeing spiritual care after 9/11; and he was the senior chaplain helping to oversee the provision of disaster spiritual care in his hometown when there was a major interstate bridge collapse in 2007.

Rev. Arthur Schmidt, DMin, BCC, is an ELCA Lutheran pastor and a certified supervisor of clinical pastoral education. He is currently president of the Association of Clinical Pastoral Education (ACPE). He has served as chaplain and educator in spiritual care for over thirty years in Colorado, California, and Washington. After a several-year stint as the coordinator of disaster response for the ACPE, Rev. Schmidt joined Theresa Becker and Greg Bodin in designing a curriculum for training spiritual care disaster response personnel for the American Red Cross Disaster Response Team. Art left this task force when he was elected president of the ACPE.

7

Spiritual First Aid

Rev. Julie Taylor, MDiv, CTR

> *It is four-thirty in the morning at a respite center for rescue and re-
> covery personnel working at the site of an airline crash. As a group
> of local firefighters end their break, leaving the respite center to re-
> turn to the debris field to search for human remains, a firefighter
> turns to the chaplain who has just handed him a cup of coffee and
> says, "Pray for me," as he walks out the door.*

Spiritual first aid is a short-term helping tool designed to mitigate the impact of the spiritual, psychological, and physical aspects of crisis that may be experienced by a person who has been affected by disaster or a critical incident. Spiritual first aid does not include advocating for any one faith or belief system, proselytizing, or imposing any beliefs or rituals; it is providing care and comfort for people during times of great need.

Assisting others is not a new concept to people of faith. Serving and caring for the needy is a spiritual tenet of all the major faith traditions, and has been practiced for thousands of years. Looking at statistics that claim 97 percent of Americans believe in God and 90 percent pray, it is not surprising that people turn to their faith or spiritual roots when experiencing crisis or stress. According to a national American Red Cross study from 2001, when respondents were asked who they were most likely or very likely to seek assistance from during crisis, 59 percent said a spiritual counselor, 45 percent said a physician, and 40 percent said a mental health professional.[1] Psychology professor Dr. George S. Everly Jr., states, "It has been commonly observed that in times of crisis and disaster, many individuals seek out religious or spiritual leaders."[2]

The International Critical Incident Stress Foundation (ICISF) has developed a wonderful curriculum called Pastoral Crisis Intervention (PCI), with levels I and II. It is my goal to expand on the PCI model, making it more accessible to a more diverse user group, beginning with a change of terms and the connection between pastoral crisis intervention and spiritual first aid. There are limited models of spiritual response to crisis that speak to the needs of responders participating from multiple faiths. Crisis interventions dealing with the spiritual response to crisis do not require a pastor. The title of "pastor" is specifically Christian and connected with ordination or a call to ministry. The use of this term in the title of a model is confusing and exclusionary, suggesting that a spiritual responder must be ordained, or Christian. The term *spiritual first aid* causes no such confusion or exclusivity. Anyone from any faith tradition, regardless of official status, can provide spiritual first aid with proper training. As written in Appendix A of Everly's book, *Pastoral Crisis Intervention,* the terms *pastoral crisis intervention* and *spiritual first aid* are used interchangeably.[3] ICISF's Pastoral Crisis Intervention Level II course goes into greater detail regarding spiritual first aid.[4]

Spiritual first aid is not pastoral counseling or therapy; it is also not a substitute for therapy. It is a crisis intervention technique used during times of acute stress. As the name implies, it is first aid, not a cure, not fixing. Physical first aid is designed to stabilize and assess an injury, to provide basic care for injuries, and if stabilization attempts are not successful, to call for a higher level of care to take over. With some physical injuries, such as a superficial cut, all that is needed is to clean the wound and apply a bandage, allowing the body to take over healing on its own. But with a heart attack, for example, administering CPR is required until paramedics arrive to transport the individual to a hospital for further treatment. The same principles apply in spiritual first aid: stabilize, assess, provide care and comfort, refer as necessary.

There is a significant difference between the long-term therapeutic process of pastoral counseling and spiritual first aid. Everly describes pastoral counseling as "an approach to the therapeutic process, wherein theology and spirituality are integrated with the principles of psychology and behavioral science to help individuals, couples, families, groups, and institutions achieve mental health and promote wellness at all levels."[5] The focus of spiritual first aid is the here and now, whereas the focus of pastoral counseling is the past, present, and future.[6] Who is spiritual first aid for? Anyone affected by disaster or critical incidents can benefit from spiritual first aid. It can be used with adults or children, survivors or family members, rescue and recovery personnel, relief workers, and the community at large. Who delivers spiritual first aid? A variety of people can be trained to administer spiritual first aid: ordained or lay clergy, faith leaders, peers, friends, even family members.

Where should spiritual first aid be administered? Venues for providing spiritual first aid could be any number of places, including, but not limited to: shelters, respite centers, disaster assistance service centers, emergency call centers or emergency operations centers, emergency first aid stations, memorial services, family assistance centers, homes, businesses, houses of worship, hospitals, combat zones, military bases, or wherever one may be working or deployed.

When is spiritual first aid best used? Generally, spiritual first aid is a tool for use in the immediate aftermath of a critical incident. It is designed as a short-term helping technique that will assist stabilizing those affected by the incident and refer them to a higher level of care if necessary.

Why is spiritual first aid needed at all? Humans are complex creations; spirituality is a realm of our experience that can be damaged during times of great pain and suffering, but it can also serve as a source of strength to draw upon during those same times. Spirituality connects us to something greater than ourselves and helps us make meaning of life—the good times and bad. For many people, religion and religious practices offer a sense of security and safety.[7]

During times of great stress, it is not unusual for people who have a relationship with a higher power or faith to use the spiritual or religious language from their faith tradition to express their distress.[8] "Such expressions do not necessarily indicate a crisis of faith, per se, rather, such expression may simply be expressions of psychological distress."[9] For these individuals, the presence of a trained disaster chaplain or spiritual care provider may be of comfort.

Basic Actions and Goals of Spiritual First Aid

As defined earlier, spiritual first aid is designed to mitigate the impact of the spiritual crisis experienced by survivors, family members, rescue and recovery personnel, and the community at large in the aftermath of a disaster. Based on ICISF's pastoral crisis intervention model, there are five basic actions to maximize the spiritual first aid standards of care set forth by PCI Level II.

- Stabilization and introduction
- Acknowledgment
- Facilitating understanding
- Encouraging adaptive spiritual coping
- Referral (as needed)

Stabilization and introduction. In this action you provide a calming ministry of presence, a caring human connection. Introducing yourself is the first step to stabilizing a situation. Keep in mind that in most disaster or crisis situations you will not have a prior relationship with the people for whom you are providing services. An introduction such as, "Hi, I'm Julie. I'm a chaplain with Disaster Chaplaincy Services. Can I get you a bottle of water?" may begin to establish rapport and give you a chance to be of immediate service. An assessment of psychological, emotional, and spiritual needs begins with making a connection. If the person you are speaking with cannot speak or answers with slurred speech, you may need to call for immediate medical assistance. This opening introduction offers many opportunities to assist in crisis.

Acknowledgment. This action involves attentive and active listening to a person in crisis. If the person you are speaking with chooses to speak about his or her experience—what happened or what is going on right now—listen. The use of reflective responses during this time signals recognition of this person's experience. For example, you could say, "It sounds like it was a complete shock," or "I see your hands are still shaking and hear that this was a terrifying situation for you." Please note that it is not advised to encourage a person to "tell their story" if they do not want to. For some people, telling their story can exacerbate the stress response. The goal of spiritual first aid is not to get to the bottom of the trauma or crisis, but to mitigate the effects of the crisis and refer an individual on to greater care if needed.

Facilitating understanding. This action involves validating the experience and providing information. Providing information on common stress reactions can help to validate the crisis reactions and emotions an individual may be experiencing. During highly stressful times, most people don't understand the psychological, emotional, and spiritual responses they or their loved ones may be feeling. All they know is that they or their loved ones aren't themselves and they don't like it. Part of providing spiritual first aid is having an understanding of typical stress reactions and being able to offer basic education materials (a pamphlet or other handout) on stress. A person's distress will often lessen once they understand the common reactions to uncommon situations and that they or their loved ones are not going crazy. This understanding can be particularly helpful for adult caretakers of children. Children often exhibit specific reactions that, while "normal," can be upsetting to adult caretakers.

Encouraging adaptive spiritual coping. In this action you promote positive coping skills and strategies, building on what works for the individual. Based on what you have heard through active listening, a spiritual first aid provider can identify some coping strategies the individual is utilizing to help get him or her through the crisis. Support the person by examining what skills he or she has tried in the past and what skills he or she is using now to get through this difficult time. Highlight the positive strategies the individual has used (such as exercising or talking with friends) and encourage that person to continue doing these things. Some coping mechanisms may feel like they are reducing stress but can actually have negative ramifications in the long run (such as increased alcohol consumption or isolation from loved ones or from work). For many people, faith and their religious traditions are strong coping mechanisms. If praying with a person or facilitating rituals are appropriate, this can be a powerful tool for both short- and long-term healing and resilience. As a spiritual first aid provider, you can create a safe space for an individual to connect to his or her faith, whether you are of that person's faith tradition or not. If there is a request for a ritual that is not of your faith, find someone onsite who can assist in providing the ritual, or make an immediate referral to someone who can.

Referral. In this action you provide a bridge to resources. While working disasters, referrals can come in many types and contexts.

There may be times when an immediate referral to an internal system is required (if you were working in a disaster assistance service center and speaking with a client who needs temporary housing, you may need to make an immediate referral to the American Red Cross or Salvation Army desk). There are also times while listening to someone that it becomes clear that they need immediate mental health assistance (such as anyone exhibiting suicidal ideation). Connecting people to their existing social supports is very important. Disaster chaplains and spiritual first aid providers, by definition, are not there for the long haul; you are there to provide immediate assistance. Therefore, it is important to get people connected to whatever resources they might need. Based on the needs presented, you may refer individuals to a funeral director, financial planner, mental health provider, grief support group, the Department of Motor Vehicles, or a licensed general contractor. The list is endless. A general rule in referrals is if you feel that you are in over your head, you probably are.

Attitudes in Action

Come to the situation with a prayerful heart: you are there to serve. I believe this to be one of the most important attitudes regarding spiritual first aid. No matter your official title at a disaster site, your role is to be of service to those who have been affected. There is no room for divas at a disaster. Be helpful. "Get the GET out."[10] *GET* stands for greed, ego, and turf; three things that inhibit disaster response.

"Handing someone a bottle of water as a spiritual response? Anyone can do that. I'm a trained professional; I'm here to help people with spiritual crisis." If a person on my team made that statement, it would be their last deployment with us. Check your ego at the door. As an ambassador of the Sacred, handing a thirsty person a bottle of water is a spiritual response. You represent something larger than yourself and all the letters that go before or after your name.

If you go into disaster or crisis work wanting to fix or believing you can fix, you will not only be unhelpful to the people you have gone to help, but you create a no-win situation for yourself. If a person says they don't want to talk or that they don't want to talk with you, leave them alone. Unless they are having a reaction that requires medical attention, it is unethical to continue to intervene.

Rabbi Jonathan Slater, a chaplain on the leadership team for Disaster Chaplaincy Services, New York, describes the attitude of a disaster chaplain as "carrying a prayerful heart into the work. Even when we are not praying with someone else out loud, the attitude we bring, the orientation we bring into that work, is a prayerful one."

> Patricia arrives at her parents' house for a visit and finds her mother is out grocery shopping and her elderly father has died. The paramedics arrive on the scene, accompanied by a chaplain who has been with them on a ride-along. The chaplain approaches Patricia and his first question is, "Had your father accepted Jesus Christ as his Lord and Savior?" Patricia is taken off guard and mumbles, "I guess so," and works to stay out of the chaplain's path until he leaves.

This story illustrates an example of the misuse of spiritual power and a complete missed opportunity for providing spiritual first aid. Patricia and her family would have been much better served had the chaplain's first words been, "I am so sorry for your loss. Is there anything I can do for you right now? Anyone I can call?" Those simple questions coming from a chaplain would have been a strong spiritual response to Patricia's suffering.

When working as a disaster spiritual care provider or chaplain, your job is to provide care and comfort. Scripture and prayer can be comforting to many people, but you cannot assume it will be comforting during a disaster. Stress creates new priorities. I have heard from clergy, "If I'm not praying with them, I'm not doing my job." Don't take people hostage with *your* need to pray. Praying silently to yourself is always okay (and a pretty good idea).

The most important thing is not what you say; it is that you are present. Your presence shows that you are willing to stay and accompany him or her, and that you won't walk away from the pain and anguish that comes along in life.

First Things First

A key guideline in providing spiritual first aid is "first things first." Spiritual first aid is not unlike medical first aid in this respect. You must stabilize a person and stop the bleeding (metaphorical and literal) before anything else can happen. As a spiritual first aid provider, it is

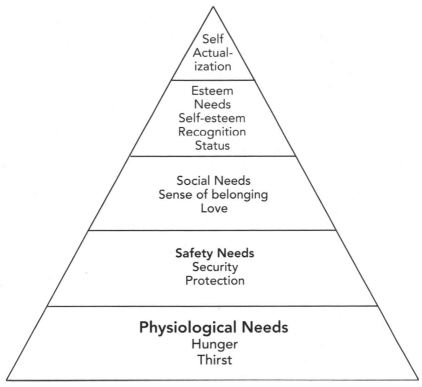

Figure 7.1

essential to note that taking care of first things first is part of the over-all spiritual response to critical incidents, emergencies, and disasters.

In 1943, Abraham Maslow published an important paper, "A Theory of Human Motivation," in which he described a ladder of basic human needs arranged in a hierarchy of pre-potency that informs and motivates behavior. There are five classifications in Maslow's "Hierarchy of Needs" (see figure 7.1). The theory states that we must satisfy each layer of need in turn, starting with the level of survival.

> For the man who is extremely and dangerously hungry, no other interests exist but food. [A] peculiar characteristic of the human organism when it is dominated by a certain need is that the whole philosophy of the future tends also to change. For a chronically hungry man ... life itself tends to be defined in terms of eating. Anything else will be defined as unimportant. Freedom, love, community feeling, respect, philosophy, may all be waved aside as fripperies which are useless since they fail to fill the stomach."[11]

When the lower level of needs is satisfied, the next level emerges. To jump to a higher level without the base of the pyramid in place is to invite a blank stare at best, a hostile interaction at worst. More than one hundred years ago, Upton Sinclair wrote *The Jungle*. The following passage describes an attempt by clergy to help, but whose assistance is focused on a level of needs much higher than their listeners are able to approach:

> The evangelist was preaching "sin and redemption," the infinite grace of God and His pardon for human frailty. He was very much in earnest, and he meant well, but Jurgis, as he listened, found his soul filled with hatred. What did he know about sin and suffering—with his smooth, black coat and his neatly starched collar, his body warm, and his belly full, and money in his pocket—lecturing men who were struggling for their lives, men at the death grapple with the demon powers of hunger and cold!—This, of course, was unfair; but Jurgis felt that these men were out of touch with the life they discussed; they had a hall, and a fire, and food and clothing and money, and so they might preach to hungry men, and the hungry men must be humble and listen! They were trying to save their souls—and who but a fool could fail to see that all that was the matter with their souls was that they had not been able to get a decent existence for their bodies?[12]

Maslow cites religion as a mechanism that can help satisfy the need for safety for some people; for others it falls into the higher-need categories. Either way, it is not a part of the base of the pyramid. The need for food, water, and sleep supersede the need for spiritual contemplation. Many of the people you will work with will not have the luxury of contemplating the Sacred while in the midst of crisis; they have to determine how to survive the next day or week or five minutes. We can hold that sacred space, all the while taking care of the most basic physiological needs first.

Cultural Issues

Culture is more than just race and religion. Age, gender, neighborhoods, occupation, sexual orientation, and education are all examples of distinct cultures. Learn about the cultures you are likely to be responding to or with, and remember, your most important tool as a spiritual first aid provider is a question—don't be afraid to *ask*. Don't assume; you never know who is in front of you. A cross around the neck does not tell you what branch of Christianity a person may belong to, or even if it is practiced. Black skin does not equal African-American.

Some cultures (including many in the United States) do not see women as spiritual leaders. I wear a clerical collar when I respond to disasters. While working at Ground Zero after 9/11, more than once a firefighter or police officer would see the collar and immediately say, "Hello, Fadda" (that's New York for *Father*), then really look at me and stutter, "Fadda, uh ... Sister, what *are* you?" The majority of first responders in New York City are Roman Catholic men; they were not accustomed to seeing a woman wearing a collar. Most of the time this humorous moment opened up a conversation, but some were offended at my "pretending" to be a priest. A time of crisis is not the time to get into arguments regarding denominational or theological differences of opinion or practice. In these instances, the best action I could take was to refer them to a Catholic priest I was working with.

Culture can be more powerful than religion. A light-haired, blue-eyed clergyperson went to an island in the West Indies to help after a hurricane. He was of the same religion as most of the people he was working with, but no one would speak with him. He eventually asked an elder in the community if he had somehow offended the people. The elder replied, "You have blue eyes. People who have blue eyes have no soul."

It is possible to work with an open heart and still find that some people will not want your help. You cannot take people's reactions to you personally. As a spiritual first aid provider, your job is to be of service; if for whatever reason you cannot be of service, it is your responsibility to refer a person to someone who can. Don't take it personally, it is about helping them, helping them where they are.

Pre-incident Education: Get Prepared, Get Training, Get Connected

"Disaster preparedness" is a phrase that has become prominent in our vocabulary over the last several years. But how many of us actually are prepared? If you do not have a disaster plan and supplies in your home and workplace, you will have a very difficult time responding to other people's needs and cries of distress. Personal preparedness is one of the responsibilities of the spiritual care provider. The American Red Cross and the federal government have excellent resources to assist with disaster preparedness. The Federal Emergency Management Agency has online training courses in the incident command system and how it works during disaster. These resources are free. Once you have your disaster plans in order (for your home and place of business), practice. The perfect plan will do no good in a crisis if it has sat quietly in a drawer, unrehearsed. Do not overlook CPR and first aid classes not only for disaster preparedness, but preparedness for the crises that can and do happen every day.

Get trained in spiritual first aid and other related interventions. Reading a chapter or even a book on the subject is not equivalent to training. Disaster Chaplaincy Services and the International Critical Incident Stress Foundation have courses designed to train individuals interested in this field. Clinical pastoral education (CPE) is not necessarily the same as crisis intervention training. If you have CPE units, they will likely help you adapt to disaster work, but even working in the most chaotic emergency room environment is different from working at a shelter right after a hurricane or at a disaster morgue. Neither one is better than the other; they are distinct and complementary skill sets. Continuing education and then regular practice of these skills is imperative.

Get connected to your local response organizations. A "lone wolf" showing up at the site of a disaster or crisis is generally not welcome. Find out if there are existing Community Emergency Response Teams in your area or get connected to your local American Red Cross chapter. There may be a network of multifaith spiritual care providers already working in your area. If not, perhaps it is time to create one. Contact Disaster Chaplaincy Services for information on how to begin that process. See chapter 3 for more about disaster preparedness.

Final Words

Crises, emergencies, and disasters are all inevitable, unfortunate realities of our world, but there are ways to help people through these trying times. Spiritual first aid is a valuable tool to add to your repertoire. It can be incredibly difficult yet incredibly rewarding work.

Reflecting back on the firefighter from the opening vignette, after being given time to rest and a cup of coffee, he is ready for a prayer. With the base of the pyramid stabilized, the next level can be explored. The presence of a trained spiritual first aid provider brings the opportunity for another level of stabilization during a time of great need. Get trained, get prepared, get connected.

Notes

1. American Red Cross national poll, October 5-8, 2001, by Caravan ORC Int. 1,000 adults over the age of eighteen living in private homes; +/- 3 percent; release date: Ocotber 16, 2001.
2. G.S. Everly, Jr., "The Role of Pastoral Crisis Intervention in Disasters, Terrorism, Violence, and Other Community Crises," *International Journal of Emergency Mental Health*, 2, no. 3 (2000): 139–42.
3. G.S. Everly, Jr., *Pastoral Crisis Intervention* (Ellicott City, MD: Chevron, 2007).
4. G.S. Everly, Jr., et al., *Pastoral Crisis Intervention-II* Course Workbook (Ellicott City, MD: International Critical Incident Stress Foundation, 2005).
5. Everly, *Pastoral Crisis Intervention* (Ellicott City, MD: Chevron, 2007).
6. Everly, et al., *Pastoral Crisis Intervention Course Workbook* (Ellicott City, MD: 2002).
7. A. Maslow, "A Theory of Human Motivation," *Psychological Review*, 50 (1943): 370–96.
8. T. Webb, "Crisis of Faith vs. Spiritual Cry of Distress," *International Journal of Emergency Mental Health,* 6, no. 4 (2004): 217–22.
9. Everly, et al., *Pastoral Crisis Intervention-II Course Workbook*.
10. The author heard this phrase from Diane Myers, the original origin is unknown.
11. A. Maslow, "A Theory of Human Motivation," 370–96.
12. U. Sinclair, *The Jungle*. (New York: Barnes & Noble Classics, 2003).

Further Reading

Everly, G. S., Jr. *Pastoral Crisis Intervention*. Ellicott City, MD: Chevron, 2007.

Everly, G. S., Jr. "Pastoral Crisis Intervention: A Word of Caution," *International Journal of Emergency Mental Health* 6, no. 4 (2004): 211–16.

Everly, G. S., Jr. "The Role of Pastoral Crisis Intervention in Disasters, Terrorism, Violence, and Other Community Crises," *International Journal of Emergency Mental Health* 2, no. 3 (2000): 139–42.

Halpern, J., and M. Tramontin. *Disaster Mental Health: Theory & Practice*. Belmont, CA: Thomson, Brooks/Cole, 2007.

Maslow, A. "A Theory of Human Motivation," *Psychological Review* 50 (1943): 370–96. http://psychclassics.yorku.ca/Maslow/motivation.htm.

McPherson, K. F. "Pastoral Crisis Intervention with Children: Recognizing and Responding to the Spiritual Reaction of Children," *International Journal of Emergency Mental Health* 6, no. 4 (2004): 223–31.

Myers, D., and D. Wee. *Disaster Mental Health Services*. New York: Brunner-Routledge, 2005.

Paget, N. K., and McCormack, J. R. *The Work of the Chaplain*. Valley Forge, PA: Judson Press, 2006.

Sinclair, U. *The Jungle*. Rev. ed. (New York: Barnes & Noble Classics, 2003).

Webb, T. E. "Crisis of Faith vs. Spiritual Cry of Distress," *International Journal of Emergency Mental Health* 6, no. 4 (2004): 217–22.

Resources

International Critical Incident Stress Foundation: www.icisf.org.

Disaster Chaplaincy Services: www.disasterchaplaincy.org.

FEMA—Incident Command System: http://training.fema.gov/VCNew/firstVC.asp.

Disaster Preparedness: American Red Cross, www.redcross.org; U.S. Government, www.ready.gov and http://www.citizencorps.gov/.

Acknowledgments

The contributor wishes to acknowledge the following people for their expertise, wisdom, experience, and guidance in writing this chapter: Marge Doherty, Derrick McQueen, Diane Myers, Diane Ryan, Rebecca Smith, Pete Volkmann, and Tom Webb.

About the Contributor

Rev. Julie Taylor, MDiv, CTR, (Certified Trauma Responder), is the executive director of Disaster Chaplaincy Services, New York. She is a member of both the International Critical Incident Stress Foundation (ICISF) and the Association of Traumatic Stress Specialists, and is an ICISF-approved instructor. Rev. Taylor has been a consultant to the New York City Mayor's Office of Labor Relations on trauma-related crisis counseling and psychoeducation. During the 9/11 recovery, Rev. Taylor was a chaplain at St. Paul's Chapel at the World Trade Center site. Rev. Taylor serves on the Hudson Valley Critical Incident Stress Management Team and is the cofounder of Chiron Associates.

8

From Honeymoon to Disillusionment to Reconstruction

Recognizing Healthy and Unhealthy Coping Mechanisms and Encouraging Resiliency

Rev. Canon William V. Livingston, MDiv, MEd.;
Rabbi Myrna Matsa, DMin; and Rev. Beverly Wallace, PhD

Following the terrorist attacks of September 11, 2001, 90 percent of Americans turned to religion as a coping response.[1] This trend will likely be repeated in future crises, and so clergy should expect an immediate response from congregational members following disasters. Due to the stress from the disaster and its recovery, most clergy will experience increased requests for counseling and see increased instances of domestic violence, addictions, and depression for which interventions are appropriate. In many instances, however, clergy will not have been adequately trained for such mental health services.[2]

Clergy can assist congregational members' resiliency and recovery in numerous ways. These include:

Offer immediate opportunities for spiritual expression. It is common after a disaster for people, whether in their own communities or in communities to which they have been evacuated, to contact area houses of worship asking for special prayer vigils or simply to use the worship space for private prayer. It is important to help facilitate all such requests.

Respond pastorally to spiritual questions. The most common question clergy encounter is "Why did God let this happen to us?"

Clergy should answer such questions with sensitivity to emotional and pastoral needs and also to the faith tradition teachings of the person asking the question. The first days and weeks immediately following a disaster is not an appropriate time for theological explanations or teachings contrary to the survivor's theological beliefs. The question is often really a request for contact and the reassurance that God has not deserted them. To emphasize this point, we have witnessed individuals whose emotional distress was greatly exacerbated when clergy persons described disasters as divine punishment of which the victims were deserving. Post-disaster is not the time for "preaching and teaching" but rather for pastoral presence alone.

Offer worship in the traditional place of worship immediately after a disaster. Even if it is not inhabitable and alternative sites will later be used, the traditional place of worship should be used for worship the day after the disaster. The need for the familiar, for the place where a person has previously found solace is a common response to the aftermath of disasters.

As an example, the first Sunday after Hurricane Katrina's landfall in 2005, many of those who had not evacuated the Mississippi Gulf Coast made their way along impassable roads to houses of worship, even if they were only concrete slabs covered with storm debris. Sunday Eucharists were offered at Episcopal parishes, where members, neighbors, and first responders gathered to participate in the weekly sacraments, to hug, to cry together, to pray. Participants recall these events as emotionally and spiritually supportive.

Offer ongoing liturgical observances. Congregations can offer liturgical observations appropriate to their styles of worship that support their members. These can include memorial services on the disaster anniversary or other appropriate times, in gathering of salvaged materials or symbols from destroyed places of worship or homes, or celebrations of new beginnings, such as the groundbreaking for a new place of worship or the blessing of a new home.

Promote resiliency. From the pulpit, in teachings, and in individual sessions, clergy should help congregants normalize their responses. As time passes after the disaster, many will assume they should no longer be having sad thoughts or times of tearfulness. Unless these behaviors interfere with their work or relationships, assuring congregants that these are common reactions to an uncommon situation gives them permission to experience the common emotions and move into healthier resiliency.

Assist in the grieving process. Clergy may encounter congregants who seem unable to process their grief because they have not identified the source. We offer two examples we have encountered: First, a woman in her mid-seventies complained to her priest that she found it frustrating that a year after Hurricane Katrina she continued to cry unexpectedly. She described it this way, "I've got friends whose insurance didn't cover their losses, but our insurance reimbursed us for our loss. Rather than rebuild on the bay, we have bought a home elsewhere. I've got everything I need. We are doing quite well. So why do I keep crying?" Pursuing this further, she identified that the destroyed home had been one she and her husband had built as their retirement home—the home in which they would grow old together and eventually die. The home they had purchased simply provided them adequate shelter and comfort but no emotional attachment. By better articulating the loss of the future they had envisioned and the memories the home symbolized, she was better able to articulate what she grieved and the coping mechanisms for those losses. Similarly, a local physician of the same age came to his clergyperson with almost the same complaint. After a couple of sessions he came to realize that his home had been built as a symbol of all that he had accomplished and that he no longer was being used as a contract physician with a local clinic since the storm. By identifying his grief of the loss of a status symbol of his success and the loss of a chance to offer a service he considered valuable, he was able to better address the source of his grief and to seek alternative mechanisms of fulfilling these needs.

Promote self-responsibility. Congregants should be encouraged to assume as much responsibility as possible for their own recovery. While it's important to help them recognize and avoid burnout, they should be encouraged to assist in the recovery efforts.

Healthy Coping Mechanisms— Helping Your Congregation

Clergy, because of their access to many aspects of their congregants' lives and because of the trust placed in them by their congregants, are well positioned to encourage and teach healthy coping among their members. Individually and corporately, clergy can support their members by encouraging them to practice the following:

- Talk with someone about their feelings—anger, sorrow, and other emotions—even though it may be difficult.
- Don't hold themselves responsible for the disastrous event or be frustrated because they feel that they cannot help directly in the rescue work.
- Take steps to promote their own physical and emotional healing by maintaining healthy practices in their daily life (healthy eating, resting, exercising, relaxation, meditation). This healthy outlook will help them and their family.
- Maintain a typical household and daily routine, limiting demanding responsibilities.
- Spend time with family and friends.
- Participate in memorials, rituals, and the use of symbols as a way to express feelings.
- Use their existing support groups of family, friends, and spiritual or religious centers.
- Establish a family emergency plan for possible future disasters. Feeling that there is something that they can do can be very comforting.

Healthy Coping Mechanisms— Helping Your Community

In a study on the "Recovery Divide," it is suggested that rather than continuing with the "conventional compensation model in which people are paid for their losses," it could be better for the individuals and for society to have a "recovery policy viewed from a development perspective."[3] Quoting the study:

1. Instituting economic development programs that incorporate significant job retraining and skill-building, as well as home-ownership development programs

2. Establishing community-based or school-based case managers to assist people in managing transitions to new schools and new communities

3. Creating a mechanism for community engagement, such as the "sweat equity" community development groups that proliferated in the 1980s and 1990s in successful urban reclamation projects, in which community residents could actively participate in rebuilding their homes and social institutions

4. Maximizing Medicaid and S-CHIP [State Children's Health Insurance Program] enrollment among eligible families and children, so as to cover a greater proportion of the uninsured children

5. Assuring ongoing mental health supports for children and caregivers[4]

As an example of a successful application of the last item is the Center for Community Resilience, which is offered to the community through the auspices of the Mississippi Mental Health Association (MHA) in Biloxi, Mississippi. Resilience training is centered in three spheres of influence: the school system, first responders, and clergy. It is targeted to these populations because they intersect across all strata of society and have the potential to positively impact the greatest number of people on the limited resources made available by a grant from United Jewish Communities and the UJA-Federation of New York. This is based on a model of resiliency training brought to Mississippi through Danny Brom, PhD, who directs the Israel Center for the Treatment of Psychotrauma at Herzog Hospital in Jerusalem, Israel, which has instituted similar programs in Israel and has consulted throughout the world.[5]

The Center for Community Resilience focuses on numerous skills, among them coping strategies, communications skills, and anger management. This training provides life skills and the means to equip children to honor and manage their feelings, which in turn equips them to handle the challenges that lie ahead.

Clergy Self-Care: Healthy and Unhealthy Coping

Clergy self-care throughout the recovery process is essential. Clergy who fail in self-care risk harming themselves, their families, or those they serve. As Flora Slosson Wuellner, a teacher, retreat leader, spiritual director, and ordained minister, said, "If a shepherd is not fed as well as the sheep, that shepherd will begin to starve and may end up devouring the sheep."[6] Sources of role strain in clergy involved in disasters include the difficulties inherent in the performance of their established roles, conflict with the performance of other roles, and inconsistent role demands.[7] Research of clergy involved as responders and non-responders has shown that compassion fatigue is directly related to the number of hours clergy work with trauma victims and their families, and preparation for this type of work through clinical pastoral education training, which reduces the influence of compassion fatigue and burnout.[8]

Clergy we observed during the Hurricane Katrina disaster went through identifiable progressions throughout the disaster and recovery process. These include:

- **Pre-disaster and disaster event:** As the warnings of the hurricane's landfall became more specific about the location, many clergy focused their energy on checking on and assisting vulnerable congregants and protecting congregational buildings and furnishings. Most clergy either honored evacuation instructions or migrated to nearby locations on higher ground with a higher probability of safety.

- **Immediate aftermath:** Even those clergy who experienced personal losses had high energy immediately following Katrina. The ability to respond to immediate physical needs, the media attention, the ability to be pastoral and express a sense of hope through their faith tradition, and the support and admiration expressed by other clergy and people across the nation resulted in increased self-esteem, energy, and endurance in the first weeks after landfall. Many can identify their moments of inspiration, their discoveries of new strengths and talents, their renewed faith, their newly formed friendships, and instances of greater involvement and cohesiveness within their congregations.

- **From honeymoon to disillusionment:** As the clean-up process dragged out from weeks to months, as worshiping in a gymnasium or another church's worship space lost its novelty, and as the demands to pastorally serve members' emotional needs, to participate in community recovery efforts, and to rebuild resulted in role confusion and the introduction of new priorities, signs of excessive stress among the clergy have become evident.

- **Signs of excessive stress:** Clergy stress most frequently expresses itself as fatigue or guilt over not meeting all expectations, frustration of not being able to determine appropriate boundaries, and depression. Depression is often expressed in more emotional attention given to negatives: delays in rebuilding the congregation's place of worship, decline in worship attendance, or grief over the absence of familiar worship. Appreciation for newly acquired or recognized skills or talents was replaced by an awareness of the lack of skills or experience to meet the challenges ahead.

- **Ability to stay the course:** At the second anniversary of Hurricane Katrina we witnessed clergy resignations from their congregations, and knew that others sought to leave when another position could be located. Most clergy who expressed a determination to remain in place through the rebuilding of destroyed congregational buildings were those who, prior to Katrina, had planned to stay at their current congregation until retirement and to retire in the local community.

- **Those who did not experience the storm:** Some of the clergy with whom we work did not arrive at their current congregations until after Katrina. Some had accepted their positions but had not started, and some accepted their positions immediately after Katrina. Regardless, response by these clergy to the stress of the disaster is very similar to those who were serving congregations at the time of landfall.

- **Stress on clergy families:** Clergy families are also significantly affected by the disaster. The stress in families is evidenced in comments from clergy spouses: "I didn't sign up for this! It's just more than I can handle." "I don't want the defining moment of the rest of my son's life to be Katrina." "I seldom saw him before the storm. Now I never do. He's either visiting those who lost their homes, attending community rebuilding committees, or at some type of parish meeting."

Clergy and congregations fairing well in the aftermath of Hurricane Katrina appear to be those that functioned healthily before the storm.

Just as families with positive communication and healthy emotional behaviors most often weather a family trauma better than families with poor communication and unhealthy emotional behaviors, the same appears to be true in congregations. Congregations experiencing conflicts within the congregation or between the clergy and congregation's lay leadership before the storm have struggled the most in the rebuilding process. They have experienced the most conflict over issues of whether clergy are sufficiently responding to pastoral and congregational needs, where to rebuild, the design of the new buildings, and the cost of rebuilding, and they have experienced the greatest turnover or contemplated turnover in clergy. For these congregations to best progress through their recovery processes, the preexisting conflicts, communication problems, or unhealthy functioning will need to be resolved.

While clergy turnover throughout the recovery process is common, attempts should be taken to prevent it. The outcome of this turnover includes:

- **Distraction and additional stress.** Clergy considering leaving feel torn between a commitment to their congregation and what is best for their family. This results in greater stress for the clergyperson and an inability to remain focused on the recovery process.
- **Failure or guilt.** The clergy leave with a sense of failure that they did not have the strength or skills to sustain the recovery process, or guilt that they have abandoned their congregation at a time of great need.
- **Negative congregational emotions.** Congregations still in the recovery process with departing often respond with anger and resentment caused by a sense of abandonment or rejection in a time of need, grief over losing a beloved faith leader, and hopelessness that this departing is another catastrophe in their already troubled lives.
- **A more complicated congregation recovery process.** In addition to having to rebuild destroyed buildings and coordinate other recovery activities, the congregation has lost the person who was coordinating these efforts and must now divert energy and resources in recruiting the next clergy leader.

SIGNS OF UNHEALTHY COPING

Through direct observation or from comments made by congregants or their family members, clergy are well positioned to identify early signs of coping difficulties. These may include the following:

- Difficulty communicating thoughts, disorientation, or confusion
- Easily frustrated
- Limited attention span
- Difficulty concentrating
- Mood swings
- Feelings of hopelessness

- Difficulty sleeping
- Increased use of drugs/alcohol
- Difficulty maintaining balance in daily routines
- Poor work performance
- Crying easily
- Overwhelming guilt and self-doubt
- Depression, sadness

- Headaches/stomach problems
- Tunnel vision/ muffled hearing
- Reluctance to leave home
- Fear of crowds, strangers, or being alone
- Colds or flu-like symptoms

When such symptoms arise, clergy may assist by offering individual or group resiliency assistance, promoting healthy coping mechanisms, and, as appropriate, referral to other professionals.

Figure 8.1

To prevent turnover, clergy, congregational boards, and judicatory authorities need to understand the importance of rest breaks for clergy that coincide with the nature of the recovery process. Though not always put into practice by those we have served, our recommendation is that clergy take breaks after each major phase of the recovery: immediate aftermath (search and rescue, food and water distribution, the retreat to evacuation sites), first phase of recovery (longer-term food distribution sites and medical clinics established, debris cleanup), recovery planning (alternative worship sites selected, recovery financial planning), initial rebuilding and long-term emotional support (pastoral support to members, establishment of plans to rebuild congregational buildings), and reconstruction (completion of new congregational buildings, significant progress made regarding community recovery).

Due to the nature of crises, breaks after the earlier phases may be only one to three days, but they should be taken nonetheless. Longer breaks should be taken after the later phases. Because of the difficulty of separating emotionally while living and working in the disaster area, these breaks need to be away from the disaster area. In Hurricane Katrina's long-term recovery, in which clergy were dealing with personal losses, pastorally serving congregants, and assisting in the broader community, clergy suffered less burnout and compassion fatigue when they took two to three days off every two to three months, and one to two weeks twice a year. To prevent congregational criticism, we recommend judicatory authorities clarify with local congregation boards the appropriateness for clergy having these breaks.

A Case Study: Katrina, the Worst Natural Disaster to Hit Our Nation

On August 29, 2005, at 6:10 a.m. local time, with sustained winds of 140 miles per hour that generated storm surges of 30 feet, Katrina left a disaster zone of 90,000 square miles in its wake—almost the size of the entire United Kingdom. The aftermath displaced more than 500,000 people, and cost estimates exceed $100 billion.[9] The immediate relief response, the initial cleanup, and the long-term recovery from this devastating storm was primarily led by local, state, regional, and national faith-based initiatives more than by the coordinated efforts of various federal, state, and local public and private entities. In many instances the local faith-based support came from congregations whose buildings were destroyed or severely damaged, whose members were displaced, and whose clergy lost their homes. Because the turnover of religious leaders substantially increases in communities experiencing major disasters and because of the scope of Katrina, we were assigned by our respective judicatory authorities to respond to the pastoral needs of the clergy and congregations, and have written this chapter through the lens of this experience.

Because this chapter focuses on the honeymoon to reconstruction phases, we offer only limited observations of the earlier recovery process and how we see this affecting the disillusionment and recovery phases. Immediately following Katrina's landfall, working independently or in coordination with one another, faith-based groups operated water, food, and clothing distribution sites from churches, schools, and empty lots throughout the devastated area. Judicatory authorities coordinated the creation of evacuation sites and processes for accepting gifts of funds and supplies and routing them and volunteers to areas with the highest need. As often happens immediately following a disaster, cultural and social barriers disappeared. As everyone needed food and water and the most basic human needs, unlikely relationships developed at food and distribution sites.

Due to the scope of Katrina, the duration of the phases of response exceeded the norms. Searches for victims and distribution sites for emergency water and food lasted for weeks, not days. Because of the loss of hospitals, the shortage of doctors, and the loss of grocery stores, some sites opened medical clinics and long-term food and clothing distribution sites—some of which operated almost to the storm's first anniversary. Also, volunteers continued to remove debris from residential and public places more than a year after the storm—a process lasting only weeks after most disasters.

Natural disasters interacting with negative human elements often result in worsened responses.[10] Katrina confirmed this observation. Failure to adequately prepare and coordinate the evacuation, uncoordinated immediate governmental response, bureaucratic delays in financial aid and recovery support, denial of claims by insurance companies, and the inability to obtain affordable future insurance coverage have all contributed to problems in the disaster recovery and exacerbated the emotional trauma. Media images of the chaos and frustration among evacuees without food or water in the New Orleans Superdome in the days after Katrina serve as a metaphor of the breakdown of the initial public response. Unfulfilled promises of public assistance to aid in rebuilding resulted in both financial delays in the rebuilding process as well as emotional distress as victims anticipate funds for rebuilding only to have those expectations thwarted. With litigation against insurance companies that denied storm damage claims continuing almost two years after Katrina, energy that would most often go into rebuilding was redirected toward legal battles. So common are these frustrations and the emotional response to them that local public mental health officials began to diagnose individuals as in "recovery stress syndrome," which will lead to more serious mental health disorders if not addressed.[11]

Higher levels of anxiety, depression, posttraumatic stress, somatic symptoms, and generalized distress occur more often in disasters with widespread community destruction.[12] Katrina victims have verbalized it this way, "I didn't just lose my house, I lost my doctor, my post office, my pharmacist, my grocery store, where my children go to school, where I go to church. I have nothing familiar." With half a million people displaced, neighbor helping neighbor or family member helping family member proved more challenging. In many instances, three generations of families and numerous siblings saw their homes destroyed.

As post-disaster communities move from the honeymoon phase into disillusionment and the start of recovery, they commonly show signs of unhealthy coping mechanisms (see figure 8.1). In the first days after the landfall of Katrina, heroic events were common. The honeymoon phase exemplified by community cohesion abounded. Volunteers and resources flowed in from all over the nation. Though reeling from the devastation, high energy and endurance was evident in most places. However, as the cumulative effect of the storm became evident—banks not able to open, mail delivery impossible, inability to reach operating grocery stores, schools unable to open—the strain began to show itself. Though still appreciated, the once welcomed outside volunteers became intrusions into survivors' private grieving; and survivors grew tired of "telling their story." Before the first anniversary of Katrina, birthdays, wedding anniversaries, Christmas, and other significant religious, family, and community events were celebrated with a sense of determination: to show that they could still celebrate, to bring a sense of joy into desolate times, to attempt to create "a sense of normalcy." After the second anniversary—with very little rebuilding having occurred, still suffering from post-storm financial difficulties—such traditionally joyful events served as reminders of all that no longer existed, that the recovery process would be much more difficult and protracted than anticipated. Due to the sheer scope of Katrina, both the severity and duration of emotional problems exceed the norms of other disasters. A study of Katrina victims conducted almost two years after the storm reveals about 14 percent have symptoms of severe mental illness. An additional 20 percent have mild to moderate mental illness, says Ronald Kessler of Harvard Medical School, who led the study. The big surprise was that PTSD, which typically goes away in a year for most disaster survivors, had increased: 21 percent had the symptoms in 2007 versus 16 percent in 2006.[13]

The social, cultural, and economic differences that had disappeared immediately after the storm returned in the months and years that followed. Those struggling the most at the second anniversary of the storm still lived in FEMA trailers, did not have doctors, did not have insurance, and continued to have difficulty in finding employment though they eagerly looked for work and were willing to be trained in new skills. Many expressed a yearning for a return to the time when all seemed equal and there was a generalized caring and sharing. They grieve the loss of the sense of hope that camaraderie brought.

"As of December 2005, estimates were that 447,827 individuals had been displaced from the impacted areas of Louisiana and Mississippi, among which were 163,106 children under the age of eighteen."[14] Not only were landmarks erased from view, familiar people also were gone. The social supports that anchor people at other times were gone. Dislocation and disorientation prevailed. Depression seeped into the landscape. People grieved their losses and relived their grief for loved ones lost before Katrina even hit.

As life slowly returned to a "new kind of normal," people demonstrated many ways of coping. Most people will come out of a disaster with the ability to bounce back and rebuild their lives. They will be changed, but the changes they experience will not prevent them from living full lives. In fact, for many the experience stimulates an inner search for meaning and purpose that empowers them to move forward and rebuild their lives. The experts call this resilience. However, there are people for whom that is not a possibility without help. Some seek psychotherapy; others go to clergy to help them cope. Some people find an unhealthy kind of help through drugs or alcohol, which numbs the senses, covering the pain of feeling useless or helpless.

Among the biggest issues for most families are housing and employment. Immediately after the hurricane, housing costs escalated significantly. There were few rentals; even temporary shelter was sorely needed. FEMA trailers did not arrive on the coast until December—almost four months after the storm. There were problems with some of these as well. Trailers had been delivered without keys to unlock the doors. Though one master key could open hundreds of trailers, keys were not made available. Some did not function. Some disabled people were given trailers that were not handicap accessible.[15] There were all kinds of logistics problems. Some people lived in trailers that were on their property; at least they were home. Others lived in FEMA trailer parks or private trailer parks. In Gulfport, Mississippi, the Sun Suites

Hotel became temporary housing for Bell Telephone employees who were in the region to rebuild the telephone grid that had been completely destroyed. They were there for months; the few other hotels that were usable were booked.

Homeowners had to jump through bureaucratic hoops set by FEMA, the insurance companies, contractors, and workers in order to begin rebuilding. There were many stories of contractors wanting money up front before beginning work and then either not completing the work and leaving town or doing a shoddy job and leaving little recourse for homeowners.The most common unhealthy coping mechanisms following disasters include substance abuse and other addictive behaviors, domestic violence, major mental illness such as depression and posttraumatic stress disorder, and suicide. Mental health care providers along the Gulf Coast reported an increase in those seeking services for substance abuse and depression.

The existence of casinos in a disaster area creates an environment for increased gambling addiction as individuals deal with boredom and disillusionment and use the casinos as a recreational diversion or think they can secure additional funds there to assist with their financial recovery. Individuals initially visit casinos for an inexpensive way to relieve the stress by "getting away." The casinos offer free liquor, entertainment, and the gambling is not expensive if visitors limit themselves to using only loose change. But that is usually not the case. It starts innocently, but people soon develop a drinking habit, begin gambling more, and spend more hours in the casino, which usually has no clocks. The casinos in the Gulf Region were the first commercial enterprises to reopen and rebuild after Katrina (which also resulted in another problem: elevated construction costs for the community since much of the available construction services were being consumed by the casinos). Various case managers have acknowledged working with Katrina victims who lost either insurance reimbursement or FEMA grants at the casinos. Not surprisingly, casinos reported higher income after the storm than before.[16]

Returning home from the casino or bar is not easy, especially when it is to a spouse who is lonely from all the time away, hassled by household responsibility, and is not happy with the errant partner. There was an increase in domestic violence as a result of this behavior, usually by the spouse who was trying to hold the purse together and pay the bills.[17]

While we are aware of suicides, the number of suicides reported by the Harrison County, Mississippi, coroner do not reflect an increase in the number of suicides since Katrina. However, only 3 percent of deaths in Harrison County were considered suicide in 2006, fewer than before Katrina, 6 percent were suicidal in 2007, and the parishes in the New Orleans area reported an 8 percent rate in 2007.[18] Also, while the current population of the Gulf Region is 30 percent less than before Katrina, the number of deaths is 30 percent above. If this does not reflect an increased suicide rate, it at least reflects increased deaths due to stress.

Katrina and Children

All of these are stressors that impact households. Children are affected by their parents' tensions. Often parents are so concerned about putting life in order for themselves and their children that they do not have the energy to devote time to the children. As a result, neither knows what the other is thinking, which creates barriers between parent and child. Children often have not been able to express their feelings to the parents. Post-Katrina findings showed that there was "a near fourfold increase in the clinical diagnosis of depression or anxiety in children" and that "the prevalence of behavioral or conduct problems doubled."[19] And children missed school. "Among elementary school children six to eleven years old, 29% had missed ten or more days of school in a given month" during the spring of 2006.[20]

Among those living in FEMA trailer parks, children were for the most part medically uninsured and had lost their primary medical connection. The disaster increased the incidence of asthma, depression, anxiety, acting out, and developmental delays.[21] Children's caregivers suffered, too, from "chronic health conditions such as hypertension, physical disabilities, asthma or other respiratory problems and diabetes. Forty-one percent of the caregivers were uninsured."[22] These conditions, too, add stress.

As stated above, people will let out tension from these stressors in various ways. In children, some of the acting out has been through aggressive behaviors toward other children or animals. Among teens this might mean engaging in risky behaviors such as sexual promiscuity, chemical addictions, and violence.

The impact this scenario has on children could be devastating. They see and feel what the parents are going through. When the parents do not take time to check in with the children, they tend to think that they are the cause of parental concerns. Kids act out partially because they may not have skills to control the frustration that could lead to rage. Elementary school nurses and teachers and nursery school administrators reported aggressive behaviors and anger issues among their population of young people.

An African greeting goes, "So! How are the children?" If one can genuinely answer, "Well!" that would indicate children are free from stress, able to explore the world around them, to learn openly, to ask questions, to feel comfortable about themselves and those who surround them. To have that answer means that the adults are doing well and their needs are being met. If the answer is, "Not well!" we will have to examine ourselves and the society that does not invest in the well-being of children. When we care for the children we make an investment in the future. If our children along the Gulf Coast miss days of school, exhibit anger and aggressive behaviors, are anxious and depressed and unable to learn, we have to worry not only about their future, but also the future of America.

Notes

1. M. A. Shuster et al., "A National Survey of Stress Reactions After the September 11, 2001, Terrorist Attacks," *New England Journal of Medicine* 345, no. 20 (2001): 1507–12.

2. A. J. Weaver, "Has There Been a Failure to Prepare and Support Parish-Based Clergy in Their Role as Frontline Community Mental Health Workers: A Review," *The Journal of Pastoral Care* 49, no. 2 (Summer 1995): 129–47.

3. D. Abramson, R. Garfield, and I. Redlener, "The Recovery Divide: Poverty and the Widening Gap Among Mississippi Children and Families Affected by Hurricane Katrina," a report of the Mississippi Child & Family Health Study, based on an August 2006 household survey of displaced and impacted families living in Mississippi (National Center for Disaster Preparedness & Children's Health Fund, February 2007).

4. Ibid, 13.

5. Y. Danieli, D. Brom, and J. Sills, eds., *The Trauma of Terrorism: Sharing Knowledge and Shared Care, An International Handbook* (Binghamton, NY: Haworth Maltreatment & Trauma Press, 2005).

6. F. S. Wuellner, *Feed My Shepherds: Spiritual Healing and Renewal for Those in Christian Leadership* (Nashville, TN: Upper Room Books, 1998), 20–21.

7. C. Bradfield, M. L. Wylie, and L. G. Echterling, "After the Flood: The Response of Ministers to a Natural Disaster," *Sociological Analysis* 49, no. 4 (1989): 397–407.

8. K. J. Flannelly, S. B. Roberts, and A. J. Weaver, "Correlates of Compassion Fatigue and Burnout in Chaplains and Other Clergy who Responded to the September 11th Attacks in New York City," *Journal of Pastoral Care & Counseling* 59, no. 3 (2005): 213–24.

9. J. Pickrell, "Special Report Hurricane Katrina: the Aftermath," http://environment .newscientist.com/channel/earth/hurricane.

10. B. L. Green and S. D. Solomon, "The Mental Health Impact of Natural and Technological Disasters," *Traumatic Stress: From Theory to Practice*, eds. J. R. Freedy and S. E. Hobfoll (New York: Plenum, 1995).

11. S. Phillips, "Katrina Still Causing Mental Health Anguish," WLOX TV, http://www.wlox.com/global/story.asp?s=6957758.

12. D. J. DeWolfe, *Training Manual for Mental Health and Human Service Workers in Major Disasters*, 2nd ed., DHHS publication no. ADM 90-358 (Washington, D.C.: U.S. Department of Health and Human Services: Substance Abuse and Mental Health Services Administration, Center for Mental Health Services, 2000):7.

13. M. Elias, "Trauma shapes Katrina's kids. The youngest find it hard to bounce back two years after their lives were disrupted," http://www.usatoday.com/news/ nation/2007-08-16-neworleans-illness_N.htm.

14. Abramson, Garfield, and Redlener, "The Recovery Divide."

15. H. D. Beiser, "FEMA: Same key could open many hurricane evacuee trailer homes," *USA Today*, http://www.usatoday.com/news/washington/2006-08-14 -fema-locks_x.htm.

16. V. Creel, "Biloxi's casino industry reported all-time record business last month [July 2007], with casinos generating $97.3 million in gross gaming revenue. In all, nine of the past 11 months have set records in one fashion or another in Biloxi," Public Affairs Manager, City of Biloxi press release, August 2007.

17. Chaplain Joe Collins, chaplain of the Harrison County Jail, Harrison County, Gulfport, Mississippi.

18. Elias, "Trauma shapes Katrina's kids."

19. Abramson, Garfield, and Redlener, "The Recovery Divide," 2.

20. Ibid., 9.

21. Ibid.

22. Ibid., 10.

Further Reading

Abramson, D., R. Garfield, and I. Redlener. "The Recovery Divide: Poverty and the Widening Gap Among Mississippi Children and Families Affected by Hurricane Katrina," a report of the Mississippi Child & Family Health Study, based on an August 2006 household survey of displaced and impacted families living in

Mississippi. National Center for Disaster Preparedness & Children's Health Fund, February 2007.

Bradfield, C., M. L. Wylie, and L. G. Echterling. "After the Flood: The Response of Ministers to a Natural Disaster," *Sociological Analysis* 49, no. 4 (1989): 397–407.

Danieli, Y., D. Brom, J. Sills, eds. *The Trauma of Terrorism: Sharing Knowledge and Shared Care, An International Handbook.* Binghamton, NY: Haworth Maltreatment & Trauma Press, 2005.

DeWolfe, D. J. *Training Manual for Mental Health and Human Service Workers in Major Disasters.* U. S. Department of Health and Human Services: Center for Mental Health Services, Publication No. ADM 90-538.

Fannelly, K. J., S. B. Roberts, and A. J. Weaver. "Correlates of Compassion Fatigue and Burnout in Chaplains and Other Clergy who Responded to the September 11th Attacks in New York City," *The Journal of Pastoral Care & Counseling* 59, no. 3 (2005).

Green, B. L., S. D. Solomon. "The Mental Health Impact of Natural and Technological Disasters," in *Traumatic Stress: From Theory to Practice,* edited by J. R. Freedy and S. E. Hobfoll. New York: Plenum, 1995.

Schuster, M. A., et al., "A National Survey of Stress Reactions after the September 11, 2001, Terrorist Attacks," *New England Journal of Medicine* 345, no. 20 (2001).

Weaver, A. J. "Has There Been a Failure to Prepare and Support Parish-Based Clergy in Their Role as Frontline Community Mental Health Workers: A Review," *The Journal of Pastoral Care* 49, no. 2 (Summer 1995).

Wuellner, F. S. *Feed My Shepherds: Spiritual Healing and Renewal for Those in Christian Leadership.* Nashville: Upper Room Books, 1998.

About the Contributors

As noted in this chapter, the three contributors were each assigned by their judicatory authorities to support clergy, clergy families, and congregations effected by Hurricane Katrina, the worst natural disaster in the history of the United States, and to participate in the broader community recovery. They encountered one another over time as they fulfilled these roles. The collegiality that developed resulted in their supporting one another emotionally and spiritually through the stress of living and being part of severely devastated communities and the isolation of leaving their former homes to work independently and to assume temporary but extended communities with which they had no connection before the storm. From this collegiality, in addition to this article, they have worked collaboratively with others to offer a resiliency conference for case managers and others involved in the recovery process, a mental health summit for mental health providers on the specific mental health needs in post-Katrina and gaps in the mental health delivery system, a clergy disaster recovery retreat for clergy of numerous faith traditions, and hope to offer future events.

Rev. Canon William V. Livingston, MDiv, MEd, serves as canon pastor-missioner for the Episcopal Diocese of Mississippi through a post-Katrina project funded by Episcopal Relief and Development. He offers individual and family pastoral support, counseling and spiritual direction to coastal clergy and their families, and has started a support group for clergy and a support group for clergy spouses. In addition, he serves as a consultant to coastal Episcopal parishes and community recovery operations funded by Episcopal Relief and Development. Prior to ordination, he worked for twenty-three years in community mental health—with fourteen of those years as CEO of the Abilene Mental Health-Mental Retardation Center in Abilene, Texas, and the Southwest Mental Health Center in McComb, Mississippi. He has served as president of the community mental health center coalitions in Mississippi and Texas, on the board of directors of the National Council of Community Centers and is a recipient of its Distinguished Service Award, and as member of the National Children's Mental Health Coalition. His academic training includes a masters of divinity from the Episcopal School of Theology of the Southwest, a masters in education in counseling from Delta State University, and a bachelor of science in psychology and sociology from Mississippi State University.

Rabbi Myrna Matsa, DMin, holds the position of rabbinic pastoral counselor for Hurricane Katrina support in the New Orleans, Baton Rouge, and Biloxi/Gulfport regions. She works closely with leaders of various faith communities, both Jewish and non-Jewish, and also laypeople within the Gulf Region providing them with direct pastoral services during reconstruction, serving as a Jewish referral resource, and interfacing with various mental health associations. She was sent by the New York Board of Rabbis in partnership with the United Jewish Communities. Rabbi Matsa has earned a doctor of ministry in pastoral counseling and pastoral care, a degree that brings together psychology and theology, and has completed four units of clinical pastoral education. Her area of concentration was in the field of dying, death, and bereavement.

As a community leader she has dedicated her life to helping people who have been at the margins of society. She has been involved in protecting children's rights, affordable housing issues, advocacy for homeless individuals and families, and other societal concerns such as substance abuse and domestic violence. Rabbi Matsa brings passion to her work as she helps to identify needs along the Gulf so that she can be counted among those who bring a source of hope and healing.

Rev. Beverly Wallace, PhD, is assistant to the bishop of the southeastern synod of the Evangelical Lutheran Church in America. Her role is to coordinate pastoral care and spiritual emotional health for the Katrina recovery on the coast of Mississippi. Rev. Wallace served as assistant pastor at Emmanuel Lutheran Church in Atlanta and Redeemer Lutheran Church in Minneapolis. Before her call to Mississippi, Rev. Wallace held a predoctoral fellowship at Elon University where she taught counseling; prior to that she was the chaplain for vocation at Hamline University, where she also taught in the religion department and in the area of social justice. The mother of two adult educators and grandmother of grandson Jaylen, Rev. Wallace received her PhD in the area of family social science with an emphasis in marriage and family therapy from the University of Minnesota. She is the coauthor of the book *African American Grief,* published by Routledge.

9

From Honeymoon to Disillusionment to Reconstruction

Pastoral Counseling—Thinking Outside the Box

Rev. Willard W. C. Ashley Sr., DMin, DH; Roberta L. Samet, LCSW; and Imam Muhammad Hatim, PhD, DMin

There is an understandable humanitarian desire to help those who are suddenly confronted with unimaginable pain and distress in the wake of a horrific traumatic event.[1]

Pastoral care and counseling that thinks outside of the box addresses not only the individual but also the systems that act upon the individual and his or her community, which are factors in that individual's ability to heal. These factors overtly or covertly alter the outcome of our testimonies and thus affect our ability to heal. Therefore, when addressing the challenges following a disaster, we are called to think outside of the box.

This chapter offers immediate help to clergy who serve congregations. What do congregants expect of clergy following a disaster or tragic event? What are common interventions and common concerns? Once basic needs are met—medical care, safety, food, shelter, and clothing—what are the next steps? You may not be a trained, licensed mental health provider, but congregants trust you as their primary caregiver. How can you be of help? When are you in over your head? When and to whom do you refer those needing further help?

Questions abound! What is pastoral counseling versus psychotherapy? What is a spiritual emergency versus a psychiatric episode? When do you refer a person or family to a mental health professional? How do you make a referral? What is the difference between a psychiatrist, psychologist, psychotherapist, pastoral counselor, or clinical social worker? What are the signs of mental distress and trauma? When is it best to think outside the box? These questions and more are the focus of this chapter. Our goal is to offer you immediate information in your role as a trusted caregiver, especially following a disaster or tragic event. We also encourage you to read chapter 2 on self-care for the clergy.

The common assumption is that clergy will have access to clinicians, mental health professionals, and hospitals or clinics to help the healing process following a disaster. We encourage you to make full use of licensed professionals as appropriate to your specific situation. There has been a shift from local clergy performing the bulk of their congregational counseling load to handing the counseling over to mental health professionals. We acknowledge this ongoing shift, along with the tension and turf wars it creates. We argue that both clergy and health care professionals must work as a team for the benefit of the congregant. Decisions should be based on what is best for the healing of the congregant or congregation. We also acknowledge that one size does not necessarily fit all. Each disaster and the resulting trauma or tragedy is different and so is each response. Racial, social, religious, cultural, economic, and educational factors do make a difference as to how best to respond to an individual's needs. Unfortunately, history tells us that these same variables factor into the available resources for rescue, recovery, and rebuilding.[2]

We seek to help you determine the best course of action for congregants who request your help. Our goal is to suggest interventions that will allow you to continue to offer quality pastoral care and counseling following a disaster. As in any field of inquiry and exploration, there are areas related to trauma that fall outside the box of expected responses and symmetrical interventions. In this chapter we will explore a few of the outside-the-box issues and attempt to offer interventions to meet these atypical situations.

What Is a Disaster?

The traditional definition of *disaster* is "an event that causes serious loss, destruction, hardship, unhappiness, or death." Disasters do happen. Sacred literature, history, and life experience record that disasters do happen, even to people of faith. To be classified as a disaster an event need not be as catastrophic as the Oklahoma City bombing, the tsunami in Southeast Asia, or California mudslides or wildfires. Car accidents, local drive-by shootings, unequal treatment in health care, and root shock, a traumatic stress reaction to the destruction of one's emotional ecosystem, are disasters that are just as tragic to the victims as the aforementioned larger disasters. So who defines what is considered a disaster? Who receives a prompt and effective response and who is left out? Who are the architects of disaster relief and clinical and clerical interventions, and where are the accountability models to ensure that interventions match need? Who actually benefits from a disaster? Who pays the heaviest price following a disaster and why?

The word *disaster* has its etymological foundation in Latin and literally means "against the stars." Within this more arcane definition lies the root of collectively induced trauma. (By this we mean trauma caused by lack of response, invisibility, outright ostracism, racism, and collective neglect.) We conclude that these experiences create yet another wave of post-disaster trauma: we blame the victim.[3]

By and large, the architects of disaster relief and "rebuilding" tend to be large governmental agencies and organizations. It seems "they" tend not to take into account the voices of those most affected.[4] In large disasters, once people have been removed from danger, hunger, and homelessness, those most at risk and most affected are rarely consulted about the process of the reconstruction of homes, communities, and infrastructure. Likewise, the architects of disaster relief and reconstruction, though well meaning, rarely resemble the populations that are most severely affected and historically have the fewest resources to rebuild their lives without outside support. We assert the aforementioned factors affect treatment outcomes regardless of technique or the clinician's skill.

Interventions

What counseling is appropriate for a clergyperson to undertake before referring a congregant to a mental health professional? Are there times when pastoral counseling is counterproductive or downright harmful? How can clergy and licensed professionals work together to help the congregant heal?

Create a Safe Space to Share What Happened

After you have accounted for all your congregants and their well-being following a disaster, it is important to gather as a group as soon as it is safe to do so. Create a safe place to share your experiences as a community. Faith-based congregations are communities. Clergy are asked to listen to the community.

On September 11, 2001, Roberta Samet was in her car, preparing to cross the Brooklyn Bridge. Here is her story:

> Just as I was about to drive on the entrance ramp, the bridge was closed and as I looked up, I saw the towers burning. We all parked our cars (interestingly enough, in front of the Watchtower buildings in downtown Brooklyn) and gasped at the burning towers. Then people drifted to their cars to listen to the radio coverage. I walked over to a woman standing by her car, and as we started talking, within a minute, we realized that we belonged to the same synagogue and that she had been married the week before by our rabbi, who happens to be one of my oldest high school friends. Though until that day I had never known this woman, we formed a deep connection based on this mutual witnessing and synagogue connection. Later that night, our rabbi called an impromptu gathering of congregants to talk, tell stories, and mostly to be together. Though I am not a very active member of the congregation, I felt a deep sense of comfort in that gathering. I needed a space to tell my story, listen to others, and recognize the collective grief and anxiety of this community.

In Cambodia, after the Khmer Rouge was finally driven out of power, a tortured population was left behind. Many of these women had been tortured, raped, violently widowed, disfigured, and generally terrorized during this regime. One of the most effective interventions for these women involved story sharing. A small group of women would sit in a circle. First, each woman told her story to the group in great detail. They were encouraged to experience their feelings as they told their story. When all the women had told their stories, the leader engaged these women in a variety of art projects. This was an attempt both to have them move through these experiences through creative outlet and also to engage the creative, life-giving forces in each of them. The final phase of the program was to help the women develop trades and work skills that would provide a meaningful and self-determined way to support themselves. The results of this intervention have been profoundly positive.

Many people find it healing and healthy to tell their story. Following the most recent disasters in the United States, we have been invited to facilitate hundreds of post-disaster support groups where survivors simply told their story. Following a disaster, all of us have a story to tell. For instance, where were you when the World Trade Center towers fell? What were you doing during Hurricane Andrew? How did the crash of flight 587 affect you? Where were your loved ones during the Columbine shootings or the Southeast Asia tsunami? Where were you during the Virginia Tech shootings? Where we were during a disaster influences our story. *One of the roles of clergy following a disaster is to create safe places for people to tell their story or to give their testimony.* Rachel Naomi Remen, MD, affirms the healing value of stories in her bestseller, *Kitchen Table Wisdom: Stories That Heal.* Dr. Remen writes, "Real stories take time. Life rushes us along and few people are strong enough to stop on their own. Most often, something unforeseen stops us and it is only then we have the time to take a seat at life's kitchen table, to know our own story and tell it, and listen to other people's stories."[5]

Talk to the Congregation

Sermons heal. Worship, sermons, and faith-based small groups serve as therapy for many congregants. Faith-based communities need to hear from their spiritual leader following a disaster. Rumors fly in the time during and immediately after a disaster. Get the facts and report them back to your congregation. You can also educate your congregation on what to expect the next couple of days and what the common reactions to a disaster are. Familiarize yourself with chapter 1 of this book,

"The Life Cycle of a Disaster," which provides accurate information on common reactions to disaster and a common timetable of responses. Know that many people turn to clergy following a disaster before they turn to a mental health professional. You can set the tone and introduce the possibility of pastoral counseling. Assure your congregation that you are available to listen, assist, and when necessary make referrals to other professionals.

Congregants tend to listen attentively to the clergy. It is well documented that physicians and other healing team members have reported frustrations over clergy "demonizing" their medical practices or prescription medications. Despite histories, personal agendas, and past failings by both professions, clergy and health care professionals must work together after a disaster. Clergy who have done their homework before the disaster know where to refer their members for culturally competent help. Let the congregation hear from you that their seeking help is in keeping with your religious practices and a component of good pastoral care.

Following September 11, 2001, Rev. Willard Ashley was asked to speak to New York City pastors about what to preach following this tragic disaster. In the seminars it was explained to clergy, contrary to the practices of some, that fire-and-brimstone sermons are not the best clinical or pastoral response to a disaster. Sermons that offer compassion, empathy, and an anchor in an unsteady world serve to help the congregation best. In some communities and demographics, sermons may need to include advocacy and prophetic action. Clergy are called upon to preach prophetically to power and unjust situations.

If you feel comfortable, you could share personal information with your congregation. Some congregants draw comfort in knowing their spiritual leader also struggles with his or her attempts to recover from the impact of a disaster. Always offer hope even in suffering. Encourage congregants to read sacred literature, pray, practice religious rituals, and focus on hope. All of us can use hope. We know hope heals.

Be a Triage Center

Hands-on clergy know their membership. If your ministry does not afford you to have regular direct contact with your membership, create small groups or some mechanism for your members to be seen regularly by someone who can follow up if something seems curious or strange. Listen with your eyes and ears. Look for signs of depression, anxiety, posttraumatic stress disorder (PTSD) or other reactions to a disaster that may need professional help to promote healing. In many cases, you are the first responder or the triage center following a disaster. Remember—do no harm.

Because you have a trusted relationship, you can make a difference, but stay within your expertise. Here are some questions to consider for the pastoral office visit following a disaster:

- What happened that led this person to seek help?
- What should you do right now: offer spiritual first aid, intervene, or refer?
- Where is this person in their spiritual journey: emergency or emergence?
- How can this person's faith perspective be of help?
- What resources are available to help with the healing process?
- What lessons and life changes are necessary for healing this person?
- What are your impressions, observations, and feelings about this person?

When clergy who are unlicensed in mental health perform pastoral counseling, the general rule is to conduct no more than three to five sessions, after which you should refer the congregant to a health care provider, mental health professional, or healing agency. *If a person expresses a desire to hurt him or herself or others, professional medical help must be sought immediately.* Again, studies have documented that people tend to turn to clergy rather than to a psychiatrist or psychotherapist after a disaster, unless there is a medical emergency. Therefore, clergy tend to be the triage center. Stay within your expertise. Do not be too proud or ashamed to make a referral to a licensed professional.

Here are tips on how to conduct your counseling sessions:

- Use reflective listening and active listening techniques. Take short breaks during the session to repeat back to the congregant what you heard him or her say to you. Use their exact words.

- Do not exchange war stories. Your job is to listen, not unload.
- Do no harm. Once the problem is outside of your expertise or comfort level, make a referral to a licensed professional.
- Do not argue with their beliefs, values, theology, or world view.
- Do not assume anything. Let the person telling their story to attach meaning to the story, not you. People make meaning out of their experiences.[6]
- Do not offer clichés, platitudes, or quick-fix answers.
- Do not judge and do not be judgmental in your verbal and nonverbal responses.
- Allow the person to express a full range of emotions.
- Allow for a spiritual emergency. A common response to a disaster is to question God, express anger at God, or ask, "How did God allow this to happen?"
- Offer religious resources that are in keeping with their faith and practice.
- Keep all information in the strictest confidence.
- Remember that pastoral counseling is a privilege—treat people with respect.
- Show compassion, empathy, and understanding of their feelings and thoughts.
- Validate their feelings of loss, anger, confusion, and despair. Affirm these are common reactions to uncommon situations.
- Practice cultural competency.
- Seek supervision and guidance.
- Offer the hope that time, resources, and supportive relationships heal.
- Make yourself available, but know your limits and set healthy boundaries.
- Utilize the rich resources of other professionals in the healing process.
- Show how much you love before you show how much you know.

Make Referrals When Necessary

A good referral is not a failure. A referral expands the pastoral care possibilities. You should refer a congregant to a licensed professional in the following cases:

- The congregant needs medical care or institutionalization.
- The congregant is severely depressed or suicidal.
- The congregant presents challenges that are outside of your skill set.
- The congregant's needs surpass your available time or training. The congregant needs long-term or intensive psychotherapy.
- You are unsure or in doubt as to the congregant's concerns or issues.
- The congregant does not seem to make any progress in three to five sessions.
- The congregant's challenges are better served by effective specialized agencies within the community.
- The congregant has severe chronic financial challenges. Agencies with trained social workers are appropriate referrals for such challenges.
- You have a strong negative reaction or intense sexual attraction to the congregant.

Below are some guidelines for making an effective referral:

- During the first counseling session, mention the possibility of a referral if you feel the challenges and concerns are outside of your expertise or skills.
- Ask the congregant to explain his or her perception of the challenges he or she faces and what kind of help is needed. Ask the congregant if he or she has sought professional help in the past. If so, what were the circumstances? How did it work out?
- Collaborate on how the congregant wants you to describe his or her challenges to your referral source.
- Help the congregant resolve his or her feelings or thoughts about calling upon the particular professional or agency recommended. "Does going to therapy mean I am crazy?"

- Explain that good self-care includes seeking help when challenges overwhelm us.
- Establish a strong trusting relationship whereby you are the bridge the congregant can travel over into another helping relationship.
- Encourage the congregant to really try a given therapist or agency, even if he or she is only mildly willing.
- Create a climate that allows the congregant to report back to you if the referral does not work out.
- Let the congregant know that your pastoral care and concern will continue both during the referral, through periodic follow-ups with the congregant and the mental health professional or agency, and after the referral.
- Encourage the congregant to ask questions of a potential mental health professional. Remind the congregant that he or she is a consumer of a service.

Following are some questions you and your congregant should ask when making a referral:

- Is this person a psychiatrist, psychologist, social worker, psychotherapist, or counselor? (See the Appendix at the end of this chapter for the differences between these professions.) What education, certification, or licenses does he or she posses?
- How does the treatment process work?
- What is the person's experience treating the congregant's diagnosis?
- What is the person's experience with the congregant's race, culture, gender, and faith?
- What can the congregant expect from the referral?
- What does the referral expect from the congregant?
- How does the congregant assess progress or set new goals?
- How soon will the congregant feel better, and what will it take?
- What are the financial arrangements for the congregant's treatment?
- How is treatment terminated? Who makes that decision?

Working with Children

Children offer a special challenge and a unique opportunity. At times children are left out of the equation when looking at trauma recovery. Ironically, it is the children who are often the window into a family or community's interactions. Some clergy are very good at counseling and understanding children, but children are usually better served by seeing a pediatrician or trained health care provider, even if working with children is your gift. If you do meet with a child, never do so alone! Keep good records of the session.

Special Challenges

Traditional wisdom and many disaster recovery programs suggest that receiving mental health care is simple: you look up a therapist or psychiatrist in the phone book, he or she administers treatment or therapy, your insurance or some government program pays the bill, and all is well.

But life is not that simple. Some congregants do not have health insurance. Some congregants have health insurance, but do not like the mental health professionals on their plan and cannot afford someone the insurance company labels as out-of-network. Some congregants have justifiable reasons not to trust physicians, psychologists, psychotherapists, or licensed professionals[7]. Some congregants find the mental health professionals in their area are simply overloaded or not available. Some congregants come from cultures where you do not share your secrets or problems with strangers. Some congregants prefer healers who hail from the same religion, race, ethnic, and cultural background, and find there are few, if any, available. There are a host of reasons a congregant may opt not to seek a psychotherapist or psychiatrist or licensed professional. We assert that before you attach some pathology to that congregant, accept that he or she may have a valid point. Psychotherapy is not for everybody. There are also dynamics that exceed the scope of traditional psychotherapy or psychiatry. So how do such congregants find healing?

Be Aware of the Politics of Healing

The exploration of grief and depression from a post-trauma perspective needs additional attention. Grief and short-term depression are normal responses to trauma and loss. Effective treatments include medication, time, talking through the experience, and sacred rituals. However, what happens when the aftermath of a trauma exacerbates preexisting depression? We are calling this "compounded depression" and define it as multiple factors contributing to despair, which will not respond to traditional treatment or counseling—psychotherapeutic interventions. This compounded depression flies in the face of resiliency. For instance, what are the long-term and compounding effects of those who lost their homes during Hurricane Katrina, were housed in an inhuman temporary shelter called the Superdome, and then placed in toxin-emitting trailers? Add to this the effects of agencies' broken promises to build new housing, effectively arbitrate insurance claims, and restore neighborhoods, which at best are slow to become reality. This is the stuff of grief that falls outside the treatment regimes of conventional psychiatric protocols. People in this category have the potential to benefit from medicine, but an area as affected as the Gulf Region following Katrina may lack psychiatric personnel to prescribe medicine, and it may take months or years before funding or political gatekeepers allow programs to be developed to increase mental health delivery capacity.

Even with available clinicians and medicines, there are situations that call for a more systemic approach to a person's healing. As one clinician instructed their patient, "I can give you medication for your depression, but what will allow your depression to diminish is a job that pays living wages and a home free of toxins, rodents, and crime." Some clinicians call this a family systems approach. When clinicians take a family systems approach they examine the individual and the environmental factors that act upon the functioning of that individual. With this approach they examine the whole versus just the individual parts. This approach suggests that, in the clinician's assessment of the patient, it is important to understand how the banks, stores, schools, media, hospitals, and community at large impact a patient's daily life. Like individuals, communities also have patterns of behavior. The core trainers from The People's Institute for Survival and Beyond[8] call this approach a "foot identification." In other words, clinicians can help people to heal from trauma when they name and remove the foot that is kicking their butt.[9] De facto institutional re-wounding requires collective responses that fall out of the scope of traditional pastoral psychotherapy. Thus, trauma recovery involves thinking outside of the box.

If Hurricane Katrina taught clergy nothing else, it was that there are times when the best therapy is a home safe from toxins, rodents, crime, agency corruption, and cultural incompetence. The clergyperson is called upon at times to be the prophet[10] who preaches against radical evil and leads in the resistance against oppressive forces. Know there are times following a disaster when the pulpit needs to become an organizing base to place pressure on government and negligent "care" organizations to change. Find your comfort level with the role of clergy as agents of change. Attend seminars and support groups where clergy get support to do this type of prophetic work.

Religious organizations have a history of being the catalyst for building schools, hospitals, and homes. In disaster work clergy have organized, raised money, and taken matters into their own hands. Sometimes the best therapy you can offer your congregants is to help navigate the maze of red tape and help accelerate the rebuilding process while licensed professionals handle the pastoral counseling load. Such a response is the clergy as advocate and prophet. Victims of disasters need strong-willed clergy who organize and effect positive change. History documents the positive influence religion can have as a tool for social change.

Learn to Identify Symptoms

The Diagnostic and Statistical Manual of Mental Disorders (DSM-IV) is the standard text that describes and defines psychiatric clinical diagnoses. In it you will find a detailed description of symptoms for every mental disorder. The list includes common post-disaster mental illnesses such as posttraumatic stress disorder (PTSD), depression, anxiety, domestic violence, substance abuse, and various other mood shifts. PTSD is a common reaction to an uncommon event, such as a disaster, and is defined as follows:

> A traumatic stress is an unusual event such as a serious harm to family members, a community disaster, a violent accident, or a wartime calamity. Following the event, the affected person re-experiences the episode in some way. This can happen by recall, dreams, or a sudden feeling that the event is recurring; it can also be set off by the incidents that remind the individual of the original trauma.[11]

Dr. Roukema, a psychiatrist trained at Columbia University, asserts,

> The syndrome includes the avoidance of anything that is related to the original trauma as well as some failure to remember significant parts of the trauma. There is a "psychic numbing"—that is, an inability to experience normal emotions and a general detachment from those who were close. In addition, persons suffering from this disorder may have sleep disturbances, anxiety and problems with concentration.[12]

Only a small percentage of people who experience trauma will exhibit these symptoms over a long period of time, and those who do often have previous histories of trauma, abuse, or severe mental illness. The vast majority of those who experience trauma will display an array of symptoms we call human reactions, which reflect common responses to uncommon situations. This can include depression,[13] sleeplessness, anxiety, irritability, temporary de-realization, work, social and sexual disturbance, fight or flight reactions, and the like. "Often a symptom of depression is passivity, and the inability to take initiative on one's own behalf. Depressed people often hold onto an idea that they are helpless and everything is hopeless, that nothing will make a difference,"[14] cites pastoral psychotherapist Margaret Kornfeld. Again, these responses are common responses to traumatic events.[15] The responses can be mild, moderate, or severe and yet still do not constitute a PTSD diagnosis. The vast majority of people who fall into this category will need soothing, reassurance, and in some cases, referral to short-term counseling or therapy.

Organizations such as the American Association of Pastoral Counselors,[16] along with other mental health professionals who are culturally competent, can play a major role in the healing process. Some people may benefit from short-term doses of medicine, but are not considered to be mentally ill or at high risk for PTSD. Most people are incredibly resilient and tend to recover over time if given culturally competent resources and sufficient support.

Respect the Value of Culture

Culture is one determining factor in what may appear to be severe or moderate nonpathological responses to trauma. For instance, in cultures where emotions are easily and fully expressed, a woman throwing herself on the floor, pulling at her hair, and screaming may be seen as experiencing a cathartic release that, once completed, could be a prognosticator of healthy recovery. In other cultures, the ability to calmly tell the story in great detail with small and slow expression of affect would be considered normal and helpful. Again, one size does not fit all, yet when best practices for trauma care are introduced to the psychiatric community rarely do they include culturally competent interventions.

Cultural beliefs inform and impact any best practices on healing. To think otherwise is either arrogant or a show of cultural incompetence. Until relatively recently, trauma literature published in the United States focused on trauma as experienced by individuals, such as domestic violence, physical and sexual abuse, and crime-related trauma, rather than by the collective. Since the Oklahoma City bombing in 1995, clinicians and researchers have contributed substantial literature and research that looks at congregate responses to collective trauma. This research has been helpful in determining how many people may be affected in the aftermath of disasters and who will require the most intensive clinical interventions.

Spiritual Emergence versus Spiritual Emergency

Roberto Assagioli, MD, a psychiatrist and student of Freud born in Venice, Italy, in 1888, found the tenets of psychoanalysis too limited in scope. He went on to formulate a psychological perspective that could consider all aspects of the human condition—mental, physical, emotional, and spiritual—and integrate them into a holistic being. Assagioli noticed a category of responses that are often misdiagnosed and mistreated that resembles psychiatric diagnosis but tends to occur in individuals with no prior history of mental illness or of psychiatric dysfunction. Christina Grof and Stanislov Grof, MD, developed the term *spiritual emergence* to describe this category of responses,[17] and Russell D. Park, PhD, and others added much to the literature studying the range of this phenomena. In 1994, the research findings of study on spiritual emergency versus spiritual emergence became the basis for the DSM-IV category V62.89, "Religious or Spiritual Problems."

Park goes on to further define the "Ten Theoretical Spiritual Emergence Typologies," which include:

1. Awakening of Kundalini energy
2. Shamanic Crisis
3. Psychological renewal through activation of a Central Archetype
4. Psychic opening that includes experiences of extrasensory perception
5. Karmic pattern or past life memories
6. Possession, where an individual assumes the facial characteristics, gestures, and attitudes of someone else, typically diabolical in nature
7. Channeling and communication with spirit guides
8. Punitive consciousness, or peak experiences
9. Near death experiences
10. Encounters with UFOs."

What is perhaps most important to note here is that spiritual emergence can mimic organic brain disorders and psychotic experiences, but they occur in individuals with no prior psychiatric history and who, upon examination, exhibit no organic or biological manifestations of clinical disease. Among these differential diagnostic references are: "1. Absence of gross organic brain disorders; 2. Absence of physical disease, which might cause similar symptoms; 3. Absence of a long history of conventional psychiatric treatment and hospitalization; and 4. Reasonably good general somatic and cardiovascular condition."[18]

Most important when dealing with spiritual emergence is to rule out organic and psychiatric histories. Grof and Park indicate that spiritual emergence can result from deep spiritual processes, accidents, health crises, and trauma. As clergy and clinicians encounter people from other cultures, non-Western faith practices, diverse parts of the world, and other psychologies, an appreciation of spiritual emergences versus spiritual emergency is crucial. A spiritual emergency is the crossroads process before one experiences a spiritual emergence. Spiritual emergence is when an individual begins to have spiritual experiences that do not significantly alter their sensorium and perception. For instance, a person walks through the woods and feels a sense of unity with all of creation. Someone is in church and the spirit "moves" them. After church they go out for brunch and are fully restored to how they were before they walked into church.

A spiritual emergency is often when an individual's perception is significantly altered on many levels—sensorium, perception, body image—and remains that way for a period of time. For instance, someone has a major kundalini awakening experience and can't open their eyes for a couple of weeks. During this time they receive spiritual information and may be extremely sensitive to sound and touch. This is a person with no psychiatric history and who has functioned up until this point. The person needs to be in a protected environment. However, if this experience is misdiagnosed, and the process is shut down with heavy psychotropic medication, it can actually do harm, both because the experience is being tampered with and also because the individual is treated as mentally ill, which is not the case. It is possible to undergo a profound crisis involving nonordinary experiences and to perceive it as pathological or psychiatric when in fact it may be more accurately and beneficially defined as a spiritual emergency.

While mainstream psychiatry diagnoses consider major shifts in sensorium and affect as pathological, when viewed through this new lens of spiritual emergence, such extraordinary responses may evidence a huge spiritual experience in which people have had mystical and deeply spiritual encounters, placing them in contact with archetypal material and spiritual understanding. What they need is to be placed in a protective environment where their basic biological needs are taken care of while allowing these extraordinary experiences to come to their own timely completion.

Take Care of Yourself and Your Loved Ones

The topic of self-care for clergy is written about in greater detail in chapter 2. We encourage you to read the chapter.

Psychotherapists use the phrase "parallel process" to refer to a situation where there are great similarities between what the client experiences and the present life experience of the psychotherapist. This was the case after 9/11 and following hurricanes Andrew, Rita, and Katrina. No one was left untouched, and psychotherapists were often sorting through their own issues and losses while sitting in front of people who mirrored their own experiences. There was no opportunity in this situation to "catch their breath." Mary Pender Greene, director of social work services for the Jewish Board of Family and Children's Services, described it this way: "What made Social Work practice so hard after 9/11 is because the Social Workers were then having feelings that paralleled their clients and that was the first time that had happened....We were all hyper-aroused on a regular basis with police activities, loud noises—now New York City is full of loud noises but you feel more sensitive to it, it really felt unbearable."[19]

When the historical issues of a client stir up the historical and highly charged emotional issues of a psychotherapist this reaction is often called countertransference. But in the post-disaster experience, we are talking about a fresh response to a fresh experience. Without support, debriefing, a good old-fashioned place to cry, and a safe space to discharge feelings, burnout and ineffectiveness are on the horizon.

Human contact and commitment to trauma relief efforts have been known to produce secondary trauma. In Western culture, when healers or clergy need some support and counseling themselves, it can be seen as a compromise to their competence. We encourage you to find a safe place and safe person with whom to debrief, cry, and get soothed.

Final Words

Faith practices, culture, context, and political will affects not only the individual but also the systems that act upon the individual and his or her community. Each of the aforementioned items are factors in a person's ability to heal. These factors overtly or covertly alter the outcome of our testimonies and thus impact our ability to heal. When addressing the pastoral care and counseling challenges following a disaster, you must think outside of the box.

Appendix

Psychiatrists are doctors of medicine who specialize in psychiatry and treating mental illness. Psychiatrists conduct patient evaluations, prescribe psychiatric medication, and order and interpret physical examinations and laboratory tests. Psychiatrists go through significant training beyond medical school, which may include training in psychotherapy, psychoanalysis, or cognitive behavior therapy. What clearly differentiates psychiatrists from other mental health professionals is their medical training. Many psychiatrists provide psychopharmacology and work in tandem with a psychologist, clinical social worker, or licensed pastoral counselor who conducts the psychotherapy.

Psychologists have a doctor in philosophy (PhD) in psychology or a doctor in psychology (PsyD). Psychologists are clinicians who study psychology, which is the systematic investigation of the human mind to include behavior and cognition. Clinical psychologists perform psychotherapy, psychological tests, and evaluations, engage in research and work with psychiatrists to help patients heal.

Clinical social workers seek solutions to challenges that individuals, families, groups, organizations, and communities face. Clinical social workers tend to consider the whole individual, which includes, spiritual, cultural, psychological, sociological, and biological needs, and the systems that affect the client's current situation. Clinical social workers focus on assessment and diagnosis, case management, psychoeducation, family interventions, relationship therapy, various psychotherapies, and clinical supervision. A social worker (MSW), has a master's degree in social work, which involves two years of study beyond their undergraduate degree. A licensed clinical social worker (LCSW) is a person who has completed his or her MSW degree and further clinical residency requirements, and has passed a state test for licensure.

Pastoral counselors are mental health practitioners who are members of a certification organization, such as the American Association of Pastoral Counselors. Licensed pastoral counselors have completed their undergraduate and master's work as well as additional course work in psychotherapy and/or marriage and family therapy or group psychotherapy, and two to four years of supervised clinical practice. Pastoral counselors are trained to provide both short- and long-term psychotherapy. What differentiates pastoral counselors from other mental health professionals is their unique focus and perspective on the intersection of spirituality and psychology in how a person functions. It is a requirement for licensed pastoral counselors to have examined their own issues in personal therapy during their training.

Notes

1. M. Gray, B. T. Litz, A. R. Olson, "Methodological and Ethical Issues in Early Intervention Research," in *Early Intervention for Trauma and Traumatic Loss*, ed. B. T. Litz (New York: Guilford Press, 2004), 180.
2. T. A. LaVeist, ed., *Race, Ethnicity and Health: A Public Health Reader* (San Francisco: Jossey-Bass, 2002).
3. A similar pattern of blame/shame is found in rape or domestic violence cases.

4. J. McQuaid and M. Schleifstein, *Path of Destruction: The Devastation of New Orleans and the Coming Age of Super Storms* (New York: Little, Brown, 2006), 67.

5. R. N. Remen, *Kitchen Table Wisdom: Stories That Heal* (New York: Penguin Books, 1996), xxxvii–xxxviii.

6. R. Kegan, *The Evolving Self: Problem and Process in Human Development* (Cambridge, MA: Harvard University Press, 1982), 3–4.

7. H. A. Washington, *Medical Apartheid: The Dark History of Medical Experimentation on Black Americans from Colonial Times to the Present* (New York: Doubleday, 2006).

8. The People's Insitute: www.pisab.org.

9. As one of the authors of this chapter is a black Baptist pastor, people on the street often respond to "Hello," with "Rev, they are kicking my butt."

10. A. J. Heschel, *The Prophets: An Introduction* (New York: Harper Torch Books, 1962), 3–26.

11. R. W. Roukema, *Counseling for the Soul in Distress: What Every Religious Counselor Should Know About Emotional and Mental Illness,* 2nd ed. (Binghamton, NY: Haworth Press, 2003), 81.

12. Ibid.

13. Depression: "Significant times of feeling worthless, helpless and discouraged." K. O'Donnell and M. L. O'Donnell, "Running Well and Resting Well: Twelve Tools for Missionary Life," in *Doing Member Care Well: Perspectives and Practices from Around the World,* ed. K. O'Donnell (Pasadena, CA: William Carey Library, 2002), 311.

14. M. Kornfeld, *Cultivating Wholeness: A Guide to Care and Counseling in Faith Communities* (New York: Continuum Publishing Company, 1998), 225.

15. P. A. Levine and A. Frederick, *Waking the Tiger: Healing Trauma* (Berkeley, CA: North Atlantic Books, 1997), 6.

16. American Association of Pastoral Counselors: www.aapc.org.

17. S. Grof and C. Grof, "Spiritual Emergency: The Understanding and Treatment of Transpersonal Crises," *Revision* 8, no. 2 (1986), 7–20.

18. R. Park, "Spiritual Emergencies: A Quantative and Descriptive Examination with an Emphasis on Kundalini and the Role of Ego," dissertation (Palo Alto, CA: Institute of Transpersonal Psychology, 1991).

19. M. P. Greene, keynote speech to the Association of Directors of Social Work, Annual Conference, May 22, 2003.

Further Reading

Canda, Edward R., and Leola Dyrud Furman. *Spiritual Diversity in Social Work Practice: The Heart of Helping.* New York: Free Press, 1999.

Farmer, Paul. *Pathologies of Power: Health, Human Rights, and the New War on the Poor.* Berkeley, CA: University of California Press, 2005.

Heerden, Ivor Van, and Mike Bryan. *The Storm: What Went Wrong and Why During Hurricane Katrina—The Inside Story from One Louisiana Scientist.* New York: Viking, 2006.

Heschel, Abraham J. *The Prophets: An Introduction.* New York: Harper Torch Books, 1962.

Kegan, Robert. *The Evolving Self: Problem and Process in Human Development.* Cambridge, MA: Harvard University Press, 1982.

Kornfeld, Margaret. *Cultivating Wholeness: A Guide to Care and Counseling in Faith Communities.* New York: Continuum Publishing Company, 1998.

LaVeist, Thomas A., ed. *Race, Ethnicity and Health: A Public Health Reader.* San Francisco: Jossey-Bass, 2002.

Leas, Speed, and Paul Kittlaus. *The Pastoral Counselor in Social Action.* Philadelphia: Fortress Press, 1981.

Levine, Peter A., with Ann Frederick. *Waking the Tiger: Healing Trauma.* Berkeley, CA: North Atlantic Books, 1997.

Litz, Brett T., ed. *Early Intervention for Trauma and Traumatic Loss.* New York: Guilford Press, 2004.

McQuaid, John, and Mark Schleifstein. *Path of Destruction: The Devastation of New Orleans and the Coming Age of Super Storms.* New York: Little, Brown, 2006.

O'Donnell, Kelly, ed., *Doing Member Care Well: Perspectives and Practices from Around the World.* Pasadena, CA: William Carey Library, 2002.

Oz, Mehmet. *Healing from the Heart: A Leading Surgeon Combines Eastern and Western Traditions to Create the Medicine of the Future.* New York: Penguin Group, 1998.

Paniagua, Freddy A. *Assessing and Treating Culturally Diverse Clients,* 2nd ed. Thousand Oaks, CA: Sage Publications, 1998.

Real, Terrence. *I Don't Want to Talk About It: Overcoming the Secret Legacy of Male Depression.* New York: Scribner, 1997.

Remen, Rachel Naomi. *Kitchen Table Wisdom: Stories That Heal.* New York: Penguin Books, 1996.

Richards, P. Scott, and Allen E. Bergin. *A Spiritual Strategy for Counseling and Psychotherapy.* Washington, D.C.: American Psychological Association, 1997.

Ridley, Charles R. *Overcoming Unintentional Racism in Counseling and Therapy: A Practitioner's Guide to Intentional Intervention.* Thousand Oaks, CA: Sage Publications, 1995.

Rothschild, Babette. *The Body Remembers: The Psychophysiology of Trauma and Trauma Treatment.* New York: W. W. Norton & Company, 2000.

Roukema, Richard W. *Counseling for the Soul in Distress: What Every Religious Counselor Should Know About Emotional and Mental Illness,* 2nd ed. Binghamton, NY: Haworth Press, 2003

Rynearson, Edward K. *Retelling Violent Death.* Philadelphia: Brunner-Routledge, 2001.

Smith, Christine M. *Preaching as Weeping, Confession, and Resistance: Radical Responses to Radical Evil.* Louisville, KY: Westminster/John Knox Press, 1992.

Washington, Harriet A. *Medical Apartheid: The Dark History of Medical Experimentation on Black Americans from Colonial Times to the Present.* New York: Doubleday, 2006.

About the Contributors

Rev. Willard W. C. Ashley Sr., DMin, DH, is coeditor of this book, a psychotherapist, and founder and senior pastor of the Abundant Joy Community Church in Jersey City, New Jersey. He envisioned and implemented the largest clergy resiliency program in the United States following the attacks on September 11, 2001, the Care for the Caregivers Interfaith Program, a ministry of the Council of Churches of the City of New York. His ministry also includes roles as an adjunct professor; a consultant on disaster recovery and clergy self-care to congregations and Fortune 100 companies; a board member of Disaster Chaplaincy Services, New York City; a board member of Christ Hospital, Jersey City, New Jersey; a former assistant dean of students and director of recruitment for Andover Newton Theological School; and past president of the Blanton Peale Graduate Institute, Alumni Association. Ashley is an ordained minister in the National Baptist Convention, USA, Inc.; Disciples of Christ; and the American Baptist Churches, USA.

Roberta L. Samet, LCSW, was the program manager for the September 11th Fund. In this capacity she oversaw the development and implementation of the long-term mental health recovery plan for New York City, the tri-state area, as well as other parts of the United States most affected by the events of 9/11. She developed 15 distinct trauma training programs reaching 7,000 mental health professionals, 3,000 primary care physicians, 2,500 early childhood educators and 2,000 clergy. She was instrumental in the development of a far-reaching mental health benefit that combined resources of the September 11th Fund and the American Red Cross. Through this program, a pool of 125,000 eligible individuals were entitled to receive free mental health and substance abuse services. Prior to this, Samet headed the AIDS Initiatives for the NYC Department of Mental Health where she served as a senior consultant to the agency. She is a past member of the board of directors of the New York City chapter of the National Association of Social Workers.

Imam Muhammad Hatim, PhD, DMin, is the director of the justice ministry for the New York City Department of Correction with the Admiral Family Circle Islamic Community of New York City; general secretary of Malik Shabazz (Malcolm X) Human Rights Institute; and a United Nations nongovernmental organization representative. He is a pastoral counseling specialist with the American Association of Pastoral Counselors, a clinical alcohol and drug counselor, and a recovery mentor associate (specializing in opiate addiction) in New Jersey. He was a Red Cross disaster chaplain at Ground Zero after 9/11 and is an intern alcohol and drug counselor in the Intensive Outpatient Program services at Team Management 2000, Englewood, New Jersey.

10

From Honeymoon to Disillusionment to Reconstruction

Working with Outside Groups to Help Rebuild a Community

Rev. John A. Robinson Jr., MDiv

More than ten years ago Ben Curran, program specialist at the Federal Emergency Management Agency (FEMA), spoke to a class of emergency managers from thirty-six states about the need for cooperation in disaster response. I will never forget his words: "How many of you think you can do this work without the voluntary organizations, churches, and synagogues in your communities?" About half the room responded affirmatively. "If you still feel that way at the end of the week, please do us both a favor and find a different line of work. You cannot do this without including voluntary agencies and houses of worship." I was stunned. I had been through a very difficult disaster response in North Carolina a few years earlier and had my offers of help and support from my church governing body shunned and ignored by federal disaster responders. An American Red Cross volunteer had helped me get connected and given me valuable guidance about how to organize my community for a response. I had come away with the feeling that FEMA didn't need the religious community in disaster; that unfortunately the faith community would have to wait until federal efforts were exhausted and then pick up the pieces for those who remained in need. When I later asked Ben about his remark, he was kind and direct: "This is a new day. We have to learn to work together."

FEMA is not the only agency or person that needs to understand the new reality in disaster response; we are all in this together and we need to work together. We need to learn to work together with outside organizations coming into the community after a disaster. And we need to work with one another as religious entities as well. Indeed, by working in cooperation with one another, the faith community can be the pivot point in a community-based response to disaster.

Learning to work with the maddening array of organizations that show up after a disaster will be essential to your effective leadership in the community after a disaster. Three things to keep in mind are the need for:

1. Clear expectations about roles
2. Prompt and respectful communication
3. Flexibility

Your job is to find out what differing groups are able and willing to do in this particular response, including what they might expect of you or your religious organization in order to work in partnership.

Helping Organizations in a Disaster

All disasters are local. The local community, including the faith community, will need to do its part and take responsibility for the overall direction of the recovery. However, outside disaster response organizations bring with them a wealth of experience and a passion for helping the survivors of disaster that can help your community recovery more quickly and with less confusion. Making those connections and developing that relationship with a multitude of organizations will be key to a successful recovery.

When disaster comes to your community, along with the media attention, the local and state emergency responders, and other disaster managers that will arrive, a variety of volunteer organizations will show up to help. Some of these organizations will be faith based, such as the Salvation Army, Presbyterian Disaster Assistance, the Southern Baptists, and the United Jewish Communities. Others will be non-faith-based social service organizations such as the American Red Cross, the

United States Junior Chamber (or Jaycees), and the National Organization for Victim Assistance. Regardless of the type of organization, each should have a defined mission, a specific period during the response that they expect to be in the field, and expectations about how they will operate in the affected area.

As the recipient of the services or supplies from these organizations, it is important to remember that no single organization will meet all of your community's disaster recovery needs, and you should not expect agencies to change their procedures or services to meet all of your needs except under the most extraordinary circumstances. Understanding the role and particular mission of partner responders will help a community use the services of disaster responders most efficiently. Communities should not expect an organization that delivers relief supplies or food to an affected area early in the recovery to stay on and help rebuild homes, and no one should think that organizations that rebuild homes are somehow "late" because they only arrive months after the event when case management, volunteer hosting, and long-term recovery systems are in place.

If the organization that is present on the site cannot respond to your need, the best you can expect is that they will attempt to help you find another organization that might help with the immediate need. The emphasis is on *might*, because you need to remember that these are all voluntary organizations. These organizations are limited by donations they have received, availability of volunteers to assist at home and in the field, and the operational capacity to meet all of their requests. They are not under the same mandate as governmental agencies or contracted suppliers.

In an attempt to bring greater coordination to the efforts of these voluntary organizations, a network of coordinating bodies have evolved from an initial core of organizations who agreed, thirty years ago, to set up the National Voluntary Organizations Active in Disaster (NVOAD, or National VOAD). The National VOAD is not an operational or programmatic agency but rather a roundtable or association for voluntary organizations that respond to disasters. Their activities revolve around the four Cs: cooperation, communication, coordination, and collaboration.

There are forty-nine members of the National VOAD (see figure 10.2 at the end of this chapter for more information). Each has a specific mission in disaster response that may include more than one role. None of these organizations will provide a community with all of the needs survivors will have in the aftermath of a disaster, and several of them will provide the same or similar support and services. This is a good thing. Many organizations, while national members of VOAD, may not have a national scope in response. They may only serve where they have a concentration of local members or offices. Not all of these organizations will or have the capacity to respond to every disaster. Some may be limited by their size, others may be limited by the requirement that the disaster have a presidential disaster declaration.

There are also sixty-four state and local VOADS (see figure 10.3 at the end of this chapter). Representatives of many of the national VOADs will also participate in the state and local VOADs. More information on all of these VOADs and VOAD members can be found at www.nvoad.org.

If there is a state or local VOAD in your area, the time to get to know the members is *before the disaster*. Typically, there will be a gathering once or twice a year to discuss planning and preparation for disaster. There is usually a small fee or dues for belonging. If you are a local or regional representative of a larger disaster organization, then that national body may cover the cost of dues and travel to attend these meetings.

After a disaster, the VOAD is a place of coordination, collaboration, cooperation, and communication, most often in the form of a conference call. During these calls, which typically last an hour, reports are exchanged about what is happening in the field, what needs are most pressing, and what specific support is needed from other organizations. This can be one of the most helpful places for a local disaster committee to be plugged in early. In order to do so, someone on the committee has to connect with a VOAD member and get the number and time of the conference call. Participating in a conference call is a learned skill. You need to plan ahead of time what really needs communicating to this coordinating body, and you need to listen carefully to what others are saying. Taking notes during the call can be very helpful. Try not to interrupt; hold questions, comments, and requests for phone numbers for follow-up until it is your turn or when there seems to be a pause in the flow of conversation.

Becoming a part of the local VOAD can facilitate this contact, but in the absence of a local VOAD, take time to meet with the local emergency management staff. These are the individuals who will be coordinating the early stages of the response. Meeting with them before the disaster can make asking for information and assistance later much easier. My experience is that emergency personnel welcome the involvement of the faith community both as a partner and a resource in disaster preparation.

Types of Organizations

Governmental

Federal, state, and local governments are now required to have a disaster-response capacity and a plan for implementing their response. The National Response Plan is being rewritten and disseminated for comment as this book is being written. The proposed new name is the National Response Framework. Regardless of what the plan for response is called, it is important to understand the current plan and the process for its implementation. For many years the national response to disaster was guided by a separate agency, FEMA. After the creation of the U.S. Department of Homeland Security, FEMA was folded into this new agency. Unlike the FEMA of old that depended on the resources of other government departments and its own resources to respond, the tendency now is to contract private vendors for services during an emergency. This new system has two consequences. First, many of the vendors being used by FEMA have little or no experience in disaster response prior to the emergency; they simply have a contract to deliver a given product or service to a given site, and doing so fulfills their contract. Understanding how the changing circumstances of the disaster may change the consequences of their actions may be missing. The second consequence is that personnel, indeed even the company, may change without notice, even in the midst of disaster. Keeping up with whom you should speak to about concerns in the delivery of goods or services becomes more difficult. This is another reason that participation in the local and state VOAD becomes more important.

States also have a responsibility in disaster response. They frequently lack the resources or delivery mechanism for an effective response without federal assistance. When a disaster strikes, the governor of the state is responsible for certifying to the president that the disaster has overwhelmed the capacity of the state to respond. When the president makes the determination that the disaster rises to the level of a federal disaster, a presidential declaration is issued. That declaration triggers the availability of a whole range of support and services to the states, localities, and individual survivors. The state's role in disaster response is to coordinate, under state law, the resources made available to it through the presidential declaration, as well as outside resources from corporations and, occasionally, foundations. Some states have set up a state-run donation site for contributions that are then funneled into governmental or nongovernmental programs.

It may come as a surprise, but the primary clients of FEMA are state and local governments, not individual survivors. The primary focus of federal activity is the coordination of the delivery of services to enable the governmental infrastructure to resume operation: roads, fire stations, and the power grid receive more funding and more federal interest during a large disaster than the immediate rebuilding of homes. The reason for this is simple: the responsibility of the federal government is to respond to the needs of government, not individuals. In recent disasters more attention has been focused on the role of FEMA in assisting individuals, but the process for accessing those resources is different in each state because states are ultimately responsible for providing funds to individuals beyond relatively small entitlement grants from FEMA and other federal programs. All disasters are local, goes the saying, but most resources come from the federal government. States are the mediator between federal and local authorities.

While state and local agencies can be the conduit for services and funding for individual recovery, that is not their primary role in disaster recovery. Their primary focus will be on the preservation of life and the protection of property. Disasters are also a public safety issue. Local and state emergency management agencies will be in control of the early response of the government to the impact of the disaster. Individual or family recovery from disaster is seen as the responsibility of the individual or family, and to a limited extent the role of nongovernmental voluntary agencies.

Quasi-Governmental

The second kind of organization active in disaster response is the quasi-governmental agency, such as the American Red Cross and its regional and local chapters. The Red Cross is chartered by Congress and mandated to provide specific services in a presidentially declared disaster. Among those services are food and shelter during the emergency stage, when survivors are not able to return to their homes. In addition they provide some limited case management that results in some support to survivors moving into homes. These benefits change from time to time, as does the manner of delivery. The best advice is to sit down with a Red Cross field representative and go over the broad outlines of what might be provided either before the disaster or soon after the emergency period is over.

The Red Cross provides emotional care at their disaster field offices through professional mental health organizations whose members have been trained by the Red Cross to be a part of the disaster response. The Red Cross will also provide coordination for spiritual care in shelters under their control. They frequently hold training and orientation sessions for local clergy who wish to have access to the Red Cross shelters to provide spiritual care.

As a faith community leader you should have access to information related to Red Cross services in your area during a disaster, but if you register as a volunteer and take courses, you will be known to the local disaster committee before disaster strikes and therefore both have influence and be more knowledgeable. This can be crucial to your community's recovery, as there is very little time for training after the disaster has struck.

Nongovernmental

The third kind of organization that you will encounter is nongovernmental organizations. These include faith-based, denominationally based and non-faith-based organizations that have either as their sole mission or a part of their mission to respond to disasters. As has been said before, no one provides everything you need. Some of these organizations provide food during the emergency period, some provide warehousing for building materials and relief supplies, and still others provide child care for survivor families so that the parents can be free to meet with case managers and service providers.

Many of these organizations are familiar to you from their exposure in the media and their own advertising. The Salvation Army, the United Methodist Committee on Relief, and the Baptist Men almost always respond even to small-scale disasters.

Faith-based organizations have some connection with a faith community or profess some specific faith commitment as a part of their work. The degree to which their faith commitment is evidenced in their work varies from group to group and from person to person. The provision of services or support from these groups should not be based upon the affiliation of the recipient or the willingness of the recipient to listen to or accept the faith commitment of the provider; however, not all volunteers may behave well in the field. If proselytizing or sharing of their views becomes a problem or uncomfortable you should contact their sending organization immediately to discuss the problem.

Response programs directly affiliated with denominations are typically a bit more formalized and have clearer expectations of local community participation. They also provide a clear point of contact for local community recovery organizations when the initial response teams have gone home.

Unaffiliated Volunteers

The last group of people that shows up in a disaster is unaffiliated volunteers. These are people who fit into one of several categories:

- They are inexperienced but well-intentioned and eager to respond.
- They have some skills that could be useful but are not connected to a faith community or volunteer agency that will make use of those skills.
- They are excitement junkies who satisfy their need for excitement by going to a disaster site and injecting themselves into a situation.
- They are people with the means and the time to spend doing something to help others and have a real willingness to support what needs to be done without having a lot of need for being in charge.
- They are people who have some previous experience with responding to disaster but no longer have a connection with a disaster response program.

Unaffiliated volunteers present a special set of challenges. If you choose to use unaffiliated volunteers be aware that you will have several issues that will need to be addressed with each volunteer (see figure 10.1):

- **Liability:** Do they have medical insurance in case they are injured on a site? If they are incapacitated and need to go home, how will they get there? Who will be responsible for transporting them?

- **References:** Volunteers rarely gives references, and doing a background check in the middle of a disaster response can be difficult without a tested system for doing so. So, how will you check the credentials, previous experience, and skills of an unaffiliated volunteer who comes with nothing more than their story and a willingness to be helpful? Once an unaffiliated volunteer is embraced by your community disaster response, you become responsible for their behavior and actions in the field.

- **Conflicts of expectations:** I frequently receive e-mails from people seeking to be a part of our disaster program. It is not always clear what their expectations are for everything from support (room and board and travel expenses) to compensation for their services. Even with volunteers, their expectation of what your program will offer them in support and what you have available may be vastly different.

- **Supervision:** Who will supervise this person? When you accept help from an organized affiliated disaster program they bring with them many, if not all, of the personnel management systems of a voluntary organization, including supervision, arrangements for personal support (such as food or housing or the responsibility to reimburse the cost), as well as the ability to take on specific tasks on behalf of your recovery and do so with minimal contact with you. Voluntary agencies are, in a sense, the volunteer subcontractors in a recovery. Each unaffiliated volunteer will require orientation to your program, personnel policies, training in the specific tasks, and terms of reference for what they are to do, in addition to a supervisor to whom they will report.

HELPFUL HINTS WHEN WORKING WITH UNAFFILIATED VOLUNTEERS

- Be selective about unaffiliated volunteers.
- Ask good questions when interviewing volunteers.
- Limit the number you use and begin training those who can stay for a time in the operation (or envisioned operations) of your program so that they can in turn assume some responsibility for leading your program.
- Always take the time to ask for references.
- Always do a background check, even at the risk of losing what may seem like a good volunteer.
- Check both criminal background and sexual offenses.
- Check their driving record and be sure their driver's license is valid.

Figure 10.1

Spontaneous and For-Profit Organizations

The American Dream now seems to include having a personal non-profit corporation or a consulting business. Disaster seems to attract both. Be very careful of organizations offering their service or support unless they are known to you from some other experience or they are affiliated with your church, synagogue, mosque, or temple. Disaster response is a specialized ministry requiring a depth of understanding for both the cycles of the disaster and the opportunities for difficulty. An effective response is a result of the provision of appropriate services in the correct sequence. While a new organization occasionally will emerge out of a specific need in disaster, or an established organization will reshape or expand their mission, this is not the usual case.

As FEMA and the individual state emergency management systems redefine their plans for response, a wider array of contracted companies are becoming involved in disaster response. Previously, a state organization such as the state National Guard unit might be deployed to provide clean water to communities using large tanker trucks or "bladders"; now, it will be just as likely that a private vendor will show up with bottles or cans of water specially prepared for an emergency under contract to FEMA or the state office of emergency management.

More and more organizations that appear to be voluntary are actually for-profit organizations seeking to sell their services or products to the nonprofit sector following a disaster. Faith-based organizations have worked for years to develop systems for eliminating the duplication of services that sometimes creeps into the provision of benefits. Now a for-profit computer software company is marketing a computer program to track the provision of benefits. Disaster is becoming a larger arena for free enterprise to find opportunities to make a profit.

Why People Help

The people who respond first to a disaster are always those closest to the event that are available to help. These spontaneous volunteers can be essential to the survivors in the first few minutes after a sudden event, such as a tornado or a bridge collapse, but people who are paid and trained to respond to the needs of survivors during the emergency period will quickly replace them.

Organizations, some of them voluntary, such as the American Red Cross, are mandated responders with specific roles and responsibilities laid out in their charter from Congress. There are other mandated organizations as well. Each state draws up a disaster response plan. In that plan specific organizations, most governmental but a few voluntary, are designated to assume specific roles in a disaster. No matter how persuasive your argument, these mandated roles are not likely to change once the disaster occurs. These responders are required either by contract or by law to fulfill only certain functions in the disaster. It is a good idea to look up the state disaster plan on the Internet and read it before a disaster occurs so that you will know who is mandated to do what in a disaster.

Another reason people help is altruism. They see the pictures of disaster on television and are compelled by compassion, their own values, or what Robert Coles, Pulitzer Prize-winning Harvard psychiatrist, refers to as "the call to service," to set aside other responsibilities in order to assist others. These people bring with them their experience, culture, and biases. Those who have had experience and some training may be more flexible, knowledgeable, and helpful than those without that experience and training, but not always. These people are motivated by an internal sense of their need to help. They are not openly looking for even a thank you, but a thank-you and a specific recognition, even in private, of the value of their service will affirm their gifts and their calling.

There are those who help because they like the excitement. Few things give both the community affirmation and the adrenaline rush like responding to an event where the overwhelming power of nature and the clear needs of survivors are combined with an open invitation for help from strangers. Helping someone find safety after a flood gives some the justification to break out of a daily routine in favor of an act of selflessness. Unfortunately, it is common for responders to display inappropriate behavior around a disaster. They might respond without proper training or authority, they might interfere with community organizational efforts by forcing themselves on others as a leader inappropriately, or they might seek to take advantage of people who are vulnerable in disaster. The problem with people who respond without affiliation and without a defined role for which they have been trained is that they run the risk of putting themselves and others either in danger or at risk of losing the essential assistance they will need to recover.

Then there are those who respond to disaster because it is an important part of their lives, because it gives meaning to their lives outside of any other benefit. These people seek to work in helpful collaboration with others. They don't look to be in the limelight or to run the show but rather to support others in doing their very best to organize an effective recovery.

Some groups come seeking the limelight, and the minute that the disaster recovery slips from the headlines, or even the inside pages, they will be gone. How to respond to these groups is difficult. On the one hand they bring with them attention, perhaps some funding, and possibly other resources. However you should be careful of providing too much credibility for a fleeting response.

Whatever background or expectation a volunteer brings to the response there will always be a dynamic tension between the gratitude you feel for their service and the volunteer's needs and expectations. Sometimes this can be a healthy and respectful relationship that affirms the work of the volunteer while maintaining the boundaries between the volunteer and the recovery program in appropriate ways. It is important to recognize the gifts of volunteers while at the same time affirming the need of the local program to own the results of operational decisions. Volunteers go home, survivors stay in the community to carry on. Survivors may not wish to become too dependent on a particular volunteer precisely because they know the volunteer will be leaving. The Red Cross has a policy of writing the exit plan for a disaster as soon as they arrive. It may not be a bad idea for the local recovery organization to develop an exit strategy for outside groups early on in the response. Some may feel that is a risky practice, but initial plans can always be changed, and having the vision of an end from the beginning keeps the recovery program from losing focus and expanding its mission inappropriately.

How to Manage Interactions with Outside Organizations

Single Point of Contact— Avoiding Being Triangulated

One of the first organizational tasks for either a congregation receiving assistance after a disaster or a community group acting together will be to develop a means for establishing relationships with outside organizations. Rather than having one person as the contact point, it may be advantageous to have several: one for material donations and relief supplies, another for volunteer teams offering to come to the area, and another for financial support. Dividing up the workload keeps any one person from being overburdened.

The urgency of the situation will leak into the offers of help. Volunteers will want to come immediately, even if you are not ready to receive them. People with material donations will want to set the schedule for when goods arrive, even if that doesn't meet your needs.

The earlier you are able to set up a system for receiving as well as requesting assistance from the outside, the easier it will be to guide those offers and responses rather than end up in conflict. A donations manager may have the most challenging job in disaster response because this person may be the only personal contact those offering assistance will have with the recovery. Make sure the donations manager is someone who can relate to a wide range of people and remain calm even under trying circumstances with difficult people.

Develop systems for referring offers to the appropriate person, and constantly remind response personnel not to ask for anything or respond to an offer of goods and supplies themselves but rather refer the caller to the donations manager. In the heat of a response, misunderstandings can take place, but reminding volunteers and responders alike that only one person can authorize the receipt of in-kind donations can minimize the confusion.

A good practice is to hand out index cards with referral information. That way all the volunteers will be able to give accurate, up-to-date information to those wanting to help. Set up a central point of contact for monetary donations. Do not allow volunteers to receive funds. Have volunteers direct the donor to a specific location or have preaddressed envelopes printed to give to donors.

Clarity about Your Own Needs

Being clear about your own needs as you go along will help with responding to offers of assistance. If your program is not going to provide food or water during the relief stage, make up your mind early on not to accept offers of food or water. Get the name of the program that is providing food and water and have it available to those who wish to give food and water.

Periodically have a meeting with other recovery groups in your area to discuss what is on offer and who needs what commodities. Never take needs on rumor. Take the time to ensure that a need is genuine before referring or accepting a gift on behalf of any disaster recovery organization.

Never accept the donation of something that you do not need in the hopes of getting another donation of something you do need from the same source later. The donor will eventually learn the truth, and the harm to your donor relations will outweigh any benefit that may have come from your lack of candor. Indeed, being a good source of referrals will more likely benefit your recovery efforts, as others will begin to see you as a reliable source of information about what is needed.

The Need for Respect

It may come as surprise to those who have not been through a disaster recovery operation, but respect can be the first casualty in an emergency. People who are normally calm, rational, and gracious can become excited, irrational, and rude. As you know by now from reading earlier chapters, irrationality can be a sign of traumatic stress for survivors of disaster. There are a few simple behaviors that can maintain respect during a response, even when times are difficult:

1. Continue to be respectful of others, even when they are being disrespectful toward you.
2. Don't raise your voice. If you are having difficulty being heard, lower your voice and people will get quieter in order to hear you.
3. Listen carefully to what the source of irritation might be.
4. Respond to the emotional context as well as the content of the communication. If a person seems angry, acknowledge his or her anger and invite that person to share what you might do to help him or her.
5. Restate what the person is saying in your own words.
6. Ask questions rather than giving a response.

There is a difference between being in charge and being in control. In a disaster you may be asked to be in charge either of the whole response, or a specific piece of the work. Being in charge means that you get to have responsibility for making decisions and hopefully consulting with others and encouraging others to work together cooperatively. You will, however, never be in control. The best that can be hoped for is to keep from being overwhelmed. The fastest way to being overwhelmed is to try to be in control.

Ask people to help you. Many people are waiting to be asked, and your request is an opportunity for them to share their gifts and feel valued by the recovery process. Ask others how they see things. This is not the same as asking someone their opinion. Asking others how they see a problem gives you the benefit, quite literally, of their perspective. Their perspective will help you understand the problem clearly.

Clarity about the Offer and the Reason for the Gift

Be careful about offers of help. While an offer of supplies may sound like a gift, unless you are very careful about saying yes, you may end up with a invoice for either the material or the transportation of the material. I have provided a list of questions at the end of this chapter to help you negotiate some of these offers.

FOB means "free on board," meaning that a supplier will provide transportation as a part of the cost of an item to a FOB point. In manufacturing, that point is frequently the factory where an item is produced. In disaster response, it is frequently the warehouse where an item is stored. Asking whether or not the delivery of something is included in the gift can make the difference between whether the gift is useful or not. Paying six thousand dollars to transport food that is free from the Red Cross is not a gift.

Some offers are a thinly veiled attempt to make a sale. I once had a water company offer me bottled water at their cost to produce, or about fifty-five cents a bottle. I declined. While it was an offer to forego profit for them, it was an expense to me, and one that I could replace with a real gift from a vendor who not only gave the product but delivered to my site for free.

Others have a true gift but like to play a kind of cat-and-mouse game by asking how you might use a gift, or will want you to inflate the price of the item for tax purposes. Avoid these offers like the plague. Never, ever change your rules of accounting for receiving a gift because of the preferences of a donor. These requests usually lead to problems down the road. Having a well-defined policy regarding gifts will save you heartache later.

Keep Good Notes from the Beginning

Get a notebook. Write "Donations" on the outside. Use one page per donor. Log the date, time, parties on the call, and content of the call, on each occasion. If you run out of pages, buy another notebook. Log your response as well as the offers of assistance.

Get another notebook. Write "Volunteers" on the outside. Use one to five pages per volunteer organization offering help. Each time you talk, pull out this notebook and keep notes on the content of the conversation, commitments made, and agreements made. Both of these books will help you later remember who promised what and when. They will give you a record and a time line.

Your Own Responsibilities

In a perfect world, the following things should already be in place before a disaster strikes. After a natural disaster these problems are frequently overlooked until they become a problem. However, as soon as possible, assign a volunteer to develop policies and procedures for a long-term recovery plan that covers everything from accounting to closing down. In addition, the following subjects will quickly come to the fore as you receive donations and begin the recovery:

Storage

At the beginning of the recovery, storage space may be provided by the state emergency management program, or by Adventist Community Services through FEMA. However, as time goes by, this space becomes smaller.

If you plan to develop a long-term recovery program, start early to find warehouse space for donations of building materials and equipment. You are responsible for storing donated materials. This is one of the advantages of an interfaith recovery program with many synagogues, churches, mosques, and temples working together. One warehouse can serve the needs of the whole program and at the same time provide support to a number of programs.

Security for In-Kind and Cash Contributions

Integrity in financial management in disaster recovery is essential. Set up proper accounting early on. Use standard computer-based accounting. Use only properly trained and accredited financial managers. Ask that all of those handling financial contributions have proper background checks and bonding. Don't hold large sums of money overnight. Make sure all of the financial transactions flow through one office. Do not allow volunteers to pay for materials with their credit cards and be reimbursed once the emergency is over. Do not allow employees to commingle personal purchases with agency purchases in the same order.

Secure in-kind donations and post signs about the limits on their use. Do not permit survivors to help themselves to supplies of donations; have a volunteer work with them to select what might be needed or make a standardized list of items that they can select from.

The Issue of Gift Cards

Gift cards can be helpful in providing materials for long-term rebuilding. They are, however, the same as cash and need to be treated as such. They do have the added value of being tracked by their PIN on the back. In this way, you can record the use of each card by attaching the receipt for each item purchased to the expended gift card. By recording the source of the card there can be an unbroken paper trail on the use of the gift.

Inventory Control

Keep track of where things go. Setting up an inventory management system sets a tone that equipment should be returned, supplies need to be accounted for, and donations should be used with care. It is far too easy for supplies to be wasted and tools to disappear unless there is a consistent system that tracks their use. You will still lose tools (power cords somehow grow legs and walk away), but the number will be less and there will be more of an atmosphere of respect for the work as well as the material when there is the expectation that equipment will be signed out and signed back in, and there will be periodic accounting of the use of supplies.

Case Management Tracking for Building Materials

Case management for long-term recovery is also essential. During the early days when clearing debris and helping families prepare for repairs, there is less urgency about case management. Once repair work can be done there needs to be adequate and fair case management.

There are now computerized systems available through organizations specializing in case management that will track the use of building materials by case. Use it. The advantage of knowing what went into a rebuilding or repair project can not only assist the survivor who will live in the house but help your program demonstrate the effectiveness of your efforts.

Documentation for Distribution of Funds or Materials

Keep receipts. Keep distribution records. Keep signatures. When you receive a donation from someone you are responsible for being able to account for where it went or how it was consumed. At some future date a donor may come to you and ask: "What happened to my (money, building materials, tools)?" An embarrassed smile will not suffice. In order for your response to have credibility, you need to be able to demonstrate care in handling other people's resources.

Return of Capital Equipment, If Appropriate

If an external program provides funds for a truck, they may expect to get the truck at the end of the response. Be sure to be clear about that when the funds are received. Most programs will provide a document that must be signed before funds are received that will cover the disposition of capital assets at the end of the response. This only makes sense. Trucks are invaluable to disaster recovery programs, but it is wasteful to keep buying new trucks for each response. Many programs "recycle" their trucks by passing them on to the next disaster.

Financial Accounting

There are few absolutes in disaster response. One of them is adequate financial accounting. Donors will hold you accountable for the use of funds. The use of funds in a disaster response can be very flexible, but the one thing that is not flexible is the need to document where the money went, what it was used for, and why. It is absolutely critical that funds be accounted for accurately. It is simply no longer acceptable to say that funds cannot be accounted for because of the disaster. Get off on the right foot by being sure that procedures are in place to account for funds that are collected and how those funds are used.

Below are several tips that will help you keep out of trouble:

- **Never, ever make cash payments directly to survivors.** If a survivor has a need that is not covered by an existing benefit, provide the commodity that is needed or the service directly. If a survivor needs gas, pay the gas station. If a survivor needs food, provide the food.
- **Do not reimburse survivors for an out-of-pocket expenditure.**
- **Keep track of disbursements on behalf of survivors in case management files.** State and federal benefits are dependent on having accurate accounting of benefits provided by others.
- **Make the provision of service need-based rather than the same benefit for everyone.** When the same benefit is provided everyone regardless of need it becomes an entitlement, not a response. Once word gets out that you are providing the same thing to all survivors the line will be at your door.

Saying Thank You in Appropriate Ways

Say thank you frequently, loudly, and repeatedly.

Say thank you to donors with letters that acknowledge their specific gift, not a form letter where someone simply fills in the blank. Keep donors up to date about the progress of the response. Donating to a disaster is the first step in a relationship that may go on for years. Behave as though you expect that relationship to be a good one by keeping the communication positive, encouraging, and truthful.

It is not necessary to give something of value in return for a gift, but an acknowledgment that allows the person to identify their participation is both valued by the donor and encouraging to other potential donors. So, a button for their shirt or a bumper sticker may be more valued than a certificate that goes in a drawer.

Be candid about difficulties without blaming others. A donor should hear bad news from you before it appears in the press or through the grapevine. If mismanagement is discovered, it should be acknowledged quickly along with an explanation of what steps are being taken to ensure that it does not happen again.

Issues

- **Know who you are dealing with.** When people offer to help with the response, ask the basic questions you would if they were driving your new car: Who are you? Can I see some identification? Who are you affiliated with? It need not be an interrogation, but you should have enough information to be sure they have legitimacy. A simple form to register their participation can gather most of the information that you need.
- **Know the responsible party in the sending organization.** Talk with whomever they said is their sponsor. Understand their connection to the sending body. Are they covered by the sending body's liability insurance? Are they staff to that organization? Are they new to the organization?
- **Have a process for resolving conflict in the field.** Ideally, you would design a process before the disaster. Conflicts

will naturally arise, so it is best to anticipate how you will handle them before they arise.

- **Remember that all help is an implicit contract.** All help comes at a cost, either financial or nontangible. Decide how much you are willing to pay for the help you receive. Some kinds of help are simply too costly. Not all offers need to be accepted.
- **Develop a long-term relationship.** Disaster response and long-term recovery require a view toward developing long-term relationships. No one agency can do it all, provide all the resources, or know how to solve all of the thousands of problems that arise in any response. The only way to have a successful recovery is to develop relationships based on transparency, respect, and collaboration. Programs that live in the solution rather than in fault finding or competition will serve more clients and evolve as valued partners in recovery.
- **Decide how much promotion of the other organization is too much.** When another organization helps your response, you need to decide ahead of time how much promoting they will be permitted to do for their own organization either in the field or after returning home. Here are a few examples:
  - Can they leave promotional material to pick up in your office or in the work site?
  - Can they solicit *your* donor base?
  - Can they use survivors to tell their story?
  - Do they have permission to recorded audio or video for the purposes of fundraising?
  - Can they distribute contribution envelopes with their aid?
  - Can they have a list of ultimate recipients for use later in fund raising?

Saying Goodbye

In the midst of a disaster response, it is easy to lose track of time. Since the long-term success of recovery depends on good relationships, it is

NATIONAL VOAD MEMBERS

Adventist Community Services

America's Second Harvest

American Baptist Men/ USA

American Disaster Reserve

American Radio Relay League, Inc.

American Red Cross

Ananda Marga Universal Relief Team

Catholic Charities USA

Christian Disaster Response

Christian Reformed World Relief Committee

Church of the Brethren—Brethren Disaster Ministries

Church World Service

Churches of Scientology Disaster Response

Convoy of Hope

Disaster Psychiatry Outreach

Episcopal Relief and Development

Feed The Children

Friends Disaster Service, Inc.

HOPE Coalition America

Humane Society of the United States

International Aid

International Critical Incident Stress Foundation

International Relief and Development

International Relief Friendship Foundation

Lutheran Disaster Response

Medical Teams International

Mennonite Disaster Service

Mercy Medical Airlift (Angel Flight)

National Association of Jewish Chaplains

National Emergency Response Team

National Organization for Victim Assistance

Nazarene Disaster Response

Operation Blessing

Points of Light Foundation and Volunteer Center National Network

Presbyterian Church (U.S.A.)

REACT International, Inc.

Samaritan's Purse

Save the Children

Society of St. Vincent de Paul

Southern Baptist Convention

The Phoenix Society for Burn Survivors

The Salvation Army

Tzu Chi Foundation

United Church of Christ— Wider Church Ministries

United Jewish Communities

United Methodist Committee on Relief

United Way of America

Volunteers of America

World Vision

Figure 10.2

STATE AND LOCAL VOAD MEMBERS

Alabama VOAD
Alaska VOAD
American Samoa VOAD
Arizona VOAD
Arkansas VOAD
California Statewide Contacts
California VOAD—North
California VOAD—South
Colorado VOAD
Commonwealth of the Northern
  Marianas Islands VOAD
Connecticut VOAD
DC VOAD—Washington D.C.
Delaware VOAD
Florida VOAD
Georgia VOAD
GuamVOAD
Hawaii State VOAD
Idaho VOAD
Illinois—Adams County VOAD
Illinois VOAD
Indiana VOAD
Iowa VOAD
Kansas VOAD
Kentucky VOAD
Louisiana VOAD
Maine VOAD
Maryland VOAD
Massachusetts VOAD
Michigan VOAD
Minnesota VOAD
Mississippi VOAD
Missouri VOAD
Montana VOAD

Nebraska VOAD
Nevada VOAD
Northern Nevada VOAD
Southern Nevada COAD
New Hampshire VOAD
New Jersey VOAD
New Mexico VOAD
New York City VOAD
New York VOAD
North Carolina VOAD
North Dakota VOAD
Ohio VOAD
Oklahoma VOAD
Oregon VOAD
Pennsylvania VOAD
Puerto Rico VOAD
Red Cloud Indian School
Rhode Island VOAD
South Carolina VOAD
South Dakota VOAD
St. Croix VOAD
St. Thomas & St. John VOAD
Tennessee VOAD
Texas VOAD
Texas—Dallas
Utah VOAD
Vermont VOAD
Virginia—Northern Virginia VOAD
Virginia VOAD
Washington VOAD
West Virginia VOAD
Wisconsin VOAD
Wyoming VOAD

Figure 10.3

important to set aside time to say goodbye to response partners as they depart the field. The observance need not be big or expensive, it just needs to happen in a way that clearly expresses your appreciation for their help and identifies the unique contribution they have made to the recovery.

Several years prior to Hurricane Katrina, a spiritual care team was sent to Louisiana to respond to the aftermath of a hurricane that affected a small community of fishermen from Southeast Asia. The team came back saying, "We went, we tried to help, but frankly, I don't know what good we did." When the community was asked about the work of the team, people from the community could not say enough good about the team and the vital importance of what they had done to help.

The good wishes of the community were passed on to the team, but it would never be the same as hearing it directly from the people with whom they had worked. The moment was passed; the opportunity to build a relationship was gone. While many in the team continue to volunteer in other aspects of disaster response, as far as I know, the connection with that community has been lost.

Contrast that experience with the hundreds of teams that have been to Louisiana and Mississippi since Hurricane Katrina. Several community-based programs not only have a time set aside to say goodbye, but they continue to be in touch with those who have come to help. Not surprisingly, many of those teams have returned over and over again to continue their work. Saying goodbye with grace and thoughtfulness is not only the right thing to do, it strengthens your response and reminds the community that they are not in the recovery alone.

About the Contributor

Rev. John A. Robinson Jr., MDiv, is the associate for disaster response in the United States with Presbyterian Disaster Assistance, Presbyterian Church (U.S.A.). He has been involved in disaster response ministry, either as a volunteer or as paid staff, since he organized Interfaith Disaster Assistance after a category F4 tornado cut through Robeson County, North Carolina, in 1984. He is a graduate of the University of North Carolina at Greensboro and Union Theological Seminary in Virginia. John lives with his wife, Helen, in Winchester, Virginia. They have two sons, John Arron and John Andrew III.

11

Anniversaries, Holidays, and other Reminders

Imam Yusuf Hasan, BCC, and Rev. George Handzo, BCC

Editors' note: This chapter is intended specifically as a resource for congregants to help them when they approach anniversaries and holy days.

Events such as anniversaries, holidays, reunions, births, and deaths are important both in the lives of individuals and in the collective lives of families. As families are spread out and often do not live near one another, so these occasions may be the major times, or even the only times, we think about and are in touch with some members of our family. They are the times when we talk to them, remember them, catch up with what is going on in their lives, and recollect our lives together as a family. In short, they are the events that keep us connected to this most important community and reinforce our identities as members of a greater whole.

Conversely, any event that impedes our ability to connect in these ways isolates us and reduces our sense of being part of a family. Disasters that directly affect members of a family will likely impact that family in a number of ways. They can abruptly and sometimes permanently separate members of a family from one another without warning and preparation. They can also bring families together as they bring other communities together to support one another. Events such as holidays, births, deaths, and other family occasions then become the opportunities for playing out these sometimes contradictory influences. If nothing else, they give us an opportunity to integrate these traumatic events into our individual and collective lives. As we prepare for and live out these family events, it is important for us to be aware of how a disaster in the family's history continues to have an influence and needs to be taken into account. We also need to be aware of how these events provide continuity and normalcy for individuals and families affected by disaster.

One Family's Story

Editors' note: The family experience described below is that of the first author, Imam Yusuf Hasan.

We have a large family spread out across the country. Some of us have been close to each other all of our lives and some of us have become closer as we have become older. Since 1984 we've had family reunions every two years. Generally about 150 people attend, often coming on chartered buses from all over the county. In August 2005 we had a major reunion in New Orleans. At that time, over one hundred members of our extended family lived in and around New Orleans, many of them in the ninth ward. I remember very vividly how we enjoyed ourselves at the amusement park and at the picnics and banquets. As always, the reunion was a time when we were happy to be together and renew our relationships.

As Hurricane Katrina approached New Orleans, an aunt who lived in New Orleans died. Many of us from outside the area purchased airline tickets and prepared to travel to New Orleans for her funeral. Needless to say, we were not able to go to New Orleans, and there was no funeral. My aunt's body, which was in a funeral home when the hurricane struck, was eventually recovered, but no funeral was ever held. So, one of the immediate and lasting effects of Katrina for my family was the inability to mourn the loss of a beloved member of the family and even to know that she was properly buried. It was particularly difficult for us not to be able to be there or get close to our family at that particular time. This loss and the inability to properly observe my aunt's death continues to be a part of our family. In this instance, a disaster interrupted our family process and prevented us from observing an occasion that would have been very important to our whole family—even to those who had not planned to attend the funeral. Our anguish over not being able to go to New Orleans and be close to our family as the storm approached was compounded by our grieving the loss of a family member. It was difficult for us to lose an aunt, a mother's sister, and never have a chance to say goodbye with a formal service.

For a long time after the storm, we did not know whether many of our family members were alive or dead. Many of them had never left New Orleans in their lives. It was traumatic to know that they were likely in another state where they knew no one, scattered about, and trying to reach each other in panic. Meanwhile, the rest of the family was collecting money to support them. Often, it was impossible to even get this support to them. Two years after the event many of our family were still not established back at home. Some were in Texas. Some were in other parts of Louisiana. For our family, Katrina remained very much both a present and a past tragedy, highlighting how long the effects of events like this can persist in the life of a family. It is also forever linked to my aunt's death.

The Role of Family Events

How can we help one another cope with the effects of these tragedies, mishaps, and calamites? How can family events be both a resource and an impediment in this process?

In August 2007 we held our first family reunion since Katrina. The coincidence of this event with the second anniversary of Katrina and the second anniversary of my aunt's death gave it special meaning. The matriarch of our family attended, along with about fifty family members from New Orleans. Of the 160 attendees, thirty-three were under the age of thirteen. Significantly, the children of the aunt who died in New Orleans attended for the first time.

In planning any family anniversary, reunion, or similar event, or in celebrating any significant family occasion in the aftermath of a disaster, several levels of need should be accommodated. You should consider the special needs of those who were directly involved in the disaster as opposed to those who were not. You should consider the needs of different age groups and those with different degrees of relationship, especially those of the same generation. You should hold in tension the need to remember and process the effects of the disaster and the need to move on. Lastly, you should always understand that individuals need to feel free to participate in the event only to the degree that they choose, no matter what others think they should do.

Needs of the Survivors

You need to anticipate that those closest to the disaster will have the most lasting effects and wounds that are deeper and therefore heal more slowly. At any point in time, they will not be as far along the continuum of returning to "normal." As mentioned, many of our family who survived Katrina were still not resettled two years after the storm, or had to relocate entirely. While many of the rest of us have been able to move on with our lives, the aftermath of Katrina is still a daily reality for them. After any kind of major loss or disaster, the first set of anniversaries, holidays, or other such events will bring its own challenges as participants work to integrate the particular loss into their routine. The first Thanksgiving dinner without the person who sat at the head of the table for years confronts the family with the reality of their loss, but also helps the family move on through seeing someone else sitting in the chair. For our family from New Orleans, the August 2007 reunion was their first chance to reunite with family from other parts of the country. For them, this was far from a routine reunion. For the whole family, this was the first reunion without our beloved aunt and sister.

Our goal was to take this dynamic seriously while not allowing it to dominate the event. We went out of our way to welcome those from New Orleans without making them feel self-conscious. We wanted to make sure that they felt loved and cared for, and that they could relax and enjoy the company of one another in surroundings that felt safe and secure. We wanted to make sure that when they returned home they would have a great memory. We honored their need to talk about what life was like for them, as well as their need to simply enjoy the fun and find something "normal" in their lives. We wanted it to be safe for them to talk about their hurt and anxieties or to simply get away from that reality if they chose.

Generational Needs

As mentioned, many of the attendees of the reunion were children. Many of them were from New Orleans. In general, children are less able to cope well with loss and exposure to disaster; some of this inability has to do with a lack of skill in verbalizing feelings and asking for help directly. Also, the everyday survival demands a disaster puts on adults often leaves them with little time or other resources to pay attention to their children. However, children do draw consolation from being in familiar groups and from doing the normal tasks of life. Children need opportunities to grieve, but also opportunities to move away from their grief to play. They express many of their feelings through activity rather than words. Family events and celebrations, such as holidays and birthdays, give children the opportunity to be assured that their life is going on. It also gives them a safe environment to process some of the feelings they do not feel free to express otherwise.

In planning our reunion, we were very aware that many of the children had lived for two years under the stress of relocation and crowded conditions with no mental health support available to them. Having the major part of the reunion in a park gave us the perfect opportunity to have an abundance of time for both free play and organized games. Children who recently had not had the opportunity to play in a safe, well-equipped environment could do so. We also had two child psychologists in attendance in case any of the children wanted to talk about their experiences. Finally, at the banquet, each child was called on individually and given a special gift so that he or she would feel special in the midst of the greater family. Even though the event was not about the children specifically, we were able to use the time and opportunity to do some things that hopefully helped their healing.

The other group we paid special attention to was the elderly. We were aware that my mother and her five surviving siblings had not had the opportunity to grieve together for their sister who died in New Orleans and never had a funeral. So, the reunion became an opportunity to do some of the work that would have been done at the funeral. We made sure they had time together for that purpose.

While using religious beliefs and practices to cope with loss is not restricted to the elderly, older people are more likely to want to incorporate religious rituals and practices into these special occasions. They may want to go to a worship service at a local church, synagogue, mosque, or temple, especially if the place itself holds special meaning for them. They may want to read their holy books alone or together.

They may want to include prayer as a part of the occasion. Even if the day itself is marked by partying, laughter, and jokes, some people might want to maintain a somber tone—at least for themselves. They might want to remember God more during those particular times.

Remembering—the Role of Ritual

It is safe to say that every special event in a family has rituals attached to it. These may be formal and religious in nature or they may be patterns of behavior that we think of as traditions and that describe the way we normally do things around a certain occasion. For example, Thanksgiving may always be celebrated at a certain family member's house. The meal may always include certain dishes prepared according to a certain recipe. Certain people may always be in charge of certain parts of the meal. It may be expected that part of the day is devoted to telephoning members of the family who are elsewhere. As children grow up and marry, the tradition is amended according to which side of the family the couple will generally spend Thanksgiving with. As members of the family die or are no longer able to fulfill their normal roles, decisions have to be made about who will take their place. Making these decisions, by whatever process, affirms the permanence of the family. It communicates, at least implicitly, that the family will go on despite losses and other changes and will continue to be a support to individuals within it.

Rituals are extremely important to our lives in numerous ways. They function as formularized interactions that affirm our relationship to each other and to powers beyond ourselves. They are patterns of behavior that we share in common. Especially in the context of disaster, they affirm and confirm that life goes on. They represent the normal and the expected. They can also represent, as in the case of a wedding or a funeral, processes for incorporating new members into the family or saying goodbye to other members. They often have ways to incorporate changes in the family experience built into them. Conversely, if rituals or traditions are interrupted, it often signals that life is unreliable, maybe even random.

After disaster has affected a family or some members of it, it is extremely important to continue treasured rituals and, to the extent possible, to observe special occasions in the usual way. At our recent reunion, in addition to the many rituals normative to the reunion itself, such as the banquet, we celebrated two birthdays. We also remembered in prayer our aunt who died and two members of the family from New Orleans who remain missing. Through these simple rituals we gave place to the grieving that Katrina had both caused and prevented us from expressing. We also reaffirmed that while Katrina could change our family, it did not destroy it. We would continue to celebrate our life together.

Moving On

At our reunion, we wanted to have an opportunity for everyone to laugh and cry together because it both helps us to remember and helps us to move on. It is about being in the moment, and getting past the moment at the same time. Some need to remember what they went through, as opposed to forgetting about it or not thinking about it. As we move on, we also need to remember that not all members of the family feel close to one another or even like one another. Rather than trying to fix this, we need to recognize it. It is important to recognize that we may not be the person to help anyone at some particular point. We might recruit someone else to be with them or someone else to talk with them. We need to recognize the helpers in the group and those who need help. If a person needs help, we need to recognize who will be helpful to them and who will not.

Respect for Individual Differences

As important as special occasions are, and as important as the family community can be in the aftermath of a disaster, one danger is that this focus can lead to a presumption that everyone has the same needs and that being fully present at a special occasion is at least part of the solution to those needs. It becomes easy to think that since these occasions are generally helpful, everyone should participate fully because everyone will be helped by them. It becomes easy for members of the family to cross the line from encouraging people to participate to pressuring people to participate and presuming that something is wrong with them if they do not. This dynamic can turn a positive, growth-producing occasion into one that effectively ostracizes certain members of the family and adds to any feelings of loss and guilt they may have rather than helping to relieve those feelings.

No two people are the same. In the context of the family group, it is always important to meet people where they are, taking into consideration how they are feeling, what they are thinking, and how they are processing the events around them. It is always good to ask how the individual wishes to be helped and to what degree they wish to participate or not participate in any activity or occasion. What does the individual want done for them and with them during these holidays and personal days? Some people cope with laughter, and some cope by lashing out. Some people want to talk continuously, and others want to be silent.

Some people try to go on with their lives and ignore that something serious has happened. While this situation can indicate that the person has needs that are not being expressed, some people truly do not need to address these issues because they are actually able to cope with them on their own. Every human being has their own coping mechanisms, and it is important for us to help them identify those and use them to the best of their ability rather than assuming we know what is best for them.

Not only do people speak differently, but they hear differently. Words that might be comforting to one person might be offensive to another. Be very careful in how you talk to individuals going through traumatic situations. As always, when unsure of what to say, simply listening is better than speaking.

Be willing to respond to the person's needs as he or she expresses them. If someone has had enough of the group and needs to go for a walk, be ready to go along. Be clear with the person that this private time is confidential. Provide safe spaces for people who have experienced traumatic situations. It is important to read body language and respond to it. This need for time away is likely to be especially important for children who are more easily overwhelmed by the emotions of the group.

While it is important to allow individuals to cope in their own way, it is also true that not all ways of coping are helpful. The person who, after a disaster, begins to consume too much alcohol at special occasions or evidences seemingly uncontrollable episodes of anger or crying is in need of assistance. Likewise, the person who used to be the life of the party but is now withdrawn and uncommunicative may not be coping well. In general, any person whose behavior changes dramatically after a disaster is a source of concern. Gentle inquires, first with those closest to the person, and then with the person themselves about how they are coping are appropriate. Especially if the person admits to not coping well, encouragement to find professional counseling is in order.

Final Words

Special occasions are important in the lives of individuals and families. They can be times of great healing, where the wounds inflicted by a disaster are tended to and processed. They can also be times that add stress to the lives of those already coping with a great deal of suffering. I have used the example of my own family and our experience coping with the losses inflicted by Hurricane Katrina in the hope that it will provide some concrete examples of the issues that need to be taken into account around these occasions and some ways we chose to deal with them.

Further Reading

Johannes, E. M. *A Flood of Emotions: The Anniversary.* National Network for Child Care, 1994. http://www.nncc.org/Guidance/flood.anniversary.html.

Anniversary Reactions to a Traumatic Event: The Recovery Process Continues. SAMSHA's National Mental Health Center, guide NMH02-0140. http://mental health.samhsa.gov/publications/allpubs/NMH02-0140/default.asp.

Kamboukos, Demy, Joel McClough, and Marylene Cloitre. *Preparing for the Anniversary of 9/11: A Teacher's Guide.* Families Forward, Institute for Trauma and Resilience, NYU Child Study Center. http://www.aboutourkids.org/aboutour/articles/911_guide_teacher_2007.pdf.

About the Contributors

Imam Yusuf Hasan, BCC, is a board-certified chaplain in the Association of Professional Chaplains. He worked with Rabbi Stephen B. Roberts, coeditor of this book, in the years prior to 9/11, helping create a disaster chaplaincy response organization in New York City, within the American Red Cross; was trained as an American Red Cross SAIR Team member; and was one of the first disaster spiritual care responders in New York after 9/11. He did his clinical pastoral education at The HealthCare Chaplaincy (HCC) and is an assistant imam at Masjid Malcolm Shabazz in New York City. Imam Hasan has been staff chaplain at Memorial Sloan-Kettering Cancer Center and St. Luke's Roosevelt Hospital, partner institutions of The HealthCare Chaplaincy, for over fourteen years. Imam Hasan is the author and coauthor of numerous articles and chapters in the area of providing pastoral and spiritual care, especially for the Islamic community. He has lectured around the country and appeared on national television, including PBS's "Religion" and "Ethics NewsWeekly" and "NBC Nightly News," numerous radio stations, and newspapers and magazines, including *Newsweek* magazine.

Rev. George Handzo, BCC, holds a bachelor of arts degree from Princeton University, a master of divinity degree from Yale University Divinity School, and a master of arts in educational psychology from Jersey City State College. He did his clinical pastoral education at Yale-New Haven Hospital and Lutheran Medical Center, Brooklyn, New York, and is ordained in the Evangelical Lutheran Church in America. Rev. Handzo is vice president of pastoral care leadership and practice at The HealthCare Chaplaincy (HCC) in New York City and leads HCC's consulting service. He was director of chaplaincy services at Memorial Sloan-Kettering Cancer Center, a partner institution of The HealthCare Chaplaincy, for over twenty years. Rev. Handzo is the author of numerous articles and chapters in the area of pastoral and spiritual care and the book *Health Care Chaplaincy in Oncology,* coauthored with Dr. Laurel Burton. He has lectured widely, including at Johns Hopkins University and the American College of Healthcare Executives Congress. Rev. Handzo is a board-certified chaplain in the Association of Professional Chaplains and is a past president of that organization.

12

Memorial Services, Site Visits, and Other Rituals

Rev. Earl E. Johnson, MDiv, BCC

How would you like your life to be remembered, celebrated, mourned? Who would you want to carry you to your grave? What would you want to be said or done at your funeral? Would you want words that are according to the rituals of your faith tradition, or an even more personal act or gesture significant to only yourself and your loved ones? What would you want done in the case that your body was never found? Death around disaster raises many questions.

How people die affects any public rituals of mourning (that is, those open to anyone beyond the immediate family). Public and private grief can be vastly different. When death is combined with a major catastrophe, the equation of public grief and private mourning becomes complicated. Politics enters the public grief equation, fueled by media.

As spiritual care providers and leaders of faith communities, it is vital that we step forward at these times. Mourning rituals are our domain and the area we know best. It is essential at times of disasters that we work hard to identify the agenda of those wishing to be involved in the mourning process. Further, at a time of unanticipated traumatic bereavement we need to work hard to keep the focus on what the deceased may have wanted, making sure those most closely related are empowered and clearly heard.

Public memorial services around disasters of any size often combine faith with power, the intensely private with the curious public, and the issues and needs of a house of worship with those of the state. There is much room for beauty and grace. There is also much room for insensitivity and outrage.

All Grieving Rituals Honored

Although site visits and memorial services may share many similarities, each is unique. Site visits and memorial services may be extremely helpful in assisting individuals and communities to mourn and celebrate the lives of loved ones and times now gone, but disaster response practitioners with little or no training, and far less common sense, may state that families need the above rituals for "closure." They believe that, somehow, visiting the site where the plane went down or the bridge fell, and then attending a funeral, will meet all the needs of survivors and family members or friends of those lost.

In reality, complex disasters cannot be equalized or defused simply through timely mourning rituals. But sensitive and safe site visits and memorial services can help the process begin. No one gets over anything. "Time heals all wounds" is a common expression. While it may be comforting to some, the conventional wisdom is that after accumulated trauma, response may be the opposite.

Listen

How disaster victims die, disappear, or are injured is critical information. However, what their families want regarding funerals, memorial services and site visits at this time needs to be honored as the primary center of attention and action.

Disasters are not simple. They are extremely complex events. Disasters, no matter their size, are ultimately local, as they occur in communities. The communities responding to those disasters are affected emotionally and spiritually (not to mention physically or materially). First responders, the fire and police, medical teams, and public safety personnel have specialized training, preparation, and screening to deal with life hazards and people to rescue and recover. They also have their humanity and their own needs. Twenty-four-hour media saturation can also victimize sensitive groups of electronic witnesses. Finally, our elected representatives who are empowered to serve and protect us also often assume, or presume, "first mourner" status with mixed results.

After a disaster, two requests are often made. The families of those affected often wish to visit the site where their loved ones were injured or died, with the request of privacy. It is also common for non–family members to exert public pressure to have a large memorial service open to the press and politicians.

The first and most important consideration that spiritual care providers have when helping facilitate either a site visit or memorial service, after the safety of the participants has been ensured, is to see that the wishes of the families and loved ones of those lost are honored. The memorial service and/or site visit should be about the families' and loved ones' needs for healing and hope, not the needs or interests of the public or the media.

Protect

Each catastrophe may bring another catastrophe, as those entrusted to our protection and safety may have been compromised by the disaster event. People may be on their own for the first three or four days after a natural disaster, many without food, shelter, or clean water. The daily hygiene and necessary medicine for both the able-bodied and the young, infirm, impaired, physically challenged, incarcerated, or hospitalized may also be nonexistent. Preexisting conditions or needs are often exacerbated by disasters.

Especially for post-disaster rituals such as site visits and memorial services, special needs populations must be considered in the planning at all stages for these events. Their safety and needs must not go unheard, particularly if they have close relationships with the deceased or injured, or if they have suffered injury themselves. Accommodations must be made to ensure they are heard and their needs are met. Protecting the needs of the most vulnerable is always part of the responsibilities of spiritual care providers helping plan these events. Your holy responsibility at these difficult times is to help ensure that all reasonable requests are honored.

Equally important, and often overlooked, is that families should be allowed to define whom they consider "family." If those in charge only consider the legal definition of marriage, vast segments of the deceased family and friends might be excluded, causing conflict and challenges that distract from the rituals at hand. Negotiations for estranged former family members can occur and accommodations made. Separation may be necessary as the intensity of the disaster may bring up much residual anger and history that, unaddressed, could impede the dignity of a site visit or memorial service. Mental health and spiritual care professional resources need to be both alerted and present to work with issues that may surface.

Keep the Focus on the Families and Loved Ones

In high-profile or publicized disasters, politicians, public officials, and even foreign dignitaries may wish to be included as representatives of the greater public good will, and to demonstrate compassion for the suffering of those now mourning. What may have been under control and manageable suddenly requires multiple accommodations for this celebrity and its accompanying media.

A seasoned events manager may need to be employed to oversee many competing entities for access to the bereaved and the evening news.

Do not be distracted or seduced by the spotlight. Work together with a team of like-minded spiritual care and mental health professionals to keep the needs and wishes of family members and loved ones primary. Only this type of focus will ensure the success of these post-disaster rituals. Listen to the family and loved ones. If they do not desire a memorial service, which is a real possibility in many disasters, do not impose one on them to endure and fake their way through, or paternalistically declare what they need or what will be "good for them" or "the appropriate thing to do."

Keep the focus on those lost. Perhaps include a litany of their names during a candle-lighting ceremony, with loved ones lighting each candle. Work hard to make sure that the focus is not on those who have chosen to attend as "representatives of the people."

Response and rescue authorities now limit access of elected officials and dignitaries to disaster events and family assistance centers. Each visit costs the rescue and recovery teams up to a day in lost time as preparations must be made to secure the perimeter and screen all who are working at the site. While the greater public may be reassured that the nation cares, many of these visits are distractions to the matter at hand. Further, they may delay the recovery of a loved one's remains and thus exacerbate the anger by survivors and family members at public officials for the disaster's occurrence. Those entrusted to our public welfare and safety may feel doubly compromised in the days and months after the disaster as investigations reveal cause. The emotional and spiritual violation of mourners can assign blame if maintenance was deferred for political expediency.

What Is "Normal"?

Everyone grieves in their own way and in their own time, and what may be considered reasonable to most, does not matter when loved ones have been lost in the horrendous ways of disasters.

Do not allow anyone's expectations or assumptions for what should happen interfere with what actually does happen when a family member or loved one arrives. Many cultures grieve loudly and physically and together in a large, extended group of mourners. Physical safety should be ensured in advance at a site visitation, as loved ones on a beach, cliffside, or similarly dangerous site may seek to "join" the deceased by entering the water or throwing themselves in harm's way. Be prepared for any eventuality and make no judgments about what is appropriate.

Survivors often become fixated on their loved ones' last minutes and relive their trauma. Health care professionals may need to provide sedation, and public safety officers may be needed for physical restraint at site visits. Hopefully other family members will intervene and provide the necessary support if needed, but perimeters of compassion and support, with well-trained and supervised personnel are essential. Nothing may be more important than recruiting spiritual care professionals who know how to claim authority and when to intervene.

Preparedness, including rehearsals and step-by-step planning with all involved, is mandatory. If you don't have time to organize and do a site visit or memorial service sensitively and well, you are inviting more grief. One contingency unconsidered—if a family member is injured or even killed during a site visit, or if people are excluded from a memorial service or ritual because of rigid adherence to an archaic state or federal law—may compound the trauma of the disaster event itself.

Issues in Planning a Site Visit

Finding the appropriate time for a site visit is important. In planning a site visit, work with the various agencies and governmental representatives in your area to help facilitate and expedite the movement of the families and loved ones who will to travel to the site of the disaster event. The decision to travel may take a few days, as families may make a decision to travel only after the reality of the disaster starts to sink in and the human compulsion to journey to the physical site where their loved ones passed on sets in. The site visit should be planned to take place only after the public agency responsible for investigating criminal acts, mechanical failures, or accidents, have ensured that all human remains have been recovered. Further, you should receive assurances that the physical site is safe for grieving loved ones to visit. Finally, make sure that the perimeter of the area remains private so that a supportive visit to a place of great loss can occur without media or politicians present. This task is often quite hard to accomplish but is essential

Transportation disasters often occur not on land but in remote areas that are inaccessible. Creative spiritual care providers in these situations should think about adapting rituals such as having baskets of fresh flowers dropped by helicopters at the disaster site and videotaped for each family, lighting candles on a secluded beach for each person killed or injured, releasing balloons for each person killed or injured, and the like. While these are all symbolic acts, these types of activities often provide essential rituals for the spiritual and emotional safety of those present.

When organizing transportation to and from site visits and memorial services plan to have spiritual care, health, and mental health professionals on every bus carrying family members. Other considerations to keep in mind are for the religious and cultural needs—such as hand washing, prayers, diet, and hydration—of those attending. Having child care provided by trained and properly screened disaster clinicians is also essential. Finally, ensure that disaster survivors, along with their families and loved ones, are separated from the families and loved ones of those who did not survive the disaster event.

After a disaster site is declared safe for a visit by family and loved ones, a tradition has developed to create a temporary "shrine" filled with pictures, notes, and flowers within eyesight of the disaster's epicenter, or Ground Zero, or site of impact. Generally, a perimeter fence or hay bales stacked can provide a point of focus for this commemoration. Remember, though, that one person's hay bale shrine may be another's stepping stone to secure a better, unobstructed view of the incident site. Plan for all eventualities. Developing a detailed plan for a site visit and a memorial service that is inclusive and sensitive to all is key.

Issues in Planning a Memorial Service

A memorial service may include many aspects of a religious service, but planners must be inclusive and accommodate an interfaith ritual without preference to a majority faith tradition. *Respect for all faith traditions, as well as those who claim no faith tradition, must be ensured.* This is a nonnegotiable characteristic of a public, nongovernmental assembly.

Skillful and diplomatic leadership is required in setting up a memorial service. Consultation should take place with current religious professionals that have preexisting relationships with family members. It is important to ensure that these faith leaders with preexisting relationships to families of those affected by the disaster can easily accompany them to the service. The most effective way to accomplish this is to have them being considered as extended members of the "family" for ID and badging purposes.

Liturgists and speakers should be recruited only after long consultations with family members, community leaders, first responder chaplains, and disaster mental health professionals. A clear understanding of the purpose of a public gathering must be stated. It is important to remember and highlight for others who may not be aware that a public memorial service for the affected community has a different purpose and desired outcome than a funeral service for individual victims or a private memorial service for family and extended family. Each assembly is unique and serves different functions.

No leader of either a public or private memorial service should impose his or her own religious beliefs or traditions on this assembly. Respect for all faith traditions as well as those who claim no tradition is nonnegotiable. Although a familiar reading or liturgy can be comforting for the majority of those present, a particular tradition should not be used to intimidate or subject that tradition over the faith traditions of others, especially at such an emotionally fraught time. To comfort some at the expense of others is not to bow to political correctness or to compromise religious tenets; it is to be insensitive at least and cruel at worst, as the speakers claim to hold their preeminence above the beliefs and wishes of some who mourn. This is a time for compassion and presence, not a time for conviction and recruitment.

Ethical spiritual leadership and shared mission of service, comfort, protection, and absence of gain from the suffering and vulnerability of others is basic. Identifying partners and team members who share the same high ethical standards and missions is crucial in developing a memorial service.

Media

Maintaining privacy of all mourners is essential. News media should be advised on pool coverage responsibilities and honor agreements. No mourners should be doubly violated by having their privacy disregarded with intrusive cameras that compromise the dignity of any event honoring the dead.

Disasters are not entertainment, especially for survivors and the loved ones of survivors and those killed. The public diet for voyeurism and curiosity about these events should not be nurtured, sold, or served. Public commerce and the need to know is secondary to the privacy and feelings of those mourning. A grieving widow or partner, a child's tears or salute, may produce a memorable photo or television image, but taken without permission at an event where the mourner has been promised safety and is experiencing intense emotional vulnerability, is an ethical violation that spiritual care providers must always protect against.

Control What Is Controllable

Depending upon the event, its scale and intensity, and the proximity of its victims and survivors and their loved ones, it may be impossible to control all aspects—the personal, the professional, and the political.

A site visit or memorial service is often taken away from the social agencies and professionals who have the experience and knowledge accumulated from numerous deployments and events. Mayors, governors, presidents, or other heads of state may decide that, as the elected or hereditary leaders of a people, they are in charge and will dictate what should occur in a public mourning ritual.

There will always be someone who self-deploys and self-promotes, someone who knows what other people need, whether those people realize it or not, and fails to listen to the families and loved ones of those injured or killed in the disaster. Be prepared.

Final Words

Disaster response may be the social action of our time. For leaders of faith communities, disaster response holds special mission and is integrated with religious beliefs and mandates.

Protecting those who survive is sacred in all faith traditions and is common sense for those of no faith tradition. Providing a ritual, a place to grieve, that is safe and where the injuries of loss cannot be compounded by further loss and injury, is also a highly held disaster spiritual care virtue. Providing hospitality for those who grieve, both the familiar face and the stranger, and tending to their needs and their dependents, are basic tenets as well as ultimate virtues and tasks. Knowing how to keep the gate, allowing those near and dear to enter without prejudice, and when to close the gate, may be based upon a lifetime of experience or the collective wisdom of like-minded spiritual care professionals.

Listen to the loved ones. Listen to what they want. Listen to their hopes. Honor and respect their feelings. Accommodate their requests and keep them safe and protected from invasive media, religious leaders, and politicians. Knowing that those we take care of today may take care of us tomorrow.

About the Contributor

Rev. Earl E. Johnson, MDiv, BCC, is an American Red Cross (ARC) Spiritual Care Response Team volunteer partner, located at ARC headquarters in Washington, D.C. Since stepping into this position in 2002, he oversees the training and deployment of almost two hundred professional board-certified chaplains who respond on behalf of their various professional chaplaincy associations through ARC to aviation and transportation incidents, as well as a variety of disasters including Hurricane Katrina, the four Florida hurricanes of 2005, and other disasters of national scope and importance. He is a board-certified chaplain and member of the Association of Professional Chaplains (APC) and the Association for Clinical Pastoral Education. In 2006 he was the recipient of the Distinguished Service Award by the APC. He is an ordained Christian Church (Disciples of Christ) minister and a former hospital chaplain in New York City and Washington, D.C.

PART II

Special Needs

13

Compassion Fatigue

Rabbi Stephen B. Roberts, BCJC; Kevin L. Ellers, Dmin;
and Rev. John C. Wilson, PhD

Editors' note: This chapter is divided into two sections. The first is practical and intended to provide detailed information to spiritual care providers on how to prevent and heal compassion fatigue. This section is both intentionally short and primarily in figure or list form so that you can easily work with and implement the suggestions. The second section is more academic and provides the research and academic background on compassion fatigue as it relates to clergy and disasters.

Section 1: Compassion Fatigue—Practical Information to Help Prevent and Overcome It

The professional work centered on the relief of the emotional suffering of clients automatically includes absorbing information that is about suffering. Often it includes absorbing that suffering as well. [1]

What is compassion fatigue? In simple-to-understand language, compassion fatigue is the "cost of caring" of working with victims of trauma or catastrophic events *that shows itself as spiritual, physical and/or emotional fatigue and exhaustion.* It comes about as a result of caregiving that causes a decrease in the caregiver's ability to experience joy or to feel and care for and about others.[2]

Who is at risk of experiencing compassion fatigue? Any person who is a "helping professional," who provides assistance or aid to others, is at risk for compassion fatigue. In addition to congregational clergy and chaplains in a variety of settings, this includes first responders such as police, firefighters, and emergency medical personnel who directly experience or witness trauma. It also includes those mental health professionals who experience trauma secondhand, such as therapists, counselors, psychiatrists, social workers, and pastoral counselors.

Why are clergy[3] at high risk to get compassion fatigue in general? Clergy, in almost all settings and all vocations, care for others day in and day out. We are often called upon to support individuals, families, and communities after a death, when families are confronted with illness, when congregants have been the victim of a violent crime, when there is violence in the schools, when communities hurt because of cultural or religious conflicts.

Understanding Limitations

A common pitfall for caregivers after a disaster is a failure to understand and define their own limits while setting appropriate boundaries relating to their capacity to care. Survivors will always have more needs than the caregiver can meet. Healthy caregivers must carefully understand and weigh the limits of their capacity to care in a given situation. This understanding is important when determining what a survivor can do alone and what they need us to help with. Known limits help prevent caregivers from attempting to carry unnecessary responsibility for outcomes over which they can ultimately have little control.

An unbalanced system of care that overextends beyond the acute crisis phase can create an unhealthy dynamic of overdependency on the caregiver. This in turn hinders a survivor's natural and essential coping mechanisms, and sets the caregiver up for compassion fatigue.

Too often caregivers wait until the emotional pileup becomes overwhelming to react, instead of draining their emotional sponge daily. It is critical that caregivers take time to do the following limit-setting exercises on a daily basis:

- Define your mission in providing care in the particular context
- Clearly define your limitations for care you can offer
- Identify what else can be done by the survivor, others, and God

- Focus on the positive impact of your care
- Leave your time of providing care by developing a ritual that allows you to reflect on your care and turning survivors over to God
- Remember that you are responsible *to* people, not *for* people

Preventing Compassion Fatigue

Preventing compassion fatigue after a disaster is both extremely hard and easy. It is easy in that the prevention steps involve basic self-care. It is hard in that after a disaster practicing self-care is often on the bottom of our to-do list. We encourage you, in the strongest terms, to read chapter 2, which covers self-care in more detail. Follow the suggestions. *Practice self-care. That is the number one way to prevent compassion fatigue.* After a disaster, when there are so many demands on your time and energy, self-care is one of the hardest things you will ever do. Preventing compassion fatigue is very much about applying the lesson from the fable regarding the rabbit and the turtle. Like the rabbit, you can go fast out of the gate, not take care of yourself by taking care of your congregation in the days, weeks, and months after the disaster, and then end up leaving the congregation and possibly even ministry. Or, like the turtle, you can go a little slower, take time for yourself, eat well, get enough sleep, converse with colleagues, and as the months go along take some vacation time so that you will remain with your congregations for many years.

Research and field findings have led to some suggestions about some very specific ways to prevent compassion fatigue. A significant issue involved with compassion fatigue is isolation. "One of the ways trauma seems to affect us all, caregivers included, is to leave us with a sense of disconnected isolation. A common thread we have found with sufferers of compassion fatigue symptoms has been the progressive loss in their sense of connections and community. Many caregivers become increasingly isolated as their symptoms of compassion fatigue increase. Fear of being perceived as weak, impaired, or incompetent by peers and clients, along with time constraints and loss of interest, have all been cited by caregivers suffering from compassion fatigue as reasons for diminished intimate and collegial connection."[4]

Below are some further areas and tools that are effective ways to prevent compassion fatigue.

Supervision

- Find a supervisor you are comfortable with, such as a clinical social worker or spiritual guide.
- You might need to meet with two or three people before you find the right person. It is more important that you find the right person than go with the first person you meet.
- Meet with your supervisor on a regularly scheduled basis, at least twice a month. After a disaster, more is better, not less.
- Practice self-supervision, such as positive self-talk, working on changing or reframing your perceptions and thoughts.
- Seek short- or long-term assistance from a professional with an expertise in compassion fatigue and the ability to resolve the personal and professional issues of compassion fatigue.

Connectedness

- Attend a clergy peer support group. Help create one if there is not already one in your area.
- Participate in a clergy peer study group. Again, help create one if there is not one already going that you can participate in.
- Attend your denomination's regional and annual gatherings. Find colleagues to share your experiences with one on one.
- Take a class not related to your work.
- Intentionally build time into your calendar for your family. In particular, set aside one night or day a week just for your spouse. Put it in your calendar as a meeting. Eat a meal together. If you have children, ask family, friends, or congregants to watch them so you have private time.

- Intentionally build time into your calendar to spend with your children. This must be scheduled time or it will not happen. This should also be a nonbusy time in which you can communicate. It does not need to be a long period of time, but it should be a regular time so your child can count on it. It could be walking the dog in the morning, taking them to school or picking them up, or washing the dinner dishes.

Self-Focus

- Follow the example of the Creator in most sacred texts— take a day off weekly.
- Religiously schedule time for practicing your spiritual tools such as prayer, meditation, and reading of sacred texts.
- Practice stress reduction and find ways to laugh.
- Remind yourself on a regular basis that your best is all you can do.
- Be intentional about maintaining a balance between the work and personal life.
- Become a nonanxious presence.
- Be intentional instead of reactive to people, places, things, and situations.
- Develop new skills and knowledge. If possible, take a class at a local seminary to remind yourself of why you became a leader of a faith community.
- Take vacation—religiously. Retreats of various kinds are helpful also.

What Are Some of the Warning Signs of Compassion Fatigue?

Warning signs and symptoms of compassion fatigue include:

- Inability to maintain balance of empathy and objectivity
- Chronic tardiness when this had not been an issue before
- Increased absenteeism or tardiness
- Losing hope
- Lowered self-esteem

- Decreased feelings of joy and happiness in general
- Decreased enjoyment of vocation or career
- Diminished sense of purpose
- Lowered frustration tolerance and increased irritability
- Outbursts of anger or rage
- Depression
- Hypervigilance
- Hypertension
- Increased substance use or abuse
- Change in eating habits
- Blaming self or others
- Extreme fatigue
- Frequent headaches
- Workaholism
- Sleep disturbances

What Should I Do If I Am Experiencing Some of the Warning Signs of Compassion Fatigue?

If you experience any of the signs of compassion fatigue, follow the practical strategies listed in the section of this chapter entitled "Preventing Compassion Fatigue." Immediately take steps to find time for you. Further, reread chapter 2 on self-care and begin to follow the suggestions. Saying "It (compassion fatigue) will go away on its own" is not a recommended course of action.

How Do I Know If I Am Experiencing Compassion Fatigue?

Compassion fatigue has many symptoms. Many are similar to those experienced by the traumatized congregants the clergy are working with. Some of the symptoms of compassion fatigue include:

- Dread of working with certain congregants
- Difficulty separating work life from personal life
- Nightmares
- Images of congregants' traumas
- Recurring or intrusive thoughts or images

- Silencing or minimizing congregants' stories
- Difficulty concentrating
- Elevated or exaggerated "startle" response
- Avoiding thoughts, feelings, conversations, or places associated with trauma
- Lack of interest or participation in meaningful or enjoyable activities
- Decreased functioning in nonprofessional situations
- Feeling a lack of skill with certain congregants about issues you previously felt certain about
- Loss of hope—hopelessness
- Lack of energy and enthusiasm
- Increased transference or countertransference issues with certain congregants
- Depression or constant sadness
- Mood swings
- Rigidity, perfectionism, or obsession about details
- Thoughts of self-harm or harm to others
- Questioning the meaning of life
- Loss of purpose in life
- Anger at God, loss of faith in God, or questioning religious beliefs
- Decreased interest in intimacy and sex
- Isolation or withdrawing from others, or loneliness
- Increase in interpersonal conflicts and/or staff conflicts

Recovering from Compassion Fatigue

Research has shown that compassion fatigue is very responsive to treatment. Seek professional help immediately with someone who has experience in this field. The hardest part of treatment is often just acknowledging you are experiencing the symptoms and accepting that you have compassion fatigue.

The most widely used model to treat compassion fatigue is the Accelerated Recovery Program (ARP) developed by Gentry, Baranowsky, and Dunning in 1997. This program is a five-session model designed to address both prevention and treatment for a broad range of professionals. Program goals are to identify symptoms; recognize compassion fatigue triggers; identify and utilize resources; review personal and professional history to the present day; master arousal reduction methods; learn grounding and containment skills; contract for life enhancement; resolve impediments to efficacy; initiate conflict resolution; and implement supportive aftercare plan.[5]

There are many other treatments also available. The professional you work with should be able to describe the options open to you.

Section 2: Research, Spiritual Care Providers, and Disasters

Compassion fatigue is a relatively new concept. The first use of the term was only in 1992.[6] It was used in an article to describe nurses' reactions to daily hospital emergencies. The first major book on the subject, edited by Charles Figley, was published only in 1995.[7] He then followed up in 2002 with a book specifically dealing with the treatment of compassion fatigue.[8] "Compassion Fatigue is the latest in an evolving concept that is known in the field of Traumatology as Secondary Traumatic Stress. Most often this phenomenon is associated with the 'cost of caring' for others in the emotional pain. There are a number of terms that describe this phenomenon. It has been described as secondary victimization, secondary traumatic stress, vicarious traumatization, and secondary survivor."[9]

Why Are Clergy at High Risk to Get Compassion Fatigue?

Research has consistently shown that religion and clergy are primary resources that people turn to when confronted with problems, particularly disasters and trauma. *The New England Journal of Medicine* reported that 90 percent of Americans turned to religion as a coping response to the terrorist attacks on September 11, 2001.[10] An American Red Cross poll taken almost a month after the 9/11 terrorist attacks indicated that close to 60 percent of Americans polled were likely or very likely to seek help from a spiritual counselor, as opposed to 40 percent who were likely or very likely to turn to mental health professionals.[11]

An article on stress and quality of life for clergy cites. "A National Institute of Mental Health (NIMH) study found that clergy members are just as likely as mental health specialists to have a severely mentally distressed person see them for assistance. (Hohmann & Larson, 1993). Clergy report that they devote 10 to 20 percent of their working time to pastoral counseling (Weaver, 1995). According to the U.S. Department of Labor, there were approximately 312,000 Jewish and Christian clergy serving congregations in the U.S. in 1992. Annually this allocation of time totals approximately 148.2 hours of mental health services, which is the equivalent to 22,000 mental health specialists delivering services at the rate of 130 hours per week."[12] Thus, clergy in general are at risk for compassion fatigue because through their daily work they are highly likely to be secondarily exposed to trauma and traumatic events.

Compassion Fatigue: Research Focus on Clergy and Disasters

The compassion fatigue self-test was originally designed and tested in 1992 and 1993 as a tool to help psychotherapists differentiate between burnout and secondary traumatic stress (STS).[13] The psychometric properties and alpha reliability scores for the original test were documented in 1993.[14] The test was expanded to become the Compassion Satisfaction and Fatigue Test in 1996, to address psychometric problems that occurred by asking only negative questions in the original test.[15] A series of positive questions parallel to the negative aspects of caregiving were developed, and a new subscale, "Compassion Satisfaction," was developed. The psychometric properties showing the expanded test's validity were generated using a pooled data set (n=374), including a small subset of Red Cross workers.[16]

An important clergy baseline study using this research tool titled "Understanding Stress and Quality of Life for Clergy and Clergy Spouses" was published by C. A. Darling in 2004.[17] The study attempted to better understand and quantify the stress in the life of clergy. The results of the study indicated that 9.1 percent of the clergy studied were at "extremely high risk" for compassion fatigue. It also found that another 7.8 percent were in the "high risk" category. However, the researchers found that 62.8 percent, the majority of those studied, were at "extremely low risk," with the remainder 20.4 percent in either the low- or moderate-risk groups.

Even in the best of times, a small but significant percentage of clergy are at significant risk for compassion fatigue. After a disaster, demand for a clergyperson's time and energy increases dramatically while at the same time many clergy often put taking care of themselves at the bottom of the list. As shown below, the results are startling and also preventable.

Rabbi Stephen B. Roberts, the primary author of this chapter, has currently produced the only peer-review research specifically focused on clergy, disasters, and compassion fatigue. Rabbi Roberts developed and then chaired an American Red Cross one-day conference for clergy and other religious leaders, held on June 17, 2002, in New York City. This resiliency training specifically addressed the impact of 9/11 and provided tools to better understand and work with those affected. The conference drew 650 attendees, who were also asked to participate in research; 437 completed the research. While clergy constituted 62.8 percent of the conference attendees, they represented 78.5 percent of the survey participants. Nonclergy included seminary students, mental health practitioners, mental health and disaster relief agency executives, and others who provided direct relief services. The research study results have been published in two different peer-review journals.[18]

What the research documented is that a disproportionately high percentage of all study participants were at risk for compassion fatigue, particularly when compared with Darling's baseline data. Figures 13.1 and 13.2 show the percentage for the baseline study by Darling compared to the results collected by Roberts after 9/11.

Figure 13.1 summary: Those who have recently experienced a disaster are much more likely to be at risk for compassion fatigue.

There are some important caveats with this data analysis. Even though both studies used the identical research tool, involved a large number of participants (Darling n=259; Roberts n=403), and the results were statistically significant, there are some significant differences. The first is that Roberts's larger group included nonclergy. Figure 13.2 corrects for this by showing the results when only clergy are included.

Figure 13.2 summary: Clergy who have experienced a disaster in the prior nine months are much more likely to be at risk for compas-

Percentage Distribution of Compassion Fatigue Risk
Comparing "Clergy Baseline" Established by Darling and
Those Studied by Roberts Affected by 9/11

RISK LEVEL	BASELINE RESULTS	POST-9/11 RESULTS
Extremely High	9.1%	27.5%
High	7.8%	11.7%
Moderate	10.0%	15.4%
Low	10.4%	12.7%
Very Low	62.8%	32.8%

Figure 13.1

sion fatigue than clergy who have not experienced a disaster in the prior nine months.

Other differences and similarities between the two samples worth noting include: the Darling study was 100 percent men, 53.9 percent were male in the Roberts study; the Darling study was almost 100 percent Protestant, 59.8 percent of the clergy were Protestant in the Roberts study; the mean age in the Darling study was 51.6 years, and 50.7 years in the Roberts study; the Darling study was located in the southeastern United States, and the Roberts study in the Northeast.

Having raised these issues, we still strongly feel that the two studies allow a good comparison between a clergy population within a short time after a major disaster and a baseline population. The results of comparing the two samples and their percent distribution of risk for compassion fatigue are a clear warning that after a disaster clergy are at a very significant risk for compassion fatigue and must work hard to prevent it.

Percentage Distribution of Compassion Fatigue Risk
Comparing "Clergy Baseline" Established by Darling and
Only Clergy Studied by Roberts Affected by 9/11 Risk Level

RISK LEVEL	BASELINE RESULTS	POST-9/11 RESULTS
Extremely High	9.1%	26.4%
High	7.8%	9.1%
Moderate	10.0%	15.5%
Low	10.4%	14.6%
Very Low	62.8%	34.6%

Figure 13.2

Preventing Compassion Fatigue

One of the hypotheses about why certain groups tested lower for compassion fatigue in Roberts's 2002 study was less isolation. In particular, those who volunteered with the American Red Cross after 9/11 participated in mandatory ten- to fifteen-minute defusing sessions at the end of each of their shifts. These sessions provided a connection with other clergy doing the same work and experiencing the same spiritual and emotional exertions. The volunteers had the ability to talk about their experiences, to listen to others as they shared similar stories, and to feel connected and understood. Further, when their volunteer service came to an end, most participated in longer debriefing programs that lasted from four hours to three days, depending on the option they chose. During the debriefing programs, participants were encouraged to share their experiences and to look within while sharing with others. The programs were specifically developed to help prevent isolation. Almost all volunteers participated in both defusings and debriefings.

The results from Roberts's study are dramatic. The group of volunteers who only assisted with the American Red Cross, and thus were less likely to be isolated from sharing about their experiences, overall had a low risk for compassion fatigue (see figure 13.3 below).[19] The next group, those who volunteered with both the American Red Cross and other agencies, overall were at the low end of the moderate risk for compassion fatigue. Then, those in the community who did not volunteer at all fell into the middle of the range for moderate risk scale for compassion fatigue. This is not surprising as most clergy in the New York region after 9/11 were involved in providing services to a large group of people. Almost four hundred thousand people were in a high-risk zone in New York on 9/11. Many experienced horrors that few Americans have ever witnessed. This group fled for their lives en masse, with many thinking they would die. Congregational clergy provided ex-

Mean Scores of Nonresponders and Responders from Roberts Study (n=403)		
	MEAN SCORE FOR COMPASSION FATIGUE*	**CATEGORY LEVEL**
Nonresponders [1]	33.0	Moderate Risk
Responders [2]		
Agencies other than ARC	36.4	High Risk
ARC and other agencies	31.1	Moderate Risk
ARC only	30.2	Low Risk

Figure 13.3

[1] Nonresponders are those who did not do volunteer work relating to the September 11th attacks with a disaster-relief agency.

[2] Responders are those who did work related to the September 11th attacks with a disaster-relief agency.

* Significant difference across groups, $p < 0.05$

tensive counseling throughout the region. Yet, oftentimes they them-selves were not provided support in the immediate weeks and months after 9/11.[20] Finally, those responders who only volunteered with agencies outside the American Red Cross overall fell into the high-risk category for compassion fatigue.

Figure 13.3 summary: Clergy who participated in defusing sessions, which lowered clergy isolation, on a regular basis when working after a disaster were at a lower risk for compassion fatigue than those who did not participate.

Talk does help prevent isolation and decreases the risk for compassion fatigue. Support groups and similar types of connectedness significantly helps decrease the overall risk for compassion fatigue. It is a lot of work to set up groups like this and then to follow through and attend them. On the other hand, to not do so significantly enhances the possibility that responders will get compassion fatigue.

Notes

1. C. R. Figley, ed., *Compassion Fatigue: Coping with Secondary Traumatic Stress Disorder in Those Who Treat the Traumatized* (New York: Brunnel/Mazel, 1995), 2.
2. Ibid. On p. 11 Figley defines compassion fatigue as: "A state of tension and pre-occupation with the individual or cumulative trauma of clients as manifested in one or more ways: re-experiencing the traumatic event; avoidance/numbing of reminders of the traumatic event; persistent arousal; combined with the added effects of cumulative stress (burnout)."
3. *Clergy* will be used to indicate all leaders of faith communities. There are a wide range of titles that leaders use. Not all leaders are ordained, and not all leaders have formal titles.
4. "Understanding Compassion Fatigue: Helping Public Health Professionals and Other Front-Line Responders Combat the Occupational Stressors and Psychological Injuries of Bioterrorism Defense for a Strengthened Public Health Response," a course offered by the Florida Center for Public Health Preparedness and the University of South Florida College of Public Health; website: www.fcphp.usf.edu.
5. J. E. Gentry, A. B. Baranowsky, and K. Dunning, "ARP: The Accelerated Recovery Program (ARP) for Compassion Fatigue," in *Treating Compassion Fatigue*, ed. C. R. Figley (New York: Brunner-Routledge, 2002), 129.
6. C. Joinson, "Coping with Compassion Fatigue," *Nursing* 22, no. 4 (1992): 116–22.

7. C. R. Figley, ed., *Compassion Fatigue: Coping with Secondary Traumatic Stress Disorder in Those Who Treat the Traumatized* (New York: Brunnel/Mazel, 1995).

8. C. R. Figley, ed., *Treating Compassion Fatigue* (New York: Brunner-Routledge, 2002).

9. C. R. Figley, *Compassion Fatigue, An Introduction,* www.grenncross.org/_Research/ CompassionFatigue.asp printed 9/5/207

10. M. A. Shuster et al., "A National Survey of Stress Reactions After the September 11, 2001 Terrorist Attacks," *New England Journal of Medicine* 345, no. 2 (2001): 1507–12.

11. American Red Cross national poll, October 5–8, 2001, by Caravan ORC Int. 1,000 adults above 18 living in private homes; +/-3 percent; release date: October 16, 2001.

12. C. A. Darling, E. W. Hill, and L. M. McWey, "Understanding Stress and Quality of Life for Clergy and Clergy Spouses," *Stress and Health* 20 (2004): 262.

13. C. R. Figley, "Secondary Traumatic Stress Disorder" in Figley, *Compassion Fatigue,* 1–20.

14. B. H. Stamm and M. E. Varra, eds., *Instrumentation in the Field of Traumatic Stress* (Chicago: Research and Methodology Interest Group, International Society for Traumatic Stress Studies). Alpha reliability scores ranged from 94 to 86; structural analysis yielded at least one stable factor, which is characterized by depressed mood in relationship to work accompanied by feelings of fatigue, disillusionment, and worthlessness. Structural Reliability (stability) of this factor, as indicated by Tucker's Coefficient of Congruence (cc), is 91.

15. B. H. Stamm, "Measuring Compassion Satisfaction as well as Fatigue: Developmental History of the Compassion Satisfaction and Fatigue Test," in Figley, *Treating Compassion Fatigue.*

16. Ibid., 11. "The overall alphas for the scales ranged from .87 to .90. These results are preliminary, but consistent with the findings of Figley & Stamm (96), which reported reliabilities of .85 to .94 on a sample of 142 psychotherapy practitioners."

17. Darling, Hill, and McWey, "Understanding Stress and Quality of Life for Clergy and Clergy Spouses," 274. Study caveats: "While a random sample of clergy was incorporated into this study, the respondents were predominately White and Methodist.... As a result, caution should be taken when interpreting these data, since the findings can not be generalized to a broad range of population and clergy. Nevertheless, the respondents in this study provided relevant information that is clearly applicable to similar clergy located in the southeastern U.S."

18. S. B. Roberts et al., "Compassion Fatigue Among Chaplains, Clergy, and Other Respondents After September 11th," *Journal of Nervous and Mental Disease* 191, no. 11 (2003): 756–58; K. J. Flannelly, S. B. Roberts, and A. J. Weaver, "Correlates of Compassion Fatigue and Burnout in Chaplains and Other Clergy Who Responded to the September 11th Attacks in New York City," *Journal of Pastoral Care & Counseling* 59, no. 3 (2005): 213–24.

19. 26 or less = Extremely LOW risk; 27 to 30 = LOW risk; 31 to 35 = Moderate risk; 36 to 40 = HIGH risk; 41 or more = Extremely HIGH risk; psychometric information—mean of group 27.8.
20. Rev. Willard W. C. Ashley Sr., coeditor of this book, helped create and implement a very effective program to address the issue of high compassion fatigue among the New York region clergy. The program started shortly after the Roberts research was completed and lasted almost another four years. There is more on this program in other chapters.

Resources and Further Reading

Compassion Fatigue and Burnout Self-Test—this test can be found on a couple of websites:
http://www.isu.edu/~bhstamm/tests/satfat.htm
http://mailer.fsu.edu/~cfigley/Tests/Compassion%20Satisfaction-Fatigue%20 Self-Test.doc

Green Cross Foundation, an organization focused on compassion fatigue started by Dr. Figley: www.greencross.org.

Figley, C. R., ed. *Compassion Fatigue: Coping with Secondary Traumatic Stress Disorder in Those Who Treat the Traumatized.* New York: Brunnel/Mazel, 1995.

Figley, C. R., ed. *Treating Compassion Fatigue.* New York: Brunnel/Mazel. 2002.

Flannelly, K. J., S. B. Roberts, and A. J. Weaver. "Correlates of Compassion Fatigue and Burnout in Chaplains and Other Clergy Who Responded to the September 11th Attacks in New York City," *Journal of Pastoral Care & Counseling* 59, no. 3 (2005).

Roberts, S. B. et al. "Compassion Fatigue Among Chaplains, Clergy, and Other Respondents After September 11th," *Journal of Nervous and Mental Disease* 191, no. 11 (2003).

Stamm, B. H., ed. *Secondary Traumatic Stress: Self-Care Issues for Clinicians, Researchers, and Educators,* 2nd ed. Lutherville, MD: Sidran Press, 1999.

Ursano, R. J., C. S. Fullerton, and A. E. Norwood, eds. *Terrorism and Disaster: Individual and Community Mental Health Interventions.* Cambridge: Cambridge University Press, 2003.

Understanding Compassion Fatigue: Helping Public Health Professionals and Other Front-Line Responders Combat the Occupational Stressors and Psychological Injuries of Bioterrorism Defense for a Strengthened Public Health Response; Course offered by the Florida Center for Public Health Preparedness and the University of South Florida College of Public Health. This is an excellent online course teaching about compassion fatigue. Further, it lists hundreds of resources. Website: www.fcphp.usf.edu.

About the Contributors

Rabbi Stephen B. Roberts, BCJC, is coeditor of this book. He is the associate executive vice president of the New York Board of Rabbis overseeing the Jack D. Weiler Chaplaincy Program. He is a past president of the National Association of Jewish Chaplains. Two years prior to September 11, 2001, he founded a partnership organization within the American Red Cross in Greater New York of what is now Disaster Chaplaincy Services, New York (DCS-NY), an independent 501(c)3. He serves DCS-NY as chairman emeritus. Since 2000, Rabbi Roberts has served as one of the five official representatives overseeing American Red Cross's national Spiritual Care Response Team. Following 9/11, he was the first national officer to set up American Red Cross spiritual care response in New York City. On June 17, 2002, in New York City, Rabbi Roberts envisioned and then chaired an American Red Cross one-day conference for clergy and other religious leaders with over 650 participants. This resiliency training specifically addressed the impact of 9/11 and the tools needed to better understand and work with those affected. He has taught extensively on disaster spiritual care and was the primary researcher for the only published peer-review research on the impact of disasters on spiritual care providers.

Kevin L. Ellers, Dmin, is the territorial disaster services coordinator for the Salvation Army in the central territory of the United States. He is also president of the Institute for Compassionate Care, which is dedicated to education, training, and direct care. He is an associate chaplain with the Illinois Fraternal Order of Police, serves as faculty for the International Critical Incident Stress Foundation, and is a member of the American Association of Christian Counselors Crisis Response Training Team. He has authored several books and teaches broadly in the topics of medic first aid, grief, trauma, disasters, and emotional and spiritual care. Ellers is a candidate for the doctor of ministry degree in the marriage and family therapy track, and is currently working on the final project for completion of the degree. He has a strong background in disasters, chaplaincy, pastoral ministries, marriage and family therapy, and social services.

Rev. John C. Wilson, PhD, is a recognized expert on disaster spiritual care focusing on the issues of the recruitment, training, and deployment of local clergy as spiritual care providers in community disasters. He serves on the American Red Cross Spiritual Care Response Team for natural disasters, aviation, and terrorism incidents, and has responded nationally to aviation incidents. He served as the acting lead spiritual care for the American Red Cross in Washington, D.C., during the 9/11 aftermath and is a member of the Spiritual Care Response Team national advisory committee. He is a national speaker on the uniqueness and need for disaster spiritual care and a regular presenter and trainer for local clergy preparing for disaster responses. He is a board-certified chaplain with the Association of Professional Chaplains and the American Academy of Experts in Traumatic Stress, and is employed as the trauma and critical care chaplain at Advocate Lutheran General Hospital, in Park Ridge, Illinois.

14

Cultural and Religious Considerations

Rev. Willard W. C. Ashley Sr., DMin, DH;
Roberta L. Samet, LCSW; Rev. Rebeca Radillo, DMin;
Imam Ummi Nur Allene Ali; Rev. David Billings, DMin;
and Rabbi Zahara Davidowitz-Farkas, BCJC

Andrew, Rita, Katrina, Columbine, 9/11, the tsunami, flight 587, domestic violence and drive-bys are names of tragedies that have changed the English lexicon. These tragedies have also served as the catalyst to change how we respond to a disaster. Confronted with the reality of cultural and religious diversity, first responders have blazed a new trail in our endeavors to evaluate our effectiveness and to explore more meaningful and more successful disaster responsiveness, namely the essential and critical need to address cultural and religious considerations.

This chapter is a brief overview as to how faith-based organizations led the charge to change the way we think, feel, and act in addressing trauma following a disaster. The American Association of Pastoral Counselors (AAPC); The Association for Clinical Pastoral Education (ACPE); the National Association of Jewish Chaplains (NAJC); The National Association of Catholic Chaplains (NACC); and the Association of Professional Chaplains (APC), had policy statements, practices, and a demonstrated track record of cultural competency prior to the tragic events of September 11, 2001. In blazing this new trail, it was their members and member organizations that worked with the Council of Churches of the City of New York (CCCNY); the Council of Religious Leaders (CORL); the New York Board of Rabbis (NYBR); the Jewish Community Relations Council

(JCRC); the Roman Catholic Archdiocese of New York, Catholic Charities; the Interfaith Center of New York; the Imams Council; the Malik Shabazz Human Rights Institute; the Muslim Consultative Network (MCN); and the Westside Jesuit Community to ensure that cultural and religious competency became integral to the response.

Generous grants from the September 11th Fund,[1] the United Way of New York, Church World Service, and the American Red Cross allowed the Council of Churches of the City of New York (CCCNY) to be the lead agency to develop, coordinate, and supervise the largest culturally competent response to a disaster in the United States of America.

The CCCNY/NYDRI[2] submitted a grant application to the September 11th Fund. As the governing agencies of the September 11th Fund, it was the practice of the New York Community Trust and the United Way of New York to take all grant applications to their boards for approval prior to any sign-off with September 11th Funds. The September 11th Fund approved the recommendation by the NYDRI search committee[3] to hire Rev. Willard Ashley[4] to be the project director of what was called the Care to the Caregivers Interfaith Project.[5] The September 11th Fund custodians were so impressed with Rev. Ashley that they increased the amount of the grant and indicated in the award letter that the grant was based on his running the project. This chapter reflects the lessons learned in organizing, planning, and implementing this project.

Introduction

Spiritual first aid[6] is our starting point. Any attempt to heal trauma must be a culturally competent, best-practices model designed in collaboration with local residents. In short, the goal is to synchronize spirituality and science in a culturally competent manner, so as to bring about healing. It is a synergy between the sacred and the secular. Cultural and religious considerations should help to facilitate resilience with compassion as they educate, equip, and empower. User-friendly, mission-driven, faith-based models must be inclusive and respectful of the community healers and leaders. If nothing else, any intervention following a disaster should do no harm.

The Hippocratic oath, "to do no harm," raises a challenge to both medical practitioners and the community leaders. In any community, the gatekeepers or leaders must discern who are the opportunists and who are the healers and compassionate caregivers. Our mission, as invited guests into a community in pain, is to avoid the temptation to be professionals scouring for clients or an agency seeking bodies to satisfy a grant,[7] or disconnected researchers looking for participants for our latest study. Instead, our mission is to help individuals and their various communities restore balance as they return to their routines, with the least amount of disruption possible given their new, post-disaster circumstances.

To accomplish our task, we must dare to venture beyond the tip of the iceberg. What makes an individual caregiver or a project/program/ intervention effective? Is it an individual's professional skills and experience, a project that creates a supportive environment, a spectacular program that provides education, or some ingredient or concept not listed here? Certainly these are important, if not essential, components necessary for effective and successful disaster care and intervention, but it is important to know that *culture, context, and collaboration mean everything.* Community leaders who show respect by honoring the cultural and religious practices of the community they are serving will be much more likely to build trust. Our project findings revealed that a major component of the clergy interventions following a disaster was based on a trusted relationship. The model we describe in this chapter represents what we learned in the largest interfaith undertaking of its kind.

Ask the Right Questions

Two past national presidents of AAPC[8] along with pastoral psychotherapists; ACPE supervisors; NAJC, NACC, APC chaplains; Carol North, MD; Barry Hong, PhD; and Roberta Samet, LCSW, collaborated with the project staff of the CCCNY to formulate the questions that needed to be asked prior to entering a faith community following a disaster:

- Who is suffering?
- To what extent is the suffering?

- How can we be of help?
- What is needed to be effective?
- Who is the indigenous leadership?
- What are the available resources?
- Who are the resident healers in the community?
- Who is not represented at the strategy/planning meetings?
- How consistent are espoused values versus actual practices?[9]
- What does the individual or community view as the needs?
- What is already being done to address the needs? How is it working?

When we ask the right questions of either an individual or a community, we should do so not with an air of a professional being the expert, but from the stance of a learner. We are in place to help. The best help we can offer is to respect the culture and religious expressions of someone whose practices may be different from our own.

Attack the Absurdity of Arrogance

Organization development expert Edgar H. Schein says, "The emphasis is on 'process' because I believe that *how* things are done between people and in groups is as—or more important than—*what* is done. The how, or the 'process,' usually communicates more clearly what we really mean than does the content of what we say."[10] Following any disaster, we reveal our arrogance and our cultural ignorance when we think we can bring healing to an individual or community without any regard for their cultural and religious norms. Going into a new community, the basic paradigm is: learn the language, respect the culture, and collaborate with the community to deliver positive outcomes. However, in a disaster, you may not have the luxury of time to learn the language. Here is where the leadership of the Care for the Caregivers Interfaith Project made a decision to hire faith-specific liaisons. We define *faith-specific liaisons* as individuals who share the same religion and know the cultural variations of a particular faith expression. Rather than our agency assuming we knew all the tenets and nuances of any given religion or faith expression, we sought out helpers from a particular community, specifically those in that community who already had established long-term, reliable, trustworthy relationships within their given religion or faith expression. We also wanted to ensure that resources went into the communities to be served rather than into outside consultants who would leave the community once their task was accomplished. The job of the faith-specific liaisons was to collaborate with the healers in their community, along with other professionals, to determine how best to heal their religious community, and who their best resource people (therapists, educators, physicians, and the like) would be. In an effort to avoid the absurdity of arrogance, Rev. Ashley hired representatives from five faith traditions in New York City.[11] These five faith-specific liaisons represented Catholic, Jewish, Muslim, Protestant, and interfaith traditions.[12] In addition to being responsible as the gatekeepers to secure the best healers and professionals for their community, the faith-specific liaisons also took on other responsibilities: teaching the other faith leaders in the project about common rituals, practices, and expectations in their culture or religious expression; designing with the Caregivers Project staff short-term and long-term recovery strategies; designing seminars and health-screening expos; helping outsiders learn the best methods of communication in their particular culture or religion;[13] and offering feedback and evaluations from their community as to the status and effectiveness of the intended recovery outcomes. The faith-specific liaisons were also on call to be a source of information in an emergency for other chaplains, health care providers, and those who sought to bring culturally competent healing.

Be a Blessing

Before you show how much you know, show how much you love. Because this is a book about disaster spiritual care, we cannot be so clinical that we forget that our first task as clergy is to show our love. Empathy is the key resource the spiritual caregiver brings to a disaster response. Pastoral psychotherapist Beverly Musgrave says, "To be present with another person in an empathic way means much more than to be in the same place with another person. Central to the practice of empathy in pastoral visitation is the art of an active 'listening presence.' Empathy, you will recall, involves truly listening to another person and being present to that person in genuine encounter."[14] In our role as an active listening presence, we must be careful not to violate cultural or religious norms. We must be sensitive to questions such as:

- How do people in their culture or religion communicate and with whom?[15]
- What are the acceptable interactions between different genders or the same gender?
- What degree of physical distance communicates respect versus a violation of personal space?
- How are gestures or body movements interpreted?
- What are the rules of ethics and etiquette?
- What methods of healing are practiced and embraced in their culture or religion?

To be a blessing is to demonstrate our love through empathy. It is also to show compassion and be comfortable with a wide range of emotions. As spiritual care providers, we must give those who connect with our spirit permission to be whole following a disaster. Our task is to abandon the script and be human. To be human in the presence of another is to take their lead and create a safe space whereby he or she or an entire community may laugh, cry, shout, dance, and engage in those human activities that remind us that we are alive.

To be a blessing is to demonstrate culturally competent hospitality. It is to value integrity, embrace fairness, seek justice yet teach mercy. Without these components we are not spiritual partners in healing.

Build Partnerships

Successful, culturally competent spiritual care is built on three words: network, network, and network. Neither you nor your agency, center, or university has all the answers. We help the healing process best when we seek the help of others and build partnerships within the communities we are deployed to help heal. If our goal is to help individuals and the community to heal, we must assess community capacity. We found this quote informative:

> Once accepted as the whole truth about troubled neighborhoods, this 'needs' map determines how problems are to be addressed, through deficiency-oriented policies and programs. Public, private, and non-profit human service systems, often supported by university research and foundation funding, translate the programs into

local activities that teach people the nature and extent of their problems, and the value of services as the answer to their problems. As a result, many lower income urban neighborhoods are now environments of service where behaviors are affected because residents come to believe that their well-being depends upon being a client. They begin to see themselves as people with special needs that can only be met by outsiders.[16]

We build partnerships when we take the stance of the Hebrew prophet Ezekiel. Before he began his prophetic task, he made a first-hand visit to the place where God would send him to be with the people. Before Ezekiel opened his mouth or began ministry, he sat where they sat. In other words, he performed a "community strength capacity analysis." When we sit where the victims and survivors have sat (and in many cases are still sitting), we communicate our willingness to be a partner who builds on their strengths and moves in the direction of independence instead of operating as drive-by professional disaster mercenaries who advocate client deficiency—dependency models.

Building partnerships shows respect for those healers who were in the community before the disaster and those who have since come to bring assistance. Building partnerships acknowledges our own limitations and declares we are better caregivers when we work together for the good of the victim, survivor, patient, or client. One of the hallmarks of the Care for the Caregivers Interfaith Project was the building of partnerships. At the very outset of the program, in addition to connecting with local healers, the staff reached out to the United Way of New York, Columbia University, New York University, The Jewish Theological Seminary of America, the American Red Cross, Lutheran Disaster Relief Services, Blanton Peale Graduate Institute, Church World Services, The Mental Health Association, the American Group Psychotherapy Association, The Federation of Protestant Welfare Agencies, The People's Institute for Survival and Beyond, Saint Vincent's Hospital, Bellevue Hospital, Catholic Charities, and the New York ecumenical community. The CCCNY Caregivers Project staff reported that their model was not accepted by all organizations on their outreach list. As a result, some organizations agreed to disagree and part company.

There is a dirty little secret in this business of disaster, as in other areas of life. Some victims are victimized twice: once by the disaster itself and a second time by those responding to the disaster who come from other regions, appointed by and salaried through some outside "official" healing agency. These people sometimes, intentionally or unintentionally, also victimize local healers and residents by taking economic advantage of them, using their invaluable experience and expertise without paying them for their consultant services, while all the while, receiving their own salaries. In terms of accountability, Marie M. Fortune and James Poling say, "It is our task within the church to face the reality that some among us exploit and damage others among us and that as a faith community, in concert with the wider community, we have the resources to confront this evil with justice and bring genuine healing in its wake."[17] We and our respective agencies detest and condemn this practice of double victimizing. We advocate for inviting local healers to the planning table and paying them for their knowledge. Do not simply "pick their brain" for free, but pay them as you would pay any consultant.

We can proudly say that the Caregivers Project paid those who came to the table. We worked to ensure they remained in leadership positions as paid contributors and consultants to the project. Let this be your testimony. Build real partnerships.

Commit to Collaborate on the Solutions

It is not enough to build partnerships alone. We must commit to collaborate on the solutions. Our collaboration must include grassroots community involvement. The goal here is not for the community to buy into a program you developed on your own, without grassroots partners. The goal is to bring in the community healers and community leaders to the planning table from day one, at the outset of disaster response. This holds true for both individuals and communities. Survivors should be active in the development of their short-term treatment plan and long-term recovery strategy.

Too many agencies, organizations, and clinicians make a fatal mistake in this area. To offer help, healing, and a hand to an individual or a community following a disaster requires work that is *labor intensive*. To commit to collaborate on the solutions means your ego and agenda must submit to the needs of the community. Said differently, this is not about you and your interests. This is about helping an individual move from temporary dependence following a disaster to long-term independence and health. Our work is not to be paternalistic but to be coequals on a journey to mutual healing. Noted psychiatrist Irvin Yalom, MD, wrote, "More than one of my patients have invoked the metaphor of the Wizard of Oz to describe their preference for the happy belief that the therapist knows the way home—a clear, sure path out of pain. By no means do they want to look behind the curtain and see a lost and confused faux-wizard.[18]

To commit to collaboration on the solutions suggests a healthy respect for the local lines of authority, mutual accountability, and shared responsibility. When trying to be sensitive to cultural and religious considerations as part of your commitment to collaborate on the solutions, three things matter: integrity, honesty, and unity. If there is a place where post-disaster havoc reigns, it is in the area of trust. Just as patients want to trust their physicians or psychotherapists, members of the various faith communities will feel you out following a disaster to discern who they can trust. Let it be said of you and your organization that it is one of integrity and honesty that embraces unity as equals.

Keep Your Eyes on the Prize

Whether you are offering counseling to an individual or designing a program to help heal a particular community or demographic, keep your eyes on the prize. What is the prize? Who pays for the prize? Who benefits from the prize? It was clear following many a disaster that the prize for some was another grant, a published work, or recognition as a leader in the field. If there was any one concern that created real resistance and reluctance on the part of a community to consider interfaith or interdisciplinary collaboration, it was the fear (and in many cases the experience) that their community was nothing more than a research study, grant project, or the latest sexy, politically correct depository for philanthropic efforts. That is not to say publications, grants, and studies are not valuable in their appropriate context. It is to say, however, that if those are your primary goals, *keep walking*. Too many people of color and others already oppressed by race, religion, or class have been the subject or, unknowingly, the silent contributors to the stardom of aspiring, ambitious academics, nonprofit executives, and organizations seeking recognition.

To keep your eyes on the prize is to know your mission. It is as Pastor Rick Warren states, to be "purpose driven." It is our prayer that your mission following a disaster is to help an individual or a community to heal. That being said, as healers, we must respect the context, values, and history of the people we are asked to serve. When we keep our eyes on the prize, our mission is to be part of a team that helps sufferers return to their dreams, goals, aspirations, and some semblance of their pre-disaster life. It is to rebuild lives, careers, homes, businesses, and institutions with dignity and respect. The prize is being part of history, to help shape how the story ends.

The Council of Churches of the City of New York worked with their interfaith partners to shape how the story ended. The story was: following a disaster, local clergy are usually overwhelmed and thus become victims of compassion fatigue.[19] People who worked on the recovery efforts following the Oklahoma City bombing indicated that two-thirds of the local clergy left Oklahoma City after the relief effort, and one-third of those left the ministry entirely. The mission of the Care for the Caregivers Interfaith Project was to offer to the clergy of New York City following 9/11 an educational and peer-support program called the Self-Care and Skill Building for the Clergy: A Unified Approach Program. Initially two thousand clergy were trained in a train-the-trainer model, which was later expanded to include a broader definition of clergy caregivers.[20] The prize was to help local clergy identify signs of posttraumatic stress disorder (PTSD), depression,[21] and anxiety. We used a presentation titled C-Flash (Clergy Frontline Assistance for Support and Healing).[22] Further, the prize was to help clergy learn self-care skills, which included clergy support groups that met every other week.[23] The prize was to be a resource to help clergy of all faiths find a place of renewal, reflection, and rest in the storm.

Rest in the Storm

Who is your cardiologist? Who is your spiritual director? Who is your therapist? Disaster work is heartbreaking. You will need your own personal team of caregivers who will give you a spiritual, mental, and physical checkup. It is difficult at best to witness the human devastation and loss of property following a disaster. Your body will need rest. Know your limits. One well-known psychiatrist offered her services to other psychiatrists, clinicians, and clergy who were part of the team searching for bodies following Hurricane Katrina. Her offer to them was, "Call me as often as you need to do each day to check in and to have a safe place to talk about what you experienced and your feelings."[24] When we do this work, we need a safe place to check in and talk about our feelings. We also need to practice good self-care. You need rest in the storm. We encourage you to read chapter 2, "Self-Care—Not an Option."

Utilize Their Spiritual Resources

Prayer, personal piety, protest, power, play, and pious practices are resources all communities of faith suggest to their practitioners. Find out what are the practices and beliefs of the persons and communities with which you work. Encourage the use and reliance upon those practices by the survivors of a disaster. One Protestant pastor called this work "ministry in the margins," meaning the use of spiritual resources is not the stuff of headlines in the news. CNN, Fox News, or *Nightline* will not run as their feature story "Cleric Prays with People Following the Disaster." You will not make the major newspapers because you sat to pray with someone who just lost their loved ones or all their property or maybe even their dignity. You will most likely not be on *60 Minutes* because you quoted one of the wisdom sayings in this book to a soul in pain. Going into some little-known village in Thailand or visiting a small town in the Gulf Region or sitting quietly to talk about faith with a Virginia Tech student is not the stuff the media follows. Handing a cool cup of water to a person who has just been left homeless following a hurricane or fire, or finding something that an injured person could conceivably find humor in is ministry in the margins. But know that in the eyes of those who are in need of healing, those margins are wide.

Final Words

The late activist and actor Ossie Davis was the keynote speaker for the kickoff of the Care for the Caregivers Interfaith Project, held at the historic

Abyssinian Baptist Church in Harlem, New York.[25] Mary Ellen Blizzard and Rev. Ashley, as project staff, served as the masters of ceremonies. The one-hundred-voice interfaith New York Metro Mass Choir provided the music. Dee Matthews, as the administrative assistant, provided the behind-the-scenes floor management essential for any successful kick-off. Forensic psychologist Jeffery Gardere, PhD, as the project's clinical consultant, handled the media, and Rev. John Hiemstra, as executive director of the CCCNY during the five-year duration of the project, welcomed the crowd of clinicians, clergy, and laypeople.

None in attendance that night knew that they were making history. The handful of pastoral counselors, psychiatrists, social workers, chaplains, and clergy from different faiths, ethnicities, and religions did not know this would be the largest interfaith undertaking of its kind. But that was not what made history. What made history was that for the sake of helping to heal a community, we learned how to respect, honor, and embrace the religious and cultural considerations of others. We invite you to do the same.

Appendix—The Ugly Specter of Race

Our chapter focused on the lessons learned in New York City, but it would be a great oversight and injustice to the topic if we did not address the issues of race. There are few places, if any, where race played such a major role in the cultural and religious considerations of disaster spiritual care as it did in the Gulf Region during the various stages of work following Hurricane Katrina.

Unfortunately, Mother Nature does not affect all people equally. Neither do tragedies resulting from political conflicts. In the United States, because of our unique history of race and racism, people of color will be affected differently than white people. Prior to Hurricane Katrina, New Orleans's black community was already reeling from vast unemployment, police brutality and lack of protection, a dysfunctional public education system where a state takeover of schools was imminent, and a severe shortage of decent low-income housing. These realities had existed for decades and even generations. Katrina made matters worse. In the storm's aftermath, caregivers descended on the Gulf Region in great numbers. To a person, it can be assumed they were compassionate and wanted to help survivors. The organizations they represented were similarly motivated by a sincere desire to deal with the trauma that victims of Katrina were living through. Few individuals or their organizations, however, understood structural racism and how it would impede the most dedicated attempts to relieve the trauma that people were dealing with. In fact, many caregivers and caregiving institutions would insist that racism had nothing to do with who suffered and how their suffering was addressed by the responders.

However, a structural analysis of systems response revealed that the same systems that failed black New Orleanians pre-Katrina would also fail them during and after. The systems were not structured to respond equitably across lines of race. Thus, in a city where poverty was as high as any urban area in the United States and many, if not most, of the poor did not own a car or know anyone who did, this reality was not factored into the plan to evacuate the city. Housing that was inadequate before the storm was nonexistent afterward. Prior to Katrina, African-Americans accounted for less than 2 percent of the wealth in the city's prosperous French Quarter and central business district. After Katrina this number became 0 percent. A congressman from Baton Rouge was quoted as saying, "God accomplished overnight what we couldn't do in thirty years—empty the housing projects of New Orleans."

The lesson we can learn from post-Katrina recovery efforts is that caregivers must understand racism and provide solace to people traumatized by disasters and the politics of violence. To not do so risks making matters worse. When the caregivers leave or do not address race, what do they leave behind?

Notes

1. The September 11th Fund was a $500 million ad hoc charity that raised and distributed funds immediately following the events of September 11, 2001. The fund was developed in partnership with the New York Community Trust and the United Way of New York. Carol Kellerman was the CEO and executive director. Roberta Samet, LCSW, was the program manager who developed and oversaw implementation of the long-term mental health recovery program for New York City and the surrounding tri-state area. She developed 15 distinct trauma training programs reaching 7,000 mental health professionals, 2,500 early childhood educators, 3,000 primary care physicians, and 2,000 clergy.

2. New York Disaster Recovery Interfaith (NYDRI) was an ad hoc organization formed by the religious leaders of New York City, immediately following the tragic events of September 11, 2001.

3. CCCNY/NYDRI was given a $175,000 planning grant to hire a clinician/clergyperson to rewrite the grant proposal and develop/implement the project. The search committee included: Rev. James O. Stallings, Rev. Dr John Hiemstra, Ausuma Mursch, Rabbi Craig Miller, and Rev. Dr Charles Straut Jr.

4. Rev. Ashely is the coeditor of this book, a graduate of the Blanton Peale Graduate Institute with certificates in pastoral psychotherapy and marriage and family therapy. He has completed eleven units of CPE through the ACPE. During the 9/11 project he was a member of the AAPC and a staff therapist at the Riverside Church, New York, New York. Prior to 9/11 he was an executive coach on Wall Street.

5. From the period of November 2002 to March 2007, the Care for the Caregivers Interfaith Project trained 4,000 clergy and 3,500 caregivers of all faiths.

6. See chapter 7 of this book.

7. In some circles these are called "disaster pimps" or "ambulance chasers."

8. Margaret Kornfeld, DMin, and James Wyrtzen, DMin, served as national presidents of AAPC.

9. C. Argyris and D. A. Schon, *Theory in Practice: Increasing Professional Effectiveness* (San Francisco: Jossey-Bass Publishers, 1974), 20–34.

10. E. H. Schein, *Process Consultation Revisited: Building the Helping Relationship* (Reading, PA: Addison-Wesley, 1999), 3.

11. Shaykh Ali, Ummi Nur, Rabbi Craig Miller, Rev. Jimmy Lim, Matthew Weiner, and Father Will Terrell.

12. The Interfaith Center of New York had established trusted relationships with Buddhists, Hindus, Sikhs, Yoruba, Native Americans, Tao, Ethiopian Orthodox, Zoroastrian, and often underserved demographics within major denominations. In addition, each year the Interfaith Center held an Interfaith Prayer Service in honor of the United Nations General Assembly and the United Nations general secretary was the invited keynote speaker. The Interfaith Center website is www.interfaithcenter.org.

13. A sign of cultural incompetence is to "advertise" screenings or conduct outreach in places the targeted groups does not visit, use language that is not sensitive to that group's norms or place ads in media sources that group does not utilize.

14. B. A. Musgrave, "Empathy: The Caregiver Looks Both Ways," in *Partners in Healing: Bringing Compassion to People with Illness or Loss.* B. A. Musgrave and J. R. Bickle, eds. (Mahwah, NJ: Paulist Press, 2003), 38.

15. Some people will not feel comfortable talking to outsiders or strangers about their problems. Some people may fear an outsider works for some government agency (e.g., immigration) with an agenda other than helping.

16. J. P. Kretzmann and J. L. McKnight, *Building Communities from the Inside Out: A Path Toward Finding and Mobilizing a Community's Assets* (Chicago: ACTA, 1993), 2.

17. See M. Fortune and J. Poling, "Calling to Accountability: The Church's Response to Abusers," in *Violence Against Women and Children: A Christian Theological Sourcebook*, eds. C. Adams, M. M. Fortune, (New York: Continuum, 1998).

18. I. D. Yalom, *The Gift of Therapy: An Open Letter to a New Generation of Therapists and Their Patients* (New York: Harper-Perennial, 2003), 99.

19. "Compassion fatigue is a more user-friendly term for secondary traumatic stress disorder, which is nearly identical to PTSD, except that it applies to those emotionally affected by the trauma of another (usually a client or family member)." C. R. Figley, ed., *Treating Compassion Fatigue* (New York: Brunner-Routledge, 2002), 2.

20. Dr. Margaret Kornfeld is an American Baptist psychotherapist and past president of the AAPC. She did significant work with the Muslim and Haitian communities during this project. At a planning meeting, she questioned our assumptions on how much actual hands on pastoral care is performed by ordained clergy.

21. "Depression is the flaw of love. To be creatures who love, we must be creatures who can despair at what we lose, and depression is the mechanism of that despair." A. Solomon, *The Noonday Demon: An Atlas of Depression* (New York: Scribner, 2001), 15.

22. The model was developed by Carol North, MD, and Barry Hong, PhD. It was refined to meet the specific needs of clergy by Rev. Willard Ashley, DMin; Mary Ellen Blizzard; Rabbi Zahara Davidowitz; Jeffery Garadre, PhD; Rev. Margaret Kornfeld, DMin; Ausuma O. Mursch, MS; Beverly Anne Musgrave, PhD; Russell Park, PhD; Rev. James C. Wyrtzen, DMin; and Roberta L. Samet, LCSW.

23. We used an instrument by Rebecca McLean and Roger Jahnke, *The Circle of Life: A Dynamic Process of Continuous Improvement for Health and Wellness* (Santa Barbara, CA: Health Action, 1997). To be more user-friendly to clergy of all faiths, it was later edited by Rev. Lois Annich (2003).

24. Phyllis Harrison-Ross, MD, founder and managing partner of the Black Psychiatrists of Greater New York.

25. During the Caregivers Project, Rev. Dr Calvin O. Butts served as the senior pastor of the Abyssinian Baptist Church, a board member of the United Way of New York and the president of the Council of Churches of the City of New York. His intervention paved the way to a million-dollar grant for our project.

Further Reading

Argyris, Chris, and Donald A. Schon. *Theory in Practice: Increasing Professional Effectiveness*. San Francisco: Jossey-Bass Publishers, 1974.

Blitz, Lisa V., and Mary Pender Greene, eds. *Racism and Racial Identity: Reflections in Mental Health and Social Services*. Binghamton, NY: Haworth Maltreatment & Trauma Press, 2006.

Canda, Edward R., and Leola Dyrud Furman. *Spiritual Diversity in Social Work Practice: The Heart of Helping*. New York: Free Press, 1999.

Figley, Charles R., ed. *Treating Compassion Fatigue*. New York: Brunner-Routledge, 2002.

Kretzmann, John P., and John L. McKnight. *Building Communities from the Inside Out: A Path Toward Finding and Mobilizing a Community's Assets*. Chicago: ACTA, 1993.

Musgrave, Beverly Anne, and John R. Bickle. *Partners in Healing: Bringing Compassion to People with Illness or Loss*. Mahwah, NJ: Paulist Press, 2003.

O'Donnell, Kelly, ed. *Doing Member Care Well: Perspectives and Practices from Around the World*. Pasadena, CA: William Carey Library, 2002.

Orner, Roderick, and Ulrich Schnyder, eds. *Reconstructing Early Intervention After Trauma: Innovations in the Care of Survivors*. Oxford: Oxford University Press, 2003.

McGoldrick, Monica, Joe Giordano, and Nydia Garcia-Preto. *Ethnicity & Family Therapy*, 3rd ed. New York: Guilford Press, 2005.

Paniagua, Freddy A. *Assessing and Treating Culturally Diverse Clients: A Practical Guide*, 3rd ed. Thousand Oaks, CA: Sage, 2005.

Schein, Edgar H. *Process Consultation Revisited: Building the Helping Relationship*. Reading, PA: Addison-Wesley, 1999.

Smedley, Brian D., Adrienne Y. Stith, and Alan R. Nelson, eds. *Unequal Treatment: Confronting Racial and Ethnic Disparities in Health Care*. Washington, D.C.: National Academies Press, 2003.

Solomon, Andrew. *The Noonday Demon: An Atlas of Depression*. New York: Scribner, 2001.

U. S. Department of Health and Human Services; Substance Abuse and Mental Health Services Administration Center for Mental Health Services. *Developing Cultural Competence in Disaster Mental Health Programs*. DHHS publication no. SMA 3828, 2003.

Yalom, Irvin D. *The Gift of Therapy: An Open Letter to a New Generation of Therapists and Their Patients*. New York: Harper-Perennial, 2003.

About the Contributors

Rev. Willard W. C. Ashley Sr., DMin, DH, is coeditor of this book, a psychotherapist, and founder and senior pastor of the Abundant Joy Community Church in Jersey City, New Jersey. He envisioned and implemented the largest clergy resiliency program in the United States following the attacks on September 11, 2001, the Care for the Caregivers Interfaith Program, a ministry of the Council of Churches of the City of New York. His ministry also includes roles as an adjunct professor; a consultant on disaster recovery and clergy self-care to congregations and Fortune 100 companies; a board member of Disaster Chaplaincy

Services, New York City; a board member of Christ Hospital, Jersey City, New Jersey; a former assistant dean of students and director of recruitment for Andover Newton Theological School; and past president of the Blanton Peale Graduate Institute, Alumni Association. Ashley is an ordained minister in the National Baptist Convention, USA, Inc.; Disciples of Christ; and the American Baptist Churches, USA.

Roberta L. Samet, LCSW, was the program manager for the September 11th Fund. In this capacity she oversaw the development and implementation of the long-term mental health recovery plan for New York City, the tri-state area, as well as other parts of the United States most affected by the events of 9/11. She developed 15 distinct trauma training programs reaching 7,000 mental health professionals, 3,000 primary care physicians, 2,500 early childhood educators and 2,000 clergy. She was instrumental in the development of a far-reaching mental health benefit that combined resources of the September 11th Fund and the American Red Cross. Through this program, a pool of 125,000 eligible individuals were entitled to receive free mental health and substance abuse services. Prior to this, Samet headed the AIDS Initiatives for the NYC Department of Mental Health where she served as a senior consultant to the agency. She is a past member of the board of directors of the New York City chapter of the National Association of Social Workers.

Rev. Rebeca Radillo, DMin, fellow in the American Association of Pastoral Counselors, served for six years on the board of directors of the association. Rev. Radillo is a licensed mental health professional (NYS); an associate professor of pastoral care and counseling at New York Theological Seminary; and founder and executive director of the Instituto Latino de Cuidado Pastoral, Inc. in New York City. Her publications include "Pastoral Counseling with Latina/Latino Americans" in *Clinical Handbook of Pastoral Counseling,* Vol. 3 (Paulist Press, 2003); *Cuidado Pastoral: Contextual e Integral* (Libros Desafio, 2007); and "A Model of Formation in the Multi-Cultural Urban Context for Pastoral Care Specialists" in *The Formation of Pastoral Counselors: Challenges and Opportunities* (Haworth Pastoral Press, 2006).

Imam Ummi Nur Allene Ali is CEO and president of Malik Shabazz Human Rights Institute; a United Nations nongovernment representative for the African Committee on Health and Human Rights; a member of the African Woman Alliance NGO; a member of the Partnership of Faith of New York City; a member of the Woman Planning Committee, Auburn Theological Seminary; a member of the Clergy Advisory Committee for Organ/Tissue Transplant Network; a committee member of the Interfaith Advisory Council, Auburn Theological Seminary; and served as a Red Cross chaplain at Ground Zero, New York City.

Rev. David Billings, DMin, has been an antiracist trainer and organizer with The People's Institute for Survival and Beyond since 1983. After thirty-five years in New Orleans, he moved to New York City in the fall of 2004 to work with The People's Institute's New York office. In the fall of 2006 he was appointed the Pauline Falk Chair on Community, Race, and Mental Health with the Jewish Board of Family and Children's Services. Rev. Billings is an ordained United Methodist minister. He also is a historian with a special interest in the history of race and racism. Over the years, Rev. Billings's organizing work has been cited for many awards, such as the Westchester County chapter of the National Association of Social Workers Public Citizen of the Year; the New Orleans Pax Christi Bread and Roses Award; the Loyola University of New Orleans Homeless and Hunger Award; and the National Alliance against Racist Oppression's Angela Davis Award for community service.

Rabbi Zahara Davidowitz-Farkas, BCJC, was the founding executive director of Disaster Chaplaincy Services, New York. She responded on September 12, 2001, to the 9/11 attacks in New York City. At the beginning of 2002 she was hired full-time to oversee the American Red Cross's (ARC) Spiritual Care Long Term Recovery program in New York City. She is a longtime member of ARC's Spiritual Care Response Team and serves on the national oversight committee. She served as dean of the Rabbinic Seminary of Hebrew Union College–Jewish Institute of Religion in New York, as the director of the Jack D. Weiler Chaplaincy Program of the New York Board of Rabbis, and as coordinator of Jewish chaplaincy at the New York Hospital–Cornell Medical Center under the auspices of the HealthCare Chaplaincy.

15

Attending to the Dead

Morgues, Body Identification, Accompanying and Blessing the Dead

Timothy G. Serban, MA, BCC

And, the humbling work continues.... Today we led at least 56 people home, to a home much greater than here. Their lives, though cut short, are still filled with the memories, the love, and blessings that they have shared. And in a few weeks from now, they will be identified and the sleepless nights that their families share tonight will be a bit less uncertain because they will know that their lost ones have been found, and I pray their grief will be assuaged, knowing that we prayed a simple prayer when each and every one of them was found.[1]

EXCERPT FROM A LETTER BY TIM SERBAN, SRT OFFICER, TO DMORT
DEPUTY COMMANDER OF THE KATRINA RECOVERY OPERATION,
NEW ORLEANS, LOUISIANA, SEPTEMBER 14, 2005

How Disasters Change the Way We Care for the Dead

Each disaster is unique and the spiritual care response must be assessed in light of the size, scope, scale, and the local cultural factors involved. The need for rituals is essential and easily overlooked when faced with the overwhelming loss of life. The Pan American Health Organization advises communities about the consequences of neglecting appropriate funeral rituals following a disaster:

When isolated deaths occur within the normal context of social development, the relatives and social groups comply with funeral rituals without hesitation, in the manner proscribed by local customs. However, when a catastrophic event occurs with many deaths, whether caused by natural phenomena or by human activity, social groups are unable to act "naturally" or "as usual."

When tens or hundreds of corpses are present, such intense social pressure results that there is a tendency to make decisions that neglect the needs of the group and individual to conduct proper funeral rituals. This has a significant impact on the mourning process. The effects of disrupting normal rituals and the unresolved mourning of a society are thought to be decisive factors in the recurrence of episodic outbreaks of violence. The map of violence in the world shows similar antecedents throughout history.[2]

The omission of a community's own rituals due to the haste caused by the pressures inherent in a disaster and because of the difficulty of carrying out rituals, presents a situation of extreme pain for the community that parallels the "invisible death" described for situations of war.[3]

This extreme pain may often be overlooked in the early weeks and months following a disaster. Yet, as the numbness subsides, families will soon return seeking to be connected once again with the loved one that died. Having a place to grieve and a way to grieve the death is essential for the healing of the community. Chaplains and disaster spiritual care providers play a vital role in ensuring that the community has a chance to begin to grieve and honor the dead. As Reyes Mate writes in his *Memoria de Auschwitz*, "For a civilization to deserve that name, all of life must be valued, including the (absent) life of the dead."[4]

Chaplains Work with Both Living and Dead

While it is common for chaplains to serve in the midst of disasters and crises, the scope of disaster spiritual care expands far beyond the ordinary scope of care in a hospital or hospice setting. In the face of a disaster, the chaplain responds to the overwhelming experience of thousands of survivors and hundreds who have died. Chaplains are called to provide professional guidance and advice on how to best care for the overwhelming numbers of the dead. Chaplains face such questions as, what should be done to honor the dead at the moment of recovery in the wake of a mass-casualty disaster? In addition, how do we honor the rituals and religious practices of the various faith traditions that have a prescribed practice for caring for the dead in a timely manner? These were the real questions experienced in the days following Hurricane Katrina and four years earlier following the September 11, 2001, terrorist attacks in New York City. The goal of this chapter is to provide a practical and concrete resource for chaplains, clergy, and those involved in recovery work from a unique view woven from these two experiences of caring for the dead in the face of great loss of life following a mass disaster.

The Interfaith Nature of This Work—Collaborating with Key Stakeholders in Faith Communities

While early preparation is ideal before a disaster strikes, no one can fully prepare to respond to the changing and fluid nature of a disaster. Many faith traditions have formal national and international disaster relief organizations within their faith communities (such as Catholic Charities USA, United Jewish Communities, Lutheran Disaster Response, or Presbyterian Disaster Relief, to name a few). Such organizations can be found through the National Volunteer Organizations Active in Disaster website at www.nvoad.org.

Professional associations of chaplains exist for the training of board-certified chaplains who serve in hospitals, hospices, health care settings, and business settings across the nation. These associations include, the Association of Professional Chaplains, The National Association of Catholic Chaplains, and the National Association of Jewish Chaplains, to name a few. Interfaith ecumenical ministerial associations are generally groups of ministers from various religious groups organized to address socioeconomic needs in the community. Engaging such groups is vital to the support of local communities in the face of a disaster especially as it relates to providing appropriate rituals for those who have died. These groups can also serve in an advisory capacity in the planning of a national memorial service. While local ministerial associations represent many faith traditions, it is important to identify if there are any other churches or faith communities that are not yet identified or represented. Some faith communities will expect disaster spiritual care providers to come to them. Due to many urgent needs, these faith communities may simply be overwhelmed caring for their own. In the early days following Hurricane Katrina in Baton Rouge, a local interfaith ministerial association held many collaborative meetings to address common concerns about the number of uninvited outside religious groups who were occupying local disaster shelters with an agenda of proselytizing. The concern was significant because their activity was taking advantage of the vulnerabilities of hurricane survivors. Additional concerns were expressed about the number of people who were dying and dead in temporary medical hospitals at the airport. The interfaith association was instrumental in coordinating clergy visits to hospitals and housing shelters. They provided additional clergy to ensure that holy days were observed and rituals were provided for members of their faith traditions. These meetings opened the door for ongoing collaboration and provided access to resources when the disaster operation transitioned to a long-term recovery effort.

In the wake of a national tragedy, it is not uncommon for rabbis, clergy, bishops, and cardinals, as well as national and international religious leaders to respond or send emissaries to support the community in their grief. Leaders of faith communities may request to visit key sites where the largest numbers of deaths occurred in order to offer prayers for blessing the dead.

Whenever possible, such requests should be coordinated with local and national officials. If there is an active rescue operation, such requests will likely be denied. Once recovery begins, however, the requests are likely to be approved. It is reasonable to request the temporary cessation of operations during these visits in order to honor moments of silence during a prayer service or blessing ritual. In honoring such requests, you should identify key government liaisons that can easily collaborate with relief organizations to support family visits to the site. Within the first four weeks following 9/11, religious leaders appeared from around the country and the world. Many sought to be as close as possible to the site where the World Trade Center towers fell. It often required an orientation to the nature of the site as an active crime scene. Family visits to Ground Zero were coordinated through the family assistance center. Families were gathered in groups of forty at a time. They were given the option of bringing flowers and stuffed animals to a designated location before viewing the full devastation. For families, visiting the site helped them connect with the place where their loved one died and for some it helped make their loss more real. Following 9/11, there were three major disaster sites: the World Trade Center, the Pentagon, and Shanksville, Pennsylvania. At each of these locations, there were multiple designated points of operations for the coordination of the recovery effort. Such sites include the recovery and reconstruction sites where debris is gathered.

No amount of preparation could prepare anyone for the massive scope and scale of the FBI operation at the Staten Island landfill in New York. This location was where the debris was taken from the World Trade Center site. During my initial deployment to this site to assess the spiritual needs among workers, a powerful image of mountains of twisted metal was observed. The first recognizable view of aircraft parts was visible here. Across this vast landscape stood hundreds of agents in biohazard suits beside huge vibrating multilevel conveyor belts that carried soil shipped by barge from the World Trade Center site. Each conveyor belt sifted the soil through smaller and smaller holes, until it ultimately ended up a fine, sandlike consistency. The low rumble of these machines was broken only by the odd but unmistakable sound of a distant bagpiper playing "Amazing Grace," as a body had been recovered and was being transferred by honor guard into an ambulance. These were the sobering sights and sounds that occupied their reverent work.

The Mass Disaster Reality—Local Faith Community Overload

In the midst of a major natural, technological, or human-caused disaster with extensive loss of life, local leaders of faith communities can be quickly overwhelmed trying to support the basic needs of survivors or providing repeated funerals or services to honor the dead. Local faith communities are often not well prepared. Those living closest to the disaster have the most difficult time maintaining healthy boundaries. The work of recovery lasts months, if not years, and the difficult task of returning to some sense of normal is nearly impossible.

One Sunday afternoon, three weeks after the 9/11 terrorist attacks on America, a New York Fire Department chaplain entered Respite Center One, located at St. John's University auditorium one block from the World Trade Center. This was a place where rescue and recovery workers came for food, rest, and support. Sunday Mass, led by one of the priest chaplains on our team, had just concluded. The fire chaplain walked in to check on things and see if we had what we needed. His eyes were bloodshot from the unending sleepless nights spent with firefighter families. He said, "I've performed thirty funerals so far and I am planning another fifteen before the week is through. The toughest part," he said, "is trying to be at so many funerals. I have one in Rockaway, one in Staten Island, and another in New Jersey all on the same day." We reached out to him in that solitary moment, hoping to help him gain a breath of rest or downtime before he had to run again. We were overwhelmed hearing what he was going through, and still, we could not imagine what he was feeling as he tried to live this incredible responsibility. In a simple way we encouraged him to take a moment for himself right here in the darkness of the auditorium to breathe. His response was, "I'm okay. Really, I'm fine. I just have so much to do and I have to be there for the families." The silence of the moment ended when his pager went off and he said, "It's an industrial fire in Brooklyn. Gotta go ..." His two minutes of rest ended, he hopped off the stage where he was sitting, and he made his way down the aisle to the exit.

This is a common example of many leaders of faith communities who face overwhelming need with a deep personal sense of responsibility. Normally, going beyond the call of duty is often seen as an honor and something that is expected of clergy. However, in the midst of major disasters and loss of life, the potential for being emotionally and spiritually drained without knowing it is dangerously high. In a disaster, local faith community leaders may be expected to be *all things to all people*. Nothing could be worse for those who serve in this capacity. This is why being closely connected to a team of professional spiritual care providers is essential. Working together as a team enables chaplains and clergy to set healthy limitations on the work we do. It gives us the chance to debrief, to check in, and to make time to feel the great emotion with the team before going off shift for the day.

Boundaries

In the face of an overwhelming disaster, one thing is clear: everywhere you look, you will see an unending sea of need. Following Hurricane Katrina in August 2005, tens of thousands of survivors were housed in shelters, on gymnasium floors, in convention centers, and in church halls. Teams of rescue and recovery workers were housed in shelters and fairground complexes. Teams of chaplains and clergy who were part of the Katrina response were embedded in shelters of five hundred or more in church gymnasiums and union halls. The needs in these shelters were great. One day, a recovery worker shared a concern for those caring for thousands of rescued pets at the fairgrounds in Gonzales, Louisiana. This animal shelter was being inundated with pet food for the rescued animals, but they barely had enough food and meals for the human rescue workers. Calls came in often from shelters requesting spiritual support for those involved in the intense evacuation of the city of New Orleans. At times, law enforcement commanders would call from the field asking if our chaplains could stay embedded with their teams for three to four more days to offer needed emotional and spiritual support. The unmet need in such disasters is limitless, and being part of a team ensures that each person has a lifeline to help limit his or her exposure to the devastation and loss of life. During the Hurricane Katrina response, we required each chaplain in the field to check in by phone every morning and every night. There were times when teams of two chaplains were deployed to remote locations with no contact for two to three days.

The role of the chaplain in the face of a disaster may be to coordinate efforts for the provision of spiritual support, provide comfort through presence, and honor people in their search for meaning in the midst of the tragic situation. In Louisiana, chaplains were teamed up with mental health professionals in shelters across the state. Many survivors struggled with daily life in shelters, meeting their basic needs, and the lack of privacy. There is a deep desire to find some sense of hope in the midst of hopeless situations. Families ask deep questions such as "Why did God let this happen to us?" They may yearn for an answer, seeking a reason in the midst of unexpected and sudden death. They may cry out for leaders of faith to "Do something! Pray, honor the life that we lost, hear our story, share my tears, walk with me in my grief, hear my questions, and honor my deep lament." Their requests often come with an unspoken word of caution: "Please do not try to fill my questions with answers. Do not make the mistake of thinking you have to answer my 'why' questions."

Do not take these moments of companionship as an opportunity to take advantage of the vulnerable and grieving by trying to recruit church members, create converts, or save souls. In the face of great disaster and devastation, clergy are called to "be present," to walk with the hurting from all faith traditions and those of no particular faith or religious tradition. In the face of great loss, it is a very sensitive time to bring the honor of ritual and tradition together. In such times, it may be more difficult not to speak than it is to rush to give an answer.

Working with People Who Might Not Be Used to Working with Chaplains

Following a disaster with mass casualties there are more levels of law enforcement agencies involved than anyone can imagine. The types of response agencies will vary depending on the nature of the disaster. For example, following 9/11 in New York, the entire site was considered an active crime scene. The State Department, FBI, and organizations that investigate international terror were mobilized, creating an entirely different level of response than what follows a natural disaster, such as Hurricane Katrina.

During a day at the World Trade Center's family assistance center at pier 94 in Manhattan, a row of agents from the State Department sat at tables processing massive amounts of paperwork. When I asked them about their role, they said, "We are processing the paperwork for the murders." This was the first time I heard the word *murder* used in relation to the event, and it was a sobering reality that this was a very different type of disaster. The scope and scale of the devastation in New York was so huge that it was difficult to comprehend the disaster as a terrorist event. Within the convention center in New York, dozens of medical examiners sat at tables to meet families and gather DNA material to aid in the identification process. Next, families were led to cubicles of lawyers who assisted them with processing information regarding last will and testaments. Chaplains found themselves not only guiding families through this maze of support, but they were called to help the legal professionals, who previously had never done something like this before. Guiding the families in this one shelter was challenging, but no one could imagine supporting tens of thousands of survivors in thousands of shelters in the wake of a natural disaster such as Hurricane Katrina four years later.

After Hurricane Katrina, the entire infrastructure of a region was devastated across 93,000 square miles, which is larger than the size of the entire country of Great Britain. The biggest question in this disaster was where to begin? The rescue and recovery efforts were complicated by mass evacuations, the threat of violence in urban areas, and the constant threat of more severe weather. Survivors struggled for basic food, water, and shelter. While efforts were being made to bring food to devastated areas, people were simultaneously being evacuated out of the entire city. The recovery process was extremely complex. In most disaster situations, the recovery phase begins only after the emergency rescue phase is complete. For example, in a building collapse, the recovery phase begins after the critical window of survivability has passed. However, following Hurricane Katrina in New Orleans, the rescue and recovery efforts were happening simultaneously due to the extreme and overwhelming nature of this disaster. Helicopters continuously flew in and out of the city, bringing survivors out of areas that were decimated.

In the midst of the pathways of rubble, teams of professional recovery workers assembled to begin the daunting task of recovering the remains of the dead. One of these teams was the Disaster Mortuary Operational Response Team (DMORT), which began in the early 1980s within the National Funeral Directors Association to address disaster situations and, specifically, mass fatality incidents. It became formalized when the United States Congress passed the Family Assistance Act in 1996, which required all American-based airlines to have a plan to assist families in the event of an airline disaster.[5] The same Family Assistance Act of 1996 was responsible for the creation of what is now known as the Spiritual Care Response Team (SRT) in the United States.

Working with DMORT teams involves an understanding of the typical layout of the disaster site. Generally, there are two types of disaster mortuaries: the temporary mortuary and the central disaster mortuary. At the World Trade Center, the temporary mortuary was established at the edge of Ground Zero in a secured tent area, and the central disaster mortuary was established at St. Vincent's Medical Center, which occupied an entire city block on a closed street with tents on either side. Medical examiners worked inside the hospital; rows of twenty-five refrigerated tractor-trailers lined the center of the street. The first two tents were designated as places of worship where leaders of faith communities had representatives offering prayers for the dead twenty-four hours a day. Conversely, following Hurricane Katrina, the disaster mortuary teams had multiple temporary transfer sites around New Orleans, and one central disaster mortuary nearly seventy miles to the north, in the town of St. Gabriel. Here, they occupied a closed elementary school, covering chainlink fences with black tarps and placing security checkpoints at the entrance. The playground was transformed into a tent city for the secured area where identification examinations occurred. Behind the buildings were rows of sleeping tents for DMORT workers.

Many of the DMORT workers we met were seasoned veterans who had been deployed a year earlier to do body recovery in Banda Aceh, Indonesia, following the devastating Southeast Asia tsunami of 2004. Very few, if any, had ever worked with chaplains in this capacity. In the weeks following Hurricane Katrina, I received a call from commanders in the field for chaplains to support DMORT teams in their recovery work in New Orleans. We were to have chaplains embedded with the four- to six-member DMORT teams who went into the field to recover bodies from locations identified by the search-and-rescue teams. The purpose of our chaplains' presence was to provide a dignified interfaith ritual of honoring the dead as each body was recovered.

Having not worked with such teams before, we had to assess the nature of this request and create a plan for our response. Like the old saying goes, "desperate times call for desperate measures." Immediately, we had to figure out what this was going to mean for our team and those in the field. Could we keep our chaplains safe? Once they were embedded, how could we ensure that they could get out of a city that was locked-down by martial law? Our first action was to meet with key leaders in the field at a rally point in New Orleans. The journey into the city unescorted through multiple military checkpoints was daunting. Street after street was abandoned, with devastation everywhere. The only way we would be able to safely leave this city was in our marked vehicle with our official identification. In the distance, the battered Superdome stood as one of the few recognizable landmarks.

Initially, we met with members of the military chaplains corps of U.S. Northern Command. They were present in an advisory capacity as we assessed this new assignment. There were numerous complicating factors involved with pulling this effort together, but success came in the skilled team of chaplains assigned to this duty. We needed to ensure that they were skilled chaplains as well as highly skilled diplomats and collaborators.

One complicating factor of working with disaster mortuary workers was that they had never worked directly with chaplains in this manner before. Chaplains, for that matter, had rarely worked directly with disaster mortuary teams beyond incidental hospital work. In addition, as the leader of the spiritual care team, I needed to ensure that those being assigned to this work were among the highest-trained chaplains due to the direct nature of this work and the reality that chaplains would be going into areas where they had previously been restricted. Each chaplain needed to have a keen recognition of their professional emotional boundaries. It would be too easy for an inexperienced disaster spiritual care provider to get caught up in the need to help and find themselves going beyond the boundaries of their assignment. Working with DMORT professionals in the field is very different from standard chaplaincy work. In health care settings, chaplains work with nurses, physicians, and caregivers. The chaplain generally enters the emotional spiritual space of the caregiver once the individual has disengaged from the heat of the crisis or critical emergency. In the midst of the crisis, all professionals must completely focus on the work at hand, ensuring that their undivided attention is given to their specialty. Any interruption or distraction could negatively affect the situation. The chaplain must carefully observe every subtle movement as the team works so as not to be in the way. They seamlessly flow into the spaces, attending to the needs as they arise. These finely tuned specialty teams have their own language and ways of communicating. They may use a simple word or cue with each other.

The DMORT teams initially feared that chaplains would tap too hard on the exterior of their teammates' defenses and potentially unravel them in the midst of a difficult recovery operation. In such situations, when a recovery worker in the field begins to talk about the emotional fallout of their experience, chaplains must be effective in applying what I call *spiritual duct tape*. The chaplain must effectively use his or her skills to help keep the recovery worker contained and focused on the task at hand until they are safely disengaged from the active disaster area. The chaplain's role is to help protect the DMORT recovery workers engaged in the active process of body retrieval. If a chaplain begins to tap too deeply into the defenses of the recovery worker in the field, the team could potentially lose the member in the most critical part of their work. In New Orleans, the recovery teams depended totally on the resources of every person on the team. If a recovery worker emotionally unraveled in the field, the burden of the physical work fell upon the shoulders of the remaining team members. With one less person, the three remaining members would have to carry the burden of this very strenuous and physical work. In the end, the chaplains and the DMORT teams found our collaboration to be successful, and commanders in the field began to seek ways to include chaplains in the future. We were able to honor the life of each person who had died with a brief yet meaningful ritual at the moment they were recovered through the entire journey of bringing them home.

In addition to partnering with DMORT in the field, the Spiritual Care Response Team served in an advisory capacity to the St. Gabriel, Louisiana, disaster mortuary support base regarding Jewish and Islamic leaders' requests for a ritual washing of the body at the end of the postmortem identification process. We determined that, in the face of this disaster, adding a washing station would not be offensive to the major Christian faith traditions and had the potential of honoring Islamic and Jewish faith communities, where this is a common practice. As a result of this collaboration, we were able to advise the DMORT team processing the bodies. They agreed to add a final washing station to their operations so that each body would be washed after all invasive procedures were complete. This washing was not meant to replace the religious ritual but to honor all traditions in the face of the extreme nature of this disaster.

As word spread about the location of the disaster mortuary, family members began to arrive at the front gate with pictures and requests to learn the fate of their loved ones. They came hoping to claim the body of their family members. It was a difficult and challenging task for the security guards and DMORT staff who were not equipped to adequately support families in their grief to face these people. Many families were simply sent away, until another role emerged for the Spiritual Care Response Team. Chaplains were assigned to the gate to provide support to families when they arrived. The family would share their story and the chaplain would honor the life of their loved one with a word or a prayer when requested. In the end, chaplains soon became a welcomed presence for these teams in the midst of this disaster.

Blessing Prayer

The blessing that was used in the Hurricane Katrina response was the same blessing used in the recovery of the victims of the World Trade Center in New York. This simple blessing is four sentences long:

> We give thanks for this person's life.
> We give thanks that this person was found.
> We give thanks for the persons that found them.
> We ask that they may be made whole in God's arms,
> And that they know peace.

The initial focus of this prayer is to honor the person's life, to express gratitude that those who were lost have been found. It includes a prayer honoring the recovery workers. It seeks to impart wholeness in the loving embrace of the God of any religious faith and, finally, imparts a prayer of final peace. If you wish, you could add a prayer for the loved ones who have lost their family member with the following line: "And may comfort surround those who have loved this person."

In a letter to the DMORT deputy commander in New Orleans, I reflected on the work that began with the disaster spiritual care providers and DMORT teams in the field, and the meaning of the work that we had accomplished in this difficult disaster. I included a reference to our prayer:

> We have established the presence of a chaplain 24 hours a day at the Disaster Mortuary; we have committed the presence of 2 chaplains to be embedded with the DMORT teams 24/7. In addition, as each vehicle arrives with the remains of those who died, the truck stops just inside the gates and a chaplain prays once more. In addition, we are contacting the local clergy of the town of St.

Gabriel in order to assist the emotional needs of this community in this disaster.

"And, the humbling work continues… Today we led at least 56 people home, to a home much greater than here. Their lives, though cut short, are still filled with the memories, the love and blessings that they have shared. And in a few weeks from now, they will be identified and the sleepless nights that their families share tonight will be a bit less uncertain because they will know that their lost ones have been found, and I pray their grief will be assuaged, knowing that we prayed this simple prayer when each and every one of them was found:

"We give thanks for this person's life.
We give thanks that this person was found.
We give thanks for the persons that found them.
We ask that they may be made whole in God's arms.
And that they know peace."[6]

While the types of rituals and traditions at the end of life vary widely across the country and around the world, we must always seek to find balance between the pressure of the immediate needs in a rescue effort with the need to ensure that every body is recovered with the utmost respect and honor. During the initial days and weeks following a disaster, clergy and professional chaplains have the opportunity to help inform recovery teams, government officials, leaders of faith communities, and families about the nature of a disaster and how their involvement can make a difference. Offering practical advice to these groups may range from providing a sacred pause in the recovery process, adding a washing station at the conclusion of the identification exam, creating a sacred place of prayer for the dead, and ensuring that families are supported with the caring presence of another person who will walk with them in the fog and haze of the tragic experience of losing someone they love.

Notes

1. Letter from Tim Serban, SRT officer, to DMORT deputy commander of the Hurricane Katrina recovery operation, New Orleans, Louisiana, September 14, 2005. http://www.dmort2.org/index.php?option=com_content&task=view&id=12&Itemid=82.
2. Reyes Mate, "El campo, lugar de la política moderna," in *Memoria de Auschwitz* (Madrid: Editorial Trotta, 2003), 78.

3. Pan American Health Organization, *Management of Dead Bodies in Disaster Situations,* series no. 5 (Washington, D.C.: PAHO, 2004), 86; http://www.paho.org/English/DD/PED/DeadBodiesBook.pdf.

4. Pan American Health Organization, *Management of Dead Bodies in Disaster Situations,* 89.

5. National Disaster Medical System: Disaster Mortuary Operational Response Teams DMORT, *How It All Started.* http://www.dmort.org/DNPages/ DMORTHistory.htm.

6. Letter from Tim Serban to DMORT deputy commander.

Further Reading

The Federation of Cyberians. *Washing the Dead Body (GHUSL).* http://www.islamabad.net/graveyard/wash.htm.

Meichenbaum, Donald. "Stress Inoculation Training for Coping with Stressors," *The Clinical Psychologist* 49 (1996), 4–7. http://www.apa.org/divisions/div12/rev_est/sit_stress.html.

National Disaster Medical System: Disaster Mortuary Operational Response Teams DMORT, *How It All Started.* http://www.dmort.org/DNPages/DMORTHistory.htm.

Pan American Health Organization. *Management of Dead Bodies in Disaster Situations,* series no. 5. Washington, D.C.: PAHO, 2004. http://www.paho.org/English/DD/PED/DeadBodiesBook.pdf.

Mate, Reyes. *Memoria de Auschwitz.* Madrid: Editorial Trotta, 2003.

Ross, Heather M. "Islamic Tradition at the End of Life," *MedSurg Nursing,* (April 2001) http://findarticles.com/p/articles/mi_m0FSS/is_2_10/ai_n18611570/pg_1.

Wikipedia, "Ritual Washing in Judaism: Contact With and Treatment of a Corpse." http://en.wikipedia.org/wiki/Ritual_washing_in_Judaism#_ref-28.

About the Contributor

Timothy G. Serban, MA, BCC, is the director of mission integration and spiritual care with Providence Health and Services in the Northwest Washington service area in Everett, Washington. He has been a board-certified chaplain with The National Association of Catholic Chaplains since 1991. He has served as an active member of the American Red Cross Spiritual Care Response Team (SRT) since 1999. Serban served in New York in a lead position with the Red Cross Spiritual Care Aviation Incident Response Team over respite centers at Ground Zero, the temporary mortuary, and the disaster mortuary at St. Vincent's Hospital and at the Staten Island landfill, where recovery work continued with debris from the World Trade Center site. In 2005, Serban served as the SRT lead chaplain in the New Orleans region immediately after Hurricane Katrina. He was responsible for the spiritual care collaboration with the Disaster Mortuary Operational Response Teams in New Orleans and morgue operations in St. Gabriel, Louisiana. He has contributed in other significant national leadership roles for the SRT and has spoken nationally on such topics as the theology of disaster at The National Association of Catholic Chaplains national conference in Columbus, Ohio. Serban currently directs a team of twenty chaplains and lives with his wife and son in Marysville, Washington.

16

Working with Children and Adolescents after a Disaster

John D. Kinsel, MS, LPCC

Webster's dictionary defines disaster as "an event resulting in great loss and misfortune." The American Red Cross goes into more detail: "A disaster is an occurrence such as a hurricane, tornado, storm, flood, high water, wind-driven water, earthquake, drought, blizzard, pestilence, famine, fire, explosion, volcanic eruption, building collapse, commercial transportation wreck, or other situation that causes human suffering or creates human needs that the survivors cannot alleviate without assistance." In other words, disasters are bad things that happen to people. And whenever people are affected by one of the multitude of types of disaster, among those affected are children.

There is a common myth in our society that says children, particularly young children, are not affected by disastrous events. The assumption is that children are either too young to understand or too preoccupied with playing to be affected or are just naturally resilient and bounce back on their own. Unfortunately, this is not the case. While children will not likely respond in the same ways as the adults around them, even infants, the very youngest of children, are affected when a disaster occurs.

All human beings respond to stress in some similar ways. When a person is faced with a threat or an actual experience of danger or loss, their brain tends to shift control from the upper brain, where rational thought resides, to the primitive brain stem, which prepares the person autonomically for one of two choices: fight or flight. How a person manages this neurological transition differs depending on multiple factors, such as previous experience, access to support systems, ability to self-regulate, and so on. For children, the stress response is often one of emotional and behavioral regression. And, as will be discussed in more detail later in this chapter, children's responses often differ markedly from those of the adults around them.

Aspects of a disaster can also affect how adults and children respond. For instance, if the onset of the disaster is sudden, such as in the case of a tornado, responses may be more extreme, as people struggle to react quickly with little or no time to prepare. Other types of disasters, such as floods, come on more slowly, allowing most to prepare in some way for what is about to happen. Another factor to consider when preparing to provide assistance to disaster survivors is the phase of the disaster at the time service is offered: impact, rescue, or recovery. Each phase is accompanied by specific needs and typical reactions.

Children and Disaster

For children, as for adults, the nature of their response to disaster is affected by both their actual experience of the disaster and their perception of the disaster. A child who was in his or her house when it was knocked down by a tornado will be more vulnerable to traumatic response than will a comparable child who returns home after being away to find his or her home destroyed. If either of these children was cared for during the disaster by a parent who remained calm and offered reassurance and hope, their response may well be mitigated. If their parent was openly distressed and anxious, the child may adopt a similar emotional response. There are a few other generalizations that can be made about children's responses to disaster.

Typical Responses

As mentioned earlier in this chapter, stress creates a fight or flight reaction in the brain by hyperactivating the brain stem. Since the brain stem is the oldest part of the brain, the result for children is often manifested in developmental regression. Milestones that previously had been mastered or nearly mastered no longer hold fast. For example, it is not unusual for preschoolers and some school-age children to "forget" they were toilet trained and begin wetting themselves, either at night or during the day, or both. Adolescents that were able to function logically and realistically may begin to act more impulsively and irrationally.

The midbrain, the part of the brain that controls emotions, is geographically and developmentally not far above the brain stem. As such, it is vulnerable to change in times of distress as well. It is not unusual for children to display increased emotionality. This may take the form of fear manifested by nightmares or a strong desire to avoid reminders of the disaster. It may appear as anger, as children become more irritable and oppositional. Other children may present with more labile mood, fluctuating rapidly from happy to sad to afraid.

Another common response to the stress of disaster is for a child to exhibit an exacerbation of previously held character and behavioral traits. If a child was active before the disaster, he or she may appear hyperactive afterward. If the child was quiet, he or she may now become withdrawn. Where there once was a talkative child, there now may be one who seems to never stop talking. If any of these characteristics were bothersome to the child's parents before, they now may be driving those parents crazy, either with concern or irritation or both.

This leads to another generalization about children's responses to disaster: they happen most often in the context of family. Any response to children in time of disaster needs to also address the needs of the parents and caregivers of the affected children. Parents and guardians experience their own stress reactions to the disaster, reactions that may interfere with their ability to attend closely to their children. They also are commonly very concerned about their children and are in need of factual information they can use to address those concerns. Parents and guardians also deserve the respect of being given information about any programs that involve their children.

A final common response by children to disaster that appears to contradict what was said earlier about the myths of children's responses is this: resiliency. Research from over thirty years of study of children in disaster suggests strongly that approximately 25 percent of children rebound quickly and regain the level of functioning they had attained prior to the disaster. These resilient children usually had at least one adult who was present with them throughout the ordeal and provided them with support and a sense of security. In addition, these children displayed mastery of the first three emotional developmental milestones: attachment, self-control, and initiative. More about the importance of these protective factors appears later in this chapter. Please be aware that the same studies suggest that 75 percent of children needed at least some intentional intervention in order to rebound from their disaster experience—a far cry from the myth that "they're just children; they'll be fine."

Age-Specific Responses

Given that children are indeed affected by and reactive to disasters, and that their reaction is often a regressive response, it is important to be aware of what children are like in the absence of disaster. Each child, each person, experiences disaster based on who they are at the time the disaster occurs. It is impossible to know the specifics of each child's life experiences: Has theirs been a stable and happy existence? Have they experienced parental separation or divorce? Has someone they know and trusted abused them? Have they experienced adults as being primarily helpful and trustworthy?

While such intimate knowledge of each child is not reasonable to expect outside a therapeutic relationship, those caring for children in times of disaster can and need to know what children of the ages being served are typically like. Although no child will fit every detail, the following age-specific generalizations describe typical children in the absence of disaster, as well as responses to disaster common to each developmental stage.

Infants

Children under age one are by definition very dependent on their caregivers. They are usually nonverbal and are limited in their ability to move around. They are in the important emotional developmental stage of establishing attachment to their primary caregivers (usually their parents). They take their cues from the significant adults around them as to how to respond emotionally in novel situations. Babies make their needs known primarily through crying, vocalizing, and gesturing. Stability, predictability, continuity, and security in terms of routines, surroundings, and relationships are very important to their emotional regulation.

Infants typically display stress responses in one of two ways: underreactivity or overreactivity. Underreactive babies move quickly through the stages of infant grief and become dull and nonresponsive. They may lie quietly for long periods without crying, even when they have a clear need, such as a diaper change or a regular feeding. They may stiffen or lie passively when picked up, not molding their bodies into their caregivers as normally would be expected. Overreactive babies may startle easily, cry frequently, and struggle and squirm when held, seemingly unable to accept the comforting an adult offers.

Toddlers

Unless hampered by a medical or developmental condition, toddlers are mobile. They are learning to walk, run, and climb. They tend to be very active as they explore the physical and human environment around them. Their primary emotional and behavioral task is to develop self-control, even as they learn how to balance being independent with being dependent at the same time. Toddlers are very new at this, and can become easily frustrated as they try to control all things and their desire to do something outpaces their capacity to accomplish it. Egocentric by nature (literally, the way their brains are wired), social engagements and niceties, such as sharing, don't come easily to them and are another common source of frustration for toddlers.

While becoming increasingly verbal over the years from one to three, toddlers are primarily grounded in the concrete, leading to a tendency to express their frustration physically in the form of tantrums. Their verbal skill can sometimes lead caregivers to believe that they can be reasoned with, but most toddlers respond best to redirection. Like infants, routines and predictability are important to toddlers, including adequate time to rest.

Also like infants, toddlers often display a dichotomy of responses to disaster. I was amazed while providing care to young children of victims of the September 11, 2001, terrorist attacks to see normally active eighteen-month-olds prefer to lie unmoving in their cribs until a caregiver returned for them. Other toddlers may become more demanding, wanting to be held often, whining to get their way. They may prefer a bottle over a cup and diapers over "big-kid" underwear.

Their play may become more disorganized, with toys being thrown or knocked over rather than being manipulated and explored. Sleep may be resisted.

Preschoolers

Between the ages of three and five, young children expand on their newfound self-control, demonstrating the capacity for initiative. This concept refers to their increased verbal and symbolic thinking capacities combined with a gradual reduction in egocentrism that allows them to play in groups, develop ideas and complex plans, and use common objects to dramatically play out their experiences and observations. This play moves from imitative to imaginative. They learn how to communicate effectively with adults and peers, though there likely is considerable unevenness in their social behavior. Having mastered cause and effect, they now respond more readily to reasoning and problem-solving when discipline is required. They are curious, love repeating things they have mastered, seek adult approval, and are generally competent in self-care and daily routines. Having both active and quiet time is important to them. They need adults around them who are attentive, positive, and provide a balance of nurture and structure.

Sadness is often expressed by preschool children as increased activity level, thus high activity levels can be expected in this age group after a disaster. As mentioned earlier, these young ones may begin to lose toilet-training skills. They may also begin to use more "baby talk." Sleep disturbance and the appearance of a variety of fears are not uncommon. Dramatic play often takes on themes associated with the disaster as preschoolers work at making sense of their experiences. For example, after 9/11 many preschool children made block towers that they could then knock down with toy airplanes. Children of this age will often have a stream of "why" questions for the important adults in their life. Emotionality often increases, with children becoming more irritable, openly upset, and oppositional. Still egocentric, the young child may believe they had a causal role in the disaster.

School-Age Children

As children move into the elementary and early middle school years, peer interactions take on more importance. They are keenly aware of friendship patterns and the opinions of their age-mates, though they still count on adults as their primary source of authority. Building on their mastery of initiative, these youngsters enjoy developing projects. Arts and crafts with a finished product versus the pure expressionism of the preschool years catch their interest. Games with agreed-upon rules and expectations that are the same for everyone characterize their moral developmental phase. They demand fairness. Adventures, mysteries, and fantasy that are separate from reality take on a new importance. Increased cognitive, language, and academic accomplishments widen their repertoire of means to perform work. Story writing and telling is now more possible. There is a desire to have reasons and explanations for phenomena that make sense to them based on their own thinking and experience.

School-age children frequently choose to draw pictures and tell stories about their disaster experiences. Like preschoolers, they may seem driven to do this and may repeat their explanations and questions over and over. Anger at the unfairness of the event may be present and may be directed at the caregiver for not preventing any loss. As with younger children, emotional regulation becomes less secure, and mood changes are common. Regression for them may include a lessening of their hold on the separation of reality and fantasy, as well as behavioral changes such as decreased cooperativeness, increased activity, or the appearance of internal preoccupation.

Adolescents

The teen years bring on sometimes seismic changes in young people. Hormones begin to flow in new ways that not only change their bodies, but also their emotions. Moodiness and emotionality are not uncommon. The egocentrism that was so active during the toddler years returns as self-absorption as teenagers consider the changes in themselves and their importance to others. Peers become even more important as standard bearers for behavior and affirmation. A push to develop their own unique identity can strain their relationships with parents and other authority figures. As their brains develop the capacity for abstract thought, the ability to "think about thinking," adolescents develop their own theories and think in new ways about the deep questions of existence. Outward appearances of certainty and experimental dress can belie an often fragile sense of self that is vulnerable to stress and criticism. Control of self and others, another vestige from toddlerhood, emerges as an important social factor. Like the toddler caught in the tension between dependence and independence, teenagers frequently present a contradictory developmental presence.

Some have suggested that the emotional volatility of adolescence makes it difficult to pinpoint stress reactions, but clear distinctions can be made after the occurrence of a disaster, often in an intensifying of traits previously present. For instance, moodiness may become increased. Teenagers may isolate themselves from their family, perhaps in part to avoid a reminder of the trauma. Rumination on the events of the disaster and their possible effect on themselves is not uncommon. On the other hand, some teens will overintellectualize, presenting their detailed rationalizations for events, disconnecting themselves from the emotions involved. Acting out with substances, suicidal ideation, and promiscuity are additional risks for this age group.

Special Situations

Children's responses to disaster can be affected by the nature of the event itself, as well as by their developmental stage. For example, a slowly approaching disaster that can be predicted and prepared for, such as a flood or a hurricane, may lead to less intense reactions, depending on the child's developmental level. Children ages preschool and up can help prepare the family for the event, either by gathering belongings together or by helping board up windows, depending on the child's capabilities. This can give the child a sense of control over circumstances and help them feel more competent to cope with what happens. In addition, an age-appropriate explanation of what is happening can be given to the child, helping them to prepare emotionally and cognitively. Most vulnerable to this type of disaster are infants and toddlers. Highly dependent and without a full grasp of cause and effect, these youngest of survivors can be confused and upset by the move from familiar surroundings into strange places with different smells, schedules, and people.

Sudden-onset disasters, such as tornadoes and terrorist attacks, catch many people off guard and not fully prepared. Even if the adults have some warning, there is usually high anxiety and little time or thought given to explaining what is happening to children. Survival becomes primary. Such disasters are often violent, with vivid damage to property and injury, possibly fatal, to people and pets. Families get separated. The status of loved ones may be unknown for long periods of time. Children may witness events beyond their capacity not only to understand, but to process. Children of all ages are especially vulnerable in such times.

When we seek to provide services to children following a disaster, it is important to understand how the phase of the disaster can affect their needs. During the impact phase, immediately after the disaster has struck, survival is of primary importance. Getting children to a safe place where they can receive shelter, medical attention, if needed, and sustenance takes priority. However, whenever possible, the emotional needs of the child survivors need to be attended to as well. Avoid separating very young children (infants, toddlers, preschoolers) from their parents or family members. If this must happen, have a plan in place to reunite them as soon as possible. Give the youngest children a simple explanation of why they are going somewhere other than home. Give older children more detail and involve them as they are able in helping themselves and others to support their sense of control and awareness of the world outside themselves.

In the days and weeks following the disaster, the recovery phase emerges. This is a time when immediate danger is past, but the children's world is still turned upside down. They are not on their usual schedule, their parents are acting differently than usual, they may be living in a shelter or other place that is not their home or in a damaged home that isn't the same. Fears of being revictimized abound. Uncertainty about the future can permeate families and entire communities. This is the time when the symptoms of distress outlined earlier in this chapter begin to appear and to be noticed by those providing care for children. It is a time to educate parents on how children respond to disasters. It is a time to help children find connections between the world they knew before the disaster and the one they will know in the future. It is a time for reestablishing routines, for encouraging self-expression, and for validating and normalizing children's perceptions, feelings, and confusions.

As time wears on into months and even years post-disaster, the phase of recovery folds over into that of reconstruction. Often these processes do not happen fast enough for the survivors. There can be bitterness and distress at the pace of reconstruction, at its unevenness across neighborhoods, at the forces that allowed the disaster to occur in the first place. There can be healing as families and communities re-build, as people come together to work side by side, as resolve and hope are experienced. Children are there in the midst of these stages as well. Those who have been called resilient are bouncing back. Those who have not mastered the events in their lives are struggling. Ongoing services are needed for children and families to get emotional as well as financial assistance. Efforts to promote the development of re-siliency need to be incorporated into systems that serve children: churches, recreational programs, schools, and day cares. The process of responding to disaster, both as survivors and as volunteers, can be a protracted enterprise.

Beyond the type and phase of a disaster, there is another special circumstance that affects a child's response to disaster that needs at-tention. The loss of a parent as a result of a disaster compounds the risk factor for a complicated stress reaction by the affected child. In the first five years of life, the greatest fear of young children is aban-donment. This anxiety about losing a parent never goes far beneath the surface of children of any age. When a parent's death occurs in the midst of all the other stressful events surrounding disasters, a child's capacity to cope is tested to the maximum. Specialized be-reavement intervention is called for. Professionals with sensitivity to age-specific needs and an attunement to an individual child and their family should be sought to intervene in an ongoing counseling relationship.

Responding to Children in Disaster

Exposure to children who have been affected by disaster tends to elicit feelings of sympathy and sadness in caregiving adults. While such feel-ings are normal and understandable, those who take on the task of working with children in disaster need to be able to manage such feel-ings in order to be able to focus on the potential of children and not solely on their loss. While children need the opportunity to grieve and work through their experiences in age-appropriate ways, the promo-tion of protective factors and reinforcement of children's strengths in the days following a disaster is essential for supporting long-term resilience.

Protective Factors

When an adult interacts briefly with a child, it is good to help them feel comforted and provide them with an avenue to express their feelings and ideas about what they have experienced. When that child has an adult that cares about them, nurtures them, and protects them over an extended and committed period of time, the experience can be powerful. Resilient children most often have the latter kind of a relationship with at least one adult. Teachers, pastors, coaches, uncles and aunts, neighbors, and, most importantly, parents can play this role for children exposed to disaster. Any program that is a temporary response to children following a disaster should attend to how the children are connected to such ongoing relationships. Adults local to the disaster that respond to children need to be aware that some children may need for them to be in it for the long haul.

Having a reliable adult in their lives is an *external* protective factor for children that goes hand in hand with the first of the *internal* protective factors: capacity for attachment. Ideally, beginning in infancy, children learn the capacity for attachment through experiences with primary caregivers who love them, are attuned to them as unique individuals, and provide them security by responding to their cues for attention. If they are hungry, these people feed them. If they are tired, the same people help them soothe into sleep. And so it goes until baby and caregiver become attached. The growing child carries these lessons about intimacy into other relationships. They learn the give and take of social existence, and they learn how to offer friendship to others. Most importantly, they learn to trust that they can seek out and build relationships with others, including adults who can support them.

For those responding to children during times of disaster, understanding the process by which attachment is developed is important so that elements of the process can be integrated intentionally into the helping response. Of primary importance is attending to each child as a unique individual and communicating that interest to the child. For infants, this means providing quality caregiving, with its features of a timely, gentle, engaging response to each infant's cues, even if it means holding an infant for a long period of time. For older children, it means offering unconditional positive regard: listening without interrupting, avoiding criticism of a child's perceptions, choice of clothing, and the like, and providing validation for any feelings they may choose to share (this includes the choice not to share!). It also means providing developmentally appropriate materials and activities that increase the likelihood of a good fit between the child's needs and the helping environment. One size does not fit all.

The capacity for self-control emerges developmentally during the toddler years, when essential baseline lessons about autonomy are learned. As toddlers move from a state of total dependence to one of a balance between dependence and independence, they are driven by an urge to explore and control. They also learn that there are boundaries on how much and what they can control. As they are repeatedly told "no" and redirected away from unsafe or socially unacceptable activity by their caregivers, they learn to inhibit their own behavior in these arenas. As they become frustrated by their own physical limitations and those imposed on them by their caregivers, they express their strong feelings in raw, physical, and poorly regulated ways: tantrums. With each successful loss of control and its associated gradual regaining of stability, they learn that emotions and behaviors can be controlled by their own volition. Often, toddlerhood is the time children also learn to control their processes of elimination, otherwise known as toilet training.

As children mature, they carry forward a sense of being able to control events and persons within certain limitations. They develop what can be called an internal locus of control, which helps protect them in a time of disaster. They believe that they are not just at the mercy of fate, but rather can become agents of change in their own circumstances. Those working with children following disaster need to support this capacity. In a practical sense, this means offering them opportunities to make choices. For toddlers and preschoolers, it means having a variety of age-appropriate materials and activities from which the children can choose. Free play, versus highly organized group activities, is preferred. Should a group activity be offered, individual children need to be made to feel it is okay if they decide to opt out and play independently. This does not mean that children are given free rein. Rather, boundaries need to be maintained, with a good amount of freedom allowed within those boundaries. Similarly, programs for school-age children and adolescents that support the capacity for self-control will offer children the option of individual or group activities, opportunities for inclusion in decision making and inquiry into what each child feels is the best way to handle whatever is going on in his or her life.

Preschoolers have as their primary emotional developmental milestone the development of a sense of initiative. With their growing capacity to think and communicate using symbols, play becomes more complex and their projects move from simple mimicry to amalgams of their own thinking, their observations of others, and their own concrete experiences. Creativity is the cornerstone element in initiative, as imagination, planning, and problem solving become regular features of the child's approach to the world. In a time of disaster, this capacity can protect children from debilitating stress reactions. Children with a sound integration of initiative feel that not only can they act on the world in their own behalf, but they also can make specific plans and come up with elaborate solutions that move them into a better future. This future thinking is a key aspect of the protective influence of a well-developed sense of initiative.

Those responding to children have a variety of choices in the ways that they support and encourage initiative in the children in their care. Offering materials that encourage dramatic play is appropriate when serving children ages three to five. Dolls, cooking utensils, transportation and rescue-themed toys, dress-up clothing, blocks, and telephones are some materials that allow for dramatic problem solving. Art materials for free expression also encourage children to practice being creative, whether the product has any deep meaning regarding the disaster or not. Older children, including teens, are also likely to respond positively to the presence of art materials. They may be more amenable to some suggestion that links the activity to the tragedy they may have experienced. "How could you use these collage materials to depict the feelings you had when you saw the damage to your house? Who would you like to send a sympathy card to and what would it look like?" are examples of prompts they might be given. The more academically advanced children may also respond to opportunities to write about their experiences. Poetry, short stories, and journaling are all options. Building on their greater social capacity and sensitivity to peers, group activities such as the creation of a mural or the planning together of a memorial also can promote the use of initiative as a potential coping mechanism.

Risk Factors

There are some conditions that put children at a greater risk for intense stress reactions and in need of more intense responses. Among these conditions are direct exposure to death, human injury or suffering (including their own injury), and violent destruction of property; loss of or unexplained separation from their primary caregivers or other significant people, such as a sibling; previous history of exposure to trauma through disaster, child abuse, or other terrifying experience; parental psychological unavailability, whether due to the parent's mental illness or strong stress reaction, or other factors; actual or perceived high risk of a recurrence of the disaster; and prolonged duration of the disruption of their life. If service providers are aware of any of these factors for a given child, a referral for further assessment by a mental health professional is indicated. Gaining knowledge of what resources for such services are available within the disaster response system and within the affected community should be a part of preparation for anyone responding to children after a disaster.

The above list of risk factors is not exhaustive, and assumptions cannot be made about a child's reactions based on the absence of the above risk factors. One study of children following the Oklahoma City bombing in 1995 found that a surprising number of children who had not experienced the disaster firsthand, but knew someone who had, displayed some symptoms of posttraumatic stress disorder. The best source of information about risk for any child is the observation of that child. Children that present with behaviors on the extreme ends of a continuum of symptoms are in need of careful attention. This would include children who are either highly or irrepressibly active or those who are extremely withdrawn; those who are impulsively raging and those who are consistently passive; or those that threaten injury to others or threaten injury to themselves. Whether presenting with extreme symptoms or not, all children require careful monitoring.

Interventions and Strategies

In the above section on protective factors, some specific strategies were detailed for the support and promotion of those factors. As individuals and groups plan to work with children affected by disaster, other interventions and activities are also called for. By attending to the developmental needs of the children served, systems and activities can be developed that accurately and fully respond to these youngsters.

Primary to any intervention program directed at children is programming that addresses the needs of their parents or guardians and families. Because children are legally the dependents of their parents, permission from parents should be obtained whenever possible before beginning direct interaction with children. Beyond this legality and liability issue is the moral obligation to attend to the parents as well as to the children. Information should be gathered about any special needs of the child. Contact with parents also affords the chance to learn about the child's cultural and ethnic orientation so subsequent programming can be sensitive to their normal experiences.

Attending to the parents' needs supports the overall goal of supporting the children. Parents are often hungry for assistance in knowing how to explain to their children what has happened. They need factual information about common child responses to disaster and trauma so they can better understand and relate to their children. At the end of this chapter is a list of resources where informational fact sheets and brochures can be obtained that are appropriate for sharing with caregivers. Parents also need an explanation of what the content and nature of the child programming will be. For some community-based programs, this may include involving parent representatives in the planning. Providing feedback to the parents about what and how their child did during the service also communicates respect.

Like the children, parents bring whoever they are and whatever response they are having to the disaster to their contact with child-serving programs. Parents may need an opportunity to tell their own story. Setting aside people and time to allow this to happen can help parents feel more comfortable about having their child participate, and feel attended to themselves. Some parents will need referrals for resources to help them with their own stress response and places where they can get specialized assistance with a child who has more intense needs.

If an organization is planning to develop their own materials or recommendations for parents, it is important that the following basic description of what children need from their parents subsequent to disaster be included:

1. **Children need to be assured and reassured that they are safe.** They need to be told directly, and often repeatedly, that their parents are going to keep them safe from becoming retraumatized. Rather than dishonestly stating that a disaster will never happen again, parents need to communicate in age-appropriate language that they, the adults, are going to take care of things and keep the children as safe as they can, so the children need not worry about handling this themselves.

2. **Even the youngest children that are verbal need a simple and truthful explanation of what happened.** This prevents them from using their imaginations to envision things as even worse than they are. It gives them something concrete to hold on to. Again, the children need not get gruesome detail but an age-appropriate, simple explanation. Many young children will gratefully accept such a response. Older children may have additional questions and want more detail. Parents should use their knowledge of their child, including their developmental level, in framing their responses. It is usually better to give too little information and get follow-up questions than to give too much and inadvertently overwhelm the child.

3. **Reestablishment of some semblance of normal routines should occur as soon as possible.** The presence of familiar practices and rituals helps children to reconnect with a sense of security. These routines could be bedtimes or bedtime stories, praying before every meal, eating together as a family, re-enrolling in day care, school, or any other routine that has meaning to a specific family.

Interventions and strategies when the population of children is very young center on the provision of a safe and secure space. Infants and toddlers need an opportunity in disaster to be minimally exposed to all the uproar and disruption that often occurs. Being surrounded by caregivers who are tuned in to them and attentive to their needs, whatever those might be, is the single most appropriate intervention for them. Part of the creation of a welcoming environment should be having supplies of diapers, changes of clothes, bottles, and snacks on hand. Whenever possible, these supplies should come from the families of the children. In this way, the taste of the formula, the type of snack, the smell of the clothes will all have a familiar feel to the child, promoting a sense of connection and continuity. Families should be encouraged to bring along favorite toys, blankets, and other "loveys," and children should be allowed to have free access to them as they so need. Separation from a caregiver should never be forced. Parents may be provided with the opportunity to stay with their children or return to check in on them whenever they choose. The focus should always be on what a given child needs at the time.

Preschoolers also may be encouraged to bring along an item that has importance to them. These items may sometimes be a bit odd. One story tells of a four-year-old who clutched a small square of old carpet, the only thing rescued from his bedroom after a flood. One child receiving care after 9/11 would not let go of an empty soda can, given to him by his mother before she dropped him off.

It is axiomatic that play is young children's work, thus play-oriented environment and programming is encouraged. Age-appropriate play materials were discussed in a section above. Besides dramatic play items, sensory and malleable materials can be provided to allow children to express strong emotions physically. Play dough can be pounded and made into shapes that then can be destroyed. Access to water and sand can help children become soothed and to explore the possibilities of these substances. Such media also may be drawn into dramatic reenactment. I once noticed while serving young children after a flood that some preschoolers had begun using paper cups in the sand table to replay the making and stacking of sandbags. Now that was initiative in action!

The presence of puzzles can help children feel a sense of control and security as the pieces fit neatly into their specified places each time the puzzle is completed. Books that are familiar preschool stories and others that tell stories of children coping with bad things happening are appropriate to have to support intervention. Information on appropriate books for children is included in the Resources section at the end of this chapter. Children should be encouraged to think of the answers to their own questions triggered by the stories. Inevitably, the natural curiosity of preschoolers will lead to some children asking the hard "why" questions about the disaster. It is okay to say you don't know. It is fine to ask the child what explanations his or her family has offered and then validate those. If pressed, a simple, factual explanation should be given and that information shared with the child's parent. Unless you are working in a specifically designated religion-oriented program, theological explanations should be avoided. Giving such an explanation that turns out to be counter to the child's own family values can promote more, rather than less, confusion for a child at a time when they need as much certainty as possible. Older children and their families should be afforded the same respect.

While play is definitely a large part of the lives of school-age children, they are more inclined than preschoolers to engage in organized play with rules and objectives. Activity-based interventions build on this developmental characteristic, as well as the children's age-appropriate interest in developing projects. Curricula for this type of programming have been developed by the Red Cross and others and are referenced in the Resources section at the end of this chapter. Those working with school-age children need to walk a fine line between encouraging them to discuss their disaster experiences and overloading them with too much detail. Children of this age are still uncertain about social boundaries and how what they are saying is affecting others. Leaders may need to guide a particularly loquacious child into talking one on one with an adult if other children are exhibiting discomfort with the discussion. Similarly, children should be encouraged to avoid media coverage of the event affecting them, as this may prolong and intensify their reaction. Such a caution is good to share with parents of children of all ages.

Since school-age children often feel most comfortable when engaged in activities, planning both group and one-on-one time centered on a shared activity can help the children to engage. Talking while doing something creates an atmosphere in which the child's defenses may be down and they may feel more comfortable talking about their feelings and experiences. While projects can take the form of writing, acting, or doing art and other creative endeavors, it also can be helpful to encourage the children to direct their creativity and problem-solving skills to an activity related to helping someone else who has been affected by the disaster. By so doing, the children are supported in thinking about solutions and positive future outcomes within systems bigger than themselves. Their own internal hopefulness benefits in the process.

Adolescents, with their natural tendency toward self-absorption, can also benefit from such altruistic pursuits. Extending beyond their own needs feeds into their capacity to develop solutions, to have their own authority, and to work together with their peers. Group discussion about the disaster events can also help adolescents to stop feeling as if they are the only one with confusion and pain. Their inclination to value the opinions of their peers combined with the paradoxical propensity to consider themselves unique and at the same time fear being different can make such group process useful in preventing disaster-related feelings getting too tangled up in the already stressful process of being a teenager.

Another strategy of particular importance when intervening with adolescents is to be honest and genuine. Teens are quick to spot inauthenticity and are generally repelled by it. A fragile trust of adults can be easily broken if these almost-grownup children perceive that they are being pandered to. With this group, you must be ready to put all issues on the table and to respond respectfully to the opinions and feelings that are offered. As with toddlers, this doesn't mean that no holds are barred. Standards and boundaries need to be established and enforced. Within those boundaries, however, the courage to be honest must reside. The calmness and forthrightness that adults provide serve as models for the children in managing their own stress.

Across all age groups and types of programming, one strategy stands out as central to effectively responding to children in disaster. Stated in other words earlier, this strategy can be described as a commitment to being in relationship with the children served. Creative projects and superbly selected materials are all helpful, but they pale in importance when compared with the human connection between caregiver and child. The capacity to be truly present with a child no matter what state they are in is as powerful a gift as any adult can give a child. To do so requires setting your own agenda aside and focusing on the child. It means intentionally putting the child's needs first, being willing to learn the child's unique cues, and being courageous enough to follow the child's lead. There is a saying from the field of infant mental health that sums up this concept as it applies to child disaster work: It's all about relationships!

Those who work closely with children who have experienced disaster, with all the myriad permutations of loss, pain, sadness, confusion, and despair, are vulnerable to feeling sad themselves. Seeing children in pain can lead to pain in those who care for them. Exposure to traumatized children can lead to traumatized adults. The technical term for this is vicarious traumatization. Preparation for the potential development of this phenomenon is part of preparing to serve children in disaster. Adults need to be attentive to their own personal care. Adequate rest, regular nutritional sustenance, opportunity for recreation, and strategies for processing your own feelings need to be intentionally addressed. Some may do this latter task best through private journaling, others may prefer group discussion, others may choose individual debriefing, while still others may find a combination of activities to be most helpful. Disaster response experience has shown that those workers who take care of themselves are more effective at taking care of others. By practicing such strategies, a worker is more likely to leave a child disaster response changed, but not harmed!

Programs in Child Disaster Work

There are many resources available to persons interested in entering the world of child disaster work. A number of these have been around for quite a long time, while others have been newly developed in response to the recent highly visible disasters of 9/11 and Hurricane Katrina. Resources can be divided into two groups: those that have a set program already developed and in operation, and those that provide specific bits of information helpful in developing and implementing programs.

The American Red Cross (ARC) has been in the business of responding to disasters for a long time. While the vast majority of their work is aimed at communities, families, and adults, they have not forgotten the children. At the disaster site, ARC partners with other response agencies to assure that the needs of children are addressed. Their Mental Health and Spiritual Care Response Teams are prepared to provide services to parents struggling with their own and their children's responses. Participating in one of the many ARC courses in disaster response can be helpful to anyone entering disaster response work. Contacting a local ARC chapter is the easiest way to get involved in such training. The American Red Cross has also developed a curriculum for use with school-age children who have experienced a disaster. A relatively recent supplement to the program is called Facing Fear and includes ideas for helping children deal with terrorism and other tragic events. You can explore this Masters of Disaster course, as well as other helpful resources, at www.redcross.org.

Since the early 1980s, the Church of the Brethren has been operating a disaster response specifically for children ages two to six. Previously known as Disaster Child Care, Children's Disaster Services (CDS) uses well-trained volunteers to set up temporary child care centers in the days following a disaster. In cooperation with the American Red Cross and the Federal Emergency Management Agency (FEMA), CDS teams enter locations where survivors must gather either for shelter or to complete applications for post-disaster aid. The CDS center provides a safe place for young children to be while their often-harried parents take care of the adult business of disaster recovery. Level I volunteers receive an intensive twenty-six-hour training that includes a simulation of being in a disaster setting. CDS also publishes brochures with information for parents about children and disaster. Spanish-language versions are available for some titles. You can obtain information about the CDS program and becoming a volunteer by calling 1-800-451-4407, extension 5 or 7.

FEMA has recently teamed with the nonprofit organization Save the Children to develop a new program to improve the lives of children and families living in temporary housing groups. The Safe and Protective Communities Project is being piloted in the Gulf Region among families affected by hurricane devastation. This project seeks to develop safe-play environments for children and to facilitate discussion and linkages between affected families and the various service agencies they must work with. The philosophy behind the project is to create opportunities for survivors to be empowered to effectively address the concerns they have about the safety of their children and other family conditions. The ultimate goal is to assist community and recovery functions that support the safety and healthy development of children. You can explore this project further at www.savethechildren.org.

In 2007, Church World Service (CWS) created their own pilot project addressing the needs of children and youth in disaster. CWS is a co-operative humanitarian ministry of thirty-five Protestant, Orthodox, and Anglican denominations, providing sustainable self-help and development, disaster relief, and refugee assistance. The program they have developed is part of their Community Arise series of educational modules that address issues surrounding disaster response. The module Community Arise: Children, Youth, and Disaster offers a comprehensive, interactive, and experiential training on many of the topics covered in this chapter. Visit www.churchworldservice.org to learn more about the ministries of CWS and to find out more about the Community Arise curriculum.

Final Words

To work with children and adolescents in times of disaster is a noble cause. It is also complicated and challenging. To do so effectively, you need to have an integrated understanding of the nature of disaster, the typical developmental characteristics of children, the common responses of each age group to the experience of disaster, and the appropriate methodology for delivering services to children. You then have to place all of that at the back of your mind in order to be able to be fully present with each individual child. In addition, you have to be able to attend to the needs of parents and to your own needs. Those who take on this somewhat staggering task can be assured that there is a reward in wait for them at the end of the experience: to see just one child cope successfully, to turn from burdened to self-confident, is enough to make the whole venture worthwhile.

Further Reading

American Red Cross. Facing Fear: Helping Young People Deal with Terrorism and Tragic Events. American Red Cross, 2001.

Augustyn, M., B. Groves, and M. Weinreb. "Confronting the Unknown." *Zero to Three* 22, no. 3 (December 2001/January 2002): 39.

Booth, C. "Untitled." *Zero to Three* 22, no. 3 (December 2001/January 2002): 52–53.

Church World Service. Community Arise: Children, Youth and Disaster. Church World Service, 2007.

Cohen, A., and R. Kaufman. *Early Childhood Mental Health Consultation.* Washington, D.C.: Center for Mental Health Services, Substance Abuse and Mental Health Services Administration, U.S. Department of Health and Human Services, 2000.

Coates, S., J. Rosenthal, and D. Schechter. *September 11: Trauma and Human Bonds.* Hillsdale, NJ: Analytic Press, 2003.

Cohen, E. and R. Kaufman. *Early Childhood Mental Health Consultation.* Washington, D.C.: Substance Abuse and Mental Health Services Administration, 2000.

Devilly, G., R. Gist, and P. Cotton. "Ready! Fire! Aim! The Status of Psychological Debriefing and Therapeutic Interventions: In the Work Place and after Disasters." *Review of General Psychology* 10, no. 4 (2006): 318–45.

Disaster Child Care. *Child Care Aviation Incident Response Team Training: Participants' Workbook.* Philadelphia: Disaster Child Care, September 1999.

Federal Emergency Management Agency. *Helping Children Cope with Disaster.* http://www.fema.gov/rebuild/recover/cope_child.

Fenichel, E., ed. "Infants, Toddlers and Terrorism: Supporting Parents, Helping Children." *Zero to Three* 22, no. 3 (December 2001/January 2002).

Fremont, W. "Childhood Reactions to Terrorism-Induced Trauma: A Review of the Past 10 Years." *Journal of the American Academy of Child and Adolescent Psychiatry* 43 (1999): 381–92.

Gramezy, N. "Stress resistant children: The Search for Protective Factor," In *Recent Research in Developmental Psychology,* ed. J. E. Stevenson. Oxford: Pergamon Press, 1985.

Halloran, E. and M. Knox. "Untitled." *Zero to Three* 22, no. 3 (December 2001/January 2002): 52.

Kinsel, J. "Notes from the President." *Baby Talk*, Special Issue: The 9/11 Terror and Beyond (October 2001). Available at www.oaimh.org.

McCaslin, S. E., et al. "How Does Negative Life Change Following Disaster Response Impact Distress among Red Cross Responders?" *Professional Psychology: Research and Practice* 36 (2005): 246–53.

Morgan, J. "American Red Cross Disaster Mental Health Services: Implementation and Recent Developments." *Journal of Mental Health Counseling* 17 (2005): 291–300.

Pfefferbaum, B. "Posttraumatic Stress Responses in Bereaved Children after the Oklahoma City Bombing." *Journal of the American Academy of Child and Adolescent Psychiatry* 38 (1999):1372–1379.

Pfefferbaum, B., et al. "Posttraumatic Stress Two Years after the Oklahoma City Bombing in Youths Geographically Distant from the Explosion." *Psychiatry* 63 (2000): 358–70.

Young, B. H., J. D. Ford, and P. J. Watson. "Helping Survivors in the Wake of Disaster." *National Center for Posttraumatic Disorder Fact Sheet.* http://www.ncptsd.va.gov/ncmain/ncdocs.fact_shts/fs_helping_survivors. 2007.

Webster's Online Dictionary. http://www.websters-online-dictionary.org/definition/disaster.

Werner, E. E., and R. S. Smith. *Vulnerable but Invincible: A Longitudinal Study of Resilient Children and Youth.* New York: McGraw-Hill, 1982.

Werner, E. E., and R. S. Smith. *Overcoming the Odds: High Risk Children from Birth to Adulthood.* Ithaca, NY: Cornell University Press, 1992.

Resources

Books for Children

Blackout by Anne Rockwell. Grades K–3. In this story, a family works together to weather a power blackout.

Carolina Hurricane by Marian Rumsey. Stranded on an island off the Carolina coast, a boy and his dog struggle to survive the fury of a hurricane.

Earthquake by Matt Christopher. Grades 4–6. A boy and his horse experience an earthquake.

Downwind by Louise Moeri. Grades 4–8. An accident at a nuclear power plant forces a family to face their fears and each others'.

Euphonia and the Flood by Mary Calhoun. Grades K–3. Euphonia puts her motto, "If a thing is worth doing, it's worth doing well," to the test as she and her pig ride through a flood, rescuing animals whether they want rescuing or not.

A Horse Came Running. by Meinder Dejong. Grades 4–6. The story of a boy who was home alone when a tornado came and the challenges he faced in coping with both the storm and its aftermath.

Little Toot on the Mississippi by Hardy Gramatky. Grades Pre K–3. Little Toot becomes a hero as he rescues animals on the flooded bayou.

Michael by Liesel Skorpan. Grades K–3. Michael's concern for a baby rabbit left outside in a thunderstorm helps him overcome his fear of storms.

Sometimes I'm Afraid by The Menninger Clinic. Grades Pre K–1. Early childhood fears are identified and normalized in gentle text and pictures.

Teetoncey and Ben O'Neal by Theodore Taylor. Grades 5–7. After a shipwreck along the Outer Banks, a young girl works through her fears.

The Big Rain by Fransoise Seignobose. Grades Pre K–4. A girl has to help move her family's belongings and make sure her grandmother is safe when a flood threatens her town.

The Big Wave by Pearl S. Buck. Grades 3–6. A child is the sole survivor after a tidal wave sweeps away his village.

The Tenth Good Thing About Barney by Judy Viorst. Grades Pre K–2. Barney the cat dies. In the process of holding his funeral, his owners face their feelings of sadness and loss.

The Terrible Wave by Morden Dahlstedt. Grades 5–9. One girl's experience during the Johnstown, Pennsylvania, flood.

Trapped in Slickrock Canyon by Gloria Skurznski. Grades 5–9. An exciting and very human story of cousins who are caught on a trail by a flash flood.

Resources for Adults

www.redcross.org/services/disaster In addition to the curricula described above, this site offers a variety of resources and information for those working with children in disaster, from background information to practical activities.

www.aacap.org The American Academy of Child and Adolescent Psychiatry offers this site that includes information of typical child and adolescent psychological issues, including a nice description of children in disaster that is suitable for handing out to parents looking for information. Look under "Facts for Families."

www.childadvocate.net/disaster This website includes a selection of materials for use by persons who work with children and their families and advocate for them.

Included is a booklet containing useful information on helping children cope with disaster, as well as associated fact sheets and a video.

www.fema.gov/rebuild/recover/cope_child Commonly asked questions by both parents and professionals about children's response to and recovery from disaster are addressed in a series of professionally written fact sheets. Available in PDF form for printing, a Spanish-language translation can also be downloaded. www.fema.gov/kids/teach_help provides lessons for teachers and parents to use in explaining disasters to children.

http://mentalhealth.samhsa.gov In a section called "Reaction of Children to a Disaster," this site details nicely age-specific issues children may have following a disaster as well as suggested age-specific adult responses. There is also a link to online publications, which include many titles related to disaster and trauma.

About the Contributor

John D. Kinsel, MS, LPCC, has been a volunteer for Children's Disaster Services of the Church of the Brethren since 1981, serving primarily as a trainer and a Level II volunteer. He is the program director of the Young Children's Assessment and Treatment Services division of Samaritan Behavioral Health, Inc. in Dayton, Ohio. A clinician and child developmentalist, Kinsel has been providing mental health services to children and their families for over twenty-five years. He is married and has two adult children.

17

The Work and Role of the College Chaplain Following a Disaster or Traumatic Event

Rev. Frederick J. Streets, MDiv, MSW, DSW, DD, LICSW

The college environment symbolizes youth and promise. Most students are naturally energetic and oriented toward the future. Parents have expectations, whether accurate or not, of how the college will respond to their sons and daughters should a disaster happen. A disaster on or off of campus, whether caused by natural phenomenon or human actions can not only shatter the student's sense of being safe in the world, but can also traumatically affect the faculty and staff who belong to that campus community.

The character of the college community is profoundly shaped and nuanced by the many different kinds of relationships students form with one another and with members of the faculty, administration, and staff. A disaster affecting the community reveals the nature and strengths of those associations. Athletic teams, fraternities, sororities, social clubs, affinity groups, and academic societies are but a few of the organizations to which students belong. It is no surprise that students will often share their concerns first with one another, particularly with those to whom they feel close, such as a best friend, team member, or the person they are dating. Sometimes the initial confidant may be a coach, residence hall counselor, or a faculty member. This network of relationships can produce a ripple effect of anxieties and fears across the campus community. Understanding and being a part of this relational matrix before a crisis strikes the community will inform and influence the effectiveness of the college chaplain's effort to provide pastoral care to students and other members of the college community after they have experienced a tragedy.

Each college is unique. The expectations and role of the college chaplain is shaped by its institutional context. In some settings, for example, the chaplain is an employee of the college and is expected to serve the entire campus community, while at another institution the chaplain may be a campus minister representing a particular religious denomination or faith and, therefore, responding on an ongoing basis primarily to the constituents of that faith community. It is essential that the chaplain knows and utilizes the various and sometimes complex relationships students and other members of the college have with one another and the institution, whether he or she is an employee of the institution or a denominational representative.

My personal experience in university chaplaincy has included responding to the impact upon the families and friends of several students who were killed together in a car accident. I have responded to the needs of students after receiving the shocking news of the death of a friend, family, or university staff member, the traumatic consequences of the attacks of September 11, 2001, the floods of Hurricane Katrina in 2005, the Southeast Asia tsunami in 2004, and the effects of war and civil unrest happening in various places in the world. Each of these occurrences affected, to different degrees, the well-being of the entire university community. There will always be those members of the campus community who do not express emotion or exhibit any signs of being directly influenced by a disaster or trauma that occurs locally or elsewhere. It is, however, difficult for them to avoid being aware of how others in their immediate environment respond to such an event.

Many colleges and universities have procedures or plans outlining what is to be done and by whom in case of emergencies or disaster. These protocols are particular to each institution and, sadly, in some situations, may not be as widely known among all of the members of the college or university. It is important for the chaplain to know this plan and his or her role in it, if one exists. It is also imperative that those who wish to and are able to assist a college community experiencing a major tragedy or disaster be invited by the college's authorities to do so. Those who wish to assist should at the very least contact the office of the chaplain, dean of students, or college or university president before attempting to arrive on campus or send emergency supplies. The good intention and appropriate desire to help can potentially cause more problems and harm to both the helper and other members of the college community if they arrive uninvited or misinformed about the situation and what is needed.

Broad Observations and Suggestions

What follows are some broad observations and suggestions for ways the college chaplain can assist the college community to cope with and heal from the spiritual and emotional wounds inflected by disaster and the aftermath of grief and trauma.

- Any disaster will have multiple variables and layers of complexity.
- It is important to meet with key individuals and convene various groupings of students, faculty, and staff to review what happened.
- Know the facts of the event and share them with others after it has occurred in a manner that is clear and sensitive and helps them to cope.
- Invite those who have gathered to share their personal reaction to what has happened. This assists them in realizing that they are not alone or the only one with the feelings they are experiencing. Good suggestions on how to proceed often come from such meetings. The chaplain has an opportunity during such meetings to observe who among them is having more difficulty coping with what has happened and to reach out or attend to them individually.
- Not everyone who has experienced a tragic or traumatic event will react to that situation in the same manner or have similar needs as they seek to cope with what has happened to them.
- Not everyone will experience posttraumatic stress disorder (PTSD) or other more serious emotional difficulties.

Not everyone will need medical, psychological, or pastoral care as a result of their having gone through a horrific episode in their lives. The chaplain, however, can alert them to the possibility that they *may* have an emotional or spiritual crisis that may be related to the affect of the earlier trauma, and that the relationship between the two might not be obvious or apparent. The chaplain can encourage them to consult him or her should this happen.

Students Supporting Students

Students are remarkable in the ways they care for one another after a disaster. These efforts must be encouraged and supported by the college community's administration. The chaplain occupies a privileged position, unique and distinct from other support services, and plays a pivotal role in facilitating that process by affirming what students do to care for one another, helping to arrange places for them to meet on the college's campus, supplying food and refreshment, and providing information about other college resources they can contact for help. No single individual has the wherewithal to give the total support and resources that may be necessary, but each of us can be a part of a bridge that links individuals in need to additional support providers.

As college and university chaplains, we can mediate the impact of trauma, grief, or a disaster by the very nature and location of our ministries, our personal relationships with those who are also affected, and our own capacity for empathy. Our individual responses to a disaster will vary, and our reactions to a traumatic event, whether it occurred naturally or is the result of human actions, are filtered through our self-understanding, which is shaped by our culture and gender. Generally, however, most people have the capacity to empathize with the suffering of others. Students and other members of the college community who are empathetic to the suffering of others need identified and organized ways to demonstrate their concern. Planning and conducting memorial services, tributes, and other communal responses that include student input provides the college community with the opportunity to express their grief and hope for the future and diminishes their sense of helplessness in the wake of a disaster or other traumatic event. The availability of such observances is very important during holidays and the many activities that occur during commencement periods. Over the years I have used a program format that consists of music and readings from diverse genres and a variety of cultural and religious traditions, moments of communal silence, commemorative candle lighting, and the reading of the names of those being remembered. Those attending were encouraged to leave at any time or stay as long as they wished.

The Chaplain's Relationship to the College Community

A sense of ownership of and belonging to a college family are strong emotional ties students have with their college. It is very important for students to be with their friends as soon as possible after a disaster. The various and complex relationships students have with one another and other members of the faculty, staff, and administration underscore the dynamic guiding the provision of pastoral care to that community following a disaster. Developing and nurturing relationships, particularly with students, before and after disaster strikes is as important to providing pastoral care as, for example, location is to the value of real estate. It is within this relationship that the college chaplain learns and discerns what the disaster means to those affected by it. Members of the college community are helped to give meaning to the disaster and find other ways to express its impact upon their lives through participating in the public remembrances of the disaster offered by the college and through the private conversations they have with the chaplain, other college personnel, and their friends and family. James E. Dittes, who has published many books in the fields of pastoral counseling and theology, reminds us in his book *Pastoral Counseling: The Basics* (Westminister John Knox, 1999) that the purpose of the pastoral counseling conversation is to help others to "reclaim commitment and clarity, to beget faith, hope, and love, to find life affirmed—this is the conversation of soul that sometimes happens in pastoral counseling."

Continuity and change typifies colleges, and this dynamic helps the college community to integrate major upheavals such as a disaster, rather than to be primarily defined by it. I have often said that a university chaplaincy is responsible for the pastoral care and reaching out to the entire university community—its parish, in effect—and helping the university to interpret and carry out its mission. Students sometimes say that college life is not the "real world." Nothing challenges this notion and the purpose of the university more than when it experiences a disaster or major trauma of some type. The affirmation of life as the work of the chaplain reflects the spirit of the college experience at its best and after its worst of times.

Ministry of Presence

We should never underestimate the importance of our being present with others after a disaster. We are not always sure what, if anything, to say at such a moment. Sometimes our wanting to speak is motivated by many things, including our own anxiety and the desire to feel we are helping. There are moments when it is appropriate and necessary to speak. Our self-awareness, sense of the campus, and our connectedness to it greatly informs what we might say. For example, I shared the following statement at one of the many gatherings we held as a university community over the weeks that followed September 11, 2001:

> The meaning of the events of September 11 eludes us. We do not know how we as individuals and a nation may change as a result of the terror that has been visited upon us. Today our grief and mourning, unimaginable three weeks ago, are profound.
>
> A space, a hole, a void, an emptiness has been created in us by the attack and murder of people in New York, Washington, D.C., and Pennsylvania twenty days ago. They were people who represented our global human community. The openness in our soul created by their loss will represent for many of us an aching void that will last our lifetime and beyond. It can also become, simultaneously, a sacred holding place where our personal grief, memory of our national tragedy, and fear of global terrorism are held.
>
> Some of us as a result of September 11 will become over time different from how we are today in ways that are now unclear to us. All of us are challenged to use our pain to transform evil into good and wrestle from destruction new life.
>
> Now, together we remember and mourn those whom we have lost and pray for those who loved them. We are thankful for all of those who escaped and those assisting in their recovery and healing.
>
> We seek through our familiar rituals and newly created ways of mourning, our heart's capacity to affirm the beauty of life, the goodness of people and to once again feel hope for the future they inspire in each of us.

College and University Responses

Colleges and universities, understandably, are initially preoccupied with a disaster as a matter of public health, security, and safety. Those affected by a disaster reflect a broad spectrum of experiences and emotions. It is the responsibility of each member of the college community to discern what the disaster means to him or her, and how they will proceed with their lives. The corporate response of a college or university to a disaster becomes a defining and educational moment for the life of that educational community. Opportunities for students to reflect on the nature of suffering and the meaning of healing, forgiveness, community, and wholeness after the disaster can help to shape their values, attitudes, and future behavior. These opportunities also help to reveal the tremendous power we have to heal ourselves, contribute to the welfare of others, and draw meaning from our experiences. These capacities for healing and renewal may be why college- or university-sponsored programs such as panel discussions, forums, concerts, art shows, and other presentations with student involvement are important communal events following a disaster.

These activities will have their own shelf life as the educational community establishes its new sense of normalcy and returns to some of its routines. The healing process and timetable, however, is different for each individual and family. The healing process is aided by the sense that the administrators, faculty, and staff of the campus care about the people of the college community and are going beyond the moment of crisis by working to make their life there better following the disaster.

Broadening the Chaplain's Role after a Disaster

We may consider broadening our understanding of our role as chaplains after a disaster by learning some of the basic psychosocial methods of assessing people's emotional and spiritual well-being and its relationship to the way their culture influences their self-understanding, ethnicity, gender role, sexual orientation, theology, and worship, as well as how their religious faith helps them to live a meaningful life. Sharing our feelings and experiences with another person and understanding that there may be a link between thinking, emotions, and physical well-being are new perspectives, concepts, and values for many people, including chaplains. Collaborating and learning from pastoral counselors and other mental health professionals in our community is a good way to increase our knowledge and skills. It is also an opportunity for these counselors to learn from chaplains more about pastoral care and the important role that religion and spirituality play in helping people to cope and recover from trauma.

Those who wish to tell their trauma story are not necessarily re-traumatized by doing so; indeed, this can be for them an act of self-empowerment. The *trauma story* of some people is not their *life's story*—there is more to who they are than the tragedies they may have experienced. Even those who have been seriously harmed are not without strengths and capacities for living. It takes courage for someone to come to us and share their pain; it is therefore important that they feel welcomed and made to feel safe in doing so. Learning to listen well to those who come to us underscores how much they can teach us about their pain and possible ways of successfully dealing with it. How people interpret an event and the meaning they give to it is crucial in understanding how they are coping with that experience. Campus chaplains can be helpful by being a bridge for those in need to additional sources of social and psychological care available at their educational institution or in the larger community. Knowing when to refer someone to additional support is an important part of pastoral care. Knowledge of the campus resources and other helping professionals on campus, and a capacity to navigate the campus's system of help or its alternatives are indispensable skills for the campus chaplains in the time following a disaster.

Some of those who suffer associate themselves with the experiences of people in sacred texts, such as Christian martyrs and the suffering and death of Jesus. A traumatic event can affect their identity, their views and beliefs about God, and ideas of fairness and justice (for example, they may focus on the story of Job). I have often heard Christians, Jews, and Muslims alike say that God does not put any more on them than they can bear. This is just one of the understandings and beliefs people may hold when they reflect upon their suffering.

Disaster and trauma can literally divide a person's sense of self and of time and history. Life's demarcation can become for them "pre-disaster" and "post-disaster." Wholeness for many trauma survivors is not about uniting these two halves but learning to live within and between them, as they attempt to make sense of and integrate their altered understanding of the world and themselves. Understanding and acknowledging people's resilience and providing suggestions on how they might accomplish this integration is a wonderful gift to those you counsel.

Altruism, Work, and Spirituality: Surviving War, Violence, and Trauma

A friend and colleague with whom I have worked for many years, Dr. Richard Mollica, MD, founder of the Harvard Program in Refugee Trauma, wrote extensively about the importance of altruism, work, and spirituality in response to disaster in his book *Healing Invisible Wounds: Paths to Hope and Recovery in a Violent World* (Harcourt, 2006). His insight has been confirmed for me in my pastoral work with those traumatized by disaster, war, and other forms of violence. Altruism, work, and spirituality are at the heart of recovery from the trauma of violence. Altruism is the type of therapeutic behavior that occurs when people help others, even when they have experienced devastation themselves. Human beings, especially when threatened under extreme conditions of violence, have an enormous capacity to reach out to one another, even if it increases their own suffering, injury, or risk of death.

Every survivor of a disaster has a story of regret or shame at not having done enough for a person in their same circumstance who suffered or died. When students are not at the place where a disaster has happened and directly affected their family or friends, their regret and guilt is compounded. These feelings of regret and shame most likely arise because altruistic behavior is a key mechanism for traumatized persons to reestablish links between themselves, their shattered world views, and other human beings. Work is not just a function of being employed, producing a product, or providing a service in exchange for money or another commodity or service. Work or other socially productive activities such as performing chores, housework, making things with our hands, and caring for children are behaviors that contribute to the healing of survivors. While remaining active on a job is critical to resisting the emotional distress of violence, participating in the daily activities of life is also therapeutic. No activity is too small or too insignificant. While it has been discovered that for traumatized people work of various forms is the world's most important antidepressant, it is an underappreciated, underutilized therapeutic activity in conflict and postconflict situations.

Spirituality is also an aspect of being human that cannot be reduced to its parts. Disasters and violence, particularly horrific or mass violence, challenge our fundamental beliefs and values about life itself, other people, and us. It shakes or destroys the confidence the victims of violence have in their values and beliefs to provide them with meaning for living. Religion and spirituality have been positive forces in the lives of many of those who have survived violence and trauma. They derive meaning for living from their sense of spirituality in addition to altruism and work.

Survivors who are actively engaged in spiritual practices, in spite of the degradation or destruction of their religious institutions, are the most resistant to the development of symptoms of posttraumatic stress disorder. Prayer, meditation, traditional healing, and other spiritual rituals and practices are prevalent in the homes and communities of many trauma survivors. The college community provides many ways that altruism, work, and religious practices can be encouraged, such as through local and national community service learning projects, volunteerism and international humanitarian work, and various forms of religious or spiritual gatherings on campus. Public or private colleges or university that have no history of providing these kinds of opportunities and pastoral care to their students and other members of their community will have to consider doing so as a result of a disaster.

There are risks involved in putting into words our traumatic experiences, but we also take risks when we maintain silence about the emotional and physical pain caused by traumatic experiences. Helping people in the college setting after a disaster means being prepared to guide them along their journey toward spiritual and emotional well-being. It means supporting them while they define for themselves the meaning of suffering, healing, community, and hope.

Prepare Before to Be Able to Respond After

It is important to periodically review your college or university's protocol for dealing with a disaster and to revise it based on what has been learned by the most recent incident there or at another campus. The college community needs to be informed about who to call and what to do in the case of such emergencies. The protocol is a dynamic document in the sense that it outlines an ongoing process for how the college will meet the needs of its community during a crisis. The college chaplain's input and experiences should inform this protocol.

About the Contributor

Rev. Frederick J. Streets, MDIV, MSW, DSW, DD, LICSW, is the Carl and Dorothy Bennett professor in Pastoral Counseling at the Wurzweiler School of Social Work, Yeshiva University, New York City. He is the former chaplain of Yale University and senior pastor of the Church of Christ in Yale, where he served from 1992 to 2007. He is an adjunct associate professor in pastoral theology at Yale Divinity School. Prior to Yale, he was for seventeen years the senior pastor of Mount Aery Baptist Church in Bridgeport, Connecticut. He is a senior consulting member of the Harvard Program for Refugee Trauma. A native of Chicago, Rev. Streets has been involved in providing pastoral care and mental health services and doing humanitarian work in urban America, Bosnia, Cuba, Colombia, Argentina, and Ghana. He will be a Fulbright Scholar during the spring of 2008 at the University of Pretoria in Pretoria, South Africa, focusing on the intersection of modern medicine and social work interventions and spirituality among families with children living with HIV and AIDS. He is the author of numerous publications and editor of *Preaching in the New Millennium* (Yale University Press, 2005).

18

Working with the Elderly after a Disaster

Cheryl Guidry Tyiska

> *The beginning of wisdom is this: Get wisdom, and whatever else you get, get insight.*
>
> PROVERBS 4:7, TNIV

It is a truism that during youth we focus on gathering information, absorbing life like a sponge. In young adulthood and middle age, the tasks of life turn to applying that information in ways that foster success in college, at work, and in relationships. In the later stages of life our goals are to take the information and knowledge acquired over the course of a lifetime and make sense of it all—creating meaning and, from meaning, wisdom. Our elders are the repositories of deep wisdom,[1] much of which may not be highly valued in today's world, particularly in developed Western society, with its insistent emphasis on youth. Still, many of us inherently know that when our older citizens, particularly those who are frail and vulnerable, are hurt by disasters and their aftermath, something precious in the fabric of our humanity is rent.

It is important at the outset to make clear that not all older people are frail, nor are they incompetent. Elderly people are often treated as though they are children, in need of others to care for them and make decisions on their behalf. Indeed, with our improved health care system, many older people live longer, healthier, more productive lives than ever before and are capable of continuing to do so even if they have been through a life crisis. Each older person is a unique individual, and each person's aging is a dynamic process, not a static state (Fahey 1990). Great care must be taken to ensure that their independence and autonomy not be automatically revoked simply because they have experienced what may well be a traumatic event. Caregivers must keep in mind that a person with many years of life experience may have endured numerous previous traumas in life, and the most recent event may not be the worst of their historic experiences. The accumulated life wisdom of older people, in fact, may provide a shining beacon of stability to younger people who turn to them for guidance on surviving a disaster. We honor our older people when we allow them to share that wisdom with us.

Having acknowledged the strengths of some older people, however, it is also true that many elderly people will not weather disaster as well as younger people. They may feel more fearful, helpless, and isolated, and less competent or resilient. The aging process itself may contribute to this sense of vulnerability. Spiritual care providers will need to be cognizant of these deficits and serve an older clientele practically, but with consummate dignity and respect. The need for spiritual care providers gifted at working with older people will only increase as our aging population continues to grow.

Aging

To my elderly brothers and sisters!

> "Seventy is the sum of our years, or eighty if we are strong, and most of them are fruitless toil, for they pass quickly and we drift away." (Psalm 90:10)

> Seventy years was an advanced age when the Psalmist wrote these words, and few people lived beyond it. Nowadays, thanks to medical progress and improved social and economic conditions, life expectancy has increased significantly in many parts of the world. Still, it remains true that the years pass quickly, and the gift of life, for all the effort and pain it involves, is too beautiful and precious for us ever to grow tired of it.

LETTER OF HIS HOLINESS POPE JOHN PAUL II
TO THE ELDERLY, 1999

As we age, we continue to develop as spiritual and physical human beings, with needs that are different from those we had when we were younger. We see this in our physical abilities. The number of visits to doctors' offices increases, as does the distance we hold the newspaper from our eyes. We become concerned about hearing loss and falling. We see this in our cognitive abilities. We forget more often and do not recall as quickly. We begin to worry that when we appear confused, others may think we are experiencing the onset of dementia. We may have had to retire and live on a restricted or fixed income. We may attend more funerals as friends and family members die, increasing our sense of isolation and a loss of shared history. We may think more of the spiritual realm, as our thoughts turn to how we have lived our lives, what our lives have meant, and what may or may not lie beyond our deaths. Time often appears to pass slowly when we are children, but as we get older, time seems to pass more quickly.

Many of us begin to notice changes related to age when we are still in middle age, during what is often considered the "prime of life" (around ages forty to sixty). These changes may shatter our illusions about our immortality and our reasonable expectations about future accomplishments and the kind of mark we will make on the world. We are at the height of our societal and financial strength and power. We are still sorting out relationships with our spouses, adult children, and our own aging parents. We (perhaps) regret the indiscretions of our youth and begin to fashion ideas about the kind of person we want to mature into.

In later middle age and "maturing middle age" (around ages sixty to seventy), we may still be dynamic and vibrant but we begin to slow down and perhaps become more introspective. Graeme Chapman (1998) suggests that all humans have a two-phased process of spiritual development, self-flourishing and self-emptying, and during these later years of life, the second phase is ascendant, in that we may well develop both "the desire and ability to pass on what we have learned about life to others." Chapman defines this as being able to "finger the edges of wisdom, accommodating a multiplicity of paradigms and living without ultimate answers." We may not acknowledge it, but we often begin to grieve the loss of our youth and the potential we never lived up to.

As we enter our elderly years (around ages seventy to eighty-five), we may focus more on our memories and our life stories. We may become more dependent and may concern ourselves with who will take care of us when we are unable to care for ourselves. Our physical world may shrink at the same time that our spiritual world may expand and may even take on an ethereal, mystical quality. We marvel at the simple pleasures of life that we may have taken for granted when we were younger and moving faster.

In extreme old age (ages eighty-five and older), we may suffer the difficulties of being unable to care for ourselves and losing our competency at even the simplest things, such as driving our car. We may be in the care of competent caregivers who love us, or in the indifferent hands of those who do not. Our dignity at such times may be a source of hope for others, but it can require a great deal of energy to maintain.

At some point, all of us recognize that aging is a process of inexorable decline in almost every sphere of our life. Sacred writings from all faith traditions speak bluntly about this painful truth.

Trauma

Spirituality and religion often provide people with a deep sense of purpose and hope. An elderly person has constructed his or her world view and understanding of the meaning of life over many years. Disaster can shatter that construct. A younger, more resilient person may be able to rebuild that sense of meaning more quickly and with more hopefulness, but when an older person's belief system has been shattered, it may take longer to reconstruct. Unfortunately, for very elderly people, time is the very quality in most limited supply.

> Reports on the responses of the elderly to disaster are inconsistent. In some disasters, they seem no more vulnerable than younger people. In others, they appear more vulnerable. Despite the inconsistency in formal research studies, there are reasons to believe that the elderly are at increased risk for adverse emotional effects in the wake of disaster. They may live alone and lack help and other resources. Depression and other forms of distress among the elderly are readily overlooked, in part because they may not take on exactly the same symptom pattern as among younger people. For instance, disorientation, memory loss, and distractibility may be signs of depression in the elderly. The elderly are also more vulner-

able to being victimized. In the context of increased stress on the family and community, meeting their special needs may take on a lowered priority. One particular issue that may appear is feeling that they have lost their entire life (loss of children, homes, memorabilia) and that, due to their age, there is not enough time left in their life to rebuild and recreate. (Ehrenreich 2001)

The impact of trauma on the elderly will vary depending on the person, just as it does in younger people. One advantage an older person may have over a younger person is that their previous life experiences often give them coping strategies and techniques they can use to cope with today's disaster. They may say, "This is a horrible experience, but I have lived through as bad or worse in the past, and I know I can survive this." Many of today's elders lived through complex events of the twentieth century. Some of those events were positive, but others—the Great Depression, the Holocaust, World War II—were devastating. They have lived through past storms, fires, and other disasters, all of which gave them a blueprint for survival. Their past may help them through today.[2]

An elderly disaster survivor may find that the world seems terribly frightening. Many elderly people who are physically ill, alone, disoriented by the disaster, living in poverty, or spiritually bereft may find themselves wondering why they should keep going on. True forms of dementia may alternate with simple bouts of normal confusion (which is experienced by almost all survivors of disaster, regardless of age). They may become depressed and may find that their faith in everything they believed and held dear has been shaken to its core. If this happens, the thin veneer of independence the older person may have maintained may give way, and they may need extensive physical, mental, and spiritual care—an exhausting task that cannot be filled by a single caregiver. It has been said that "raising a child takes a village," but it is also true that caring for a traumatized elderly person likewise takes a team of helpers. Elderly survivors may not know about services available to them. They may require help to utilize those services, and they may refuse help because of embarrassment or a fear of losing their independence (Langer 2004). Connecting elderly survivors to other caregiving resources is often one of the most difficult tasks for primary and spiritual care providers.

Elderly survivors may have already lost so much—other loved ones, their careers, their health, their being "needed" by others, their independence, their homes and treasured possessions—that the additional losses caused by disaster may seem overwhelming. They may retreat into memories of a safer past, where they will be comforted. They may also be deeply concerned about the whereabouts and condition of their friends and family members, especially their grandchildren, who represent their future. If younger members of their families have died because of the disaster, the older person may feel ashamed and guilty for having survived. The deaths of their loved ones may cause them to seek out spiritual comfort and answers.

While many will receive comfort from their faith leaders and trained spiritual care providers, others may be frustrated with the spiritual care they receive. They may lash out at spiritual care providers and at their God or Creator. They may be deeply offended and angry if they receive pat, condescending responses to questions that have no easy answers. Some elderly people will even find it difficult to conceive of a good reason to prolong their own lives in the face of such insurmountable pain. Caregivers need to acknowledge the reality of this existential quandary. When elderly people question the value of life, their concerns should not be minimized.

> The National Interfaith Coalition on Aging (1981) defines spiritual well-being as "the affirmation of life in relationship with God, self, community, and environment that nurtures and celebrates wholeness." Such affirmation becomes vitally important when much that has meaning is threatened or lost in old age. When everything is lost, including one's health, the spiritual capability to reach out to God remains an effective weapon to combat meaninglessness and despair. In dying, the spiritual task of transcendence becomes even more important. (Wong 1989)

Posttraumatic Stress Disorder

Research on disaster-related posttraumatic stress disorder (PTSD) in elderly people is sparse and conflicting. For example, in 1996, Stephen Ticehurst reported on the results of a survey of survivors of an Australia earthquake and stated, "Older people may be more at risk for experiencing posttraumatic stress reactions despite having fewer disaster-related experiences. They may also underutilize support services following a disaster. Older women in particular and people with an avoidance coping style appear to be the most vulnerable." Other studies disagreed.

An early longitudinal study involving elderly survivors of the Lockerbie aviation disaster (Livingston 1994) indicated that the course of the disorder lessened in the majority of elderly survivors diagnosed with PTSD but that more than one in seven continued to experience significant dysfunction five years after the bombing of Pan Am flight 103. Interestingly, these results were similar to those of younger trauma survivors in the study.

A study of elderly survivors of a hurricane in Honduras from varied socioeconomic backgrounds who experienced different levels of exposure to the storm concluded that "no evidence was found for a differential vulnerability on the part of the elderly as compared with younger adults. Among the elderly increasing age was not a factor" (Kohni 2005). A study by Man Cheung Chung (2004) agreed with this conclusion, and stated, "Following exposure to technological disasters, young, middle-aged, and elderly community residents could display similar posttraumatic responses and employ similar coping strategies, which contradicts the vulnerability hypothesis and the inoculation hypothesis." A follow-up study by Chung (2005) corroborated this result. Chung found that age had little to do with the level of PTSD. The factors that were most important were level of exposure to traumatic stimuli and that the type of exposure had a direct correlation to the type of PTSD symptom that was predominant.

While some older people may be at higher risk for trauma-related PTSD, that risk may not be associated with age, but with other factors. It is also important to keep in mind that some PTSD may be the result of a traumatic experience that occurred earlier in life but that was reactivated by a recent disaster (Weintraub 1999) and may hinge on how well the earlier trauma was resolved. Weintraub suggests that, in fact, "there is even evidence that the elderly are less likely than the young to develop the disorder."

Given the paucity of research on this subject, the Western bias of the research, and the varied conclusions of the researchers, spiritual care providers should not assume anything about the posttraumatic stress reactions of older disaster survivors.

Working with Elderly People after a Disaster

In 1996, I was part of a volunteer crisis team responding to survivors of the massacre of Srebrenica in Bosnia-Herzegovina. During that 1995 massacre, more than 7,000 men and boys were marched out into the woods and killed. My task was to enter classrooms in abandoned schools that had been turned into shelters for internally displaced persons to provide crisis intervention. One of my most poignant memories is of an elderly secular Muslim woman who agreed to talk to me. I asked her if she could tell me about the impact of the war on her life. I will never forget her words. She shook her finger in my face and said, "I will tell you about what happened to me and my entire family, although it will do me no good. What I want you to do is to take my testimony. You must bear witness to my horror. Once I tell it to you, it will belong to you, too, and you will carry it with you wherever you go. My story will live on in you, and I want you to take this story back to the United States and tell others, so that what happened here will never be forgotten."

CHERYL TYISKA, PERSONAL EXPERIENCE

The first obstacle for spiritual care providers is to locate elderly disaster survivors. Heat waves in Chicago in 1995 and in France in 2003, which resulted in the deaths of thousands of mostly elderly people, were poignant wake-up calls that the elderly are often invisible and forgotten. They will be found in congregate settings (emergency, special needs, or homeless shelters), nursing homes, hospitals, apartment communities, and private homes. Those with no working method of communication, no transportation, or no personal care aide to help them may be more difficult to locate. Some elderly people with disabling conditions may wait in increasing anxiety for help to arrive. The disaster may have destroyed their medication, and their eyeglasses, hearing aids, orthotic devices, and other medical equipment may have been lost or damaged.

Once help arrives, some elderly people may refuse to leave their homes, even if their home has been severely damaged. That home, as palatial or as modest as it may be, contains the remnants of a lifetime of memories. They may fear looters or they may be concerned that once they are transported to a shelter or nursing facility they will never be allowed to return home. In reality, there may be no home to return to, and they may end up being relocated several times until a suitable permanent home can be arranged. They may also fear the evacuation diaspora that removes them, perhaps permanently, from longtime friends and neighbors. According to the South Florida AAA director, after Hurricane Andrew in 1992, "Sixty percent of the elderly who left Dade County before the storm never came back, never informed any city agency of their whereabouts, and never requested services for which they [were] eligible" (Stokesberry 1993). Rather than going to an unfamiliar and perhaps frightening location, the elderly may be willing to withstand bad weather and the lack of food, water, and medical care to remain and protect what little they have left.

A second dilemma faced by spiritual care providers is that they may be confronted with many older people with serious confusion or actual symptoms of dementia. Some will be so overwhelmed by the disaster response systems that they cannot focus on their emotional or spiritual concerns. It may be important that their immediate survival needs be met first, before spiritual care can be truly effective. Helping to get elderly disaster survivors entered into the disaster case management system will ensure that their other needs will be known and addressed by those who perform that type of work.

Spiritual care providers must be able to assess when a disaster survivor is experiencing those trauma reactions that are considered "normal" under the circumstances and those that may tax the individual's ability to cope. In the elderly, this limit may be reached quickly. It is extremely useful for spiritual care providers to work in partnership with disaster mental health care providers to provide a spiritual assessment and a mental health assessment in tandem.

As a result of trauma or disaster:
- Faith is reinforced
- Faith is challenged
- Faith is rejected
- Faith is transformed

DISASTER MENTAL HEALTH FIELD MANUAL, 2006

There is no precise how-to checklist for any caregiver on working with a disaster survivor, and the caregiver must use his or her own skills of observation, assessment, and human compassion to determine how to intervene. However, some basic considerations might be helpful when working with elderly people who have lived through a disaster.

- **Emphasize their abilities rather than their disabilities.** What can they do for themselves? Are there any internal pockets of strength or resilience they can access?
- **Realize that elderly people may process the physical, emotional, mental, and spiritual impacts of the disaster more slowly.** Give them space and time. Be patient.
- **Speak and enunciate clearly.** Yelling will not help a person with a hearing impairment to hear you.
- **If an elderly person has questions about the disaster or its aftermath, answer them honestly if the information is known.** The likelihood is strong that a caregiver will not have many definitive answers.
- **Remember that questions asked do not require an answer.** They simply need to be voiced. Practice humility. Caregivers do not have to know everything.
- **Encourage elderly disaster survivors to tell their stories.** Listen to them. Bear witness to their horror. Often, the stories they choose to tell may be about past traumas. Perhaps the current trauma rudely reawakened memories of those past events. Listening to all of the stories helps to weave the new trauma into the fabric of a long life.
- **Listen at least twice as much as speaking.** Words are important, but so is what is behind the words. Discern what the older person is trying to convey to you.
- **Do not be invasive or ask probing questions.**
- **Be mindful of an older person's increased need to sleep and perhaps their decreased need to eat much.** Encourage rest and good nutrition.
- **With their permission, do not be afraid to touch them.** Hold their hands. Give them a hug. Appropriate, caring physical contact can help to lessen the human sense of iso-

lation many older people experience.³ Touch lets them know they are cared for and that they are not alone.

- **Do not fear laughter.** Elderly people may well be able to discern humor and irony even in the midst of difficult days.
- **Likewise, do not fear silence.** Elderly people may need quiet time with a safe companion in order to reminisce and contemplate.
- **Give them a teddy bear, a plant, or a small gift.** Bringing a gentle pet for the older person to stroke may be calming. Tangible items they can hold can provide a sense of security. If they have photos or mementos of loved ones, put them in visual sight or place them nearby.
- **Background music can provide a soothing or enlivening environment.** A radio or television may provide an older person with contact with the larger outside world.
- **Read to them from works of their choice.** Books on cassette or CD can be enjoyable and can take the older person's mind off the tragedy for a while.
- **Provide them with privacy. Treat them with dignity.** They may appear to have regressed to a more dependent, child-like state, but they are not children.
- **Do not make trite, condescending comments that minimize the depth and the impact of the event.** These comments are a testament to a caregiver's discomfort with the awful truth. Affirm their reality.
- **Do not discourage them from speaking of death.** Death is a reality, and we do honor by listening to them as they prepare for this final stage in their journey on earth.
- **Focus on what the older disaster survivor believes that is helpful and hopeful.** Explore their beliefs with them, and how those beliefs have been altered by their experiences.
- **Remember that providing round-the-clock care often exhausts an older person's primary caregivers.** They may experience a whirlwind of emotions—sadness, anger, guilt, frustration—at the same time that they are physically battered and overwhelmed. Particular concern here comes from a study undertaken after Hurricane Floyd that suggests that

domestic violence increased after the flood, and that the elderly were among the most affected group (Clemens 1999). Therefore, for many reasons, it is important that those who care for older survivors receive respite and spiritual support as well.

Care of Spiritual Care Providers

As mentioned above, those who provide primary care for elderly survivors will need care themselves. This is also true for spiritual care providers who may serve many survivors over a short period. It is important for spiritual care providers to create their own personal or communal rituals for replenishing their spirit and rejuvenating their soul in order to carry on with the work of serving multiple traumatized victims. The work of providing spiritual care is enriching to most, but it requires that the caregiver be in touch with his or her own mortality and vulnerability. It can, as it does for many disaster survivors, cause a reassessment of the caregiver's life and priorities, which can be a positive experience. Still, it can take a physical, emotional, and spiritual toll that must be recognized.

Deborah Proffitt (2007) studied thirty members of the clergy (Jewish and Christian). Her hypothesis was that "use of religion-based coping strategies following a difficult life event was expected to facilitate posttraumatic growth, and posttraumatic growth was, in turn, expected to result in greater current well being. Both predictions were supported. In addition, higher levels of rumination soon after the event were associated with greater posttraumatic growth." Spiritual care providers who are trained to understand the dynamics of disaster mental health are at an advantage over caregivers and clergy without such training.

The Power of Ritual and Prayer

A useful ritual I learned when I first became a hospice volunteer is the hand-washing ritual. It has helped me many times. When I enter the presence of a hospice patient, wherever that may be, I take a moment to wash my hands. Not only is this medically hygienic, but it serves a spiritual purpose. As I wash my hands, I purposefully "wash off" the outside world and remind myself to focus on the person I am about to encounter. I put aside all other thoughts and worries so I can attend to that one human being. Then, when my visit is over, I repeat the process, and I "wash off" the experience I had with my patient so I don't take it back out into the world with me. The hand-washing ritual helps me to set boundaries and to focus my energies on one person at a time.

CHERYL TYISKA, PERSONAL EXPERIENCE

Even without a disaster to contend with, aging itself may be a frightening experience, as elderly people begin to acknowledge that they are nearing the end of their physical time on earth. Questions that may have been ignored for years can no longer be ignored. Who am I? Why am I here? What has my life been about? Will I be remembered after I am gone? Why did this disaster happen? Why did I survive when other, younger people died? What am I supposed to believe now?

Aging people of faith often hold on to their faith for solace. Their community of faith may be a source of sustenance and support, and their faith-based rituals and spontaneous and memorized prayers can give them a sense of belonging to a community of like believers. Those who profess or practice no faith may be searching for truths that can connect them to something greater than themselves, and some may begin to attend religious services or pray for the first time—or for the first time in a long time.

Prayer may provide an opportunity for older people to give voice to their thoughts, concerns, hopes, and fears. It provides "someone" to talk to and with about what is troubling them, "someone" to ask questions of or help from. It can give them an opportunity to give thanks for blessings received, express contrition for shortcomings and failings, and may even provide an outlet for the expression of anger (even anger toward God or their Creator).

In addition to its spiritual benefits, prayer has physical benefits. Repetitive or meditative prayer, for example, can help calm people and reduce stress, as can guided imagery. Prayer requires a certain amount of contemplation and introspection, so it can help people to process the disaster event cognitively. Unfortunately, older disaster survivors may be unable to remember the words to prayers they have said all their lives, or they may not be able to concentrate on longer prayers. Even their conversational prayer may be agitated. If this occurs, it might be helpful to encourage the elderly survivor to focus on just one or two words or sounds.

> The relationship between murmuring and meditation ... points to the role of voice (and hence breath) and repetition in meditative practice, seen as an effort to transcend two dichotomies: between mind and body and between present and future. The study of repetitive voicing—whether purely internal or physically enacted—establishes a historic sequence that links Biblical, Greco-Roman, medieval, and early-modern wisdom literature.... Murmuring, as Brian Stock reminds us, is a form of meditation. Returning to the Hebrew Bible in his wide-ranging account of meditation, reading, and healing in the Western tradition, he tells us that the root *haga* means "to murmur in a low voice" and that this act is translated sometimes into Latin as *meditatio*. (Lyons 2006)

Rituals are often part of a family or faith community's traditions and can serve to remind an older person of their connection to a distant past. The realization that the rituals will still be performed long after they are gone may "connect" them to a future they will not be present to experience. They also may serve as reminders of beliefs that may have been temporarily forgotten in the confusion and the chaos of the disaster and its aftermath.

For elderly disaster survivors who are not able to participate in communal faith rituals and services, perhaps due to health issues or lack of transportation, it might be useful to videotape such services and make the tape or DVD available so he or she can participate in the experience vicariously. Spiritual care providers may also want to explore the possibilities of providing or coordinating services in congregate emergency settings (such services are particularly common in shelters run by faith-based organizations).

> Spiritual processing embraces a holistic view of the person ... as the individual analyzes the traumatic event, personal behavior, and emotional experiences in terms of seven essentially spiritual dimensions: (1) distrust and fear, (2) rejection and betrayal, (3) futility, (4) alienation and estrangement, (5) loss and grief, (6) guilt and shame, and (7) isolation and withdrawal. (Parlotz 2007)

Make No Judgments

Spiritual care providers need to respect the vulnerability of elderly disaster survivors and be cognizant of the trust invested in them by people who look to them for spiritual guidance. While it is important to provide spiritual care, or to find someone of their faith tradition who can provide such care, it is equally important for the caregiver not to impose his or her beliefs on the elderly survivor. Even if the older person is angry with God, spiritual care providers, perhaps more than any other caregivers, are a reminder of a loving presence.

There has been less research on elderly trauma survivors than has been performed on survivors of other age groups. Anecdotally, many spiritual care providers can recount stories of elderly people who were unable to adapt to the disaster and others who accommodated yet one more crisis in their life story. We may assume that elderly people are not as strong or as resilient as other people, but as spiritual care providers, this is not for us to judge. We are simply to follow where they lead. They are the prophets of our own future.[4]

Notes

1. Lest we be too idealistic about this notion, however, it is useful to note that an elderly person may be capable of as much foolishness and lack of wisdom as a person of any other age!

2. It is important to recognize that this is a generalization. Not all elderly people developed effective coping strategies based on past life experiences. If their repertoire of coping mechanisms were unhealthy when they were younger, they may continue to be ineffectual and unhealthy in old age.

3. Many medical facilities and hospice programs routinely use lavender hand massage as a treatment with their older patients. Gentle, circular-motion hand massage is provided using a natural oil (such as sesame oil from a grocery store) with several drops of essential lavender oil. Lavender is said to have calming properties. Such massage could be helpful in establishing rapport with an older disaster survivor and the calming aspects of this activity could have spillover benefits for the caregiver as well.

4. This sentence is reminiscent of a poem written by slain El Salvadoran Archbishop Oscar Romero and has poignant relevance to the issue of spiritual care providers for elderly disaster victims. The poem, "Prophets of a Future Not Our Own," reads as follows:

It helps now and then to step back and take a long view. The kingdom is not only beyond our efforts, it is even beyond our vision.

We accomplish in our lifetime only a small fraction of the magnificent enterprise that is God's work. Nothing we do is complete, which is another way of saying that the kingdom always lies beyond us.

No statement says all that could be said. No prayer fully expresses our faith. No confession brings perfection. No pastoral visit brings wholeness. No program accomplishes the Church's mission. No set of goals and objectives includes everything.

This is what we are about: We plant the seeds that will one day grow. We water seeds already planted, knowing that they hold future promise. We lay foundations that will need further development. We provide yeast that produces effects far beyond our capabilities.

We cannot do everything, and there is a sense of liberation in realizing that. This enables us to do something, and to do it well. It may be incomplete but it is a beginning, a step along the way, an opportunity for the Lord's grace to enter and do the rest.

We may never see the end results, but that is the difference between the master builder and the worker. We are workers, not master builders; ministers, not messiahs.

We are prophets of a future not our own.

Further Reading

Chapman, Graeme. *Spirituality for Ministry.* Retrieved from http://www.mun.ca/rels/restmov/texts/gchapman/sfm/SFM23.HTM.

Cheni, Hongtu, et al. "Religious Participation as a Predictor of Mental Health Status and Treatment Outcomes in Older Persons." *International Journal of Geriatric Psychiatry* 22 (2007): 144–53.

Chung, Man Cheung, et al. "Coping with Posttraumatic Stress: Young, Middle-Aged and Elderly Comparisons." *International Journal of Geriatric Psychiatry* 19 (2004): 333–43.

Chung, Man Cheung, et al. "Differentiating Posttraumatic Stress Between Elderly and Younger Patients." *Psychiatry* 68, no. 2 (Summer 2005): 164.

Clemens, P., Hietala, et al. "Risk of Domestic Violence after Flood Impact: Effects of Social Support, Age, and History of Domestic Violence." *Applied Behavioral Science Review* 7, no. 2 (1999): 199–206.

Disaster Mental Health Intervention Field Guide. Indianapolis: Family and Social Services Administration, Division of Mental Health and Addiction. Job 4655.

Ehrenreich, John H., and Sharon McQuaide. *Coping with Disasters, A Guidebook to Psychosocial Intervention,* rev. ed. Retrieved from http://www.mhwwb.org/CopingWithDisaster.pdf.

Fahey, Charles J., and Mary Ann Lewis. "Principles of Integrating Spiritual Concerns into Programs for the Elderly." *Generations* 14, no. 4 (1990): 59–62.

Kohn, Robert, et al. "Prevalence, Risk Factors and Aging Vulnerability for Psychopathology Following a Natural Disaster in a Developing Country." *International Journal of Geriatric Psychiatry* 20 (2005): 835–41.

Langer, N. "Natural Disasters that Reveal Cracks in Our Social Foundation." *Educational Gerontology* 30 (2004): 275–85.

Letter of His Holiness Pope John Paul II to the Elderly, 1999. Retrieved from http://www.vatican.va/holy_father/john_paul_ii/letters/documents/hf_jp-ii_let_01101999_elderly_en.html.

Livingston, Hilary M., et al. "Elderly Survivors of the Lockerbie Air Disaster." *International Journal of Geriatric Psychiatry* 7, no. 10 (1992), 725–29.

Lyons, John D. "Meditation and the Inner Voice." *New Literary History* 37, no. 3 (2006): 525–38.

New Revised Standard Version Bible. 1995. Anglicized Edition.

Parlotz, Robert D. "Trauma Pastoral Care: Part 1—An Affective-Cognitive-Spiritual Adaptation Theory," 1999–2007. Retrieved from http://www.geocities.com/frbobparlotz/drbobparlotz.html.

Proffitt, Deborah, et al. "Judeo-Christian Clergy and Personal Crisis: Religion, Posttraumatic Growth and Well Being." *Journal of Religion and Health* 46, no. 2 (2007).

Stokesberry, John. "South Florida AAA Director Shares Lessons Learned in Hurricane's Wake." *Aging* 365 (January 1, 1993): 0002–0966.

Ticehurst, Stephen, et al. "The Psychosocial Impact of an Earthquake on the Elderly." *International Journal of Geriatric Psychiatry* 11 (1996): 943–51.

Weintraub, D., and P. Ruskin, "Posttraumatic Stress Disorder in the Elderly: A Review." *Harvard Review of Psychiatry* 7, no. 3 (1999).

Wong, Paul P.T. "Personal Meaning and Successful Aging." *Canadian Psychology* 30, no. 3 (1989): 0708-5591.

About the Contributor

Cheryl Guidry Tyiska is a nationally certified crisis responder, crisis response trainer, and victim advocate. She is director of victim-witness services for the Anne Arundel County (Maryland) state attorney's office. She served as interim executive director of National Voluntary Organizations Active in Disaster and was president of its board of directors. She served as interim executive director of the National Organization for Victim Assistance, was its deputy director for two years, and was its director of victim services for eighteen years. Tyiska has responded to many crises and has performed numerous trainings and speaking engagements in the United States and other countries.

19

Working with Police, Firefighters, and Other Uniformed Personnel

Rev. Charles R. Lorrain, DMin

In today's society, clergy for the most part do not have the opportunity to interact with members of the police or firefighting professions. Unlike one hundred years ago when people probably knew the beat cop by name, their only interaction now is probably negative and revolves around a traffic citation or medical emergency.

Since clergy do not work regularly with these groups, they often don't understand the nuances of their professions. How, then, at times of disaster, can clergy expect to be able to work with these emergency service personnel? This chapter will hopefully answer those questions and give insight into who these people are beneath the badge.

Group Characteristics and Uniqueness

Disasters, whether human-caused or natural, bring together a large number of highly trained emergency services personnel: police officers, firefighters, EMTs, and the like. Each of these remarkable individuals share a commonality of having a different "personality type" from those who populate the non-risk-taking job sector.

For example, emergency services personnel are action oriented. They are required to make decisions very quickly and to take action on those decisions even when the risks are high. They have a strong desire to be needed and tend to have "rescuer" personalities. Lastly, they have a strong need to be in control. These and other traits set emergency services personnel apart from the general population (see figure 19.1).[1]

TRAITS OF EMERGENCY SERVICES PERSONNEL

- Risk takers
- Easily bored
- Action oriented
- Highly dedicated

- Need to be needed
- Rescuer personality
- Need to be in control
- Need for immediate gratification

Figure 19.1

To be able to work effectively on-scene during a disaster alongside uniformed personnel, you need to understand the group you are ministering to or you will run into walls or being escorted off-scene and not know why.

Subcultures

Most uniformed service groups are subcultures. They are paramilitary in organization and often they don't trust people outside the group or those inside who have not "paid their dues." To have paid your dues means you have worked around them long enough that they have seen who and what you are and have come to a point where you are trusted and accepted into the group. In law enforcement we call this "breaching the thin blue line." Much like going into a foreign culture in the mission field, entering the world of emergency services personnel will introduce you to new languages, rites, rituals, and idiosyncrasies that must be learned if you are to be invited into their world and be effective. This is especially true if you do not have the opportunity to work with them on a regular basis and you are not known by them.

How different can they be, you ask? Well, you will see them pray in the midst of profanity, you will see them relieve stress by using humor that most wouldn't understand, and you will see courage and strength that defies logic. These are the people who will be running into a disaster when everyone else is running away. That takes a very special kind of person.

Vulnerability/Image Armor

Most people will never get the chance to see who the brave men and women are beneath the badge. To be able to do their job well, emergency services personnel put a protective shell around themselves that is sometimes called "image armor." This shell allows them to insulate themselves from the horror and trauma they deal with daily. However, the protective measure that allows them to function at a high level is also their vulnerability. The same armor that shields them from the emotions of the job often keeps them from purging the destructive and toxic nature of its outcome. It is a truly a Catch-22.

When police or fire personnel are at work on-scene, they are on autopilot and suppressing emotions to be able to do their job. Trying to break into their image armor at that point could be detrimental to them. Timing is critical when ministering to uniformed personnel.

Ministry of Presence

Much of what a clergyperson does around uniformed personnel is what we call a ministry of presence, not pressure. It is being on-scene, but not being in the way; it is reading the eyes and emotions of those around you and being available as they need you; it is a timely word of encouragement, a hand on a shoulder, a prayer for strength and courage; it is compassion personified. But it is never proselytizing, preaching, or pushing the officer into an emotional corner.

There are four abilities that fit into the ministry of presence:

- Availability
- Visibility
- Adaptability
- Credibility[2]

Availability means you are there with them, ready to go wherever and whenever asked. *Visibility* is simply being seen. They need to see you function as a clergyperson before they will feel comfortable asking you for help. If you are not visible, you will definitely be out of their minds. *Adaptability* is being willing to change. Disasters are fluid, changing almost hourly. If you are too rigid and can't adapt to changes quickly, you will never make it in a disaster scenario. Last, *credibility* comes as you are being real with people. Law enforcement personnel are trained to spot fakes. They will have no respect for you if you don't walk the talk.

Jurisdictional Issues

In the United States police and fire departments work within different spheres of responsibility in different geographical areas. These responsibilities are mandated by federal, state, county, or city law and are called "jurisdictions" or "the range of legal authority."[3] Generally, federal laws supersede all others jurisdictionally and are at the top of the heap. State, county, and city jurisdictions go in descending order all the way down to the bottom.

During disasters, many agencies may respond to the affected areas, and the pushing and shoving starts almost immediately as to who has jurisdiction over the incident. Oftentimes, several agencies might exercise areas of jurisdictional control and a system has to be set up to integrate services so they are provided in a seamless manner. Sometimes the jurisdictional issues are so complex and difficult to define that power struggles ensue.

Why is jurisdiction important to clergy responding to the disaster? First, if you are just responding to volunteer your services and you do not belong to a particular disaster response group that is recognized by the group exercising jurisdictional control over the disaster, it is possible you may be denied entry. This is especially true if the event is a human-caused disaster that is deemed a crime scene.

Second, the same might be true if you are working with a local group or even a state agency and the disaster is deemed under federal jurisdiction, as only credentialed people recognized or authorized by that particular federal agency will be allowed in. This does not mean, however, that all avenues of service will be cut off. For example, the American Red Cross is always looking for local disaster volunteers to work in an affected area. They will screen, orient, and credential you for the disaster as needed. Other groups provide similar services as well.

The thing to keep in mind is that no matter how much you think you should be in the middle of a disaster scene because you are a member of the clergy, your desire to be there doesn't carry any weight when it comes to the legality of the disaster response. The best course of action is to be proactive and prepare ahead of time to be able to work with one of these disaster response groups. It saves a lot of time and effort when a disaster is in full swing.

Training—Preparation, Preparation, Preparation!

You have probably heard the old adage that the key to successful real estate is location, location, location. When it comes to successfully dealing in disasters with uniformed personnel it is preparation, preparation, preparation!

You must take a proactive approach and obtain training *before* the incident occurs or you will be too far behind the curve. Don't be a fair-weather clergyperson that does nothing all year long and then expects to go to the big show when disaster strikes. Be proactive and prepare! There are several specific trainings that you should consider taking to equip yourself to work with these special groups.

General Pre-disaster Training: The first training that would be helpful to obtain is general pre-disaster training. This encompasses general instruction on the dynamics of disasters, how they affect different populations, things you will need to know to work within those environments, self-care, and the like. This is the foundation for all other training. General pre-disaster training may be obtained from the American Red Cross or other similar disaster response agencies.

Critical Incident Stress Management: Critical Incident Stress Management, or CISM, is an intervention protocol developed specifically for dealing with traumatic events. It is a formal, highly structured and professionally recognized process for helping those involved in a critical incident to share their experiences, vent emotions, learn about stress reactions and symptoms, and give referrals for further help if required. It is not psychotherapy. It is a confidential, voluntary, and educative process, sometimes called "psychological first aid."[4]

There are ten elements that comprise the CISM system:

1. Pre-incident education
2. On-scene support services
3. Defusings
4. Demobilizations
5. Debriefings
6. Specialty debriefings
7. Informal discussions
8. Significant other support services

9. Individual consults
10. Follow-up services

Clergy who will be working in a disaster setting must be able to recognize the traumatic stress symptoms that could be exhibited by uniformed personnel working on-scene. This will aid the clergyperson in assisting these individuals both during and after the disaster. Any clergyperson wishing to take a CISM course may find course information listed on the International Critical Incident Stress Foundation's website at www.icisf.org.

Pastoral Crisis Intervention: The term *pastoral crisis intervention* (PCI) has been defined by George S. Everly (2000) as "the functional integration of any and all religious, spiritual, and pastoral resources with the assessment and intervention technologies typically thought of as crisis intervention."[5] The PCI course aids clergy in learning how ministry in disasters differs from the general ministry given to their parishioners. Clergy wishing to take a PCI course may find course information listed on the International Critical Incident Stress Foundation's website, www.icisf.org.

National Incident Management System: On February 28, 2003, President George W. Bush issued a homeland security presidential directive that mandated the secretary of homeland security to develop and administer a National Incident Management System (NIMS). This system provides a consistent, nationwide template to enable federal, state, local, and tribal governments and private-sector and nongovernmental organizations to work together effectively and efficiently to prepare for, prevent, respond to, and recover from domestic incidents, regardless of cause, size, or complexity, including acts of catastrophic terrorism.[6] Clergy who might work on-scene during disasters within the incident command structure should take the basic NIMS classes IS-100 and IS-700. Both classes may be taken free online through the Federal Emergency Management Agency website at www.fema.gov.

On-Scene Protocols

There are some very specific issues regarding on-scene protocols that need to be addressed if you are going to be working around police and fire personnel. These dos and don'ts will help you stay out of trouble!

Self-Deployment

The number one all-time worst thing a clergyperson can do is self-deploy to the scene of a disaster. I cannot stress this fact strongly enough. Clergy, like mental health providers, are a compassionate group of people who are always ready to respond to human need. However, self-deploying during times of disasters can make you a liability, not an asset.

Most will remember the bombing of the Alfred P. Murrah Federal Building in Oklahoma City in 1995. After the disaster, countless clergy and mental health providers swarmed Oklahoma City from around the country to lend aid. Sounds like the right thing to do, doesn't it? Unfortunately, it was the absolute worst thing to do.

During disasters there are incident-specific people that are needed on-scene, as determined by the agencies that have jurisdictional control over a disaster. When people choose to self-deploy, they use up limited resources that are needed by those incident-specific personnel.

In the Oklahoma City bombing disaster, airlines were booked full by people trying to get to Okalahoma City, hotel rooms were taken by people just showing up, restaurants were packed, and rental cars were unavailable. All the limited resources needed by the people that were properly deployed to the disaster were being utilized by well-meaning but misguided people that self-deployed to the scene.

If you are not deployed to the scene by a recognized disaster response agency—*stay home!* Stay home and pray for those affected by the disaster. Stay home and send money to the organizations working the disaster. Contact the American Red Cross and inquire if they have need of local disaster volunteers. *Just don't self-deploy and take up valuable resources needed by disaster response personnel.*

Confidentiality

When dealing with police and fire personnel, confidentiality is of the utmost importance. When you finally arrive at a place where you have gained their trust and they will open up and talk to you, there is an absolute expectation that it will remain confidential. A breach of confidentiality will not only destroy any hope you have of ministering to them, but it will probably hinder or destroy the efforts of all clergy involved in the disaster response. Word spreads very fast through these professions, and if it is found out that you cannot be trusted, you are through!

You need to remember that these men and women are confiding in you because of trust, not because of your title, education, or credentials. If you loose your credibility, you have nothing.

Another issue that you have to be very careful about is the confidentiality of information you might overhear from conversations between officers, investigators, or the like because of your proximity to the incident. There is a legitimate excitement for you to want to share what is going on with your family and friends back home, but sharing the wrong information could jeopardize aspects of an operation. Law enforcement often holds back from the public key bits of information that is discovered through the course of an investigation. This is a useful tool in the investigation and possibly in the prosecution at a later date. You do not know what information is reported to the media by law enforcement. Should you accidentally leak information in your exuberance, it could have a negative impact and compromise an investigation. So remember, what you see, hear, and are told, and information you might be privy to *must* be kept in the strictest of confidence.

When to Talk with Uniformed Personnel

As mentioned previously, uniformed personnel are on autopilot when working on-scene during disasters. They are focused, driven, and task-oriented, which is necessary for the successful completion of the operation. If you are working on-scene around uniformed personnel, do not try to get them to come out of their shell and open up to you emotionally. They are very vulnerable at this time and you could create a bad situation for them.

When a disaster recovery effort uses the CISM system, there will be defusing sessions on-scene or near the scene of the disaster, demobilizations between shifts if necessary, and formal debriefings when appropriate. Your job is to be available, supportive, comforting, and encouraging. Just a "How are you doing?" or "Can I get you something to drink?" often speaks volumes of care and concern.

Sometimes you will find emergency services personnel to be silent as they process the barrage of information from an incident. There is an old saying: "If you can't improve on silence, don't." Silence often makes us feel uncomfortable, and we feel the need to engage people. But we cannot let our own comfort level dictate conversation that might exacerbate trauma to another. When they are ready and feel it is safe to do so, they will open up. Remember, people deal in time and God deals in timing. Ours is having enough wisdom to recognize the difference.

Media

Any major disaster, whether human-caused or natural, is a media circus. You might be asked or even hounded by the media for a sound bite. Very simply, do not speak to the media unless directly told to do so by someone in authority. The best course of action is to direct them to a uniformed officer or the public information officer (PIO). Emergency services personnel do not look kindly on those seeking media attention.

Crime Scenes versus Natural Disasters

Although all disasters are monumental and overwhelming in scope, there are some differences between how human-caused and natural disasters are handled. These differences are mainly concerned with human-caused disasters that are deemed crime scenes. When working around crime scenes with police and fire, there are important dos and don'ts to remember. You do not want to be the one who compromises a crime scene.

Yellow tape: You are probably familiar with the yellow crime scene tape you see on television crime shows. This tape is an important tool in setting up an inner perimeter and keeping the crime scene from being contaminated. The safe rule is to never cross the yellow tape unless directed to do so by a uniformed officer. If you are invited in for some reason, follow the exact entrance and egress path used by uniformed officers or investigators so as not to contaminate the scene. Do not wander around the scene like a tourist.

Scene contamination: Scene contamination can compromise forensic evidence vital to an investigation. Do not take in or remove anything from a crime scene. Keep your hands in your pockets and do not touch anything, as you might taint evidence. Remember, on any disaster scene under federal jurisdiction, it is a violation of federal law to remove anything from the scene. This is one place you can ill afford to go.

Phones: If there are phones within the crime scene, do not use them. They may be of investigative value for either forensic evidence left on the phone or by the last number dialed. It is always better to be safe and use a cell phone or a landline outside the inner perimeter.

This also brings up another point about using cell phones. Cell phones are not a secure link. Their signal can be intercepted by scanners that are often used by the media or other groups of people. If you need to obtain or pass on information that is sensitive in nature, seek out and use a landline phone. Remember, information leaked even by accident can compromise an investigation or create a hardship for people if the media obtains certain information before it is ready for dissemination.

Photographs and souvenirs: If you have ever worked on the scene of a major disaster, you were probably awestruck with the devastation. So much so, you may have wanted to take pictures or souvenirs to help you remember it. While this is legally permissible on the scene of natural disasters, although possibly insensitive if done in the sight of victims, it is a definite no-no for crime scenes. Cameras and film may be confiscated on the scene of any human-caused disaster determined to be a crime scene.

It bears repeating that taking items from a crime scene could subject you to criminal charges. Unfortunately, this has happened to members of the clergy who did not use discretion. So a word to the wise—just don't do it! It is not worth the heartache.

Final Words

It is an honor and privilege to be able to work alongside the brave heroes beneath the badge during disasters. The work they do is extremely difficult and they pay a heavy price to do it. If you desire to be truly effective in your ministry with them, take the time to prepare properly. If you do so, it will make your ministry much more rewarding, and the impact you will have on their lives will be immeasurable.

Notes

1. G. P. Bray and J. T. Mitchell, *Emergency Services Stress: Guidelines for Preserving the Health and Careers of Emergency Services Personnel* (Englewood Cliffs, NJ: Prentice-Hall, 1990), 21.
2. D. W. DeRevere et al., *Chaplaincy in Law Enforcement: What It Is and How to Do It* (Springfield, IL: Charles C. Thomas, 1989), 15.
3. *Webster's New World Dictionary,* 4th ed. (Cleveland: Webster's New World, 2002).
4. "What Is CISM?" http://www.criticalincidentstress.com/what_is_cism_.
5. *International Journal of Emergency Mental Health* 2, no. 3 (2000): 139–42.
6. *National Incident Management System,* http://www.fema.gov/pdf/emergency/nims/nims_doc_full.pdf.

Further Reading

Bray, Grady P., and Jeffery T. Mitchell. *Emergency Services Stress: Guidelines for Preserving the Health and Careers of Emergency Services Personnel. Englewood Cliffs,* NJ: Prentice-Hall, 1990.

DeRevere, David W., et al. *Chaplaincy in Law Enforcement: What It Is and How to Do It.* Springfield, IL: Charles C. Thomas, 1989.

Friedman, Cary A. *Spiritual Survival for Law Enforcement.* Linden, NJ: Compass Books, 2005.

Kirschman, Ellen. *I Love a Cop.* New York: Guilford Press, 1997.

———. *I love a Firefighter: What a Family Needs to Know.* New York: Guilford Press, 2004.

Mitchell, Jeffery T., and George S. Everly. *Critical Incident Stress Debriefing: An Operations Manual for the Prevention of Traumatic Stress among Emergency Service and Disaster Workers,* 2nd ed. Ellicott City, MD: Chevron, 1996.

Panton, Douglas, and John M. Violanti. *Traumatic Stress in Critical Occupations.* Springfield, IL: Charles C. Thomas, 1996.

Resources

International Conference of Police Chaplains (ICPC)
P.O. Box 5590
Destin, FL 32540
850-654-9736
www.icpc4cops.org

Federation of Fire Chaplains (FCC)
85 County Road 1602
Clifton, TX 76634
254-622-8514
www.firechaplains.org

Federal Emergency Management Agency (FEMA)
500 C Street S.W.
Washington, D.C. 20472
800-621-3362
www.fema.gov

International Critical Incident Stress Foundations (ICISF)
3290 Pine Orchard Lane, Suite 106
Ellicott City, MD 21042
410-750-9600
www.icisf.org

About the Contributor

Rev. Charles R. Lorrain, DMin, is the executive director of the International Conference of Police Chaplains (ICPC). Rev. Lorrain is a certified master chaplain with the ICPC, having served twenty-five years in field ministry to local law enforcement and also national events such as 9/11, the crash of American Airlines flight 587, Hurricane Katrina, and others. He is a board-certified expert in traumatic stress, a diplomate with the American Academy of Experts in Traumatic Stress, a board-certified crisis chaplain, and board-certified in emergency crisis response. He also serves on the American Red Cross Crisis Response Team and the ICPC's disaster response team.

20

Resources in a Disaster

Accessing Them for the Congregation and Congregants—Suggestions on Ways for a Congregation to Get Involved That Strengthen It, Not Destroy It

*Rev. Thomas H. Davis Jr. and
Rev. Lloyd George Abrams, DMin*

Following Hurricane Katrina, Church World Service announced a campaign to raise $9.4 million for Gulf Region recovery and relief efforts. In recent history, other organizations have announced multimillion-dollar campaigns for recovery efforts following a disaster. News of these large-scale efforts has given the false expectation that money and resources are readily available following a disaster.

The reality is that *disaster recovery is primarily up to the individuals and communities that have suffered the loss.* They are the ones who must find the money to finance their own recovery. Unfortunately, there is no one who will wave a magic wand and restore them to their previous condition. As will be described later in this chapter, there are some government agencies, voluntary agencies, and faith-based organizations that will help with some of the recovery, but the bulk of the recovery depends upon the person or organization affected by the disaster.

Long-term recovery from disaster continues long after the news media leaves. The general rule is that if disaster response is four days, the disaster relief phase will last forty days and the recovery phase will last four hundred days. The goal is to return the congregation and the individuals affected by disaster to their pre-disaster condition. Help will be needed from as many resources as possible to handle all of the immediate needs. There is no such thing as too many resources.

The Congregation's Starting Point—Insurance

Financial recovery from a disaster is a large issue. All houses of worship should have insurance on their building and contents. *Insurance provides the best means for recovery following a disaster.* That is why it is so important to contact the insurance agent as soon as possible following a loss. There is no other system in place in our culture that can provide as much immediate financial recovery as the insurance we own.

In the case of houses of worship, there may be both primary and secondary insurance available. Primary insurance will insure the building up to a certain dollar limit. The primary insurance may even be self-insurance through the religious connectional system.

Secondary insurance takes over after the primary insurance limit has been reached. For example, an organization such as the Boy Scouts of America may have primary insurance up to $15 million. Beyond that limit, a group such as Lloyd's of London may provide secondary insurance for damages beyond the $15 million limit.

It is very important after a disaster to wait for an inspection from the insurance agent before making any repairs. The property owner can and should take action to prevent further damage, which can involve temporary repairs made by volunteers. Even with temporary repairs, it is wise to take pictures before and after they are made to document the condition of the building. If the volunteers offer to make permanent repairs, ask them to wait until your insurance company approves the repairs. It is equally important to delay permanent repairs until after an inspection from state and federal representatives. In the case of federal inspection, it is the verification of the damage that helps qualify the homeowner for federal financial disaster relief. To start the federal inspection process, register with the Federal Emergency Management Agency (FEMA) by making a telephone call.

A congregation may also set money aside for a possible disaster—this is known as self-insurance. Such financial reserves for disaster recovery can be held in an endowment fund. Church policy often prevents spending the principal of an endowment fund for any reason short of a disaster. Such a financial reserve provides a cushion that can be coupled with an insurance settlement for repairs and replacement.

Maintain and review insurance policies on an annual basis. Insurance is your first line of defense in protection against total loss and bankruptcy caused by a catastrophic event. Other than emergency housing, FEMA will not provide assistance until an insurance claim has been filed and the claim is paid or denied. It is very important for individuals to file their insurance claims immediately following a disaster. Insurance claims are placed in a queue and processed in the order in which they were received.

Identify attorneys within the congregation or community who may be willing to become involved in insurance litigation. Sometimes, a memo on the letterhead of an attorney can expedite insurance claims. Additionally, there may be a class action suit that your congregants may need to become involved in. If this is the case, you will want a reputable attorney to represent your best interest. Your attorney will also be aware of any legitimate class action law suits that may emerge following a disaster.

The maintenance of good insurance is an act of stewardship. Those who manage their insurance do not become a burden to the recovery process and thus allow the limited resources of the donations to nonprofit organizations and the faith-based community to be used for those who are truly of greatest need in our society.

Finally, as you file your congregation's insurance claims, be aware of members who have special age, health, emotional, physical, or mental needs. Help those with special needs notify the insurance company. People who otherwise function well may have a difficult time coping with all of the paperwork that will face them following a disaster. Providing help with the completion of the insurance forms, the FEMA application process, or filing out Small Business Administration loan forms is a very helpful service to your congregants affected by disaster.

How to Ensure That Your Congregation Does Not Go Under

Before we begin the discussion of congregational survival in the context of disaster and its effects on congregational life, we should be reminded of Ecclesiastes 3: "For everything there is a season, and a time for every matter under heaven: a time to be born, and a time to die ... a time to break down, and a time to build up." In the cycle of life, a disaster may not be the time for some congregations to survive. There are always limited funds for rebuilding or repairing in the life of any community affected by a disaster. Sometimes it is not the most prudent use of those limited funds to enable a congregation to survive that may need to come to the end of its life cycle. This is a difficult message that may not make emotional sense when a congregation is suffering the pangs of their loss.

Again, preparedness is at the heart of hardening your congregation against the potentially devastating affects of disaster. Basic disaster preparedness is a must for the individuals and families in the membership of your congregation and for the congregation itself. There are many very good resources for this purpose (see chapter 3 for detailed ways to prepare).

Develop a congregational plan of response to disaster. Set aside seed moneys for start-up. *Be prepared to be self-sustaining for at least three months with no income stream.* Through adult education, engage in disaster preparedness activities. Administratively, maintain an up-to-date mailing list and calling trees. Develop collaborative community relationships.

Do not neglect the care for the caregiver. *Burnout and attrition rates of clergy can be high following a disaster and can cause a congregation to fail!* Many national faith-based institutions recognize the value of taking care of the clergy and the caregiver. Emotional and spiritual care, training, and support for clergy or other leaders within the faith community may be provided by national or regional judicatories.

Take care of your family first. Caregivers who do not provide the needed care for their own families will be caregiver who are distracted and will not fully be able to provide the best service to anyone concerned.

In the same manner, take care of your house of worship first. Your place of worship is an important touchstone for its members and the community as a whole.

Take care of the members of your congregation first. Volunteers from within your faith tradition are often willing to give aid to their family of faith without regard to income and won't require their friends to file for insurance or aid from the American Red Cross, Salvation Army, or FEMA before providing assistance. Volunteers respond more out of compassion and their need to be helpful than the basis of need. Allow volunteers to work with your congregants as soon as possible. After you have secured your family and your extended family, you will have more time and energy to respond to the community at large.

An important tool for a congregation to survive a disaster comes from looking to modern technology to gather your congregation in a virtual world. Develop an interactive website with a members-only section that can be turned into a weblog or bulletin board for posting information about the needs and whereabouts of the members of your congregation. After Hurricane Katrina in 2005, several pastors reported success in locating members of their congregation in remote locations through the use of their website. In the midst of a disaster you will want to be certain to have a local volunteer manage and continue to develop your website. Other helpful web-based communication tools might be Yahoo Groups, Google Groups, MSN Groups, or other instant-messaging tools. YouTube, a video sharing site, and MySpace, a web networking site, may also be useful tools for communication. Be mindful of who and what you list or post on MySpace and YouTube; law enforcement and potential employers have been known to view its contents. One New York City police cadet ran into difficulty when one of the people she listed in her circle of community on MySpace was a person of interest for law enforcement. Finally, use the postal service to find your relocated congregants. Send a mailing with address corrections requested. You will pay the equivalent of first-class postage to be notified of a change in address, but the post office will provide you with whatever change of address they have on file for that person.

Look to the inside and outside of your congregation. In the time of disaster, special offerings to support those in need are appropriate. Other congregations within your geographical area may also be willing to take special offerings or provide volunteers for feeding or clean up.

Sources of Disaster Funding Directly Available to a Congregation

There are many ways to raise money for a congregation's own disaster recovery. Sources of disaster funding available to a congregation include their denomination, nonprofits, and sometimes even government assistance. If the congregation is a part of a larger connectional system, they may receive donations from other connected congregations in the area and from the national organization of their congregations.

National faith-based organizations such as Church World Service, United Methodist Committee on Relief, Presbyterian Disaster Assistance, Islamic Relief USA, Catholic Charities USA Disaster Response, Christian Reform World Relief Committee, United Jewish Communities, and Lutheran Disaster Response are just a few of the many faith-based domestic and international relief agencies. Different financial restrictions may apply in each group.

Some national programs may not allow disaster funding to be used for their own congregational property. The policy may require congregational property damage repair financing be raised from within by a parish-wide appeal. A telephone call can easily determine issues of protocol.

We started this chapter with the question "Who finances a congregation's recovery?" While some resources are available, *the bottom line is that much of disaster recovery rests upon the congregation and the individuals affected*. Nothing is more important than procuring adequate insurance and setting money aside in a disaster reserve account before disaster strikes. Even with adequate funding, disaster recovery will still be a long and arduous journey. Only financial planning and education can make the response easier.

Becoming a Community Resource During or After a Disaster

"I have a facility, but not the budget to respond—where do I turn?" The opportunities for your congregation to become a community resource during or after a disaster are limited only by your imagination. There are many ways in which a facility can be used at little or no cost. Don't let the fear of cost inhibit your creativity. These opportunities are an important way to help both your congregants and the larger community.

Houses of worship can be used as a storehouse for donations, as a place for emergency services personnel to relax when not working, or as a training and screening center for volunteers. These are just a few of the many ways religious centers have been used in the past.

Below is a list of various uses for a worship facility. Few of these ideas have any associated costs; most only need some coordination to be a tremendous service to a grieving, disaster-affected community.

When a congregation is being used to provide any of the services listed below, it is advisable to assign someone to be the public relations representative for the faith community. It is important to select a person who has prior experience or training. Being a part of the rescue and recovery phases of a major disaster will probably thrust the congregation into the national spotlight. Some enterprising reporter will want to interview a spokesperson from the worship center. This representation should be undertaken by a person with education and or experience in public relations rather than the church secretary or the pastor who is already late for another appointment. The national and international press can be vicious and determined. The general rule is that you control the press, or the press controls you.

Being a service to your community by providing facilities is a mission experience. It is a task that should be undertaken with planning and preparation. It is an opportunity that should not be overlooked. We are called to love our neighbor. Nothing is more loving than helping your neighbor when they need assistance following a disaster.

Become an American Red Cross shelter. There is no financial cost in becoming an American Red Cross shelter. Prior to a disaster, contact your local American Red Cross (ARC) and seek a memorandum of understanding that your congregation's facility can be used as a shelter or disaster recovery center. There are minimal standards that you must be able to meet in order to have your facility used: you must complete an application and pass an inspection. Following acceptance, a shelter kit with necessary supplies will be delivered to the building to be stored there. This kit includes signs, registration forms, and other materials. American Red Cross staff, including mental health workers and medical personnel who assist in the psychological physical healing of those affected by the disaster, will run the shelter. The ARC is most likely to use organizations that they have preexisting relationships and agreements with in the event of a disaster, so be proactive and complete the application and inspection process before a disaster strikes. The ARC also provides training for disaster preparedness.

Contact your local public health department. Determine what their needs might be and how you can partner with them.

Volunteer your facility to provide meeting space for Citizen Emergency Response Training. Neighbors are the first responders to any disaster. Being a good neighbor is to become trained in how to be most helpful to your neighbor in the event of a disaster. It is also important to be recognized by the emergency responders as they arrive on the scene of a disaster. Citizen Emergency Response Training provides the appropriate training and relationship-building with your local emergency management agencies.

Use your space for volunteer management. Voluntary organizations need just the right size building for volunteers to gather and be screened. A large building may be used for a large disaster and a small facility for a small disaster. Following screening, volunteers need to be given an orientation about what it means to be a volunteer. For example, if the volunteer is being asked to work for the American Red Cross, they will need to understand the protocols for working as an ARC volunteer. They will also need some basic training in an introduction to disaster work and mass care. The worship center's classrooms may be the perfect place for such activities.

Use the building for community memorial services. This is a use of worship spaces that is often overlooked. It sometimes requires a very large building, but not always. When two professors at a university were killed in a car accident, two joint memorial services were held in that community. A large service was held on the university campus, and another service was held in the church where one of the professors was a member. In small towns, the funeral home is often too small for the funeral or memorial service of a pioneer of the community. A house of worship in the small farm community of St. John, Washington, has made it their mission to provide space for funerals and memorial services for any person in town. In the town of Moscow, Idaho, the congregations organized a series of evening worship services following the ambush shooting of some police officers. Each worship or prayer service took place in a different worship center around town.

Provide meeting spaces for community groups after a disaster. Many worship centers have a number of classrooms or meeting rooms. These rooms can be the perfect space for regular meetings of community organizations such as Kiwanis, Rotary Club, Lions, 4-H, and

Alcoholics Anonymous who may have to move their meetings to a new space if a disaster destroys their usual meeting space. A new community group that may be looking for meeting space after a major disaster is the Long Term Recovery Organization. This group of five to eight people matches the needs of the disaster victims with the resources of the community.

Offer your building as a feeding station. Inner-city congregations are often familiar with this use of their building, but suburban congregations may not be. Even congregations with small kitchens can provide tables, chairs, and shelter to people being fed by large mobile kitchens. The Southern Baptists are famous for feeding scores of people who can then take their food into the education building of a worship center for a place to sit. As the feeding station moves around the community from church to church, a great number of people can be fed. The Salvation Army is another faith-based organization that seeks out space to conduct its feeding programs. A parking lot in the right location may be all they need.

Become a food distribution center for a national food bank. If the regular community distribution center is heavily damaged or destroyed, a worship center could become the new local food bank. For example, in the small town of Randle, Washington, the United Methodist Church has built a food bank into one wing of their new church building.

Serve as a respite center for emergency services personnel. A respite center is a place where police officers, firefighters, EMTs, and other emergency services workers can rest and recuperate following twelve hours or more of disaster response. In New York City, St. Paul's Chapel was very close to the World Trade Center towers. Following the 9/11 terrorist attacks, the chapel became a respite center. Each pew was furnished with a blanket, a pillow, a teddy bear, and chocolate for the tired rescue workers. The chapel continued this program for more than six months.

Provide nursery care for small children. This may be a service you already provide during your worship services. Some houses of worship even have preschools. It should not take much coordination to open the nursery or preschool as a temporary child care center following a disaster. A temporary shelter for children provides a needed relief to overstressed parents and children. The Church of the Brethren, who specialize in disaster child care, may even staff the facility for free.

Both the Brethren and the American Red Cross will provide mental health and spiritual care for the children and their parents.

Open your worship center for adult grief counseling. Mental health workers from the American Red Cross and Salvation Army, as well as community mental health centers, welcome small classrooms for one on one counseling.

Function as a community warming center. During a power outage, some houses of worship may be spared a loss of power due to the setup of power grids. That worship building can function in a new way as a community warming center. If the kitchen is large enough, it can also distribute hot meals. The meals do not have to be made in the kitchen. They could be preprepared meals from the Salvation Army, Southern Baptists, or other that are kept hot in the kitchen until distribution.

Use your storefront congregation for donations management. These houses of worship in former grocery stores have the loading docks needed to move large amounts of clothing and other donated goods. It is highly recommended that a professional donations manager be employed, perhaps through the combined help of several churches. Donations can easily get out of hand and become the "second disaster." No one wants to be flooded with piles of dirty, moldy clothing. In Minden, Louisiana, two church members saw the need for donations management and obtained the use of an abandoned Wal-Mart on the edge of town to be the donations center. Within two weeks, the volunteer staff of congregational members had served over two thousand people.

Use the parking lot as a staging area for emergency personnel. A staging area is where police officers and firefighters gather for planning and organization before deployment. Being a staging area requires very little effort or liability on the part of the congregation. In Springfield, Oregon, the Lutheran church across from the high school was used to park ambulances following a school shooting. The ambulances would arrive behind the church, wait in line to pick up a patient from the front of the church, and then make a run to the hospital. They returned to the parking lot in the back of the church for their next patient pickup and delivery. In the first hours, just a few ambulances delivered twenty-two children to the local hospitals.

Become a replacement center for medical supplies such as eye glasses, hearing aids, and the like. Many of these medicals aids are lost in a tornado or destroyed in a flood or wildfire. Medical supply centers are eager to offer replacement devices but may lack the space and shelter for distribution or fitting.

Preparing and Responding to Disaster— Creating or Finding Resources

Gilbert Furst, retired director of Lutheran Disaster Response, has said, "You are a physical sign of God's love for disaster survivors. Your presence as a volunteer brings the gift of hope and new life to those suffering from a catastrophe."[1] The greatest spiritual care that can be provided to a disaster survivor is that of your presence. Financial support, physical support, and volunteer support are the greatest spiritual gifts to be offered in the midst of disaster recovery. Providing food, housing, and clothing is the provision of spiritual care.

A common theme that is being heralded in this chapter is prepare, prepare, prepare, prepare. The question if a disaster befalls your community is never "How will we be ready to respond?" Rather, the question is "When a disaster befalls our community how well will we be prepared?" It is often extremely difficult to convince those who prepare budgets for the religious community to plan for a disaster. It simply does not seem to them to be good stewardship to set aside funds for something that may or may not happen. Here are some suggestions on how a congregation or worshiping community can better prepare itself for the likely event of a natural or human-caused disaster striking near or in the midst of their community.

Arrange memorandums of understanding (MOU) with other religious communities and institutions in your community prior to a disaster. A MOU will help determine how you will communicate and share limited resources in the event of a disaster. Organizations with which it is important to have a MOU might be your local clergy association; social ministry organizations such as Catholic Charities, Jewish Community Centers, Lutheran Social Services, and the Salvation Army; faith-based colleges and universities; church camps; and faith-based medical facilities. Issues to be considered might include: Who has a kitchen that can feed large numbers of people on short notice? Who has the facility to house dislocated people for a short period of time? Who can become a communication center? Who can coordinate and receive volunteers who will come from outside or within your community?

Prior to a disaster, learn who the private individuals are in your community who may own generators or have a reputation for being especially helpful. You may be able to call upon them in a time of need. In particular, knowing this information may help you find refrigeration for those who have medications that must be refrigerated at all times. Knowing this in advance can save lives within your congregation.

Budget for a disaster prior to a disaster. Establish a disaster response fund in your annual budgeting process. It is commonly understood to be wise for households to have savings that can sustain them in an emergency for at least six months. It is important for our faith-based communities to set aside a portion of its receipts for emergencies as well. Consider the story of Joseph. Joseph won the favor of the pharaoh by interpreting the dreams of the pharaoh and predicting a great famine. The pharaoh set aside a portion of the country's harvest in preparation for the famine. The result was that the people of Egypt did not suffer in the time of pestilence and famine.

Congregational appeals for the establishment of a disaster fund may be in order. A simple appeal to seed a disaster preparedness fund may offer your worship community the opportunity to establish your congregation's emergency fund.

Determine in advance the appropriate uses for funds that are set aside for disaster preparedness. Will priority for receiving these funds be given to congregants? How will you consider immediate need while keeping in mind the more difficult long-term recovery need? How will need be identified? How will you partner and work with other community organizations to meet the needs of your congregants and the members of the community at large?

After a disaster, explore funding resources for response and recovery outside of your congregation's assets. National or regional religious structures related to a congregation often will have funding available for congregational use during the time of a disaster. This type of funding is likely made available for individual assistance and may not be available for structural damage to the church, synagogue, or place of worship. Through this funding you may be able to offer emergency grants of two to five hundred dollars to congregants affected by the disaster.

After a disaster, provide meals and child care for those affected by a disaster. In the weeks following the impact of a disaster, the affected individuals will become overwhelmed with the initial and ongoing tasks of recovery. Not only will they need to begin the process of cleanup, but they will also be faced with a mountain of confusing paperwork, claims to insurance, and registration for federal assistance if the disaster becomes a federally declared disaster. Among the unseen needs that emerge are the need for well-balanced meals and child care. Taking care of the children of your congregation and making sure that everyone is eating a well-balanced meal becomes an invaluable gift. This is a need that may continue for weeks. Groceries and other food items can be provided by Second Harvest or other local food banks. You will also find local grocers who would be willing to establish donation deposit boxes in their store for in-kind food donations.

Find support from local service clubs. Often local Lions, Rotary, Kiwanis, Elks, or other service clubs will have limited funds to help offset the unexpected costs of immediate response in a disaster. Keep service clubs involved and informed of your response work. Not only are some of them able to provide financial assistance, but they also may be willing to lend a helping hand. During the 2006 winter storms in Washington State, Kiwanis built a new handicapped-accessible front porch for a homeowner whose back was broken as the result of a falling tree. Nonprofits may have fewer financial restrictions than government agencies and may be especially helpful for financial needs not covered by any other source of relief.

Invite the media to report on the needs of your community. Be careful not to request used clothing or furniture. These items are difficult to screen during a disaster and pose a hardship in finding warehouse or storage facilities. Make use of Disaster News Network (www.dnn.org) to tell your story and to seek consultation on dealing with local media outlets.

Join the emerging Long Term Recovery Organization (LTRO). Within two weeks of a disaster, a local LTRO may begin to take form. These organizations may be faith based or community based in their structure. A LTRO will leverage money, volunteers, and resources to assist individual and families in identifying and meeting their unmet needs.

Assist the less well-educated to fill out forms and gather necessary documentation for the application process. Money usually comes only after mountains of paperwork. Pay special attention to those with mental health or dementia issues and those who may be unable to read.

Consider asking neighboring communities for financial or volunteer support. The spirit of helping your neighbor is a compelling value in this country. Communities of faith will provide spontaneous donations and will want to do whatever they can to help. Volunteers will emerge as neighbors seek to offer a helpful hand. It is important to become the conduit for the provision of care to the people of your community.

Organize repair and cleanup teams within your congregation. Preplanning and education in disaster response are important. Training will help volunteers understand the spiritual crisis of disaster and appropriate responses for volunteerism, as well as issues of safety and liability. Only repair your congregants' damaged buildings against adverse weather after taking pictures of the damage. The repairs should only be temporary until inspected by your insurance company and by government inspectors.

Governmental Agencies

Much has been written about government agencies in disaster relief. Government agencies often focus their relief on individuals rather than faith-based organizations. However, helping the people in a worship community obtain financial relief is often the first step in returning the faith-based organization to financial stability.

Two leaders in disaster relief are the Federal Emergency Management Agency (FEMA) and the Small Business Administration (SBA). Together they try to provide assistance for housing. FEMA can provide small grants for housing up to a certain limit, and the SBA has individual and business low-interest loans available up to a certain limit. The objective is to help people have a home environment that is safe, sanitary, and secure.

Other federal assistance not as widely publicized includes Health Services, the Internal Revenue Service (IRS), and Housing and Urban Development (HUD). Health Services may have disaster food stamps available for immediate relief following the loss of income occasioned by a disaster. If the person affected by disaster paid taxes last year, they may be able to deduct this year's property loss from last year's taxes and get an immediate refund. This financial relief may help in obtaining a rental house through HUD.

State government may provide "other needs assistance," such as help with medical, dental, and funeral expenses, as well as other disaster-created expenses. "Other needs assistance" is usually not income related.

Other Ways for Your Congregation to Become Involved during and after a Disaster

Become involved in your local or state Voluntary Organizations Active in Disaster (VOAD). In times of crisis, we tend to gravitate toward the partners we know. If you are not known in the disaster response community as a partner, you will not easily gain access to critical information and communication as the recovery process begins to move forward.

Look beyond the faith-based community and become involved with disaster preparedness and training that your local emergency management may offer. Emergency management is at the heart of the initial response to a disaster. They operate the command and control center for disaster response. It is important that you have a good relationship with your local emergency management group. There are several ways that this task can be accomplished.

Develop neighborhood watch groups. The neighborhood watch provides an additional level of security to your community. It also brings neighbors together in such a way that they get to know each other and a relationship will be built prior to an emergency.

Map your neighborhood. Mapping your neighborhood is an additional activity that introduces and involves your congregation with local emergency management in preparation exercises for a disaster. Guidelines for neighborhood mapping are available from most state emergency management agencies, if your local community does not already participate in a mapping program.

Disaster education can be obtained at relatively low cost. Educational services are available through the American Red Cross, the U.S. county emergency management, the Salvation Army, and the Department of Homeland Security. Disaster conferences are offered nationwide almost every month, and the registration is often considered a business expense and thus tax deductible. The American Red Cross charges a nominal fee for their first aid, CPR, and disaster preparedness classes. Disaster preparedness material for both home and business (including congregations) is available from the organizations that offer the training classes.

When Rebuilding Is Not an Option

Our basic assumption in this chapter is that with the proper insurance, initiative, and inspirational drive, congregations and congregants can rebuild their lives following a disaster. The chapter reflects our thinking that there are programs in place and if you diligently seek those programs, rebuilding is possible. Our experience in the field reflects that such outcomes are common and the stuff agencies love to include in their annual reports.

Recent history and mass-media journalists have brought to light a new response to trying to rebuild following a disaster. There are times when there is not the political will to rebuild, or it simply is not prudent. What happens when, as in the case with Hurricane Katrina, congregants and congregations relocate to various parts of the United States? What happens when, even if you followed our suggestions as outlined in this chapter, decisions are made outside of your control not to rebuild, or if you did rebuild the population or demographics have changed?

We also acknowledge the reality that congregations serving in economically challenged neighborhoods often have great difficulty securing insurance. The insurance companies who do venture into the aforementioned neighborhoods usually charge a much higher premium for congregations and congregants who live below the poverty line. In neighborhoods where crime, unemployment, and poor educational systems are commonplace long before a disaster strikes, leadership may be confronted with difficult choices about what is needed for a congregation's basic survival—paying the electric bill, paying the mortgage, paying insurance, or paying a clergyperson at part-time or full-time status? There are no magic answers. We suggest if a congregation disperses, congregants should call their clergyperson to report their current living status and plans for the future. Clergy may need to consider rebuilding in another location or moving on to a new congregation. Life is not always linear, and at times our choices are difficult but necessary for our survival.

Notes

1. *Meeting God in the Ruins: Devotions for Disaster Relief Volunteers* (Minneapolis: Augsburg Fortress, 2003), 6.

About the Contributors

Rev. Thomas H. Davis Jr. is an ordained minister with the Christian Church (Disciples of Christ). Currently he is the chair of the Emotional and Spiritual Care Committee of the National Voluntary Organizations Active in Disaster. Since 2002, he has worked with Church World Service as a disaster response specialist. In this position he has consulted with multiple communities in twenty-one states and territories on capacity building for long-term recovery following disasters. He has also developed a retreat for clergy and caregivers following a disaster designed to offer renewal and reflection of their disaster response. Rev. Davis's work has focused on community-based recovery involving social service organizations and the faith-based community, including congregations and judicatories.

Rev. Lloyd George Abrams, DMin, is a certified trauma specialist with the Association of Traumatic Stress Specialists and a senior chaplain with the International Conference of Police Chaplains. He has extensive experience in both disaster response and law enforcement. Currently, he is a voluntary agency liaison, disaster assistance employee with the Federal Emergency Management Agency. He is a longtime disaster response coordinator with the Pacific Northwest Conference United Methodist Church and also a longtime member of the American Red Cross Spiritual Care Response Team. He has responded to numerous disasters around the United States.

Index

Judaism / Christianity / Interfaith

Show Me Your Way: The Complete Guide to Exploring Interfaith Spiritual Direction
by Howard A. Addison 5½ x 8½, 240 pp, Quality PB, 978-1-893361-41-6 **$16.95**

Talking about God: Exploring the Meaning of Religious Life with
Kierkegaard, Buber, Tillich and Heschel *by Daniel F. Polish, PhD*
Examines the meaning of the human religious experience with the greatest theologians of modern times. 6 x 9, 176 pp, HC, 978-1-59473-230-0 **$21.99**

Interactive Faith: The Essential Interreligious Community-Building Handbook
Edited by Rev. Bud Heckman with Rori Picker Neiss
A guide to the key methods and resources of the interfaith movement.
6 x 9, 400 pp (est), HC, 978-1-59473-237-9 **$40.00**

The Jewish Approach to Repairing the World (*Tikkun Olam*)
A Brief Introduction for Christians *by Rabbi Elliot N. Dorff, PhD*
A window into the Jewish idea of responsibility to care for the world.
5½ x 8½, 192 pp (est), Quality PB, 978-1-58023-349-1 **$16.99** (a Jewish Lights book)

Modern Jews Engage the New Testament: Enhancing Jewish Well-
Being in a Christian Environment *by Rabbi Michael J. Cook, PhD*
A look at the dynamics of the New Testament.
6 x 9, 400 pp (est), HC, 978-1-58023-313-2 **$29.99** (a Jewish Lights book)

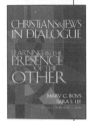

Disaster Spiritual Care: Practical Clergy Responses to Community,
Regional and National Tragedy
Edited by Rabbi Stephen B. Roberts, BCJC, & Rev. Willard W.C. Ashley, Sr., DMin, DH
The definitive reference for pastoral caregivers of all faiths involved in disaster response.
6 x 9, 384 pp, Hardcover, 978-1-59473-240-9 **$40.00**

The Changing Christian World: A Brief Introduction for Jews
by Rabbi Leonard A. Schoolman
5½ x 8½, 176 pp, Quality PB, 978-1-58023-344-6 **$16.99** (a Jewish Lights book)

The Jewish Connection to Israel, the Promised Land: A Brief Introduction for
Christians *by Rabbi Eugene Korn, PhD*
5½ x 8½, 192 pp, Quality PB, 978-1-58023-318-7 **$14.99** (a Jewish Lights book)

Christians and Jews in Dialogue: Learning in the Presence of the Other
by Mary C. Boys and Sara S. Lee; Foreword by Dorothy C. Bass
Inspires renewed commitment to dialogue between religious traditions.
6 x 9, 240 pp, HC, 978-1-59473-144-0 **$21.99**

Healing the Jewish-Christian Rift: Growing Beyond Our Wounded History
by Ron Miller and Laura Bernstein; Foreword by Dr. Beatrice Bruteau
6 x 9, 288 pp, Quality PB, 978-1-59473-139-6 **$18.99**

Introducing My Faith and My Community
The Jewish Outreach Institute Guide for the Christian in a Jewish Interfaith Relationship
by Rabbi Kerry M. Olitzky 6 x 9, 176 pp, Quality PB, 978-1-58023-192-3 **$16.99** *(a Jewish Lights book)*

The Jewish Approach to God: A Brief Introduction for Christians
by Rabbi Neil Gillman 5½ x 8½, 192 pp, Quality PB, 978-1-58023-190-9 **$16.95** *(a Jewish Lights book)*

Jewish Holidays: A Brief Introduction for Christians
by Rabbi Kerry M. Olitzky and Rabbi Daniel Judson
5½ x 8½, 176 pp, Quality PB, 978-1-58023-302-6 **$16.99** *(a Jewish Lights book)*

Jewish Ritual: A Brief Introduction for Christians
by Rabbi Kerry M. Olitzky and Rabbi Daniel Judson
5½ x 8½, 144 pp, Quality PB, 978-1-58023-210-4 **$14.99** *(a Jewish Lights book)*

Jewish Spirituality: A Brief Introduction for Christians *by Rabbi Lawrence Kushner*
5½ x 8½, 112 pp, Quality PB, 978-1-58023-150-3 **$12.95** *(a Jewish Lights book)*

A Jewish Understanding of the New Testament
by Rabbi Samuel Sandmel; new Preface by Rabbi David Sandmel
5½ x 8½, 368 pp, Quality PB, 978-1-59473-048-1 **$19.99**

We Jews and Jesus: Exploring Theological Differences for Mutual Understanding
by Rabbi Samuel Sandmel; new Preface by Rabbi David Sandmel A Classic Reprint
6 x 9, 192 pp, Quality PB, 978-1-59473-208-9 **$16.99**

Spiritual Practice

Soul Fire: Accessing Your Creativity *by Rev. Thomas Ryan, CSP*
Shows you how to cultivate your creative spirit as a way to encourage personal growth.
6 x 9, 160 pp, Quality PB, 978-1-59473-243-0. **$16.99**

Running—The Sacred Art: Preparing to Practice
by Dr. Warren A. Kay; Foreword by Kristin Armstrong
Examines how your daily run can enrich your spiritual life.
5½ x 8½, 160 pp, Quality PB, 978-1-59473-227-0 **$16.99**

Hospitality—The Sacred Art: Discovering the Hidden Spiritual Power
of Invitation and Welcome *by Rev. Nanette Sawyer; Foreword by Rev. Dirk Ficca*
Explores how this ancient spiritual practice can transform your relationships.
5½ x 8½, 192 pp, Quality PB, 978-1-59473-228-7 **$16.99**

Thanking & Blessing—The Sacred Art: Spiritual Vitality through
Gratefulness *by Jay Marshall, PhD; Foreword by Philip Gulley*
Offers practical tips for uncovering the blessed wonder in our lives—even in try-
ing circumstances. 5½ x 8½, 176 pp, Quality PB, 978-1-59473-231-7 **$16.99**

Everyday Herbs in Spiritual Life: A Guide to Many Practices
by Michael J. Caduto; Foreword by Rosemary Gladstar Explores the power of herbs.
7 x 9, 208 pp, 21 b/w illustrations, Quality PB, 978-1-59473-174-7 **$16.99**

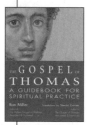

Divining the Body: Reclaim the Holiness of Your Physical Self *by Jan Phillips*
8 x 8, 256 pp, Quality PB, 978-1-59473-080-1 **$16.99**

Finding Time for the Timeless: Spirituality in the Workweek
by John McQuiston II Simple stories show you how refocus your daily life.
5½ x 6¾, 208 pp, HC, 978-1-59473-035-1 **$17.99**

The Gospel of Thomas: A Guidebook for Spiritual Practice
by Ron Miller; Translations by Stevan Davies
6 x 9, 160 pp, Quality PB, 978-1-59473-047-4 **$14.99**

Earth, Water, Fire, and Air: Essential Ways of Connecting to Spirit
by Cait Johnson 6 x 9, 224 pp, HC, 978-1-893361-65-2 **$19.95**

Labyrinths from the Outside In: Walking to Spiritual Insight—A Beginner's Guide
by Donna Schaper and Carole Ann Camp
6 x 9, 208 pp, b/w illus. and photos, Quality PB, 978-1-893361-18-8 **$16.95**

Practicing the Sacred Art of Listening: A Guide to Enrich Your Relationships
and Kindle Your Spiritual Life—The Listening Center Workshop
by Kay Lindahl 8 x 8, 176 pp, Quality PB, 978-1-893361-85-0 **$16.95**

Releasing the Creative Spirit: Unleash the Creativity in Your Life
by Dan Wakefield 7 x 10, 256 pp, Quality PB, 978-1-893361-36-2 **$16.95**

The Sacred Art of Bowing: Preparing to Practice
by Andi Young 5½ x 8½, 128 pp, b/w illus., Quality PB, 978-1-893361-82-9 **$14.95**

The Sacred Art of Chant: Preparing to Practice
by Ana Hernández 5½ x 8½, 192 pp, Quality PB, 978-1-59473-036-8 **$15.99**

The Sacred Art of Fasting: Preparing to Practice
by Thomas Ryan, CSP 5½ x 8½, 192 pp, Quality PB, 978-1-59473-078-8 **$15.99**

The Sacred Art of Forgiveness: Forgiving Ourselves and Others through God's Grace
by Marcia Ford 8 x 8, 176 pp, Quality PB, 978-1-59473-175-4 **$16.99**

The Sacred Art of Listening: Forty Reflections for Cultivating a Spiritual Practice
by Kay Lindahl; Illustrations by Amy Schnapper
8 x 8, 160 pp, b/w illus., Quality PB, 978-1-893361-44-7 **$16.99**

The Sacred Art of Lovingkindness: Preparing to Practice
by Rabbi Rami Shapiro; Foreword by Marcia Ford 5½ x 8½, 176 pp, Quality PB, 978-1-59473-151-8 **$16.99**

Sacred Speech: A Practical Guide for Keeping Spirit in Your Speech
by Rev. Donna Schaper 6 x 9, 176 pp, Quality PB, 978-1-59473-068-9 **$15.99**
HC, 978-1-893361-74-4 **$21.95**

Prayer / Meditation

Sacred Attention: A Spiritual Practice for Finding God in the Moment
by Margaret D. McGee
Framed on the Christian liturgical year, this inspiring guide explores ways to develop a practice of attention as a means of talking—and listening—to God.
6 x 9, 144 pp, HC, 978-1-59473-232-4 **$19.99**

Women Pray: Voices through the Ages, from Many Faiths, Cultures and Traditions
Edited and with Introductions by Monica Furlong
5 x 7¼, 256 pp, Quality PB, 978-1-59473-071-9 **$15.99**

Women of Color Pray: Voices of Strength, Faith, Healing,
Hope and Courage   *Edited and with Introductions by Christal M. Jackson*
Through these prayers, poetry, lyrics, meditations and affirmations, you will share in the strong and undeniable connection women of color share with God.
5 x 7¼, 208 pp, Quality PB, 978-1-59473-077-1 **$15.99**

Secrets of Prayer: A Multifaith Guide to Creating Personal Prayer in
Your Life   *by Nancy Corcoran, CSJ*
This compelling, multifaith guidebook offers you companionship and encouragement on the journey to a healthy prayer life.   6 x 9, 160 pp, Quality PB, 978-1-59473-215-7 **$16.99**

Prayers to an Evolutionary God
by William Cleary; Afterword by Diarmuid O'Murchu
Inspired by the spiritual and scientific teachings of Diarmuid O'Murchu and Teilhard de Chardin, reveals that religion and science can be combined to create an expanding view of the universe—an evolutionary faith.
6 x 9, 208 pp, HC, 978-1-59473-006-1 **$21.99**

The Art of Public Prayer: Not for Clergy Only   *by Lawrence A. Hoffman*
6 x 9, 288 pp, Quality PB, 978-1-893361-06-5 **$18.99**

A Heart of Stillness: A Complete Guide to Learning the Art of Meditation
by David A. Cooper 5½ x 8½, 272 pp, Quality PB, 978-1-893361-03-4 **$16.95**

Meditation without Gurus: A Guide to the Heart of Practice
by Clark Strand 5½ x 8½, 192 pp, Quality PB, 978-1-893361-93-5 **$16.95**

Praying with Our Hands: 21 Practices of Embodied Prayer from the World's
Spiritual Traditions   *by Jon M. Sweeney; Photographs by Jennifer J. Wilson; Foreword by Mother Tessa Bielecki; Afterword by Taitetsu Unno, PhD*
8 x 8, 96 pp, 22 duotone photos, Quality PB, 978-1-893361-16-4 **$16.95**

Silence, Simplicity & Solitude: A Complete Guide to Spiritual Retreat at Home
by David A. Cooper 5½ x 8½, 336 pp, Quality PB, 978-1-893361-04-1 **$16.95**

Three Gates to Meditation Practice: A Personal Journey into Sufism, Buddhism,
and Judaism   *by David A. Cooper* 5½ x 8½, 240 pp, Quality PB, 978-1-893361-22-5 **$16.95**

Prayer / M. Basil Pennington, OCSO

Finding Grace at the Center, 3rd Ed.: The Beginning of Centering
Prayer   *with Thomas Keating, OCSO, and Thomas E. Clarke, SJ; Foreword by Rev. Cynthia Bourgeault, PhD*
A practical guide to a simple and beautiful form of meditative prayer.
5 x 7¼, 128 pp, Quality PB, 978-1-59473-182-2 **$12.99**

The Monks of Mount Athos: A Western Monk's Extraordinary
Spiritual Journey on Eastern Holy Ground   *Foreword by Archimandrite Dionysios*
Explores the landscape, the monastic communities, and the food of Athos.
6 x 9, 256 pp, 10+ b/w drawings, Quality PB, 978-1-893361-78-2 **$18.95**

Psalms: A Spiritual Commentary   *Illustrations by Phillip Ratner*
Reflections on some of the most beloved passages from the Bible's most widely read book.   6 x 9, 176 pp, 24 full-page b/w illus., Quality PB, 978-1-59473-234-8 **$16.99**
HC, 978-1-59473-141-9 **$19.99**

The Song of Songs: A Spiritual Commentary   *Illustrations by Phillip Ratner*
Explore the Bible's most challenging mystical text.
6 x 9, 160 pp, 14 b/w illus., Quality PB, 978-1-59473-235-3 **$16.99**; HC, 978-1-59473-004-7 **$19.99**

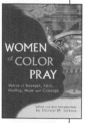

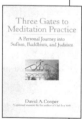

About SKYLIGHT PATHS Publishing

SkyLight Paths Publishing is creating a place where people of different spiritual traditions come together for challenge and inspiration, a place where we can help each other understand the mystery that lies at the heart of our existence.

Through spirituality, our religious beliefs are increasingly becoming a part of our lives—rather than *apart* from our lives. While many of us may be more interested than ever in spiritual growth, we may be less firmly planted in traditional religion. Yet, we do want to deepen our relationship to the sacred, to learn from our own as well as from other faith traditions, and to practice in new ways.

SkyLight Paths sees both believers and seekers as a community that increasingly transcends traditional boundaries of religion and denomination—people wanting to learn from each other, *walking together, finding the way.*

For your information and convenience, at the back of this book we have provided a list of other SkyLight Paths books you might find interesting and useful. They cover the following subjects:

Buddhism / Zen	Global Spiritual	Monasticism
Catholicism	Perspectives	Mysticism
Children's Books	Gnosticism	Poetry
Christianity	Hinduism /	Prayer
Comparative	Vedanta	Religious Etiquette
Religion	Inspiration	Retirement
Current Events	Islam / Sufism	Spiritual Biography
Earth-Based	Judaism	Spiritual Direction
Spirituality	Kabbalah	Spirituality
Enneagram	Meditation	Women's Interest
	Midrash Fiction	Worship

Or phone, fax, mail or e-mail to: SKYLIGHT PATHS Publishing
Sunset Farm Offices, Route 4 • P.O. Box 237 • Woodstock, Vermont 05091
Tel: (802) 457-4000 • Fax: (802) 457-4004 • www.skylightpaths.com
Credit card orders: (800) 962-4544 (8:30AM–5:30PM ET Monday–Friday)
Generous discounts on quantity orders. SATISFACTION GUARANTEED. Prices subject to change.